DESCARTES AND HUSSERL

SUNY series in Philosophy
George R. Lucas, Jr., Editor

DESCARTES AND HUSSERL

THE PHILOSOPHICAL PROJECT
OF RADICAL BEGINNINGS

Paul S. MacDonald

State University of New York Press

Published by
State University of New York Press, Albany

© **2000** State University of New York

For information, address State University of New York Press,
State University Plaza, Albany, NY 12246

Production by Michael Haggett
Marketing by Dana Yanulavich

Library of Congress Cataloging-in-Publication Data

MacDonald, Paul S., 1951–
    Descartes and Husserl : the philosophical project of radical
beginnngs / Paul S. MacDonald.
        p.   cm. — (SUNY series in philosophy)
    Includes bibliographical references and index.
    ISBN 0-7914-4369-8 (hardcover : alk. paper). — ISBN 0-7914-4370-1
(pbk. : alk. paper)
        1. Husserl, Edmund. 1859–1938.   2. Descartes, René, 1596–1650—
Influence.   I. Title.   II. Series.
    B3279.H94M225   1999
    193—dc21   99-15027
                                                            CIP

10 9 8 7 6 5 4 3 2 1

CONTENTS

v

ACKNOWLEDGMENTS

To Professors David Cooper and E. J. Lowe, University of Durham, for their unflagging support and encouragement over the course of this research. Their detailed criticisms have made this a better piece of work than it would have been otherwise. To Professor Peter Simons and Mr. Chris Long who each read the entire manuscript and made many valuable suggestions.

To the British Academy for a two-year Research Grant during which much of the present research and writing was accomplished. To the Editor of *Philosophy and Theology* (Marquette University) for permission to reprint material. To Jane Bunker and two anonymous readers at the State University of New York Press for criticisms and suggestions, especially on chapters 2 and 3, which stimulated me to readdress certain overlooked issues.

To the Thought Gang—Martin Connor, Stuart Hanscomb, David Mossley and Barry Stobbart—for many long discussions, in and out of the pub, for four years; their friendship has made a solitary endeavor much less lonely and far more enjoyable.

To my wife Fiona for her kindness and good humor, but most of all for her love and good faith.

ABBREVIATIONS

Full citations for these works will be found in the Bibliography.

Editions of Descartes' Works:

CSM I, II   *The Philosophical Writings of Descartes,* 2 vols. Translated by Cottingham, Stoothoff, and Murdoch.

CSM III   *The Correspondence of Descartes.* Translated by Cottingham, Stoothoff, Murdoch, and Kenny.

AT   *Oeuvres de Descartes.* Edited by Adam and Tannery. 12 vols. New Edition.

Editions of Husserl's Works:

CM   *Cartesian Meditations.* Translated by Dorion Cairns.

Crisis   *The Crisis of European Sciences and Transcendental Phenomenology.* Translated by David Carr.

Early   *Early Writings in the Philosophy of Logic and Mathematics.* Translated by Dallas Willard.

EJ   *Experience and Judgement.* Edited by Landgrebe. Translated by Churchill and Ameriks.

FTL   *Formal and Transcendental Logic.* Translated by Dorion Cairns.

HSW   *Husserl: Shorter Works.* Edited by McCormick and Elliston.

Ideas I   *Ideas First Book: General Introduction to a Pure Phenomenology.* Translated by Fred Kersten.

Ideas II   *Ideas Second Book: Studies in the Phenomenology of Constitution.* Translated by R. Rojcewicz and A. Schuwer.

Ideas III   *Ideas Third Book: Phenomenology and the Foundations of the Sciences.* Translated by T. E. Klein and W. E. Pohl.

IP   *The Idea of Phenomenology.* Translated by W. P. Alston and G. Nakhnikian.

LI   *Logical Investigations.* 2 vols. Translated by J. N. Findlay.

PP   *Phenomenological Psychology.* Translated by J. Scanlon.

PL   *The Paris Lectures.* Translated by Peter Kostenbaum.

TS   *Thing and Space: Lectures 1907.* Translated by R. Rojcewicz.

Time   *The Phenomenology of the Consciousness of Internal Time.* Translated by J. B. Brough.

HUS   *Husserliana: Gesammelte Werke.* Edited by Walter Biemel et al. Vols. I–XXIX.

The closeness of the network of which this nexus [within the *Meditations*] is constructed, and the extreme polyvalence that results for each of its elements, imparts to the Cartesian text a unique density and intensity. Leibniz had likened God to a savant who puts the most matter in the least volume. The comparison can be redirected, and the Descartes of the *Meditations* can be assimilated, for philosophy, to a Leibnizian God. . . . From the small, dense and laconic book of the *Meditations,* which has often been ill understood, in spite—if not be-cause—of the accumulation of commentaries, has flowed the rivers of modern philosophy. When a book is that rich, it suffices for us to glimpse only a small part of its riches, in order for it to manifest an infinite wealth.

Martial Gueroult
Descartes According to the Order of Reasons

The understanding of the beginnings is to be gained fully only by starting with science as given in its present-day form, looking back at its development. But in the absence of an understanding of the beginnings, the development is mute as a development of meaning. Thus we have no other choice than to proceed forward and backward in a *zig-zag pattern*; the one must help the other in an interplay. Relative clarification on one side brings some elucidation on the other, which in turn casts light back on the former. In this sort of historical consideration and critique, then, which begins with Galileo (and immediately afterwards with Descartes) and must follow the temporal order, we nevertheless have constantly to make *historical leaps* which are thus not digressions but necessities.

Edmund Husserl
The Crisis of European Sciences

I

INTRODUCTION
CONVERGENCE AND DIVERGENCE

Few thinkers in the twentieth century have had such a profound influence on philosophy and related disciplines as Edmund Husserl (1859–1938). Through his work and teaching, he has shaped many of the areas of inquiry and tools for analysis which today occupy prime places in the philosophy curriculum. It is relatively uncontentious to observe, as several recent writers have done, that a list of his students and their students reads like a who's who of twentiety-century continental philosophy. Husserl's prodigious influence extended far beyond the scope of standard philosophical research and motivated ground-breaking reorientations in a variety of disciplines. His lectures, writings, and personal contacts had a critical impact on Gestalt Psychology, Structural Linguistics, the French 'New' Anthropology, and Existentialist Literature, among others. The single figure to whom Husserl himself accords unreserved respect, to whom he returns again and again over a thirty-year period, is René Descartes. This otherwise untypical admiration and the repercussions which Cartesian-inspired phenomenology generated has been much commented upon by Husserl scholars since the 1930s. This distinctive and explicit philosophical guidance is so well known that it has inspired a dozen articles and book-chapters, and then . . . silence. Paul Ricoeur's authoritative commentary[1] on Husserl's *Cartesian Meditations*, first published in 1954, and Jan Patocka's brilliant piece, "Cartesianism and Phenomenology,"[2] provide exemplary case studies of informed interpretation of Husserl's Cartesian inheritance. Among other scholarly efforts on this topic, John Burkey and Walter Soffer deserve special mention, having both recently highlighted the significance of Husserl's characterization of some ninteenth-century psychology as a disguised skepticism and relativism.[3] However, they do not extend this insight beyond the range of Husserl's own texts in order to show that the arguments which

1

Husserl had to contend with are congruent with Descartes' background problems. Perhaps more can be said on Descartes' inspiration of an original thinker by paying attention to those areas in Husserl's work where there is no explicit reference to Descartes.

If the Western philosophical tradition can be thought of as a twenty-five-hundred-year-old conversation, then some voices have gone silent, some are louder and more strident, others are not only preemptive but are backed with a chorus of approval. How does one *begin* to philosophize? How does one enter this conversation where most of the parts seem to be taken already? One way to begin is to acquiesce to the importance of current issues and terms of discourse, and then to make a contribution, a positive addition to the general forward movement. Another way is to announce that the subject matter and vocabulary, the standard moves in the philosophical 'game,' are no longer acceptable and that it is time to start a new discourse. Both Descartes and Husserl repeatedly call for a complete demolition of previous philosophical achievements and a return to the beginnings in order to better determine what counts as an intelligent conversation. Pierre Thevanez' exceptional article on "The Question of the Radical Point of Departure" provides an insight into the meaning of *beginning* in the philosophical sense for these two thinkers. If one defines philosophy as the search for what is first, this first has two senses, two dimensions into which it opens. It is either a nontemporal *arché* or *proton*, whose priority is logical or ontological, i.e., it is a science of principles; or it is a temporal *arché* whose priority is chronological, i.e., a science of the beginning, concerned with taking the first step, a search for a method or route.

> In the second sense, the *arché* is an open question; it is the uneasiness of the philosopher who is anxious to take root in the truth, in an original truth; it is the anxiety of not missing the entrance, of finding his footing, like a mountain climber. Here it is a question of philosophy as something to be done, as a task and as a search. . . . Therefore, the beginning is a problem, not an insoluble problem or even a false problem, but a *radical* philosophical question in the proper sense of the term. The awareness of this situation of a problematic beginning is precisely philosophy become a radical question to itself.[4]

With Descartes and Husserl as our guides, this work explores the theme of a radical return to beginnings, a theme marked by three decisive reversals. The first moment occurs when Descartes makes a radical turning against late scholasticism and resurgent skepticism, and toward the foundation of certain knowledge within subjectivity. The second takes place where Husserl makes a radical turning away from a Cartesian-inspired philosophy and against the skepticism and relativism inherent in empirical psychology. And the third is where Husserl in his later works, especially *The Crisis of European Sciences*, effects a reversal against his own previous phenomenological conclusions, a program secured as a result of his previous radicalization of the Cartesian project. This investigation is, however, far more than a comparison and contrast of the overt similarities between Descartes and Husserl. It is, for example, more than the assertion that the phenomenological reduction finds its historical source in Cartesian doubt, or that they both construe the significance of their projects as the establishment of *prima philosophia*. The mere citation of methodical doubt in the *Meditations* as the starting point for Husserl's initial conception of the reduction has been well documented, not least by Husserl himself who repeatedly calls upon Descartes as his "spiritual forefather." Nor is it the brief of this study to show that Husserl employs a fabricated "Descartes" in terms of which he elaborates his own transcendental turning. In contrast with this rarefied exemplar, this highly stylized provocateur, Husserl also devoted a considerable amount of his lectures as early as 1905 to a detailed historical interpretation of the Cartesian project.

It is plausible that English-language commentary, on the detailed relations with Descartes which Husserl elaborated over his lengthy and productive career, has been constrained by the relative unavailability of Husserl's original texts. It is worth reminding readers that two of the most important sources for Husserl's multifaceted views on Descartes were not published until recently. The *Lectures on First Philosophy* (from 1923/24) were not published in German until 1956– 59 (HUS VII & VIII), and though translated into French by A. Kelkel in 1970, they have not yet been translated into English. Fortunately, Ludwig Landgrebe (Husserl's personal assistant in the 1920s) has provided a detailed thirty-page summary of the second half of this monumental work, translated into English as "Husserl's Departure from Cartesianism."[5] The next best primary source, the *Lectures on Logic and Theory of Knowledge* (from 1906/07) was published only as recently as 1985 (HUS XXIV) and remain unavailable in English. In addition, some of Husserl's discussions of issues highly pertinent to this inquiry, such as the notion of first philosophy as transcendental phenomenology and the viability of a universal science founded on *a priori* principles, still remain in manuscript.[6]

A number of introductory books on Husserl and Pure Phenomenology do little more than summarize Husserl's appropriation of Descartes in Husserl's own terms. Whereas the accuracy of such a summation is indeed an important issue in critical scholarship, there is not a great deal *at issue* in commentators' discussion of Husserl's "Descartes." It is a relatively straight-forward task, though without doubt a complex and lengthy one, for a good Husserl scholar to collate the many textual references and synopsize a fairly good picture of Husserl's picture of Descartes. On the other hand, Cartesian scholars are devoted to an explication of their subject matter in depth, in the course of which a variety of interpretations emerge on highly specific and sometimes open-ended topics. It does not seem to be the case, for example, that a reputable Cartesian scholar would take for granted the charge that Descartes committed a vicious circle in reasoning for the existence of God, or that there is an insurmountable problem regarding the interaction of *res cogitans* and *res extensa*. It is true of course that someone might conclude a critical analysis of the relevant texts with a statement compatible with either standard interpretation. What is missing in current debates on such issues as Husserl's exposition of Cartesian doubt, the concept of intentionality, mind-body union, and so forth, is quite simple and clear-cut—an unprejudiced and well-informed knowledge of Descartes. With a thorough and intimate understanding of Descartes as a starting point, it is then possible to segregate what Husserl claims Descartes says with what Descartes actually says, or can be plausibly construed to say on open-ended issues. It would then also be possible to show that it is often precisely Husserl's divergence from Descartes' position which generates his most profound insights.

Let me expand on this last statement so that the significance and scope of this divergence is entirely clear. It seems rather uncontentious to show that where Husserl says he follows from or re-engages a Cartesian point, *this* is what Husserl meant by such-and-such a claim *in his own terms;* and the same of course, where Husserl departs from or disengages from what Descartes said. Although such a textual exegesis is a precondition for a proper understanding, this is not what is here indicated by Husserl's convergence or divergence from Descartes. It will be one of the principal claims of this thesis that it is (sometimes) precisely where Husserl *misidentifies* Descartes' position on a specific issue that the most interesting Husserlian insights are generated. Thus, for instance, Husserl's assumption that there is indeed a vicious circle in Descartes' demonstration of God's existence as the guarantee of the certitude of clear and distinct seeing allows Husserl, in the rejection of an unknowable transcendent deity, to postulate unknowable other subjects lying beyond any possible intuition. Where Descartes *seems* to need God's existence in order to make his argument work, so also it *seems* that Husserl needs the presumptive presence of conscious others in order to secure claims made by the transcendental ego.

In contrast with Husserl's overt indications of Descartes' influence on specific phenomenological themes, it is my contention that there is a pervasive and systematic parallelism between their respective projects, which is only more obvious at the specific points indicated by Husserl. Beneath the surface, however, this thematic continuity flows onward, occasionally diverging but usually converging on those topics where a comparable treatment by the philosopher is required. And the reason that this happens is due to a profound congruence in their respective points of departure, methodological procedures, and idealized destinations. One of the most common metaphors employed by both thinkers for the philosophical enterprise is that of a voyage of exploration. In terms of this grand metaphor, the old world left behind, the narration of the voyage itself, and the discovery of a new world are articulated in compatible vocabularies. The very fact that this narrative is called a journey is something which they both feel distinguishes their enterprise from that of their predecessors and contemporaries. Descartes explicitly names this format the "order of reasons," to counterpoise it with the building or edifice of the natural sciences, the "order of essences"—the same distinction which Husserl makes between the "order of cognitions" and the "order of beings."

The intellectual backgrounds which provoked Descartes and Husserl to in-augurate such large-scale enterprises are strikingly similar in several respects. First, the renewed skeptical arguments of the late sixteenth and early seventeenth century which incited Descartes to search for an indubitable foundation for human knowledge bear remarkable similarities with the relativist and positivist tendencies in empirical psychology against which Husserl struggled. Second, they both approached metaphysics as the discipline which was most appropriate for sorting out such skeptical problems after years of detailed investigations into mathematics. Descartes' *Rules for the Direction of the Mind* (1628) and the essays appended to the *Discourse on the Method* (1630–35) occur at approxi-mately the same stage in his philosophical development as do Husserl's work in the foundations of mathematical cognition between 1887 and 1895. Third, they both envisioned the most fruitful course forward as springing from a first phi-losophy which would be an all-embracing science of sciences (*mathesis universalis*), or more accurately, a theoretical model of scientific cognition—a model which both were to abandon as untenable in later works. Even their most intractable difficulties show distinct parallels. For both thinkers, the most elabo-rated form of their mature philosophy almost foundered on the subject's inter-face with the world. For Descartes, the most stubborn impediment centered around the mind's interaction with physical bodies in the material world; whereas for Husserl, it centered around the ego's confrontation with the givenness of other egos in the intersubjective world. These pervasive thematic parallels, pur-sued in the following investigations, account for remarkable resonances through-out considerations of specific philosophical problems.

This thematic parallel can be illustrated by the relative positions of various texts within each author's corpus considered as a whole. Descartes intended the *Discourse on the Method* to be a ground-clearing study for the three lengthy essays, which are applications of this method to particular topics. In the same fashion, Husserl's *Logical Investigations* comprise six detailed researches into specific areas, preceded by the justly famous "Prolegomena to Pure Logic," which is both a refutation of the psychologistic interpretation of logical laws and the outline of a new eidetic psychology—phenomenology. Just as Descartes took the central message of skeptical attacks on knowledge claims to its limit in order to overturn any possible skepticism, so Husserl employed the most rigorous extension of exact psychology to describe the *a priori* conditions for the occurrence of cognitive acts and their contents and thus to disprove any claim for their origin in contingent matters-of-fact. The touchstone for cognition which is immune to doubt in these early stages, against which both Descartes and Husserl evaluate other epistemic claims, is that of the intuition of mathematical truths. And the formal ontology which they both need in order to make sense of the kinds of intuition and intuitable contents which are disclosed in other cognitive modes are very similar; for Descartes, simple and complex natures, and for Husserl part-whole theory.

The skeptical milieu in which Descartes opens his quest for an indubitable foundation for a universal science has a striking parallel with the confusion and uncertainty in psychological enquiries at the end of the nineteenth century. The skeptical crisis of the early seventeenth century largely revolved around sustained attacks by Protestant theologians against the primacy and authority of the Catholic Church, and Catholics' defense tactics against these charges. Luther, Calvin, and others denied that the "visible church" was the final arbiter in issues of religious faith, especially with respect to the interpretation of holy scripture. The Reformers argued that the truth of a religious claim should be based on the inner conviction of the claimant and argued against a version of *petitio principii* (or circular reasoning) in the Catholic Church's position. They pointed out that if the criterion for the truth of an interpretive statement about doctrine or scripture was whether it accorded with the dictates of the official church (i.e., the Pope), then the church itself derived its primacy in deciding such issues from scriptural sources, that is, from their own unilateral interpretation of a specific doctrinal injunction.

The late sixteenth century saw the appearance of a number of publications which further exacerbated theological controversies and spilled over into debates on virtually every subject. The startling appearance in 1562 of Sextus Empiricus' *Outlines of Pyrrhonism*, previously thought lost in antiquity, provided more or less ready-made arguments on an immense variety of topics. Montaigne's *Essays*, four editions of which came out between 1580 and 1595, became an exceptionally popular epitome of skeptical tropes and anecdotes, bolstered with his dyspeptic observations on human nature. Standard remarks about sensory illusions, the waking/dreaming dilemma, and the fallibility of human reason were supplemented by broader and deeper questions. At least with respect to

Descartes' contemporaries, the intellectual situation seemed to be highly unstable and, according to some alarmists, portended a surge in atheism. From his early days, Descartes had seen that his task was not to counter each particular skeptical argument, while standing on shifting ground, but rather to radicalize (i.e., to capture the root of) the entire philosophical enterprise itself. The search for a certain foundation would generate "little by little" one well-proved point at a time, securing a science which would provide the means to refute any skepticism whatsoever. It was his extraordinary insight to take doubt to the extreme limit (but not beyond) and then turn its full force against the fulcral point of the cogito in order to accomplish this ambition.[7]

In the Seventh Replies to the *Meditations*, Descartes responds to his most obdurate critic:

> We should not suppose that sceptical philosophy is extinct. It is vigorously alive today, and almost all those who regard themselves as more intellectually gifted than others, and find nothing to satisfy them in philosophy as it is ordinarily practised, take refuge in skepticism because they cannot see any alternative with greater claims to truth. (CSM II, 374)

The main tenets of a psychological derivation of logical laws, which Husserl was to identify as the most persistent anti-philosophical trend in the nineteenth century, are to be found in their most explicit form in the work of John Stuart Mill, Theodor Lipps, and Christoph Sigwart. The main thrust of their position is that the truths of logic (and other "exact" sciences) are based on empirical observations of discriminable phenomena, where invariant regularities in their occurrence indicate lawlike rules which observers can follow in order to determine whether other instances are in accord or discord with these rules. The only kind of observation which could be called upon in the empirical investigation of logical statements is introspection, which for these psychologists, was indeed a sort of visual inspection turned inwards. The mental origin of specific logical postulates was the genesis of their definition, and their validity resided in the subject's cognitive ability to explicate them. The fact that such mental occurrences took place in human cognition, which was governed by definite protocols of psycho-physical formation, meant that these postulates were also governed by the same laws. The most productive parallel to be drawn between seventeenth-century skepticism and nineteenth-century psychologism can be shown by highlighting the conflation between two epistemologically disparate notions: on the one hand, the contingent, factual occurrence of logical cognitions in a human subject; and on the other hand, the necessity and ideality of what those cognitions are about irrespective of who (if anyone) has them.

Husserl's mature reflection on these matters in his lectures from 1925 strikes a chord resonant with Descartes' attitude towards half-hearted skeptics who couldn't see that a truly radical skepticism undermined the ground beneath their own feet. In the elaboration of descriptive psychology into a genuine phenomenology, Husserl appropriated the skeptical overtones of his psychological adversaries and then directed it towards the very method upon which they had based their conclusions. In doing so, he overturned the empirical, contingent grounds for generating the indubitable veracity of mathematical or logical axioms and established the validity of the 'objective' content of these self-same "mental facts."

> It could come to pass that a very radical scepticism could be directed against this [naturalistic] psychology ... such as could never be directed against the exact science of nature. . . . The most radical sceptical reaction . . . shall interest us here. This sceptical critique turns towards nothing less than the entire methodology of this psychology insofar as it ever raised the claim actually to explain the facts of the life of the mind mentally. (PP, 3)

Both Descartes and Husserl envision an overall response to the skeptical challenge as a demand to renovate the principles under which claims to "scientific" knowledge are made at all. For each thinker this involves demolishing a false picture or model of what a scientific theory of the world would seem to require a mind to be: for Descartes the mind was another 'object,' but of a unique kind; for Husserl, the mind could never be another kind of object encountered in the world. Their radicalization of pregiven structures of scientific knowledge disclosed an entirely new world accessible only after methodical doubt's fulfillment and the phenomenological reduction's completion. It is significant that for Descartes and Husserl, this entails not simply a new way of looking at an old problem, or new terms for expressing an accepted distinction, but rather an entirely new philosophical discourse in which that problem or that distinction can be articulated. For Descartes to characterize an account of his quest for certainty via universal doubt as a fable is, in some sense then, to give a history of this new world. Although he suppressed publication of *Le Monde* in 1633 when he learned of Galileo's condemnation, he summarized these issues in 1637 in Part Five of the *Discourse*. "I did not want to bring these matters [physical laws] too much into the open, for I wished to be free to say what I thought about them without having either to follow or to refute the accepted opinions of the learned. So I decided to leave *our world* wholly for them to argue about, and to speak solely of what would happen in a *new world*" (CSM I, 132; emphasis added).

It is in "our world," obscured with "a fog or mist" of prejudices and received opinions, that theologians dispute about the criteria for religious truth and skeptics undermine what little has been established in the nascent empirical sciences. In the bright "new world" revealed by the subjective certitude of thought reaching its 'object,' any traveler who enters there has had the way cleared for him. In contrast with the objective certitude of the natural sciences, that for each lawlike thought there is state of affairs to which it corresponds, this certitude is unique to its domain—that for each thinking act there is something thought. "For a while then, allow your thought to wander beyond this world to view another world; a wholly new one which I shall bring into being before your mind in imaginary spaces." And further, "My purpose is not to *explain*, as they [the learned] do, the things which are in fact in the real world, but only to *make up* a world in which there is nothing that the dullest minds are incapable of conceiving" (CSM I, 90, 92, emphasis added). This introduction to the new world is accompanied, so to speak, by an invitation for each reader to enter along with him, in much the same way that Descartes enjoins the readers of the *Meditations* to meditate along with him.

This old world is the world of the natural attitude, so vigorously called into question by methodical doubt, and the new world is the universal consequence of just that purification and clarification. This is the same metaphor which Husserl employs to characterize devotion to the task of phenomenological analysis. "Our procedure is that of an explorer journeying through an unknown part of the world, and carefully describing what is presented along his unbeaten paths, which will not always be the shortest. Such an explorer can rightfully be filled with the sure confidence that he gives utterance to what must be said, . . . even though new explorations will require new descriptions with manifold improvements" (Ideas I, 235). This theme of "losing the world in order to gain it" epitomizes Descartes' and Husserl's summons for radical conversion in the philosophical enterprise. And the most potent metaphor to signal this dramatic transformation is that of philosophy as a path or road and the philosopher as an explorer.

About to depart from the old world, with his vision firmly fixed on the new, Descartes remarks, "It will be enough if I open the way which will enable you to discover them [physical laws] yourselves. . . . So I shall be content to continue with the description I have begun, as if my intention was simply to tell you a fable" (CSM I, 97–98). Even when Husserl comes to depart from his own previously argued for departure from Cartesianism, citing Descartes' overlooking of transcendental subjectivity as too damaging for this way, he still uses the same imagery. "The proper sense of the discovery Descartes could not seize for himself. Behind the apparent triviality of his well-known phrase *ego cogito, ego sum* there open up in fact depths all too dark and deep. It was with Descartes like Columbus, who discovered the new continent, but knew nothing of it, merely believing to have discovered a new sea route to India" (HUS VII, 63). To be fair to Husserl, he definitely uncovered vast domains in the nature of consciousness unexplored by Descartes, but to be fair to Descartes—and unfair to Husserl's unfairness to Descartes—the Cartesian way did reveal some of these "depths dark and deep," to a greater extent than Husserl would admit. And to be scrupulous with Husserl's own simile, whatever Columbus discovered about this new-found land could have been accurately depicted, irrespective of the fact that he mistook it for India.

Throughout his philosophical career, from the *Rules for the Direction of the Mind* to the *Passions of the Soul*, Descartes consistently exemplified the twofold orientation of philosophical activity with the same dual metaphor. Long before his first explicit discrimination of the order of reasons and the order of essences in the "Second Replies," he makes the same segregation in an implicit fashion using the images of philosophy's path and science's building. The first glimpse of this occurs in Rule XII of the *Rules*: "When we consider things in the order that corresponds to our knowledge of them, our view of them must be different from what it would be if we were speaking of them in accordance with how they exist in reality" (CSM I, 44). In a letter to Mersenne of April 1630, after abandoning work on the *Rules*, he describes an abrupt change of direction in these terms: "I was forced to start a new project [*Le Monde*] rather larger than the first. It is as if a man began building a house and then acquired unexpected riches. . . . No one could blame such a man if he saw him starting to build another house more suitable to his condition" (CSM III, 21). It is an historical irony that he felt compelled to vacate this new house three years later after learning of Galileo's condemnation, since the astronomical physics in this work endorsed the heliocentric picture.

Only rarely does one image occur in a passage without the other: a building is consistently used to illustrate the cobbled-together character of both halfbaked "scientific" enterprises (such as alchemy and astrology) and the fanciful metaphysics of the scholastics; a path is always used with a positive overtone to illustrate a new way of conducting philosophical enquiries. There are numerous instances of this dual metaphor in the *Discourse*, where Descartes cautions against borrowing or adding to a gerry-built edifice and commends instead the right following of the path. "It is not enough to have a good mind, the main thing is to apply it well. . . . Those who proceed but very slowly can make much greater progress, if they always follow the right path, than those who hurry and stray from it" (CSM I, 111). It is this falling away from the right path which so disconcerts the thinker in the *Meditations* after he has purged all his prejudices and withdrawn from the sensory world. "So serious are the doubts . . . that it feels as if I have fallen unexpectedly into a deep whirlpool which tumbles me around. . . . Nevertheless, I will make an effort and once more attempt the same path which I started on yesterday" (CSM II, 16).

The persistence of the building and path metaphors throughout his writings indicates a thematic continuity in the manner in which Descartes understood his own philosophical activity. The building image is usually phrased in the third-person, about some other writer, and concerns the construction of an alleged science, little by little, from simple statements to more complex, cross-referenced structures. Not until the "Seventh Replies," where Descartes claims that his method imitates that of the architect, and Part One of the *Principles*, which is an expression of the results of that method, will Descartes commend the procedure of building. On the other hand, the path image is almost always phrased in the first-person, with respect to the thinker's point of view and signifies the unique perspective of moving forward in an unknown land. The sense of this image should be quite evident—having secured each point along the way and kept one's bearings through backward-glancing assessments, the next step can be clearly fixed and known in advance as the one required. One of the tasks of this current study will be to show that visualizing a radically new philosophy as a journey of exploration is founded on the discrimination between order of reasons and order of essences and that this is prefigured by the imagery of science's building and philosophy's path.

The task of charting such unknown territory and of making its novel features intelligible to fellow travelers involves the use of a terminology which is not burdened with accreted layers of meaning. Both Descartes and Husserl are at some pains to carefully disassociate their vocabulary from that of their predecessors. But this can never be just a matter of coining new terms—old wine in new bottles—as though one could Humpty-Dumpty-like call anything by any name one chooses. To a large extent new terms are required insofar as one's conceptual analysis picks out new things which can then be distinguished. As mentioned earlier, such a fundamental analysis of the structures of consciousness relies heavily on a primitive notion of intuition, i.e. direct cognitive acquaintance. This intuition, the mind's grasp of that which is presented precisely *as* it is presented, does not operate solely within the domain of sensory perception—it is not literally another form of "seeing." Rather, it is the most basic cognitive relation toward any kind of mental 'content,' whether perceptual, imaginative, signitive, or otherwise. Within the entire sphere of cogitata considered purely as the correlate of thinking acts, a primitive distinction can be made between two sorts of 'things' presented, and two ways in which they can be related: an x is either a part (of a whole) or a whole with parts, an x is either dependent or independent of other parts and wholes.

In only one text does Descartes deal explicitly with the basic building blocks of his new world, and that is in Rule XII of the *Rules*. After distinguishing between the two basic operations of the mind, intuition and deduction, and the ways in which the innate cognitive power combines with images to produce the various faculties, he introduces eight basic theorems regarding simple and complex natures. The kinds of simples and composites, and the ways in which they can be related, comprise a conceptual framework which he appeals to again and again, most notably in the *Meditations*, as Jean-Luc Marion astutely observed.[8] The eighth theorem, in fact, explicitly stipulates that all of the previous theorems' discussion of simples and composites can be recast as analyses of different types of parts and wholes. It is our contention that this formal ontology functions within Descartes' project in much the same way in which Husserl's part-whole theory functions in his. The third of the *Logical Investigations* is devoted to a formal ontology of parts and wholes, their relations of dependence and independence, and the ways in which parts and wholes form larger wholes. Husserl's mereological study occurs in just the same place in his overall project as does Descartes': after investigation of mathematical cognition, before the discovery or inception of universal doubt, and before embarking on a journey of exploration.

Descartes' unprecedented employment of methodical doubt in clearing the way for a radical rethinking of the meaning of certainty in human knowledge is perhaps the principal topic (along with mind-body dualism) which has generated the greatest amount of commentary. It would seem that, even with regard to Husserl's reworking of this in the phenomenological reduction, there just would not be anything more to say. A number of issues seem to have been exhausted through scholarly treatment: methodical doubt itself, the three stages which universalize this, and the problems which are elided due to Descartes' silence on specific features. But this is to ignore another exceptional component of Descartes' program, his novel theory of ideas, in terms of which it is possible to look again at the method of doubt. Previous discussions by eminent commentators such as Hintikka, Gewirth, and Kenny have focused exclusively on what is called into doubt, the thoughts, beliefs and opinions which are not immune to the query: Is it possible that this idea could be false? Descartes often discusses this under the rubric of 'minimal condition' for doubt, that is, if an idea or thesis admits the least ground for doubting its truth he will consider such an idea *as if* it were false in order to discover what remains.

But in the preface he has already warned the reader that there is an ambiguity in the word *idea* itself. "Thus 'idea' can be taken materially, as an operation of the intellect, in which case it cannot be said to be more perfect than me. Alternatively, it can be taken objectively, as the thing represented by that operation" (CSM II, 7). In the "First Replies," he explicitly discriminates "the determination of an act of the intellect by means of an object [from] the object's being in the intellect in the way in which its objects are normally there" (CSM II, 74). The reader ignores this injunction at his peril, and one would be best advised to look again at the use of the term *idea* throughout the *Meditations*, specifically with respect to the sections on doubting. A number of recent scholars, including Calvin Normore, Lilli Alanen, and Vere Chappell, have made a strong case for a primitive notion of intentionality in the "Third Meditation." In its simplest expression this means that the 'objective' reality of an idea indicates the cognitive content, or objectual correlate; and the 'formal' reality pertains to the status of the cause which produces the idea whose 'objective' reality it makes reference to. Thus the 'material' aspect indicates the cognitive act, or act correlate, of the whole process of having a thought. This may seem a very strange use of the term 'material,' which one would ordinarily associate with the building blocks of the physical, extended world, but his usage accords very well with Husserl's bisection in *Ideas First Book* of intentional correlates into 'material' and 'quality.' Although careful adjudication of textual evidence is required to firmly establish this distinction in Descartes' thought, its consequences on methodical doubt are what most concern us here. I hope to show that new insight into Cartesian doubt and a richer understanding of the *Meditations* can be gained by considering various stages (or phases) in the act of doubting, that is, with regard to the cognitive mode or 'material' aspect of doubtful ideas.

There are six distinct phases in the full cognitive process of methodical doubt; these might be considered as the purely intellectual analogue of the stages or stations in devotional exercises. These phases are abandoning prejudices, detachment from the senses, abstention from judgement, clear and distinct seeing, an act of will, and attentional regard. First, it is the natural light, the source of God-given eternal truths, which reveals that prejudices must be abandoned before one can begin to know where to look for a certain foundation for knowledge. Second, one must detach oneself from the world of the senses in order that one is not predisposed to locate this source in the world of extended things. Third, one must abstain from affirming or denying judgements based on sense-derived ideas, since these may be "infected" by worldly instabilities (such as illusions), from which one has just withdrawn and detached. Fourth, the stability and epistemic centrality established thereby allows one to clearly and distinctly grasp whatever resists the destabilizing and decentering influence of the uncertain, of anything which is open to the minimal condition of doubt. Fifth, by an act of will, one endorses all that which has been clearly and distinctly seen, or can be posited as such; one endorses also, as the source of this freedom, the perfection and infinitude of God. And finally, by holding in steadfast mental regard all the previous phases and their necessary connection, one not only retains the certainty of every prior intuition which forms a link in the chain of reasons, but also recapitulates these cognitive "moments" whenever a new concern calls forth the argumentative certainty which this chain endows.

During the period when Descartes composed the *Meditations*, the religious connotations of this title would not have been lost on any reader. L. J. Beck[9] was perhaps the first English language scholar to point out that devotional or spiritual exercises would have been readily familiar to the reading public of that time. The Exercises of Ignatius Loyola, the founder of the Jesuits, would have been especially well-known to the young Descartes who first studied philosophy at the Jesuit College of La Fleche. These exercises were meant to be carried out in complete solitude and endorsed several ascetic precepts—poverty, chastity and obedience—to which the *Meditations* also subscribe. In the context of Descartes' mature thinking, these precepts are *poverty* in the solitary thinker's renunciation of prejudices and received opinions, *chastity* in his complete disengagement from the sensuous world, and *obedience* to the dictates of the "natural light" which reveals God as the guarantor of certitude. Descartes' ascetic orientation towards his own life is quite evident in his choice of a personal motto— *Bene qui latuit, bene vixit*, "He who is well concealed (or lives quietly), lives well." (CSM III, 43; see also, III, 300). In the seventeenth-century context of religious controversies regarding the correct way in which to express one's true faith, usually evinced in the church to which one gave allegiance, the expression of an individual's orientation toward philosophical issues could readily be framed in terms of a radical conversion in that direction. "I am vain enough to think that the [Catholic] faith has never been so strongly supported by human arguments as it may be if my principles are adopted. . . . And so I resign myself to do for my part whatever I regard as my duty and submit myself for the rest to the providence which rules the world." (CSM III, 88).

There are so many respects in which Descartes' and Husserl's projects are congruent that it should come as no surprise to read Paul Ricoeur's sketch of phenomenology as a "spiritual discipline [*ascese*]" and that "a true skeptical crisis is at the origin of the phenomenological question . . . How can [consciousness] move beyond itself and encounter its object with certainty?"[10] It would seem then that both the theological-skeptical crisis of the seventeenth century and the psychological crisis of the nineteenth century motivated a radical rethinking of the legitimate scope of philosophy as such, and that this rethinking was conceived by its originators as a form of conversion. After the publication of the *Logical Investigations* in 1900 and before the public avowal of transcendental idealism in *Ideas First Book* in 1913, Husserl was to experience a personal revaluation of his mission in the light of persistent doubt. "I am unable to live in truth and veracity. I have tasted sufficiently of the torments of obscurity and doubt where I am tossed about in every direction. I must achieve internal coherence" (HUS II, xv). In addition to this internal coherence, researches carried out to expose the autonomous *a priori* structures of consciousness require enormous efforts, strenuous labours expended "in the face of our philosophical poverty in which . . . we are vainly fatiguing ourselves" (Ideas I, 115). In a marginal note to this passage, he remarks that, "These considerations produced for me the insight that a transcendental epoché can be effected, which makes a well-founded and independent philosophy possible." And, of course, Husserl situates the historical and conceptual origins of the epoché in Descartes' procedure of methodical doubt.

If the Cartesian method of universal doubt is that moment in his journey which initiates a radical conversion, it is indeed a turning-with (*con-verto*) the one who first and foremost meditates according to the order of reasons. It is thus at once a turning-against the scholastic tradition and the skeptical challenge, and a turning-toward that which grounds scientific cognition in certitude. Although Husserl will repudiate the consequences of this maneuver as leading to a denial of the already pregiven world, he will embrace the principle of abstention prior to this. It is through a neutralized holding-in-place of that which is abstained from (or, in his own words, the bracketed within the brackets), that the phenomenological reduction is distinguished from Cartesian doubt. As such, in light of phenomenology's projected course as a "spiritual discipline," the epoché assumes the guise of an individual turning-with the thinker himself.[11] In his most mature work, during reflections on the vocation of one who is called or summoned to carry out such work, Husserl is quite explicit about this connection. "Perhaps it will even become manifest that the total phenomenological attitude and the epoché belonging to it are destined in essence to effect, at first, a complete personal transformation, comparable in the beginning to a religious conversion" (Crisis, 137).

If we concede that the individual's decision to activate the epoché is indeed a form of personal conversion for the philosopher, and thus a turning-away from the errors of previous thinkers, Husserl makes no second-order claim for his philosophy that any other philosopher who worked on a grand scale would not also make. One cannot imagine Hume or Kant, for instance, *not* demanding that the reader rethink central issues in light of the program being advanced. In the sense that this is a summons for those who follow to turn-towards "a new region of being never before delimited in its peculiarity," this summons is perfectly congruent with every major shift in the philosophical tradition. Is there something else, something beyond the demand to put aside one's prejudices and start again from zero, that Husserl seems to be calling for that no other philosopher would not also call for? Exception has been taken by some commentators to the epoché as a procedure for achieving a cognitive orientation where it has been likened to a quasi-mystical state.

In an otherwise well-balanced and informative book, David Bell is quite dismissive in this regard: "The reduction itself is a procedure for inducing in us a particular state of mind of which no adequate conception can be formed by those who have not already successfully performed the reduction and thus achieved that state."[12] Let's say that the fact that one has attained this reduced state of mind is a necessary condition for clarifying structures of consciousness and the constitution of meaning, this in no way invalidates the content of what this reduced cognitive state is now in a position to grasp—either a claim made from this point of view is cogent or not. To conclude from one's contingent inability to follow this procedure that what is gained under its auspices is of dubious value is to commit a psychologistic fallacy, the kind of confused reasoning which Husserl was at such pains to expose. Such a fallacy is the inverse of the claim that the ability to cognize a specific logical relation, e.g., commutability of identity, confers legitimacy on what is posited in that cognition. Bell goes on to state that, "there is . . . something dismal and dogmatic about a philosophy whose utility, cogency and plausibility depend essentially . . . on the individual philosopher's having undergone some esoteric experience the nature of which he is then in principle unable to communicate."

Such a caricature of the phenomenological method relegates it to the literary domain occupied by crackpots and eccentrics. Certainly David Bell and other critics do not in fact treat the results of most phenomenological investigations with such disdain. It is a contingent feature of any thinking subject that it is capable of achieving, or recognizing that it has achieved, the epoché; and although the eidetic insights secured thereby are dependent on this attainment, the truth of these insights is not thus dependent. This insightful dependence is not confined to the epoché: conceptual distinctions between "sense" and "reference," for example, or "necessary" and "sufficient condition," are achievements of higher-order reflection, where what was vague and confused becomes clear and distinct. In other words, understanding occurs where each term is both completely significant and sharply separated from the other term. Every one who has engaged in philosophy has had these moments of clarity, the resolution of a conceptual aporia, and though this disclosure may be misplaced or forgotten, the fact that it was achieved and what was disclosed within it are not lost. At a global level, the epoché is a world-bracketing conceptual alteration whose central unlocking mechanism is the concept of intentionality.

Before proceeding to discuss the Cartesian notion of intentionality, we can allow Husserl himself to answer the charge of esotericism:

Consciousness of something is therefore something obviously understandable of itself and, at the same time, highly enigmatic. The *false paths* into which the first reflections leads, easily generate a *skepticism* which negates the whole troublesome sphere of problems. Not a few already bar access by the fact that they cannot bring themselves to seize upon the intentive mental process. . . . If the right attitude has been won, and made secure by practice, above all however, if one has acquired the *courage to obey* the clear eidetic data with a radical *lack of prejudice* so as to be unencumbered by all current and learned theories, then firm results are directly produced, and the same thing occurs for everyone having the same attitude; there accrue firm possibilities of communicating to others what one has himself seen. (Ideas I, 212; emphasis added)

In contrast to Cartesian methodical doubt which pretends that the actual world may be illusory and thus that all knowledge derived from that world has to be treated as if it were false, Husserl's epoché holds in suspension all that appears to consciousness, irrespective of whether or not it is founded on an actual world. If Descartes then seeks to recover a world clarified and made distinct through the dual guarantee of the cogito and God, Husserl seeks to uncover the meaning of this appearing or being presented to consciousness and the epistemological conditions which make this possible. Such conditions, their attendant cognitive structures, the different layers of meaning, the genesis of the ego and its habits—all these issues spring from the incontrovertible characteristic that consciousness always exhibits intentionality. It is not enough to say of this crucial notion that consciousness always indicates being conscious *of*, for it also always indicates being conscious *to*, a unifying and unitary subject. This dwelling or abiding within the sphere of consciousness, which will reveal the domain of transcendental subjectivity, is that fateful discovery initiated by the unprecedented maneuver of the phenomenological reduction.

It is almost fatuous to assert that though Descartes and Husserl are both motivated to radicalize and transform the nature of philosophical enquiry, they differ with respect to *this thing*, or that Husserl goes further than Descartes with respect to *that thing*. It is quite patently within the purview of the present work to exhibit convergent points of departure and divergent destinations. But beyond that, it is our aim to show that there is already more of a Husserlian radicalness in Descartes than Husserl (or his commentators) will admit, and that Cartesian moments on Husserl's journey occur at unremarked places, especially when Husserl does not explicitly acknowledge this influence. The present study is not an exercise in the "exact science" of hindsight, permitting us to isolate and underline curiously prescient statements in Descartes which foreshadow elements in Husserl, since Husserl himself quite openly refers throughout his career to Descartes as his "spiritual forefather." As far as Husserl's construction of an exemplary "Descartes," e.g., in the *Cartesian Meditations*, his Descartes is far less a radical rethinker of first philosophy than Descartes would give voice to, and far more of a phenomenological explorer. In this respect, at least, we entirely agree with Walter Soffer's adroit summation: "The precise nature of Husserl's neo-Cartesianism is thus hard to specify. To the extent that Husserl's view of his relation to Descartes is correct his claim as a neo-Cartesian depends upon the distinction between motif and doctrine. To the extent that his view of the relation is incorrect . . . Husserl's claim can ironically be supported in some measure."[13]

Particular features of the seventeenth-century skeptical milieu and ninteentth-century empirical psychology will account for Descartes' and Husserl's divergent situation of the thinking subject, the notion of scientific knowledge, and the trajectory of a radical return to first principles. Nevertheless, both the Cartesian and the Husserlian enterprise will require the elimination of theoretical prejudices, an Archimedean point from which to begin one's quest, the attainment of an incorrigible domain of knowledge, and the return to a previously abandoned world, now purged of all that is not clearly and distinctly evident. Each of these moments has a different meaning (in the broadest sense) for the two thinkers, but the overall process, symbolized as a journey, is one of losing what is already given, going outward or away from that, and then returning with a new-found understanding.

The skeptics and reformers of the early seventeenth century were in orbit around the problem of the certainty of knowledge and the criterion of religious truth, stabilized in their trajectory by the gravity of the problem's insolubility. Their only surety was through an act of faith which instantly transported them into the sun of God's illumination, an image which occurs in philosophical discourse under the rubric of the "natural light." Descartes was in fact quite fond of astronomical metaphors and his progress through the stages of the *Meditations* can be recast in these terms. His method of universal doubt, which took skepticism to the limit, allowed him to reach escape velocity and free-fall about the sun, then back again to a new world—this is a description of the parabola of a comet.[14] It seems strange then that the progress of methodical doubt should be termed *hyperbolic* (a rhetorical figure for exaggeration) when its observable trajectory is *parabolic*. If any project had a hyperbolic course, it would lead one into the cold and unlighted regions beyond our solar system. These are the dark regions of occultism and atheism which Descartes feared would await those who did not fully understand the purpose of such methodical doubt or when to put it aside. "I was afraid that weak minds might avidly embrace the doubts and scruples which I would have had to propound and afterwards be unable to bring them back." (CSM III, 53). This last phrase underlines the sense of his philosophical project as an outward and return journey, a sense synopsized in the programmatic motto: in order to gain the world one must lose it first.

Of all the scholars who have discussed Descartes' influence on Husserl, Pierre Thevanez should be singled out for his highly evocative, condensed imagery regarding their interconnection. It is one of the oddest features of this seminal article that the comparisons he elicits are so enlightening, so startling in their rendition, that one wishes they were accurate. Thevanez picks up on this same extroverted imagery of a return journey when he asserts that the radical point of departure for Descartes is the center of a centripetal motion, while for Husserl it is the terminus of a centrifugal motion. However, he is quite wide of the mark when he continues, "thus we find in Descartes the virginal beginning and the linear method, going forward without return or recovery, following the order of reasons which are irreversible. While in Husserl we see a circular movement which revolves around its point of departure, radicalizes it progressively without ever truly leaving it."[15] If this is an accurate image of the Cartesian project according to the order of reasons, then it is mistaken with respect to what is uncovered in this course which, according to the order of essences, establishes the certitude of knowledge and the infinitude and perfection of God. If one rejects this linear account of the Cartesian journey then the alleged circularity in reasoning regarding God's guarantee of clear and distinct seeing can be understood as one instance of the reversibility of the ordered reasons which have demonstrated these particular essences. A close reading of the *Meditations* shows that this interpretation accords well with Martial Gueroult's reaction to Thevanez' statement. "It seems that when sketching, with great philosophical talent, his parallels between Descartes and Husserl, Thevanez has not succeeded in exorcising the classical fiction of a linear Descartes, the inventor of a fictional world, who has been able to forget the real because of mathematics and who goes straight forward as a maker of abstract theorems."[16]

At the end of the "Second Meditation," the meditator shows some concern for his readers who have been brought to a pitch of hyperbolic doubt and may fear that they will never have a sure anchorage in the old world again. After his rejection of the deceitful power of the evil genius and the revelation of the cogito's certainty, he has isolated that thing which thinks (*res cogitans*). Amongst those things which this thinking being thinks about is the world of the senses whose openness to illusion and error had first inspired the program of universal doubt. "I see that without any effort I have now finally got back to where I wanted" (CSM II, 22). In this passage he definitely implies that he already had some notion of where he wanted to arrive before he started out; and more than that, that this would involve a turning-away from the world in order to then return to it. "Descartes also says . . . that the doubt is not to be carried into everyday life. . . . That judgement, moreover, is not simply retrospective, something to be recovered when one has come out at the other end; rather, it is an observation about the nature of the project."[17] It will not be until the "Sixth Meditation," however, with the second proof for God firmly in place, that the external world's material support for clear and distinct ideas of substances will be reconfigured on the grounds of an objectively verifiable evidence.

Paul Ricoeur interjects a comment on the phenomenological reduction during his discussion of the Cartesianism of Husserl's project, a comment which contains an implicit criticism of Thevanez' remark that there is no world regained by the meditator.

> The kinship is evident between the Cartesian doubt and this suspending of the belief in being which we apply to the world. Contrary to Descartes' Sixth Meditation, however, no world will be found again. The epoché does not consist in stretching an ontological bond in order to be more assured of it; rather it claims to dispel irrevocably the realistic illusion of the in-itself. Only the intersubjective perception of [Husserl's] Fifth Cartesian Meditation will change the 'for me' into 'for others' . . . and then the world will be found (or regained) again.[18]

If Descartes' project is to establish the foundations for an entirely new realm of being, whereas Husserl's project is to disclose an entirely new sense of the world, then these outward and return movements will have parallel trajectories but divergent destinations. It is specifically with reference to the epoché that Husserl's rhetorical terminology incorporates this metaphor. The epoché suspends or brackets all acts of belief-positing in the natural attitude so that one is able to seize upon what could have effected this alteration. "That then is what is left as the sought for phenomenological residuum; though we have excluded the whole world with all physical things, living beings and humans, ourselves included. Strictly speaking, we have *not lost* anything but rather *have gained* the whole of absolute being which, rightly understood, contains within itself, constitutes within itself, all worldly transcendencies" (Ideas I, 113; emphasis added).

A synoptic image may be of some help in understanding the overall thematic parallel between Descartes' and Husserl's philosophical enterprises. One can think here of Descartes' reference to abbreviated representations, e.g., astronomers' imaginary circles, in order to construct such an image. Imagine then, if you will, a world-sphere which the meditator turns away from and leaves behind by carrying through the process of methodical doubt. The journey narrated in the *Meditations* describes a parabolic course outward and into deep space (or, in this case, a plenum). But before it is lost forever, the meditating ego is captured by the infinite epistemic force of God as first truth in the order of beings and turns back towards its worldly origins. But the world it returns to is not the same: there are now two spheres, *res cogitans* and *res extensa*, which perfectly coincide in the thinker himself. Where before there had been a profusion of sensuous qualities, now there are precise configurations of continuous quantities. Lest the explorer ever think that he may lose his bearings in this new world, he can always retrace his course through the order of reasons. And he is always capable of doing this in the certain knowledge that God has indeed provided the ground for all this-worldly truths.

In Husserl's case, there are three courses away from this world, as outlined in *The Crisis of European Sciences*: the psychological, the ontological, and the Cartesian. Our concern here is only to point out the path traced by the last course. In some sense, the enterprise initiated by the phenomenological reduction is not an outward and return journey. Imagine instead a world which remains sharply in focus, but where the 'act' of focusing is itself thematized, that is, made the 'object' of reflective thought. In cinematic terms, this would be a reverse forward zoom, where the camera backs away while the lens zooms in on the subject; the outward motion is exactly coordinated with the optical forward closure. The effect for the viewer is one of canceling or annulling the two polarized movements—and yet the subject itself remains just as before. What has changed is the frame, the background and foreground, all those features which provide the essential context for situating the subject. The startling effect of this visual transformation can be appreciated only if one attends to its continuous unfolding; a before and after picture would be entirely inadequate. In the same fashion, the bracketing of the world leaves intact what is in the brackets, but makes its situation or placement, and hence its meaning, stand out. This is the significance of Husserl's remark that where Descartes discovered an entirely new world of being, Husserl himself was concerned to uncover an entirely new sense of the world.

The significance of a purified sense of the world as an "acceptance phenomenon," one which is subtended by the general thesis of the world's being, can perhaps be made more clear by dramatically rephrasing the question, What does the epoché accomplish? What does it mean to say that the whole world is gained *in a new way* once it has been lost? For the phenomenologist, philosophical enquiry is not a matter of apprising oneself of the facts in the case, as though the source of knowledge of the world were a puzzle whose answer was hidden somewhere. Rather, it is a matter of surprise that the world appears just this way and not otherwise, a radical contingency signified by Husserl's reference to "the irrational fact of the rationality of the world." Insofar as the philosopher considers the mind's empirical, circumstantial connection with the world, it will always be the case that the world looks just like the philosopher's terms describe it to be. There is not anything else against which a "bridging theory" of the mind's awareness of the world could be adjudicated. "As traditional theory of cognition shows, this enigma [of cognition] cannot be solved as long as immanence and transcendence are regarded in the form of an ontologically grounded opposition which could only be overcome by constructing a connecting 'bridge.' "[19] For example, granted Spinoza's hypothesis of one infinite substance with two principal attributes which have infinite modes, each of his further claims about particular features will make sense in terms of this world-picture. What is it then about the world and the mind such that this fulfilment or correspondence would always take place? One way to answer this question would be to study the various frameworks in which thinkers articulate their vocabularies, for example, an archaeology of philosophical discourse. Since it is not possible to ask what the world would be like disengaged from consciousness, another approach to this question would be, What would consciousness be like disengaged from the world? This disengagement is the task of the phenomenological reduction, and the domain uncovered thereby is the proper subject matter of a transcendental phenomenology.

2

SEVENTEENTH-CENTURY SKEPTICISM VERSUS NINETEENTH-CENTURY EMPIRICAL PSYCHOLOGY

It is one of Descartes' lasting achievements that, confronted with the skeptical crisis of the late sixteenth and early seventeenth centuries, he did not participate in the controversy as either a proponent of the recently revived Greek skepticism nor as an adherent of a dogmatic philosophical viewpoint. In stark contrast to Montaigne, Gassendi, and others, Descartes does not quote from, borrow, or depend in any way for his arguments upon previous writers. None of his works show the reliance which his predecessors and contemporaries placed on the authority of other writers, especially the ancient authors. Even Galileo attempted to disguise (in some degree) the originality of his heliocentric theory by resort to the testimony of ancient cosmographers. It has long been established that Renaissance and Reformation writers had an entirely different attitude toward the work of previous writers than the post-Enlightenment obsession with originality and accurate citation of references—a position of indebtedness we now take for granted.

In his immensely popular *Essays*, Montaigne borrowed liberally from Sextus Empiricus, Cicero's *Academica,* Guy de Brues' *Dialogues,* and the works of many others, usually without acknowledgment; Pierre Charron borrowed from Montaigne and Sextus Empiricus; Gassendi from Montaigne, Charron, and Sextus, and so forth. This was very much the ordinary editorial practice of the period, so how much more extraordinary must the *Meditations* have been when they appeared in print in 1641. Aside from its astounding ambition to establish the possibility of certain knowledge in the sciences upon an indubitable chain of reasons, this was to be accomplished without recourse to any outside testimony; in fact, of course, such external support was prohibited altogether.

Many of the criticisms directed against Descartes (especially by Gassendi in the "Fifth Objections") included the charge that he ignored what "many learned men" had said on some topic or other, and his response was brusque and constant. The mere fact that N. asserts that it is obvious that such-and-such is the case bears no relation whatsoever to the certitude of such-and-such. If the meditator and some other thinker are in agreement on the topic at hand, it is no more than a fortunate by-product of the certainty of the very proposition under question.

> Those who seek learning from standard texts and indexes and concordances can pack their memories with many things in a short time, but they do not emerge as wiser or better people as a result. On the contrary, there is no chain of reasoning in such books, but everything is decided either by appeal to authority or by short summary syllogisms, and those who seek learning from these sources become accustomed to placing equal trust in the authority of any writer . . . , so little by little they lose the use of their natural reason and put in its place an artificial and sophistical reason. (CSM III, 222)

The Seventeenth-Century Skeptical Background—Basic Features

Recent research[1] has emphasized the unprecedented manner in which Descartes confronts the skeptical challenge, primarily in terms of the complete control of the skeptical position which he exercises for purposes unforeseen by any skeptical proponent. For the interpreters of Cicero's *Academica,* skeptical arguments were deployed to demonstrate that nothing certain could be known, that it was futile to engage in the search for truth in the sciences. For the Pyrrhonian followers of Sextus Empiricus, the claim that any given epistemic assertion could be countered with an equal-weighted assertion for the opposite (*isosthenia*), was sufficient to persuade the wise man to suspend judgment (*epoché*), and attain a position of equanimity (*ataraxia*). In either version of skepsis, the arguer must be prepared to counter any assertion presented to him and show how this assertion leads to either nonsense, circular reasoning, or an infinite regress; but in this format, the skeptic is not in control of which specific knowledge claims are being made. The repertoire of standard arguments is purely defensive and makes no constructive attempt to explain what sort of conditions might be required in order for a knowledge claim not to be ruled out. Descartes will completely turn the tables on his skeptical opponent by appropriating the position of total ignorance, calling into doubt every conceivable condition for knowing, and then showing that only through the founding of certain knowledge can one avoid circular reasoning and an infinite regress.

It is not the purpose of the present study (at the moment anyway) to reiterate or argue further for the extraordinary manner in which Descartes overturns any possible skepticism. Nor is its task to illuminate the transmission of ancient skeptical material in the works of sixteenth and early seventeenth century humanists, reformers, and counter-reformers. Rather its task is to highlight specific lines of thinking in those writers who most influenced and shaped the skeptical crisis of this period. Only in this manner will it be possible to elucidate the claim that Descartes adopts the position of the most relentless skeptic and, in taking this to the limit, thus overturns skepticism. Husserl, in his attack on nineteenth-century psychologism and relativism, will characterize his own standpoint as a "descriptive psychology" which does not hesitate to go further than any other empirical psychology, and in doing so, invalidate any alleged empirical foundation for logic. Aspects of particular seventeenth-century skeptical disclaimers about the origin, validity, and relational character of knowledge (or the fallibility thereof) bear remarkable parallels with particular claims by nineteenth-century empirical philosophers about the similar character of logical constructions. It is highly significant in this respect that Husserl, in his summary position regarding previous researches in the empirical psychology of cognition, will describe his own phenomenological inquiry as "radical scepticism" (PP, 3). Indeed, it is the skeptical procedures of the natural sciences which empirical psychologists did not take far enough into their own domain; they "suspended judgment" at the point where indeed all factually occurring mental events are intrinsically relational and origin-dependent, hence their hypotheses are inconclusive.

> Natural science has become great by unhesitatingly setting aside the luxuriant growth of ancient skepticism and refusing to conquer it. . . . Natural science has taken half a step backwards again whereby it has given room to new skeptical reflections and let itself be limited by skeptical tendencies in its possibilities for work. . . . The right position . . . is that position which sets aside with full awareness all skepticism together with all "natural philosophy" and "theory of knowledge," and takes cognitive objectivities where one actually finds them. (Ideas I, 47)

In order to contrast a groundless skeptical orientation with the grounded certitude of Cartesian 'universal science,' it will be necessary to examine specific arguments and positions held by contemporary seventeenth-century skeptical writers. In the historical context in which the rule of faith, papal infallibility, and the Church as arbiter of theological doctrine had been called into question by Luther and Calvin, the publication of Sextus Empiricus' compendium of ancient skepticism added further fuel to an already heated debate. A great deal of groundbreaking research on the transmission and influence of skeptical arguments on the writers of this period has been done in a number of books over the last thirty years by Richard Popkin, whose synoptic starting points are adopted here. Latin editions of Sextus' *Outlines* by Henri Stephanus in 1562 and by Gentian Hervet in 1569 made available for the first time a vast array of skeptical material which far surpassed what had been previously provided by Cicero's *Academica* and Diogenes Laertius' *Lives*. Montaigne was the first great popularizer of Sextus' and Cicero's materials and the several editions of his *Essays* in 1580, 1588, and 1595, especially the "Apology for Raymond Sebond," spread his trenchant criticisms beyond the Latin-speaking community. Pierre Gassendi (1592–1655), close associate of many of the libertines, Marin Mersenne, and other influential writers, published his first work, the *Exercises,* in 1624 and was one of Descartes' most rebarbative critics.

Another skeptical writer in this historical context is Francisco Sanchez (1550–1623) whose *Quod Nihil Scitur*[2] of 1581 is quite distinct from the previous writers both in style and depth of argument. Where Montaigne and Gassendi write in a discursive, rambling fashion, interspersing lengthy polemics against the stupidity and arrogance of mankind with brief synoptic arguments presented almost like factual anecdotes, Sanchez clears the table of the new skeptics' banquet of ancient ideas and presents a rigorous and systematic attack on the conviction that one can attain certitude in knowledge on the basis of reason alone. "This book differs radically from the [other] works . . . in that it is a philosophical work in its own right. Sanchez is more interesting than any of the other skeptics of the sixteenth century except Montaigne in that his reasons for his doubts are neither the anti-intellectual ones of someone like Agrippa, nor the suspicion that knowledge is unattainable just because learned men have disagreed up to now."[3] Charles Schmitt also singles out Sanchez as one of the most important figures pointing the way towards the skeptical crisis of the seventeenth century.[4]

Although Sextus' outline of the ten tropes or modes of skeptical argument has been amply discussed elsewhere,[5] they will be worth some attention now in order to clearly mark out the sort of assertions which have strong connections with Husserl's critical targets. Sextus defines skepticism as "an ability, or mental attitude, which opposes appearances [*phainomena*] and judgments [*noumena*] in any way whatsoever, with the result that, owing to the equipollence [*isosthenia*] of the objects and reasons thus opposed, we are brought firstly to a state of mental suspense [*epoché*] and next to a state of quietude [*ataraxia*]."[6] This summary definition comprises virtually all of the key terms in ancient Pyrrhonian skepticism, aside from the concept of the criterion, which has two senses: "In the one, it means the standard regulating belief in reality or unreality . . . ; in the other, it denotes the standard of action by conforming to which in the conduct of life we perform some actions and abstain from others."[7] The former sense brings with it more complex epistemological problems which will extend much further and deeper than the ten tropes' surface counter-claims, or to which the ten tropes themselves are methodically reduced. The latter sense is the synoptic notion which embraces the moral maxims whereby the skeptic lives his life; this is taken up again in the tenth trope.

Sextus then presents the ten tropes, also called arguments or positions, each of which capitalizes on the relativity of the perceiving subject and object perceived. The eighth mode has a second-order status which subsumes the previous seven modes, since it stands as a generic trope to their specific charges. There are at least two broad arguments from relativity, for which abundant anecdotal evidence is cited under the heading of one or another trope. The first (reconstructed) argument is this: the same things produce different impressions in different subjects (including animals) and human subjects express differing judgments on these same things. The production of different impressions, and hence judgments, is due to differing conditions under which the thing appears (e.g., well-lit, far away, close by, etc.) and/or differing dispositions in the subject (e.g., drunkenness, illness, senility, etc.). It is impossible to decide which impressions should be given greater credence; thus, although it is possible to give an adequate account of how the thing appears to the subject, it is not possible to demonstrate that this appearing "corresponds with" or adequately represents the thing as it is *in itself.* The most appropriate decision then is for the subject to suspend judgment on the true nature of the thing.

In "Against the Logicians" Sextus reworks the material of the ten tropes[8] in presenting the subject, the object and the relative conditions before the "seat of judgment," in his juristic metaphor, to inquire which of the contesting positions should be the "magistrate" in sorting out such diversity of opinion. This magistrate's decisive power indicts the problem of the criterion discussed at great length in the "Outlines" where it is attacked on two main fronts.[9] A candidate for the criterion that would settle which of the many conflicting appearances indicates the "true nature" of the underlying object, must make an assertion about the veracity of the appearance. If this assertion is not to be counterbalanced with a contrary assertion, it must demonstrate a proof for this assertion's assent. Since such a proof will also have only appearances to rely on, it will also itself have to be proved, and hence generate an infinite regress.

It is not to our purpose to consider skeptical arguments regarding specific theories about the correspondence (or lack thereof) of appearances with underlying things, but rather with the rejection (or acceptance) of judgments allegedly based on those theories and the reasons adduced for such rejection (or acceptance). Thus it is not an issue here to uncover the epistemological presuppositions in the skeptic's theory of perception and the ontological diremption between that which is presented [*phantasia*], appearances [*phainomena*], and the underlying reality [*hypokeimena*]. "The skeptic does not divide the world into appearances and realities so that one could ask of this or that whether it belongs to the category of appearance or to the category of reality. He divides questions into questions about how something appears and questions about how it really and truly is, and both types of question may be asked about anything whatever."[10] It just doesn't seem to have occurred to the skeptics to adjust their theory of what it means to have knowledge of the world in order to take account of these divergences. In any case, discursive efforts to isolate specific aspects of the skeptical analysis of judgments will underline salient features of the problem of the criterion.

In response to Voetius' charge that his works "open the way to scepticism," Descartes replies:

> If you are referring here to the actual time at which an act of faith, or natural cognition, is elicited, you are destroying all faith and human knowledge, and are indeed a sceptic. . . . But if we are talking of different times . . . this merely shows the weakness of human nature, since we do not always remain fixed on the same thoughts. . . . For I was speaking not of any certainty that would endure throughout an entire human life, but merely of the kind of certainty that is achieved at the moment when some piece of knowledge is acquired. (CSM III, 223)

In the outline devoted to the existence and nature of cause [*aition*][11] one of Sextus' arguments is that someone who asserts that there is some cause of some thing, either asserts this absolutely, i.e., without basing his assertion on any rational cause, or he does so due to certain causes. If he asserts this absolutely, his statement is "no more" weighted than the assertion of the opposite statement, in light of neither having any rational cause. Whereas if he asserts this on the basis of certain causes, then he will be assuming that which he wishes to prove. This is an important moment, a crucial conflation of the notion of physical causation with the notion of psychical motivation. The kind of causal relations between things is not the same kind as those "reasons" which might be based on observation of physical causation, which convince or motivate a person to make a specific knowledge claim. One feature of Descartes' program in the mapping of the physiology of perception, memory, and imagination will be to carefully mark out this distinction. Although it is true that the activity of the "animal spirits," insofar as they are an operative principle in corporeal memory and imagination, occurs in a manner equivalent to the operation of causal regularities in the physical world, the connection between ideas and their expression in judgments cannot be subsumed under the laws of physical causality. The certitude of clear and distinct ideas is the result of, among other factors, their being grounded in a domain which has, from the start, been divorced from the entire world of sense impressions and preconceived judgments about physical causality.

In his dissection of the empirical psychologists' derivation of logical laws from factual mental events, Husserl will underline a similar interpolation from one domain to the other and make this trenchant criticism. After pointing out the first confusion, in identifying logical laws as contents of judgments with the judgments themselves, the second confusion is that "We confuse a law as a term in causation with a law as the rule of causation. In other fields too, we familiarly employ mythical talk of natural laws as presiding powers in natural events—as if the rules of causal connection could themselves once more significantly function as causes, i.e. as terms in just such connections" (LI, 102). It is definitely a case of mythical talk for Sextus to so collapse physical causality into the force of rational persuasion and to consider these laws as "presiding powers" in the operation of human thought.

In order to disprove the existence of physical bodies Sextus resorts to a similar equivocation between the mathematical concept of a limit and the actual boundaries of a physical body.[12] He adduces a spurious "proof" which is only plausible if there is a systematic equivocation between "parts" of a geometrical object, which are its functional predicates, and "parts" (in some atomistic sense) of the boundary of a physical thing. This particular version of terminological slight-of-hand is found in a number of his arguments purporting to refute the physical laws of motion, and so forth. The enigma of abstract parts of an abstract whole vis-à-vis dependent parts of a physical whole will exercise all of Descartes' ingenuity in attempting to reconcile the Christian mystery of transubstantiation of the body of Christ in the Eucharist with his principles of physics (CSM II, 173–78).

Gorgias is quoted with much approval in his elimination (or disavowal) of nonexistent things which are merely thought of (fictitious entities, e.g., the chimera) and the consequent inability of a speaker to communicate anything about either nonexistent things or sensible things of which one does not have any direct experience. Let us disregard the highly sophistical "arguments" regarding the ontological status of existent and nonexistent things, whether thought or not thought. It is, however, worth noting the unexpected consequences of this position on human speech about such alleged 'objects,' and hence, of course, on what judgments are formed thereby.

> For the means by which we indicate is speech, and speech is not the real and existent things; therefore we do not *indicate* to our neighbors the existent things but speech,

which is other than the existing realities. Thus, just as the visible thing will not become audible, and vice versa, so too, since the existent subsists externally, it will not *become* our speech, and not being speech it will not be made clear to another person.[13] (emphasis added)

It is a serious distortion of whatever sense is conveyed by "indication" that speech as the means of communication indicates nothing more than the fact that speech occurs, due to the fact that whatever it is you are communicating about is not the same sort of thing as the process of communicating. This distortion has repercussions on other philosophical debates; it shows up, for instance, in the disavowal of intelligible speech as a distinguishing feature of human beings. Montaigne and Gassendi will make much of the alleged overstatement of speech as human specific in their anecdotal evidence for communication between animals. Of course, it's only through language that the concept of sensible thing can mean something to a sentient being and hence figure as a link in an inferential process. As part of his general scheme for the founding of the sciences, Descartes will restore signifying speech to its preeminent place as a uniquely human prerogative (CSM I, 140).

If speech were to distinguish humans from other animals (but doesn't, according to the skeptic), then perhaps the faculty of sensation would distinguish animals from nonliving things. In the endless and repetitive search for an infallible criterion by which any perception or judgment could be evaluated as evident or true, reason in the apprehension of intelligible things, and sensation in the apprehension of sensible things will each be discounted. The former is discarded in light of the pretheoretical assumption that there is nothing in the intellect which has not already been presented to the senses, and the latter in terms of the following argument, attributed to Carneades. All sensation occurs due to the impact of evident things, and insofar as anything is presented to sense, this being-sensed will indicate both itself and the appearance. This presentation occurs as an alteration in our sense faculty whereby one *perceives* both the alteration, i.e., the presenting as such, and that which is presented in the presenting, i.e., the appearing thing. "But since [cognition] does not always indicate the true object, but often deceives and, like bad messengers, misreports those who dispatched it, it has necessarily resulted that we cannot admit every presentation as a criterion of truth, but only that which is true."[14] Such a disqualification of sense as a potential criterion (whatever its other demerits) is the result of having treated the act of presentation as the same sort of thing as that which is presented; that is, of requiring from the psychical occurrence of some presenting act the veracity of which only the presented content is capable. To modify Carneades' metaphor, it would be to accuse the messenger of lying (or being mistaken) because he had correctly reported the occurrence of a falsehood (or a mistake).

Several specific lines of skeptical argument have been isolated for examination for two purposes. The first is to throw some light on challenges to dogmatic knowledge which would later be reinvigorated by Montaigne, Gassendi, and other 'neo'-skeptics. The second is to explicate conceptual confusions which point the way towards the kind of wrong-headed thinking which will be the target of a thorough-going refutation by Descartes and, reworked under the aegis of naturalistic psychology, the target for Husserl as well. If it has not been thought necessary in this present study to consider all of the main skeptical arguments, Descartes himself rejected a point-by-point rebuttal of skeptical tropes. On the other hand, it is not possible to treat skepticism as a unified philosophical position in order to attempt to refute it as Descartes did. If it is accurate to claim that Descartes took control of skepticism in order to bring it to an extremity of self-purgation, for this study to take complete control in this manner, analyses of specific skeptical arguments would indeed evaporate. Some of these conceptual confusions and collapses would survive the Cartesian overthrow and, like a persistent contagion or infection, reappear in mutated forms throughout the next two hundred years. Having "evolved" in parallel with the progress of the natural sciences, some of them reemerge in the nineteenth century in empirical investigations into the psychological origin of logical laws.

Characteristics of Neo-Skeptical Arguments

Montaigne is justly credited with being the first modern writer to consistently and thoroughly treat himself as the theme of an "empirical investigation." His subject matter is not the nature of the human mind in general, but the nature and growth of this one person, through the story of his education, travels, illnesses, and other all-too-human trials. With more influence and as much insight as any other sixteenth-century writer, Montaigne assimilated the skeptical arguments of Sextus Empiricus and Cicero's *Academica,* especially in the "Apology for Raymond Sebond," written in the 1570s and appearing in each of the expanded editions of the *Essays.* As well as an idiosyncratic disquisition on his own convictions and fallibilities, Montaigne was also responsible for an unprecedented deployment of arguments from cultural relativism. Having read accounts of the Spanish discovery of the New World, as well as recently published compendia of curious practices in the Orient, and having access to sailors' and natives' first-hand reports of North America, he was in an unrivaled position to make

comparisons with customs and beliefs completely alien to the European tradition. This cultural relativism, combined with his vigorous advocacy of skeptical
doubt, was to give Montaigne's popular writings an extraordinary influence on
skeptical writers for the next two centuries.

Montaigne begins the "Apology for Sebond" by defending Sebond's Natural
Theology against two charges: that Christians are wrong to attempt to support
their religious beliefs with human reason, and that Sebond's arguments are weak
and unsuited for what he wants to demonstrate.[15] Guided by Augustine's insistence on the human need for the light of divine grace, Montaigne will take up
the challenge and go further than merely meeting his critics' presumption. Close
attention to the arrogant claims for the power of human rationality teaches the
lesson that "the weakness of their reason can be proved without our having to
marshal rare examples; that reason is so inadequate, so blind, that there is no
example so clear and easy as to be clear enough for her; that the easy and the
hard are all one to her; that all subjects and Nature in general equally deny her
any sway or jurisdiction."

Human beings, he declaims, are vain and presumptuous to consider that the
faculty of reason could set them apart from other creatures, arrogant to think that
reason could show the way to certainty in questions of knowledge. If rationality
is held out to be that feature distinctive and unique to human beings, by means
of which they and they alone can presume to have certain knowledge, one
avenue of attack for Montaigne is to demonstrate that this alleged rationality is
not unique to human beings and thus does not give them any privileged access
to truth. Later in the "Apology," he will attack the second half of this claim—
even if rationality were unique to humans, it is fallible, prone to error and
misuse, and cannot attain to any such certitude. Montaigne cites numerous examples, drawn mostly from ancient authorities, of the intelligence, faithfulness,
probity, and so forth of many animal species. In stark contrast, only humans
show willful ignorance, cowardice, vengeance, and sexual voracity beyond the
bounds that any animal would exhibit. It is strange to consider that just where
Montaigne situates human deficiencies as illustrations of humans' inferiority
to other animals, it would perhaps be more pertinent to cite such behavior
as evidence of human reason's ability to deny and override merely biological
constraints.

Philosophy is singled out as the paragon of human reason and numerous
instances brought forth, similar to the humble comparisons with animals, to
demonstrate that even the most eminent philosophers disagreed about every
conceivable issue, and that having the rules of logic at their command did not
prevent them from suffering in the way that any other human would. "When men
are demented their very actions show how appropriate madness is to the work-

ings of our souls at their most vigorous. . . . Do you want a man who is sane, moderate, firmly-based, and reliable? Then array him in darkness, sluggishness and heaviness. To teach us to be wise, make us stupid like beasts; to guide us you must blind us."[16] It stark contrast to this, it is the possibility of madness which will help clear the way for Descartes at an early stage of methodical doubt, and it will be laziness or sluggishness which pulls him away from clarity and distinctness attained through this doubt (CSM II, 13 and 15).

It is in the second half of the "Apology" that Montaigne begins his extensive borrowings from Sextus' *Outlines* and Cicero's *Academica.* Montaigne approves of the skeptics' goal of *ataraxia,* freedom from disturbances—perplexities which cause fear, envy, pride, and other conditions due to which humans commit the most "inhuman" acts. The skeptics' technique consists in their ability to counterpose any assertion with another assertion of equal weight, i.e., one of equivalent support by the evidence. "This is doubt taken to its limits; it shakes its own foundations; such extremes of doubt separate them completely from many other theories." And then, "Other people are prejudiced by the customs of their country, by the education given them by their parents or by chance encounter: normally, before the age of discretion, they are taken by storm and, without judgment or choice, accept this or that opinion of the Stoic or Epicurean sects."[17] This formulation has echoes in the opening lines of the "First Meditation" on the prejudices of childhood and the need to demolish everything in order to start at the foundations; and in Descartes' comments in response to the "Seventh Objections," that those who find nothing in philosophy to satisfy them are taken in by the skeptical sect (CSM II, 374).

Descartes will deftly extract some of Montaigne's figures of speech,[18] reworking some of these images from the ancient skeptics, and then redirect them to attack the position that knowledge is unattainable. One of Montaigne's best-known metaphors likens a human mind to a blank tablet: "No system discovered by man has greater usefulness nor a greater appearance of truth [than Pyrrhonism] which shows us man naked, empty, aware of his natural weakness, fit to accept outside help from on high. . . . He is a blank writing-tablet, made ready for the finger of God to carve such letters on him as he pleases."[19] It is precisely to this "stripped" subject, naked, empty and aware of prejudices that Descartes will turn for the subject most suited to the reception of clear and distinct ideas and the operation of intellective seeing. The image of the "blank writing-tablet" will reappear again in Gassendi and most famously in Locke's *Essay* a century later.

Montaigne will later mock detachment from the senses: "One fine philosopher even poked out his eyes so as to free his mind from visual debauchery . . . but by the same standard he ought to have blocked up his ears. . . . Eventually he would have to deprive himself of every other sense, for all the senses can have this dominant power over our reason and our soul."[20] This is exactly the motivation which impels Descartes to carry this out, if only as a thought experiment. "I will now shut my eyes, stop my ears, and withdraw all my senses. I will eliminate from my thoughts all images of bodily things" (CSM II, 24). Insofar as Montaigne would refuse to carry this out and instead holds to the conviction that all knowledge is acquired through the senses, his image for the mind is that it is like "a tool of malleable lead or wax; it can be stretched, bent or adapted to any size or to any bias; if you are clever, you can learn to mold it."[21] Such an image would indeed be conducive to the notion that reason has no fixed basis in itself and shifts with the infinite shiftings of the things which it apprehends. It is the reverse image which Descartes employs to demonstrate the operation of reason—that through all its material and apparent changes, the piece of wax remains the same piece of wax and is perceived as such by the mind alone (CSM II, 20–21).

It is the factual contingency of discrepant judgments expressed with regard to appearances that leads Montaigne to one of his most damaging (and fallacious) statements. "The *fact* that there is no single proposition which is not subject to controversy among us, or which cannot be so, *proves* that our natural judgment *does not grasp* very clearly even when it does grasp, since my judgment cannot bring another's judgment to accept it, which is a *sure sign* that I did not myself reach it by means of a *natural power* common to myself and to all men."[22]

This conclusion depends for its rhetorical force on an invalid inference from the empirical fact that a proposition is open to disagreement to the 'proof' of human inability to grasp the content of a proposition. In other words, its purported validity rests on the necessary dependence of the judgment's certainty on the psychical occurrence of such judgments in individual subjects and their psychical "power" to accurately express these judgments. This highly spurious hypothesis bears an uncanny resemblance to similar claims made by J. S. Mill, Sigwart, and others in the mid-nineteenth century in their exposition of the nature of judgment—a revealing parallel which we will return to later. The point to be drawn here is that Descartes will be able to defend clarity and distinctness as criteria of cognitive grasp by founding these criteria on *a priori* 'primary notions' which make possible the insight into the compatibility or incompatibility of judgments based on them.

Montaigne returns to the themes of madness and dreaming as exemplary instances of the extent to which human beings have fallen away from the truth. "To be convinced of certainty is certain evidence of madness and of extreme unsureness." One can only be uncertain whether Montaigne deliberately wanted to attribute the status of certain evidence to the connection between the conviction of certainty and the experience of madness. He is also quite certain as to where such fallenness will lead: "Our waking sleeps more than our sleeping; our wisdom is less wise than our folly; our dreams are worth more than our discourse; and to remain inside ourselves is to adopt the worst place of all."[23] After purging himself of sensory illusions, the waking/dreaming dilemma, and so forth, it is within himself that Descartes will find the place to apply the Archimedean lever to shift the entire world. Despite beginning the "Apology" with support from Augustine, Montaigne seems to have abandoned Augustine's dictum that "Truth dwells within the inner man." Nevertheless, through his paraphrases of Sextus, Montaigne resuscitated the Greek skeptics' arguments on doctrinal relativism, suspension of judgment as conducive to quietude, sensory illusions, the alleged veracity of thoughts in dreaming, and that the search for a criterion leads to either circular reasoning or an infinite regress.[24]

Montaigne concludes his skeptical attack on rational aspirations for certain knowledge with weary resignation. "There is no permanent existence either in our being or in that of objects. We ourselves, our faculty of judgment, and all mortal things are flowing and rolling ceaselessly: nothing certain can be established about one from the other, since both judged and judging are ever shifting and changing."[25] This climactic formulation assimilates both the subjective and the objective domains, the world of being and the conditions of knowing, into an all-embracing Heraclitean flux, wherein the bewildered human's only sure anchorage will be provided by faith through divine grace. If Montaigne's motives had been to counter violent sectarianism and overzealous enthusiasm, his trenchant and extensive critique of the poverty of reason was almost too successful. If he had wanted to highlight the virtues of skeptical suspension in order to point the way to fideistic belief, the "Apology" was often read as a testimony to negative dogmatism and the adoption of an atheistic position.[26]

Pierre Gassendi was also strongly motivated by the skeptic's practical approach to an ethical life and his earliest work, the *Exercises* of 1624, praises Charron, Montaigne, Lipsius, Seneca, and Cicero, and states that but for lack of worldly experience, he would consider himself a disciple of Sextus Empiricus.[27] The *Exercises* is a very curious and precocious work, since it embraces quite a wide variety of scientific, theological, and philosophical positions. Gassendi is in many respects one of the earliest empiricist philosophers and elaborated a detailed if confusing theory of knowledge based on experience and *a posteriori* reasoning. He accepted the Copernican revolution in astronomy and the anti-Aristotelian conception of atoms and the void, and developed some of the most virulent, if not most persuasive, arguments against standard logic, universal statements, and the primacy of mathematical principles. And yet he would have adhered to a complete relativism and solipsism if not rescued from total darkness and ignorance by the surety of divine illumination. On a number of points he prefigures Descartes' *Discourse* in his reworking of skeptical doubt and the epoché, but was sufficiently biased by the standard interpretation of Sextus that he failed to see that his own doubts about sense experience did not go as far as Sextus' original doubts.[28] It is certainly an anomaly of the *Exercises* that many of the conceptual confusions and conflations which are being highlighted here reach their "clearest" formulation, that is, the confusions become more pronounced and eccentric, and incommensurate epistemic claims are stretched to the breaking point.

In introducing these "indigestible compositions of mine," Gassendi seems to start out in a promising manner with an invocation made more memorable by Descartes in the *Discourse* and the *Meditations*. "In the beginning it seemed to me that I would need great mettle to break free where so few have tried to stand on their own feet, to rid myself of so many habits contracted since childhood from exposure to common men, to shake off the shameful yoke of this prejudice."[29] But this promising start is sadly diminished when it becomes apparent that his purpose in "starting afresh" is to redress the balance between the ancient skeptics and their current adversaries by rehabilitating the skeptics' tropes and restoring their original charm. He revives Sextus' and Montaigne's derision of the worth of logic by imputing circular reasoning to the logician's attempt to arrive at the nature (or essence) of any species of material thing. In sum, where the logician recommends definition and division of examples of a particular in order to unravel its specific nature, the skeptic responds that one already has to have some notion of the thing in order to pick out examples to be analyzed. The chemist knows far more about gold and fire, the farmer about crops, etc. than any logician ever could. This is a peculiar notion of the proper domain of logic, to say the least, but his remarks also extend to analyses of the grammar and usage of sentences.

The same argument is brought forth to show the inappropriateness of logic to an understanding of words and propositions, since it is only words' actual usage and the grammatical structure of sentences which reveal their correct interpretation. Throughout the examples he adduces from anatomy, military tactics, music, and geometry, Gassendi relies on several ingredients for his dismissal of logic: first on the physical composition and internal relations of the things which words "represent" or stand for; second, on empirical observation of what parts they are actually composed of or could be divided into; and third, most importantly, on his assumption that it is experience alone which can provide the criterion according to which the predication of specific features (and parts of wholes) can be judged to be true or false. Gassendi's vague and hazily defined concept of experience will have far too much work to do, especially in discussions of universal concepts, common nouns, and the proper domain of mathematical entities. For example, "Universals are nothing more than what the grammarians call common nouns, or ones that can be applied to more than one object, e.g. 'man' or 'horse.' " And because of his extremely limited account of the origins of knowledge, since everything that one perceives in the world is unique, *where* is the location of a universal term which serves to mark this thing out as an instance?[30]

In this early work, Gassendi briefly considers whether or not it would be legitimate to construe as genuine knowledge one's own experience of the appearance of things, but not with reference to any underlying reality. "When I say that I know that I am now seated rather than standing, that it is day rather than night, that I am fasting rather than full, at home rather than in the marketplace" could this be called knowledge?[31] He hesitates precisely at the point where Descartes, seated in front of the fire at the start of the "First Meditation," calls such appearances into doubt and takes one step further along the road to certain knowledge. Gassendi backs away from the precipice and asserts that only through direct acquaintance with its cause or through proof derived from this cause is there certain and evident cognition of a thing. M. F. Burnyeat has accurately pointed out that "the idea that truth can be attained without going outside subjective experience was not always the philosophical commonplace it has come to be. It was Descartes who made it so, who (in the second Meditation) laid the basis for our broader use of the predicates 'true' and 'false,' whereby they can apply to statements of appearance without reference to real existence."[32]

In Gassendi's rebuttals to Descartes' Replies, one of the reasons which would prevent subjective appearance from being construed as a candidate for genuine knowledge is the explicit identification of intellective ideas with the mental images of corporeal things. Since indubitable knowledge of things can only be founded on ideative cognition of a thing's essence and, since the images the mind receives are only of accidents and not of substance, there can be no certain knowledge of any thing whatsoever. This deselection of the merely apparent is further undermined by the derivation of the meaning of a general notion from the operation of the understanding in particular circumstances, that is, its reduction to the factual origin of the notion in some experienced state of affairs.[33] With regard to mathematical concepts, this prolapse is exacerbated by the equation of the psychical formation in the imprinting of an image of a triangle, with the idea of triangularity itself. Only in a pre-Cartesian framework would it be possible to seriously contend that geometrical propositions "counted as appearances"—"for to demonstrate is nothing more than to point out what needs to be considered."[34] This reduction of the meaning of a geometrical axiom (or a logical rule) to the mere empirical observation that every actual instance of the geometrical 'object' accords with the statement of the axiom or rule is a prime example of an early psychologistic fallacy. Ralph Walker commends Gassendi's vigorous repudiation of *a priori* knowledge as an anticipation of the arguments of J. S. Mill and W. V. Quine (compare Quine on direct acquaintance)[35]—an ironic conclusion, since this anticipation of empiricist theory of knowledge formation in logical laws is precisely what Husserl will condemn.

In his later work, the *Syntagma* of 1658, Gassendi is more explicit about this: "Thus to consider the proposition everyone continually cites, that every whole is greater than its parts: we assent to it at once because right from the start . . . we have never *compared* a whole with one of its parts without *noticing* that it contains other parts as well and is therefore larger and greater than it"[36] (my emphasis). The resolution of the question regarding the truth of a logical rule about parts and wholes, for example, is not the result of the fact that, in an indefinite series of pertinent observations about wholes and parts, no given case arises which contravenes the rule. Even if there never were such a case, the question should be (per Descartes), what conditions of knowing directed toward this object render it impossible that it could be cognized otherwise? Only under these suppressed conditions will it be possible to elucidate why *this* instance is pertinent to the field of objects to which the rule is applied. Husserl will remark three hundred years later:

> One should not confuse the psychological presuppositions and bases of the knowledge of a law, with the logical presuppositions, the grounds and premises, of that law. . . . No one can seriously hold that the concrete singular cases before us, on which our insight into a law is grounded, really function as logical grounds or premises, as if the mere existence of such singulars entailed the universality of law. Our intuitive grasp of the law may require two psychological steps: one glance at the singulars of intuition and a related insight into law. Logically, however, only one step is required; the content of our insight is not inferred from singulars. (LI, 108–9)

Gassendi's most notable example, comparable in its position in his chain of reasoning to Descartes' example of the piece of wax, is that of an apothecary's theriac (antidote) contained in a casket with a label.[37] Theriac or "Venice treacle" is cited later by Sanchez as a well-known instance of a compound of poisons which resisted all other poisons, and hence seemed to contravene its real nature.[38] Demonstrations of geometrical propositions, and *mutatis mutandis* all other basic mathematical laws, amounts to no more than showing that the label (= the rule) does indeed correspond with (= holds true of) the thing contained within (= the abstract object). Gassendi's skeptical design has been to point out that human beings may fail to see what is shown in the demonstration of some rule, not that the showing itself is doubtful, and hence that such rules can hold with certainty. "The demonstration that he offers you or the means he uses is not the cause of the thing's being as it is, but merely makes it obvious to you that the thing is so. . . . If it did not base its conclusion upon triangles appearing in some material form, it would only be chasing chimeras since no other triangles but these can exist."[39]

If his early work in the *Exercises* of 1624 was entirely critical in its vigorous advocacy of a thorough skepticism, his more mature work in the *Compendium* of the 1640s shows a concerted effort to find a middle way between the skeptics and the dogmatists.[40] Despite his propensity for pedantry and his almost complete evasion of the questions and arguments brought forward by Descartes in his "Replies," Gassendi was a dedicated and assiduous scientist. Twenty years of his own experiments, coupled with close scrutiny of those of Copernicus and Galileo, led him to a notable advance in dealing with the problem of the criterion. It is no longer "obvious" that every attempt to establish a criterion by which the "weight" of a claim could be evaluated would lead invariably to either circular reasoning or an infinite regress. At least as important as his resolution to ground the criterion of a scientific claim on experience and verification by experimental observation is his stipulation of a normative basis according to which such claims could be evaluated. One should give credence to "an argument that cannot be legitimately contradicted," and regarding matters that need no further proof, "when things are so clear that merely stating them convinces us of them."[41] This is a worthy attempt at an escape from the standard skeptical arguments which Gassendi had so well marshaled against himself and others. But in propounding a nascent empirical theory of scientific procedure, he will not have been prepared to consider the complex and profound problems involved with cognition of a self-evident proposition and how it is possible for experience alone to serve as a criterion for our knowledge of sensible and intelligible things.

Francisco Sanchez' *Quod Nihil Scitur*, first printed in 1581, is quite distinct from Montaigne and other late sixteenth-century adapters of Sextus' Pyrrhonian skepticism. There is no evidence that Sanchez employed the standard tropes from the recent Latin translations of Sextus, though he was thoroughly conversant with Cicero's *Academica* and Diogenes' *Lives* which included a summary of the principal skeptical arguments. He had an extensive background in medicine, particularly Galen's popular works, and an exhaustive knowledge of Aristotle. His main targets in *Quod Nihil Scitur* are the epitomes and textbooks of Aristotelian logic heavily used in schools and universities, and the dogmatic, unquestioning reliance of their authors on "the master"; a sentiment echoed by Descartes (CSM I, 182). Where contemporary Protestant reformers were contesting papal infallibility, Sanchez was dismayed and angered by philosophers' conviction in the infallibility of Aristotle as the method setter for the natural sciences.

As a professor of medicine at Toulouse and a practicing doctor at the Hotel-Dieu for thirty years, Sanchez would have been attracted by Carneades' skeptical probablism, initially formulated in response to practical problems in the diagnosis of diseases. Whatever the epistemological questions regarding appearances and reality and the shakiness of the faculty of reason, the physician's attitude toward the practical treatment of his patient was that when specific symptoms were present, it was more likely that the patient had a specific disease than that he did not. "The goal of my proposed journey is the art of medicine, which I profess, and the first principles of which lie entirely within the realm of philosophical contemplation."[42] This is a statement of general intent echoed by Descartes at the end of the *Discourse*: "I have resolved to devote the rest of my life to nothing other than trying to acquire some knowledge of nature from which we may derive rules in medicine which are more reliable than those we have had up till now" (CSM I, 151).[43]

Descartes devoted some detailed attention to Galen's medical works (CSM III, 81–83), in addition to his well-remarked studies in mathematics under Isaac Beeckman the year before his 'miraculous discovery.' After his initial fascination with mathematics, he turned away in search of solutions to more fundamental metaphysical questions. In his early quest for a reliable path to certain knowledge, he reflected that, "Of all those who have hitherto sought after truth in the sciences, mathematicians alone have been able to find any demonstrations, that is to say, certain and evident reasonings; I had no doubt that I should begin with the very things that they studied" (CSM I, 121). Sanchez also arrives at a comparable stage on the road traveled in his pursuit of knowledge: "I had long searched through the realms of physics and mathematics but I had not found truth there. As I continued my investigations into this matter, some men said that truth had established itself in an intermediate zone between the natural and the supernatural worlds, that is to say, in the realm of mathematics."[44] Henri Gouhier argues that Sanchez may have had an indirect influence on Descartes' early studies while a student at the College of La Fleche in 1606–14.[45] Other scholars have suggested that Sanchez had a more direct impact on the *Discourse,* since Descartes was in Frankfurt in 1619 (several months before the famous dream of November 1619), one year after the publication of the Frankfurt edition of *Quod Nihil Scitur.*[46]

The similarities between Sanchez' "Preface to the Reader" and Part One of the *Discourse* are striking; Etienne Gilson, in his commentary on the *Discourse,* indicates numerous convergences with skeptical writers, particularly Sanchez.[47] On a number of points, both in terms of topical matter and their route to these questions, the convergence between Sanchez and Descartes is quite striking; some of these points (not Gilson's) are worth further explication. (1) The fruits of their search are the results of seven (or nine) years gestation for Sanchez; and nine years for Descartes' *Rules* and eight years for the *Discourse*. (2) They were both hungry for knowledge and speak of book learning as nourishment. (3) Eventually this was unsatisfactory, and they withdrew into themselves and began to doubt all that they had learned. (4) Although they admired the conceits and elegant figures in fables and poems, they considered these to be misleading in the search for truth and to be avoided in philosophical discourse. (5) Considering the diverse opinions of so many learned men, it is impossible that more than one could have arrived at the truth, and anything probable might as well be considered false. (6) Syllogisms are of little use, for either one already knows the truth of the premises, or one uses sophistical reasoning to convince another of what one is completely ignorant of. (7) The false sciences, such as alchemy and astrology, are the displays of jugglers and tricksters to persuade you of more than they actually know, and to provide you with a notion that their method for attaining the truth is the same as that of the natural sciences. (8) To construct a science based on an improper method and the mere accumulation of scholastic "proofs" is like erecting a building on an unstable foundation or effecting small repairs on one that is about to collapse.

Despite the striking parallels in the expression of how they came to a search for truth in the sciences, the framework and methodology of the search itself are quite different. Sanchez opens his attack on the proponents of an Aristotelian theory of knowledge with the statement that if he and his interlocutor are already in disagreement and cannot understand one another, this is because it is not possible to comprehend the nature of *things,* rather every definition and almost every inquiry is about *names.* Throughout his rigorous cross-examination of the dogmatic adherent, Sanchez repeatedly asks questions such as, What do you *mean* when you talk about "being" or "nature," etc.; What does it *mean* to say that you know something? If you use syllogistic reasoning to demonstrate that you know something about x, although the form of your inferences may be correct, the matter or nature of x is not revealed in this process. If you want to predicate something of a substance, e.g., "man is rational," you must know more than one thing, but knowledge of singulars is gained only through perception which presents one thing at a time. Hence what you might predicate of some thing depends on what you remember having known in some previous perceptual context; but to remember something is not to understand it. Sanchez's querent then resorts to the Platonic doctrine of reminiscence: that the demonstration of a truth draws out only what you already knew beforehand, when incarnate in a previous soul. But if memory is the source of the soul's knowledge, much the same could be said of that previous soul, and the one before—which leads to an infinite regress. A similar treatment is accorded to the proposition that knowledge is understanding something by means of its causes, in the sense of efficient and final causes.

In Sanchez' *That Nothing is Known,* there is also an early, and highly condensed, statement of what later became known as the hermeneutic problem.[48] There are not two kinds of knowledge, one of the things themselves and another of first principles, but rather there are two ways in which knowledge can be acquired. One from simple things which are not further divisible, such as matter, form, and spirit; the other of complex things, which are divisible into simple things. Through the analytic understanding of the simples, one can come to knowledge of the complex, but sometimes one can only have known those simples precisely as parts of the complex whole. This is extended by analogy to an understanding of any given single science, which borrows from and contributes to other sciences, and hence can only be known by understanding all the sciences together. This part-whole interdependence is used again by Sanchez to show that if human being is the union of body and soul, one cannot know the whole without first knowing the two parts, and vice versa. This claim is quite similar to Descartes' point about first knowing the principal attributes of mind and body before attempting to explain their union.

Sanchez derogates any attempt to understand the meaning of words by recourse to etymology, since philology reveals that naming is arbitrary and irrelevant to the essence of things. Nor can human reason be guided by the meaning of observed rituals and customs, since these reveal such an astonishing diversity that there can be no unifying truth behind them. In discussing many of the standard skeptical examples regarding misleading and deceptive appearances, Sanchez compares skepticism to the many-headed Hydra and bemoans the fact that there is no one to vanquish this monster. (See Husserl's image below.) He then analyzes the act of knowing in terms of its functional constituents: the apprehending subject, the apprehended object, and the medium through which cognitive apprehension takes place. In a style similar to the skeptical relativity trope, he shows that each of these is open to such variability in its conditions, that even if one of these were to have a solid purchase on the truth, the other conditions would completely undermine the whole cognitive process of understanding.

Descartes' Reaction to the Skeptical Challenge

The unprecedented nature and scope of Descartes' encounter with skepticism in the *Meditations* can perhaps be better appreciated in light of these kinds of doubts which contemporary skeptics were promulgating. In the "First Meditation" he is concerned to rid himself of errors and prejudices accepted since childhood in order to establish something stable and lasting in the sciences. He will not do so by grappling with each and every skeptical thesis which might have inspired these several errors, but by demolishing the foundations of the "building" which houses such erroneous beliefs—then it will collapse of its own accord. He has until now accepted the doctrine that knowledge is acquired either from or through the senses, but on some occasions the senses may deceive. Even such obvious sensations as one's bodily dispositions may be doubted by madmen. No sane person would deny that we are sometimes deceived by our senses, but is it impossible that any given perception may be deceptive in such a way that we are not even aware of being deceived? The visions that we have in dreaming are so similar to ones that we have when waking that there are no sure signs by means of which we could distinguish one state from another. But even dream visions are constructed out of shapes and colors which, whatever their imaginary recomposition, are also the real components of the same sort of things to be found in corporeal nature.

One way out of the waking/dreaming dilemma will be to consider that any discipline, e.g., the Galilean science of extended things, which is strictly founded on mathematical truths will be immune to methodical doubt. Regarding assertions beyond this domain, the doubter will withhold assent or suspend judgment in much the same way as he now would treat all his previous beliefs. He will be tempted by habitual opinions to give assent to those beliefs which seem the most probable, but by an act of will he will push them away until they are counterbalanced and the way cleared for perceiving things correctly. In order to bring about a cognitive state which is immune to his powerful conviction regarding mathematical knowledge, he will need an even more powerful doubt. He will thus suppose a malicious demon who systematically deceives him in every belief, including those regarding the existence of his own body, as one of those corporeal things. Although the 'objects' of mathematical insights are not open to doubt, his memory of having attained those insights may have been interfered with. Is there anything at all of which he could now claim to have indubitable knowledge?

Having extended skeptical doubt from the occasional deceptions of the senses, the relative disposition of the subject's own faculties, and the equivocation of persistent deception in dreaming to the very being of his own corporeal nature, Descartes has rendered the skeptic speechless. In the "Second Meditation," having appropriated the ground on which to develop a new theory of knowledge, and not just adopted a stance to defend attacks which arise from an antitheoretical position, Descartes will begin to build on this extremely reduced acquisition—that there is some "thing" which is deceived. The malicious demon can never bring it about that that which is deceived, insofar as it is a deceivable thing, does not exist. Wherein consists this being able to be deceived, that is, this *being*, which is able to be deceived?

What is this *thing* that can be deceived in so many other ways, but cannot be deceived into thinking that it doesn't exist? In order to uncover the nature of this "I," let us consider what it was believed to be before the inception of doubt and then "subtract" any attribute which cannot withstand this rigorous process. If the answer should be "a man," defined as a rational animal (or anything else, for that matter), the doubter is aware that this will lead down "a slippery slope" and he has no time to waste on subtleties of this sort, i.e., on the ready-made skeptical tropes which lead to circular reasoning. The first *thought* he has regarding his nature is that he has a corporeal body, by which he means a thing with a determinable shape and location. This is a conception of one's own body which is entirely novel and situated in the Galilean universe of extended things organized by the geometric method. And yet all of those features of corporeal bodies most intimately associated with one's own will not survive the stages of methodical doubt. Only the feature of thinking resists "subtraction" and thus "I am then *in the strict sense* only a thing that thinks." What else, what other features could this thing have?

One cannot rely here on memory since that is the repository of all the prejudices which have been banished and, as well, its contents could have been created out of nothing by the demon. Let us turn then to the other faculties, which I as a thinking being, most assuredly have. Imagination will have to be discounted since that is no more than contemplating the images of corporeal things and is freely able to invent nonexistent things (chimeras) which do not even have the minimal feature of being an existent thing, a feature already secured at a prior stage. In turning next to sense perception, Descartes introduces a startling term in the chain of reasons, which does not occur in this context in any previous thinker. Whether awake or asleep, in seeing light, hearing noise, or feeling heat, it is still true of these sensations that one *seems* to see, hear, or be warmed; and in this restricted sense, seeming is simply being aware of. This seeming is the mere appearance of an object, irrespective (for the moment) of whether it refers in some way or other to an underlying reality. Where the skeptics were so fond of likening the mind to a malleable piece of wax, here it is the apparent piece of wax which will direct the thinker to the 'nature' of a material substance and to a higher-order conception of what it means for a substance to have an invariant essence.

According to an entirely subjective point of view, the piece of wax undergoes many changes in shape, taste, temperature, etc., and yet it is grasped, throughout these changes, as one and the same piece of wax. Sensory impressions are of the wax's many appearances, and the imagination is incapable of running through all of those not already presented; and yet this thing is "grasped" as extended, flexible, and changeable. The perception one has of it, or rather the act whereby it is perceived, is a case of "pure mental scrutiny" that is, it is grasped by the intellect alone. In distinguishing the wax from its outward forms, it is as though it were cognized naked, without its clothes—an ironic reversal of the standard skeptical image of a human being, "naked, empty and ready for God's grace." Through this analogy, one's understanding of the self is not only more certain than that of a corporeal thing, but also more distinct and evident in that its invariant essence is thinking, and this includes doubting, believing, and assenting. The results of the experiment with the wax may be extended to all other corporeal bodies and thus "applied to everything else located outside me"—the first historical use of this phrase to delimit "external reality" from the purely psychical domain.

The Skeptical Basis of Nineteenth-Century Empirical Psychology

In *First Philosophy*, Husserl acknowledges the Greek Skeptics, Plato, and Descartes as the three great beginners in the history of European philosophy (HUS VII, 7). "Ancient skepticism, begun by Protagoras and Gorgias, calls into question and denies *episteme,* i.e., scientific knowledge of what is in-itself. 'The' world is not rationally knowable; human knowledge cannot extend beyond the subjective-relative appearances. Starting from this point, . . . it might have been possible to push radicalism further; but in reality it never came to this." Recall Descartes' statement in a letter of 1638: "Although the Pyrrhonists reached no certain conclusion from their doubts, it does not follow that no one can." (CSM III, 99). For Husserl in *The Crisis of European Sciences,* the greatest benefit of the skeptical challenge was overlooked by everyone before Descartes, and most of those who came after him did not learn the lesson so indelibly printed in the text of the *Meditations*—Husserl's reproach in this matter has an unusually theological overtone. "The skepticism which was negativistically oriented toward the practical and ethical (or political) lacked, even in all later times, the original Cartesian motif: that of pressing forward through the hell of an unsurpassable quasi-skeptical epoché towards the gates of the heaven of an absolutely rational philosophy and of constructing the latter systematically." (Crisis, 76–77).

It is highly significant in the development of Husserl's thought after the *Logical Investigations* that the term "epoché" enters his philosophical vocabulary after the publication of Raoul Richter's *Der Skeptizismus in der Philosophie* (1904) and Albert Goedeckmeyer's *Geschichte des Griechischen Skeptizismus*

(1905). According to Rudolf Boehm's checking of Husserl's own copies, they show intensive markings of the relevant passages; in addition, Husserl corresponded with Richter on the key term "epoché."[49] Moreover, we now know, due to the recent publication of his private diary for 1906–7, that at this time he went through a serious personal crisis in which all his previous work was subject to severe reassessment. Husserl finds praise for ancient skepticism in bringing up the problem of the subjective conditions for truth and praise for Descartes in his initial treatment of this in the "First" and "Second Meditations." It is in the "Third Meditation" that Husserl will take exception with Descartes' analysis of the essential constitution of the *res cogitans*. It is this moment in the chain of reasons that will lead Husserl to a radical divergence in his explication of the intentional structure of consciousness and the origin of transcendental subjectivity. Nevertheless, Descartes' overthrow of skepticism was a necessary condition for any progress in the establishment of a *mathesis universalis*.

> The novelty of Cartesianism and thus the whole of modern philosophy consists in its struggle against skepticism, which remained unsurpassed in the general course of its development. Cartesianism confronts this again in an entirely new spirit, in which it radically grasps skepticism at its ultimate principle roots and in so doing finally seeks to overcome it. . . . Modernity begins with Descartes because he first sought to theoretically satisfy the indubitable truth that lay at the basis of the skeptical arguments. He was the first to make theoretically his own the universal field of being, the very one which the extreme skeptical negations presupposed, and turn the argument back on them, namely, on their own certain knowing subjectivity. (HUS VII, 60–61)

The diverse strands of skeptical critique traced thus far—sensory illusions, the problem of the criterion, the waking/dreaming enigma, diversity of judgments, etc.—formed a virtual Gordian knot which Descartes would not attempt to unravel, but would sever at one blow. Or in Husserl's metaphor, the skeptical tradition was "the hydra ever growing new heads" (HUS VII, 57), which set Descartes the Herculean task of slaying it once and for all. Myles Burnyeat succinctly poses three questions[50] which point to this explosive new beginning, stimulated by the press of skeptical assault and allowed to emerge by its demise. (1) How did it come about that philosophy accepted the idea that *truth* can be obtained without going outside subjective experience? (2) When and why did philosophers first claim *knowledge* of their own subjective states? (3) When and why did *one's own body* become for philosophy a part of the external world? (Given that no ancient or modern skeptic ever doubted the *existence* of his own body.)

The answer to all three questions can be found in Husserl's tour-de-force exposition of Galileo's mathematization of nature (Crisis, 21–60) and its consequent splitting of the world into physical bodies, which are subject to causal laws on a geometrical model, and the mental world of humans beings, who are comprised not only of physical bodies but also of lived-bodies, and hence not comprehended in this scheme. In a prescientific manner, the world is given to each person in a subjectively relative way; each one has his own appearances which count for him in a way in which they do not count for another. But simply because of this, we do not postulate an indefinite number of worlds, but just the one world, filled with spatio-temporal shapes. All these shapes of physical bodies coexist and belong together in such a manner that there are intuitively given determinate regularities, in terms of which each person may make discrepant observations. The mathematization of this natural world of shapes by Galileo, extended indirectly to other qualities of physical bodies besides extension, allowed the grounding of a science in ideal objects, governed by rigorous laws of causality. The Galilean (and later Newtonian) system uncovered a plenum of self-contained entities or substances whose interconnections could be exhaustively and comprehensively explicated in a geometrical manner. But what has happened along the way to humans who, aside from being physical bodies (and thus objects) in this plenum, are also the subjects for whom appearances occur within the horizon of open-ended possibilities for knowing?

> In his view of the world from the perspective of geometry, the perspective of what appears to the senses and is mathematizable, Galileo *abstracts* [cf. Descartes' *subtraction* of essential features] from the subjects as persons leading a personal life.... The result of this abstraction is the things purely as bodies; but these are taken as concrete real objects, the totality of which makes up a world which becomes the subject matter of research. One can truly say that the idea of nature as a really self-enclosed world of bodies first emerges with Galileo. A consequence of this . . . is the idea of a self-enclosed natural causality in which every occurrence is determined unequivocally and in advance. Clearly the way is thus prepared for dualism which appears immediately afterward in Descartes. (Crisis, 60)

The pregiven world of experience has now split into two *new worlds*: the world of nature and the psychical world of its living inhabitants. Just as the ancients, including the skeptics, had no universal science for a closed domain of physical bodies, so also they had no comparable understanding of the psychical domain as a self-enclosed totality of sense-giving constructions. Descartes will accomplish for philosophy what Galileo had mapped out for the physical world: (1) he will demonstrate that "scientific" truth can be found entirely within the realm of subjectivity without recourse to the positing of an "external" world; (2) that knowledge can be obtained from an adequate understanding of the normative character of certain ideas in the psychical domain; and (3) that one's own lived-body (as distinct from the merely physical body), with all its habits, passions, and practices, having survived the stages of doubt, can be the "subject" of scientific researches in a manner similar to its physical aspect treated as the object of physiology.

The two separate and distinct substances, *res cogitans* and *res extensa,* now have clearly delimited horizons for investigation. But in this splitting of the world only the geometrical treatment of nature has been established, and with this physicalist model as an exemplar of explanation, "scientific" research into the psychical domain will attempt to describe its workings in an entirely inappropriate manner. Husserl traces this new discipline, with its tacit acceptance of mind-body dualism, to its origins in the protopsychology of Hobbes and Locke, from which the naturalization of the psychic descends to the present day. This tracing of a double problematic is why he can describe Descartes as *both* the spiritual mentor of his transcendental phenomenology *and* as "the progenitor of the psychologism which saturates the whole of modern philosophy" (HUS VII, 338).

Martial Gueroult would definitely want to defend Descartes from any charges of psychologism even if these charges are the result of a misconception of his achievement and a retrospective slight-of-hand in positing a false origin for psychology as a science of introspection. Fortunately for our case, Husserl does not accuse Descartes of any such psychologistic interpolation of the nature of consciousness, but rather of originating a dualistic schema which could be misconstrued in just the way Gueroult describes.

> In effect, by substituting ordinary psychological consciousness for mathematico-rational intelligence, as the essence of thought, we are led [by misreading] to see in Cartesian knowledge of self only a pure and simple introspection based on our attentiveness . . . and we are led to see the *Meditations* as solely an intellectual biography, an account, the history of an experience, etc. We are brought in this way to see the Descartes of the *Meditations* as a psychologist. . . . One is brought, in addition, to subordinate the main thing to the accessory thing, the basic doctrine to the literary presentation, because of the charge imposed on the philosopher by the necessity to persuade a rebellious reader captured by the imagination. Thus the spirit of Cartesianism is finally destroyed at its roots, a spirit that is not psychological but geometrical, thus a psychologism without rigor is substituted for it.[51]

Just as Descartes felt that he had to demolish his own previous convictions, Husserl also felt the need to discontinue his mathematical researches until he had succeeded in reaching a decisive clarity on the basic questions of epistemology and in the critical understanding of logic as a science (LI, 43). The exhaustive analyses of empirical psychology of logic comprise the first volume of the *Logical Investigations,* "Prolegomena to Pure Logic." This book-length treatise has a complex structure (HSW, 143–47) which can perhaps best be explained by a parallel exegesis of Husserl's principal queries, the answers offered by prior theories of logic, and Husserl's refutation or critique of these. Recent researches[52] have sought to establish with greater accuracy the historical milieu and scholarly communication between German, English, and American exponents of empirical psychology. Schnadelbach[53] has concisely outlined the emergence of sociology and psychology in the early nineteenth-century German institutional framework and the tremendous influence of the German translation of J. S. Mill's *System of Logic.* "Psychologism in logic, according to which the structure and validity of the principles of logic are based on the organization of the human psyche, can be regarded as the standard opinion of philosophers from the middle of the last century up until well into our own: Gottlob Frege and Edmund Husserl were fairly isolated in their campaign against it." Anton Dumitriu[54] has cited the origins of this trend at the historical intersection, in the late eighteenth and early nineteenth centuries, of the British empiricist tradition in epistemology and the German neo-Kantian conception of natural science. Martin Kusch's recent work[55] in the academic history of accusation and counteraccusation among German philosophers and psychologists has highlighted a serious problem in adequately identifying the alleged character of psychologism as a charge leveled against poor reasoning.

A detailed synopsis of the salient arguments of Husserl's critique of empiricism's background assumptions will provide the setting for comparisons with Descartes' counterskeptical strategies. In chapter 1 of the "Prolegomena," "Logic as a Normative and as a Practical Discipline," the theoretical incompleteness of the separate sciences can be remedied by a correct understanding of a comprehensive and foundational theory of science as logic. Husserl borrows a famous image from Sextus Empiricus[56]—"The setting forth of truths . . . must reflect the systematic connections of those truths, and must use the latter as a ladder to progress and penetrate from the knowledge given to, or already gained by us, to ever higher regions of the realm of truth" (LI, 62). In chapter 2, "Theoretical Disciplines as the Foundation of Normative Disciplines," the historically attested fact that logic arose out of practical motives is traced back to the nascent science of the ancient Greeks and their need to repel the attacks of the sophists and skeptics. Scholastic logic still lives under the spell of this tradition, but assuming the role of a false methodology for other disciplines, it entered mistaken pathways and achievements were attributed to it in the late Renaissance for which it was essentially unqualified. Numerous modern proponents of logic as a method for the physical sciences are cited, but Husserl echoes Descartes' reaction to the multiplicity of skeptical positions: "We do not intend to assemble and to subject to a critical analysis any and every argument historically advanced for this or that conception of logic" (LI, 81]). His attention will be focused instead on the basic standards or principles which give unity to the concept of a normative science.

Chapter 3, "Psychologism: Its Arguments and its Attitude to the Usual Counter-Arguments," presents the most controversial thesis for this grounding of logic as a normative science and the sort of principles which give it theoretical unity. This then comprises an introduction to the psychologistic position in the fullest sense, for which chapters 3-8 provide Husserl with an opportunity to expose the contradictory consequences and endemic prejudices which result from this position-taking. In this context he quotes from J. S. Mill's highly influential textbook: "Logic is not a science separate from and coordinate with psychology. To the extent that it is a science at all, it is a part or branch of psychology, distinguished from it on the one hand as the part from the whole, and on the other hand, as the art is from the science. It owes all its theoretical foundations to psychology, and includes as much of that science as is necessary to establish the rules of the art."[57]

For the empirical psychologist, logical thought is unable to think beyond or be applied further than the factual manner in which thinking takes place. This echoes the skeptic who argues that it is not feasible for anyone to claim to know the things themselves irrespective of how they appear to the knower. Charges that this commits a fallacy of circular reasoning, that a science of logic grounded on contingent laws would have to first establish the validity of rules which it presupposes, are no more cogent than the skeptics' resort to charges of circularity in dismissing attempts to establish a criterion. This charge rests on an equivocation in the term "presuppose," that is, between assuming the validity of certain rules as premises versus establishing the rules in accordance with which science must proceed. "Both are confounded in our argument for which reasoning *according* to logical rules, and reasoning *from* logical rules count as identical. There would only be a circle if the reasoning were *from* such rules. . . . An investigation may construct proofs without ever having recourse to logic. Logical laws cannot therefore have been premises in such proofs. And what is true of single proofs is likewise true of whole sciences" (LI, 95).

Skepticism and Relativism Remove the Very Basis for Theory Construction

No matter how psychology may be defined—as the science of psychic phenomena, the facts of consciousness or internal experience, etc.—three empiricist consequences arise which lead to absurdity, as outlined in chapter 4. First, since psychological laws lack exactness, so will the logical laws founded on them—and this is preposterous. Logical laws rely for their continued validity in every possible context on thorough exactness which would be vitiated by any dependence on contingent circumstances. Second, if the response should be to deny that such psychological laws are not vague but are as exact as any other natural law, it is simply not true that a natural law can be known *a priori,* nor given by insight or intuition. A natural law can only be established and justified by induction from the singular facts of experience; but induction does not guarantee the holding of the law, only the probability of its holding. The probability and not the law itself is justified by insight, and thus logical laws, established in this manner, would be no more than probabilities. This is the same criticism which Descartes directed against the skeptics' founding of mathematical proofs on probable premises (CSM III, 352).

The third consequence is that if logical laws have their origin in psychological matters-of-fact, these laws must also be psychological in content, both by being laws for such mental states and by presupposing the existence of such states. But it is patent nonsense to assert that a logical law implies a matter-of-fact of any kind whatsoever, even conscious presentations and the judgments formed therefrom. If the rejoinder should be that logical laws could never have been posited if there were not someone for whom these presentations occurred and who abstracted those basic logical concepts, this is irrelevant since it conflates the psychical components of the assertion of a law with the logical moments of its content. This leads Husserl to one of the most crucial formulations of his refutation.

> Logical laws have first been confused with the judgments, in the sense of acts of judgment, in which we may know them: the laws as *contents of judgment* have been confused with the *judgments themselves.* The latter are real events, having causes and effects. Judgments whose contents are laws are, in particular, frequently operative as *thought motives.* . . . A second confusion is added to the first: we confuse a law as a *term in causation* with a law as the *rule of causation.* In other fields too, we familiarly employ *mythic talk* of natural laws as presiding powers in natural events as if the rules of causal connection could themselves once more significantly function as causes, i.e. as terms in just such connections. [LI.102]

Chapter 5, "Psychological Interpretations of Basic Logical Principles," comprises an examination of the specific interpretation of the laws of noncontradiction and the hypothetical syllogism from the psychologistic viewpoint with particular reference to their exposition by David Hume, J. S. Mill, F. A. Lange, and Christoph Sigwart. Husserl archly points out that these thinkers have never been afraid of being inconsistent and that it is only through a persistent misunderstanding that this empirical trend has held such a dominant position. Much as Descartes remarked that skepticism brought to its intrinsic conclusion would bring about its own downfall, so Husserl comments on psychologism: "To think it out to the end, is already to have given it up, unless extreme skepticism affords an example of the greatly superior strength of ingrained prejudices to the most certain deliverances of insight" (LI, 111).

J. S. Mill's *System of Logic* typifies an exemplary psychologistic explanation for the law of noncontradiction, which applies *mutatis mutandis*, to other logical axioms.

> I consider it to be, like other axioms, one of our first and most familiar generalizations from experience. The original foundation of it I take to be, that belief and disbelief are two different mental states, excluding one another. This we know by the simplest observation of our minds. And if we carry our observation outwards, we also find that light and darkness, sound and silence, motion and quiescence, equality and inequality, preceding and following, succession and simultaneousness, any positive phenomenon whatever and its negative, are distinct phenomena, pointedly contrasted, and the one always absent where the other is present. I consider the maxim in question to be a generalization from all these facts.[58]

What an extraordinary statement!—and one that Carneades or Antiochus, Sextus' skeptical paragons, could have claimed as their own. "All the gods seem to abandon Mill's otherwise keen intelligence. Only one thing is hard to understand: how such a doctrine could have seemed persuasive" (LI, 112). Husserl remarks that the factual pairs cited in this passage are not contradictory propositions and that the concept of exclusion has already entered into the definition of the correlative terms, positive and negative phenomena. Mill has substituted for the logical impossibility that the propositions should both be true, the real incompatibility of the corresponding acts of judgment by a thinking person.

In the "Appendix" to his exposition of this psychologistic misconception, Husserl makes an explicit connection between extreme empiricism of this type and extreme skepticism. Each of these destroys the possibility of the rational justification of mediate (i.e., non-self-evidential) knowledge and thus completely undermine its own possibility as a scientifically proven theory. His specific demonstration of this is to show that the skeptical attack on the criterion, which reduces its truth claim to a species of fallacious inference, itself appeals to a *petitio principii*. "If however, all proof rests on principles governing its procedure, and if its final justification involves an appeal to such principles, then we should either be involved in a circle or in an infinite regress if the principles of proof themselves required further proof; in a circle if the principles of proof used to justify the principles of proof were the same as the latter, in a regress if both sets of principles were different" (LI, 116).

This is the same line of argument which Sextus' Pyrrhonian advocates will employ to demonstrate the untenability of any standard being used as a criterion of certain knowledge. Similar expositions of the law of noncontradiction are found in F. A. Lange[59] and Christoph Sigwart,[60] two of the principal exponents of the empirical derivation of logical laws.

In chapter 7, "Psychologism as Sceptical Relativism," Husserl distinguishes two main types of skepticism (LI, 135–37), epistemological and metaphysical, both of which he detects as undercurrents in the ancient Greek tradition. In the former type, all such claims as that there is no truth, no knowledge, no proof, and so forth, depend entirely on the assumption of a position which tacitly denies the conditions for any assertion to be intelligible—and as such it is absurd. There are two subtypes of this skepticism: subjective or noetic and objective or logical. Noetic skepticism violates the subjective conditions of its own possibility as a viable theory since there is no way in which it can distinguish between an evident and veracious assertion and an arbitrary and unwarranted one. Logical skepticism relies on the meaningful use of the notions of truth, judgment, property, relation, etc. and at the same time violates the laws which embrace these notions and without which no theory can have a coherent sense. Metaphysical or inauthentic skepticism, on the other hand, would limit knowledge to what is merely apparent, while denying the existence or knowability of the thing-in-itself. As such, it is not absurd or nonsensical, but it is readily confused with the former variety.

This second main type is not a concern for Husserl in the *Logical Investigations* but will become so after the introduction of the concept of epoché or "bracketing" of the given world. (Which as we have seen occurs after his reading of the Pyrrhonian account of suspension of judgment.) This is the world given with all its prejudices, already constructed meaning formations, and other valued products of purposive activities. One of Husserl's pivotal points of departure from Descartes will be focused on that point in Descartes' chain of reasons where the thinking subject encounters the world of appearances, a world filled with discrepant perspectives. Instead of working around such discrepancies as sense illusions, problems of the dream state, ambiguous meanings, and so forth, they should be built into our understanding of this world as the way such things are in fact always already given to us. One of the valued products, so to speak, of this meaningfully structured world is the philosophical diremption of subject and object as distinct substances, and this is the legacy of the Cartesian overcoming of epistemological skepticism.

In order to understand this skeptical attitude as it relates to human subjects (and thus attempts to derive laws of judgment from the species-specific laws of human cognition), Husserl discriminates between individual relativism and human-specific relativism, which he calls "anthropologism." The former is such a "bare-faced and cheeky scepticism" that no one has seriously propounded it in modern times. Any person who asserts that his theory of knowledge expresses only his own viewpoint and is only true for the speaker, relegates himself to silence and has nothing further to contribute. All claims derived from the position that the laws of thought are dependent on the particular constitution of human beings qua human are self-canceling and inherently absurd. In this context, the psychologistic doctrine is a collection of statements intrinsically dependent on contingent features of human-specific *psychical* constitution and its factual operations. The "General Introduction" to Sigwart's *Logic* is a cornucopia of this species-specific relativism:

> If . . . we deny the possibility of knowing anything as it is in itself—if the Existent is only a thought of our production—it still remains true that the ideas to which we attribute objectivity are those which we produce with a consciousness of necessity. The fact that we regard anything as existing implies that all other thinking creatures of like nature with ourselves . . . would also be forced with the same necessity to regard it as existing. [And] logical investigations should [not] entirely abstract from and ignore the general nature of the matter and presuppositions of actual thought. Of thought developing entirely from itself in the particular individual we have no knowledge; we know it only under the general relations & conditions, and with the general purposes of human thought.[61]

It is simply not possible for the truth of a judgment to be relative to any given species, such that it might be false for a differently constituted species, since this would render the *content* of what is expressed in the judgment—which must be the *same* judgment, otherwise it could not be picked out from the other species' discourse—both true and false. And this consequence violates the sense of the terms "true" and "false" assumed in the original thesis. This thesis is no more correct when the judgment is considered relative to an individual's own mental processes; the concept cannot be construed as a real part of the factual occurrence of a psychical event—it can be *meant* but not *produced* in one's cognition. In such wise, all attempts to explain the compatibility or compossibility of logical laws on the principles of the association of ideas are doomed to failure, since if this were the case, how could any judgment which denies these laws arise through their actual operation. The restriction of the universal validity of logical laws to human beings or any given subject's cognition must be completely dismissed.

I can compel nobody to see what I see. But I myself *cannot doubt;* I once more see, here where I have insight, i.e. am embracing truth itself, that all doubt would be mistaken. I therefore find myself at a point which I have either to recognize as the *Archimedean point* from which the world of doubt and unreason may be levered on its hinges, or which I may sacrifice at the peril of sacrificing all reason and knowledge. I see that this [the former] is the case, and that in the latter case . . . I should have to pack in all rational striving for truth, all assertion and all demonstration. (LI, 159; emphasis added)

Husserl's Confrontation with Dilthey's Historicist Understanding

The *Logical Investigations*, first published in 1900, included commentary on virtually all the principal German works in logic to that date, including Theodor Gomperz's translation of J. S. Mill's *System of Logic*. The most notable omission is Wilhelm Dilthey, whose *"Ideen zu einer beschreibenden und zergliederden Psychologie"* was published in 1895.[62] In his "Lectures on Phenomenological Psychology" from 1925, Husserl explains the circumstances under which he had considered it unnecessary to read "Dilthey's great work" (PP, 24–25). The strong tendency toward positivism which Husserl had detected in Dilthey's earlier work, *"Einleitung in die Geisteswissenschaften"*[63] put him off any further examination; an inclination reinforced by "Ebbinghaus' brilliant rebuttal" of Dilthey's *Ideen*.[64] But in later correspondence (HSW, 198–209), Dilthey expressed such delight on reading the *Logical Investigations* and claimed such remarkable congruence with his own theoretical conception of psychology, that Husserl was provoked into reading the *Ideen* for himself, as well as the author's later *"Der Aufbau der geschichtlichen Welt"* (1910)—"the last and most beautiful of his writings." "Dilthey was in fact right with his judgment which had so greatly astonished me, concerning the inner unity of phenomenology and descriptive-analytic psychology. His writings contain a gifted preview and preliminary level of phenomenology" (HSW, 198–209). It is pertinent then in the context of our overview of Husserl's discussion of skepticism as relativism to consider his postponed treatment of Dilthey.

Dilthey's *Ideen* was "the first assault against this naturalistic psychology [and was] characterized by genius, though also incompletely matured" (PP, 3, 14). His critique of the rationality of physiological and experimental psychology centers on its explicit emulation of the methodology of the exact sciences, in that this psychology "wants to subordinate the appearances of psychic life to a causal nexus by means of a limited number of univocally determined elements." In order to accomplish this, such a discipline has to construct hypotheses by means of inferences which transcend experience. Such a framework is entirely appropriate to the natural sciences, where sensory experience gives us spatio-temporal things external to consciousness. But this transcendent foundation is entirely inappropriate to the psychical domain which is given only through internal experience. Such knowledge is given through lived experience (*Erlebnis*) in which the individual's own psychic being is constituted by complex intertwinings which belong to every concrete phase of an ongoing psychic life. A teleology or directedness runs through psychic life as such, directed toward happiness, purposeful activities, and valued objectivities which are manifest in the arts, science and religion. A form of psychical causality operates here (motivation) which can be brought to light and made intelligible by an insightful reconstruction of the social-historical context in which the inner-directed meaning was produced. Only through a systematic analysis of such purposeful and meaning-giving activities can descriptive psychology distinguish itself from natural science which explains physical phenomena, by making intelligible a person's understanding of psychical phenomena and its ordered expression in such purposive activities.

In 1911, after the publication of Husserl's "Philosophy as Rigorous Science," Dilthey wrote to Husserl to clarify his position on historical understanding and to point out that they were in essential agreement in their antipathy to a naturalistic conception of psychology, though Dilthey objected to being considered a skeptic in this regard (HSW, 203)—in fact, Dilthey characterized his empiricist opponents as skeptics. Husserl took some pains to reassure Dilthey that his criticisms in the *Logos* article were not directed at him, and that they had independently arrived at a complementary position in their attempts to overcome a false metaphysics, though from divergent philosophical orientations (HSW, 207). In fact, Dilthey in the 1895 *Ideen* had disparaged any attempt to found psychology on the model of the natural and experimental sciences. The second chapter of this treatise is devoted to a general survey of results in psychophysical and naturalistic psychology which brings out the repeated failure of specific researchers to achieve the solid and coherent foundation which they had demanded of this emergent discipline; much in the same way that Husserl surveys their collateral work in logic.

> The profit in using the hypothetical character of our explanation of nature in the interest of an arid *skepticism*, or a *mysticism* in the service of theology, is cut off. [How similar to Husserl's remark on "natural powers" above.] . . . Present-day science is caught in the following dilemma, which has contributed enormously to the development of *skepticism* and a superficial and sterile *empiricism*, and thus to the increasing separation of life from knowledge. Either the human studies make use of the foundations which psychology offers . . . or they strive to fulfill their task with-

out the support of any scientifically ordered view of mental affairs, by depending only on a subjective and equivocal psychology of life. But in the first case, explanatory psychology imparts its wholly hypothetical character to the theory of knowledge and the human studies.[65]

Husserl's critique of Dilthey's concept of understanding a meaning-directed act centers on the essential necessity implicit in mental genesis, the origination of expression, and so forth. As much as he praises Dilthey's unprecedented contributions to the first adequate distinction between the natural-scientific and the social-scientific, he deprecates Dilthey's weakness in logical precision and thinking through exact concepts: "he does not penetrate to a clarity of principles concerning its own peculiar sense and the limits of its possible results" (PP, 7). The analytic turning to inner experience and the description carried out in pure internal 'seeing' make possible the understanding of an individual mental act and its product in terms of its own inherent necessity in the unified and unifying historical nexus of that given individual. Even granted the most comprehensive and precise understanding of the motivation for this meaningful activity, i.e., given such-and-such conditions, this person could only have acted in this way. This understanding then cannot be construed as a general psychical law since it requires contingent factual premises for its interpretation.

A rigorous psychological science will have to be able to account for universal laws according to which individual cases, in carrying through a particular instance of lawful necessity, become intelligible. The best scenario, the most valid extension of descriptive "understanding," would be a typology or classification of human cultural, artistic, and religious activities. And though this typology is indeed an advance over simplistic, relativist models, it returns the scientific status of psychology to one based on a comparative natural history, whether of personalities, habitual tendencies, or associations. Since Dilthey's conception of this new psychology depends on direct 'seeing' in inner experience, itself founded on a universal form of absolutely inviolable necessity—made use of in projective understanding—he is confounded in paradox.

> The theory of knowledge wants to make intelligible, generically and in principle, how cognitive activity in its psychic interiority can succeed in producing objective validity. But how could it ever solve such a problem if it depended upon a psychological empirical procedure which would supply it with only natural-historical universalities instead of inviolable and intuitively evident necessities? Principles of knowledge cannot possibly be clarified by vague biological universalities of types. Thus in every respect, a psychology which provides necessities is a desideratum. (PP, 13)

Husserl's Refutation of Psychologism Congruent with Descartes' Overcoming of Skepticism

If the earlier chapters of the *Logical Investigations* have drawn out the absurd and countersensical consequences of a psychological explanation for logical laws, chapter 8 turns to an uncovering of its principal arguments in establishing this explanation. Husserl's analysis of the three main "prejudices" point up distinctive convergences with Descartes' treatment of the prejudices inherent in the skeptical attack on knowledge. The first prejudice (LI, 168–71) is that prescriptions which regulate what is psychical, including logical laws, must obviously have a psychical basis. It is thus self-evident that the normative principles of knowledge must be grounded, i.e., must be fully explicable in terms of the psychology of knowledge which is the science of the psychical basis for any normative expression.

The problem here is that logical laws are not normative propositions whose content informs one how one should judge, rather they are laws which depend on normativity for their cognitive content and which assert its universal necessity. Those prejudiced in this manner would want to claim that the laws of logic and mathematics have distinctive meaning-content, in contrast to less exact normative rules in other disciplines, which gives them a natural right to regulate our thought. Such a prejudice persuades them to place too much value on the subjective aspect of science as the methodology of the human acquisition of knowledge, to the detriment of its objective aspect as the coherent ideal of the theoretical unity of truth. Thus "they ignore the fundamental difference between the norms of pure logic and the technical rules of a specifically human art of thought. These are totally different in character in their content, origin and function" (LI, 168–71).

In the *Rules for the Direction of the Mind*, Descartes made a parallel distinction between the "dialectical" protocols which guide our thinking in specific matters and the rules of inference which reasoning must presuppose in order for our thinking to express a true judgment. The method which he proposes demonstrates the correct employment of cognitive insight and deductive inferences— adhering to these will prevent one falling into needless skeptical anxiety.

> [But] the method cannot go so far as to teach us how to perform the *actual operations* of intuition and deduction, since these are the simplest of all and quite basic. If our intellect were not *already able* to perform them, it would not comprehend any of the rules of the method, however easy they might be. As for other *mental operations* which dialectic claims to direct with the help of those already mentioned, they are of no use here, or rather should be reckoned a positive hindrance, for nothing

can be added to the clear light of reason which does not in some way dim it. (CSM I, 16; my emphasis)

The second prejudice discussed by Husserl (LI, 177–84) is not one which is confined to logical laws but extends also to mathematics. According to this way of thinking, logical demonstrations are concerned with syllogisms and proofs, truth and probability, ground and consequent, etc. and as such what they refer to can only be manifested or experienced in judgments. This manifestation can only take place as the content of a psychical event, and psychology provides a coherent and reliable account of how these psychical events take place. Husserl's dismissal of this further attempt to rehabilitate a psychological grounding for logical laws employs a mathematical analogy regarding counting and number. The psychical act of counting takes place with respect to a possible concrete object of presentation, whereas number and numerical operations refer to ideal species whose concrete instances are found in what becomes objective in certain acts of counting. Numerical concepts (as well as logical terms) which constitute mathematical and logical laws have no empirical range, but are exclusively one of ideal singulars and genuine species. The second prejudice is no more than a subterfuge to reintroduce validity into a form of psychologistic explanation which had already been unmasked in the previous exposition of the crucial distinction between the factual occurrence of a judgment and the essential content expressed through the judgment.

The third prejudice (LI, 187–96) relates to the *feeling* of inward evidence or a conviction of the certitude which accompanies the psychical act directed towards a logical truth. As an observation on the sort of cognition which takes place in the logician's construction of an inference, for instance, this feeling may have some heuristic value, but it is another thing to claim that the presence of this feeling somehow guarantees the truth of the judgment to which it is attached. Practical directions which assist in picking out the occurrence of such evidential indices may in fact lead one to achieve judgments and construct inferences which are indeed certain and valid, but this is incorrectly extended to an explanation of the grounding of such logical laws as certain and valid. Sigwart gives an exemplary statement of this position:

> The possibility of determining the criteria and rules of necessary and universally valid procedure in Logic depends upon our ability to distinguish objectively necessary thought from that which is not necessary, and this we find in the *immediate consciousness* of evident truth which accompanies necessary thought. . . . There is, in the last instance, no answer but an appeal to our subjective experience of necessity, to the *inward feeling* of certainty by which some of our thought is accompanied,

to the consciousness that, starting from the given premises, we cannot think otherwise than we do think. Belief in the truth of this feeling and in its trustworthiness
is the last anchorage of all certainty; for the man who does not acknowledge it there
is no knowledge—nothing but accidental opinion.[66]

The striking parallel between this psychologistic explanation for certainty
and validity and the position of the sixteenth-century Protestant reformers' doctrine of "inner persuasion" can be illuminated by replacing "logical law" with
"religious claim" (in the above passage) and reading a theological connotation
for the term "thought." Just as Calvin[67] would be unable to refute a charge of
circularity in his appeal to "inner persuasion" as the criterion in determining a
conflict of interpretations in theological doctrine, so also the empiricist logicians
were unable to see the commission of a *petitio principi* in the spurious grounding of logical truth on a feeling of conviction.

Husserl's refutation concedes that every law of pure logic does permit an
inwardly evident transformation in the psychical domain which allows one to
isolate the conditions of inward evidence. It is true, for instance, that one and
only one of two mutually contradictory judgments can manifest inner evidence,
because one and only one can be true. But the inner evidence of these sorts of
judgments does not depend on psychological conditions, which are contingent
and external to the judged content, but on ideal conditions.

> Each truth stands as an ideal unity over against an endless, unbounded possibility of
> correct statements which have its form and its matter in common. Each actual
> judgment, which belongs to this ideal manifold, will fulfill . . . the ideal conditions
> for its own possible inward evidence. The laws of pure logic are truths rooted in the
> concept of truth, and in concepts essentially related to this concept. They state, in
> relation to possible acts of judgment, and on the basis of their mere form, the ideal
> conditions of the possibility or impossibility of their inner evidence. (LI, 192)

For Descartes the situation is very similar, since it is not possible to clearly
and distinctly perceive an unclear and indistinct idea, though it is possible, under
specifiable conditions, not to clearly and distinctly perceive what would constitute a clear and distinct idea. It is not an act of self-reflection which *confers*
clarity and distinctness, but rather through or by means of self-reflection, the
clarity and distinctness of what is thought in the thinking act can be brought
forth. Such self-reflection uncovers the originary manner in which only clear and
distinct ideas can be presented. The subject matter towards which our cognitive
seeing is turned may be obscure, but this obscurity can itself become firmly
grasped as that which must be abstracted in order to cognize (and hence judge)

clearly and distinctly. The formal reason which induces one to assent to such an idea consists in a certain "inner light" which is divinely inspired, and when one's cognition is illumined by this, there is the guarantee that what one assents to, in clear and distinct seeing, is indeed a clear and distinct idea (CSM II, 105). This "objective perfection" manifest through the natural light as guarantee of the clarity and distinctness of that which is cognitively seen is very close indeed to Husserl's concept of apodictic (or perfect) evidence, which discloses itself to critical reflection as having the unique feature of being the absolute inconceivability of its nonbeing and thus excluding every doubt as object-less and empty. And this closeness in the treatment of the meaning of logical laws is the direct result of their congruent treatment of the skeptical attitude which provoked a radical rethinking of the grounds and conditions for a philosophy which aspires to a scientific certitude.

ORDER OF REASONS VERSUS ORDER OF ESSENCES; OR, SCIENCE'S BUILDING AND PHILOSOPHY'S PATH

Some years ago I was struck by the large number of falsehoods that I had accepted as true in my childhood, and by the highly doubtful nature of the whole edifice that I had subsequently based on them. I realized that it was necessary, once in the course of my life, to demolish everything completely and start again right from the foundations if I wanted to establish anything at all in the sciences that was stable and likely to last. (CSM II, 12)

The opening lines of the *Meditations* and one of the most famous incipits in modern philosophy; from this will be launched a ground-breaking revolution in seventeenth-century thought. And embedded within these lines is the most persistent and significant of all the philosophical metaphors which Descartes will employ from the *Rules* (1627) to the *Principles* (1644–47). To liken the construction of grounded scientific knowledge into a coherent whole to the architecture of a building is a clear and succinct metaphor and, in many instances, functions as no more than a rhetorical device or figure of speech. And yet his recurring commitment to this image elevates it to the status of a thematic concern, and this for three reasons.

First, in almost every instance, the building metaphor is coupled with the contrasting figure of the path or the way which one must take in the process of philosophizing in this new manner, that is, the one unfolded in the *Meditations* itself. Second, that if in many cases this has seemed to be no more than a rhetorical figure, in the "Seventh Replies" to Bourdin's "Objections," he states that, "throughout my writings I have made it clear that my method imitates that of the architect" (CSM II, 366). For twenty-four pages (in the Adam-Tannery edition), Descartes recapitulates the stages of his philosophical enterprise in great detail, equating each to a stage in the construction of a great building. And third, the building and path metaphors are an expository or literary analogue for the format of presentation, better known under the rubrics, order of essences and order of reasons.

As a rhetorical device, the building metaphor was not original or unique to Descartes and, like Sextus' image of the "ladder" of syllogisms, had found its way into contemporary writers' discussion of method, that is, as the elaboration of a coherent and self-contained corpus of knowledge. Sanchez' concerted attack in *Quod Nihil Scitur* (1584) on the scholastic followers of Aristotle concluded with this sustained analogy to a crumbling building:

> They never stop writing them [treatises on dialectic], revealing new collapses every day, like some ancient building that keeps threatening to fall down, or else one built on sand and an unstable site, with foundations made up of fragile materials; a building that must be continually shored up with wooden props, or reinforced with stone, mortar, and so forth, since cracks keep continually opening in its structure on this side or that. Just so, as the syllogistic discipline continually crumbles . . . its inhabitants and craftsmen continually struggle to prevent it.[1]

In a similar fashion, the "Announcement" which opens Francis Bacon's *Instauratio Magna* (1620) sets the stage for his comprehensive taxonomy of the sciences in these terms:

> Human knowledge itself, the thing employed in all our researches, is not well put together nor justly formed, but resembles a magnificent structure that has no foundation. And whilst men agree to admire and magnify the false powers of the mind, and neglect or destroy those that might be rendered true, there is no other course left but, with better assistance, to begin the work anew, and to raise or rebuild the sciences, arts and all human knowledge from a firm and solid basis.[2]

If this image characterizes the poorly built and groundless structure of accumulated knowledge, oblivious to errors and prone to prejudices, so also its opposite typifies the results of scientific researches conducted according to proper methods and eschewing all previously unexamined conclusions. However, Bacon in the next paragraph employs a different image to characterize the point of view of the inaugurator of this new scientific enterprise, and those who carry out its program, in terms of the philosophical process by which such results are achieved.

> He thought it not right to desert either the cause or himself, but to boldly enter on the way and explore the only *path* which is pervious to the human mind. . . . For it is wiser to engage in an undertaking that admits of some termination, than to involve

oneself in perpetual exertion and anxiety about what is interminable. The ways of contemplation indeed, nearly correspond to two *roads* in nature: one of which, steep and rugged at the commencement, terminates in a plain; the other, at first view smooth and easy, leads only to huge rocks and precipices. (emphasis added)

A brief digression into the contemporary development of one scientific enterprise will illustrate the preeminence of this conception of science's standing. Parallel to the late sixteenth- and early seventeenth-century philosophical confrontation with the resurgence of Greek skepticism, from Montaigne to Pierre Gassendi, was the struggle in astronomy to establish and validate the heliocentric model first promulgated by Copernicus in 1543, though circulated among his friends as early as 1510. Although this model was formulated as an explanation of the actual workings of the celestial bodies, the printed edition was prefaced with a statement by Andreas Osiander that Copernicus' theory was no more than a mathematical hypothesis, and as such could not come into conflict with the tenets of the Christian faith.[3] Despite the fact that this prefatory disclaimer was probably written with the best intentions, to spare Copernicus from the presumed interdiction of the Papal Curia, it had the unfortunate though short-lived effect of reducing Copernicus' discoveries to the status of one unfounded claim competing against other disparate claims.

With the proviso that it is only a mathematical hypothesis, the heliocentric model could have been counterposed against any other model in the same way in which, for example, the Stoics confronted the Skeptics with regard to the problem of the criterion. With good fortune though, most of the significant astronomers from the mid-sixteenth century until Galileo, ignored this spurious disclaimer and considered Copernicus' model as the only theory which could adequately explain both observable phenomena and their undisclosed consequences, e.g., the discovery of other planets. This was in contrast, of course, with competing geocentric theories which saved only the observable phenomena and had to readjust their basic premises when confronted with emergent elements. Several notable figures in this period felt obliged, however, to counter Copernicus' detractors on their charge that it was no more than an hypothesis. Kepler was inveigled by Tycho Brahe to defend the elder famous astronomer against the mathematician Nicolai Baer (pseudonym "Ursus") who had attacked Tycho's work using several standard skeptical arguments.[4]

Kepler's *Defence of Tycho Against Ursus,* written in 1600, though not published until much later, bears serious comparison with Descartes' *Discourse on the Method* for several reasons.[5] Kepler's defense does not rely in any way upon the usual scholastic terminology or arguments in its construction of an epistemological framework in which to situate the results of astronomical observations. It is directed towards any conceivable skeptical assault, and not just Ursus' sometimes face-tious criticisms, against a scientific theory which would construe theory-building as no more than an hypothesis open to equal-weighted counterhypotheses. It also demonstrates an unprecedented comprehension of previous astronomical theo-ries in terms of the historiography of scientific thought, and its general method is to begin with axiomatic first principles from which all further postulates could be derived.

Kepler opens the first chapter by remarking that Ursus "writes as if hypoth-eses had been established merely for the amusement of mankind"; that they do not have any greater epistemic weight than a fiction or literary invention. Kepler's first task then is to correct this misconception of the meaning of hypothesis by a comparison of this concept with that which is used by geometers. One should be reminded here of Sanchez's attempt in *Quod Nihil Scitur* to elucidate an intelligible meaning for the term "knowledge." Kepler begins his defense with this scene-setting metaphor:

> Before the birth of logic as a part of philosophy, when they [the geometers] wanted to expand their demonstrations by the natural light of the mind, they used to start their teaching from some established beginning. For in *architecture* the builder is content to lay down foundations below the ground for the future mass of the house, and he does not worry that the ground below might shift or cave in. Just so in the business of geometry, the first founders were not, like the Pyrrhonians who followed later, so obtuse as to want to doubt everything and to lay hold on nothing upon which as *foundation,* sure and known to all, they would wish to build the rest.[6]

One possible source for this immensely popular rhetorical figure is Demosthenes' *Orations,* a standard Greek text for university students of the period. *Scientia* as an edifice would almost certainly have been as familiar to literate readers as Sextus' ladder of syllogisms or Ariadne's thread through the labyrinth. It occurs early in Demosthenes' text, in the "Second Olynthiac Ora-tion": "It is impossible to acquire a solid power by injustice and perjury and falsehood. Such things last for once or for a short period. . . . As a house, a ship, or the like, ought to have the lower parts firmest, so in human conduct the principle and foundation should be just and true."[7] Among other suggestions as to the origin of this image, Dalia Judovitz claims that "Descartes' architectural metaphor is based on the passage in the Republic [Book 6, 501a] where Plato compares the construction of the perfect city to the work of a painter using a divine model. . . . For Descartes, the perfect city is no longer built on a divine model, but rather on a self-made and self-invented rational model."[8]

An even more likely source, however, is in Galen's *Ars Parva,* one of the most popular medical works of the Renaissance, and by an author whom Descartes had thoroughly studied (CSM III, 81–83). Galen argued that medicine was one of the productive arts (*techné*) and compares it to architecture or the building of houses. Just as one comes to understand the finished house by means of analysis, one understands the human body through anatomy. However, physicians differ from house builders in having to understand not only the parts of their subject matter, insofar as the parts make up the whole, but also the operations or functions of each of the parts considered on its own.[9] In this genealogy of rhetorical imagery, one should also bear in mind that throughout sixteenth- and seventeenth-century discussions of method, the writers concerned were aware of its etymology in ancient Greek texts. Aristotle and Plato usually employed this term in its originary sense: *meta* + *odos,* "to follow the path." If in Plato, this indicated the dialectical structure of discourse, in Aristotle this concept is refined to a definite manner of inquiry about any province of knowledge, *via ac ratio inquirendi.*[10]

For Descartes, the general sense of the *building* image is the aggregate of interrelated knowledge claims about a specific subject matter, e.g., the human body, the celestial spheres, or the origin and domain of *scientia.* He usually employs this image to typify the sort of dogmatic, uncritical position held by other theorists and usually with derogatory connotations; with the obvious exception of the "Seventh Replies." On the other hand, the general sense of the path image refers to the ongoing activity of the philosopher, having stripped himself of prejudices and abstained from the uncritical acceptance of any particular doctrine. This is the most common manner in which he talks about his own philosophical activity and thus admonishes those who either cannot or will not follow along with him.

The first use of the path image is in Rule II of the *Rules* and here it may be an oblique reference to the excesses of ancient skepticism. "Perhaps without guidance they might head towards a precipice, but so long as they follow in their master's footsteps (though straying at times from the truth), they will surely hold to a course that is more secure" (CSM I, 11). He may have had in mind the well-known stories told about Pyrrho himself, whose associates had to traipse around with him in order to prevent him being run over by carts or falling over cliffs.[11] It was in the context of pointing out the absurdities inherent in the complete withholding of assent to appearances that Aristotle remarked: "For why does a man walk to Megara and not stay at home, when he thinks he ought to be walking there? Why does he not walk early some morning into a well or over a precipice, if one happens to be in his way? Why do we observe him guarding against this, evidently because he does not think that falling is equally good and not good."[12] Walking toward a precipice is the result of allowing skeptical doubt to spill over into everyday affairs, something which Descartes repeatedly cautions against. But it is also the result of not following the right path, or not following the path in the right manner.[13]

For the student to follow a teacher around for no better reason than that his guide is accorded the status of a pathfinder is as risky as being a disciple of Pyrrho or any other person who does not observe moderation in doubt. "So blind is the curiosity with which mortals are possessed that they often direct their minds down untrodden paths, in the groundless hope that they will chance upon what they are seeking; rather like someone who is consumed with such a senseless desire to discover treasure that he continually roams the streets to see if he can find any that a passer-by might have dropped. This is how almost every chemist, most geometers, and many philosophers pursue their research" (CSM I, 15). He is equally disparaging of those who transfer or reemploy this haphazard process of finding the truth to their elaborate construction of models which incorporate those truths. Those ignorant of proper scientific method, "frequently examine difficult problems in a very disorderly manner, behaving in my view as if they were trying to get from the bottom to the top of a building at one bound, spurning or failing to notice the stairs designed for that purpose" (CSM I, 20–21).

Rule XII includes the first mention of what will later become the crucial distinction between analytic and synthetic methods of exposition. It is not germane to our present concern with the building and path metaphors to undertake a review of the complex ancestry of synthesis and analysis from its origins in the fourfold methodology of Aristotle's *Organon* and Euclid's *Elements*.[14] It is enough for our purpose that the conceptual distinction between *ordo rationarum* and *ordo essendi* corresponds with the rhetorical figures of the path of first philosophy and the building of the sciences. "When we consider things in the order that corresponds to our knowledge of them, our view of them must be different from what it would be if we were speaking of them in accordance with how they exist in reality" (CSM I, 44). The fullest explication of this correspondence will become apparent in the maturation of Descartes' thought through the *Discourse*, the *Meditations*, and the *Passions of the Soul*.

In a letter to Mersenne of April 1630, after abandoning work on the *Rules,* he describes an abrupt change of direction in these terms: "I was forced to start a new project [*The World*] rather larger than the first [*Rules*]. It is as if a man began building a house and then acquired unexpected riches and so changed his status that the building he had begun was now too small for him. No one could blame such a man if he saw him starting to build another house more suitable to his condition" (CSM III, 21). Although he is confident and reassures Mersenne that he will not change his mind again, he could not have foreseen the condemnation of Galileo's *Dialogue on the Two Chief World Systems,* which he learned about while working on *The World.* Ironically then, he does have to vacate this house, and after an interim period, make another assay at building a suitable structure, in the *Discourse on the Method.* Part One of the *Discourse* opens with a sketch of the author's education and travels, including a summary estimation of ancient writers' positions on science and ethics. "I compared the moral writings of the ancient pagans to the very proud and magnificent palaces built only on sand and mud. . . . As for the other sciences, in so far as they borrow their principles from philosophy, I decided that nothing solid could have been built upon such shaky foundations. Neither the honour nor the riches they offered was enough to induce me to learn them" (CSM I, 114–15). However, in the practical domain so often demarcated by Descartes from the abstract and metaphysical discipline of the philosopher, he commends the right following of the path in everyday affairs. The moral maxims adduced in Part Three of the *Discourse* are only the most famous example of his careful segregation of metaphysical certainty from practical common sense. "It is not enough to have a good mind, the main thing is to apply it well. . . . Those who proceed but very slowly can make much greater progress, if they always follow the right path, than those who hurry and stray from it. (CSM I, 111).

The first thematic presentation of the dual metaphor, in contrast to its use as a mere rhetorical figure, occurs immediately after his cryptic mention in the *Discourse* of the now famous dream of November 1619. This context perhaps is not so surprising since the path is one of the key motifs in episodes of the dream itself. Near the start of the third dream episode, a mysterious figure enters his chamber and displays a book open to a poem whose title is *Quod vitae sectabor iter?* (What path in life shall I follow?). The dreamer interprets this not only as a moral maxim, but also as part of his "marvellous discovery" on the road towards a new science.[15] Among his initial thoughts after the dream was the realization that there is greater perfection in any given work, whether material or abstract, if it is the result of one person's efforts rather than many working together. "Thus we see that buildings undertaken and completed by a single architect are usually more attractive and better planned than those which several have tried to patch up by adapting old walls built for different purposes," (CSM I, 116). In this extended treatment several important analogies are drawn. Ancient cities which have grown gradually from small villages to large urban centres display disorderly and haphazard arrangements of buildings and streets, in contrast to newer cities which are planned as a whole in advance of their construction.[16]

As a corollary, Descartes observes that those societies which have grown gradually from half-savage to civilized bring in new laws on an ad hoc basis, i.e., only according to circumstances, in contrast with those states where a single wise lawgiver has thought out all the basic laws, embodied perhaps in a constitution. A second corollary pertains to religious doctrines which are contained in the true religion (Christianity), articulated by the one true God alone, where the pagan religions had to contend with a multitude of conflicting deities. And a third corollary from this initial image pertains to the corpus of alleged scientific knowledge contained in textbooks, the accumulated sediment of many researchers cobbling things together on the basis of their predecessors' works.

He is convinced that in the ethical conduct of his own life and in the metaphysical domain of the philosopher, it is far better to start from first principles and then proceed to more complex problems. Public institutions, which one would encounter in practical affairs, are an obvious example of social structures which are so cumbrous and unwieldy that they cannot be rectified; custom alone will smooth away these excrescences. "It is almost easier to put up with their imperfections than to change them, just as it is much better to follow the main roads that wind through the mountains . . . than to try to take a more direct route by clambering over rocks and descending to the foot of precipices." (CSM I, 118).

In the next paragraph, he chastises those headstrong persons who never have the patience to carefully consider the issues and order their thoughts. "If they once took the liberty of doubting the principles they accepted and of straying from the common path, they could never stick to the track that must be taken as a shortcut, and they would remain lost all their lives" (CSM I, 118). He may here have had in mind Thomas Campanella, the author of *De Sensu Rerum* (1620), of whose writings he remarked in a letter to Huygens of March 1638 "that to go astray through fondness for the most out-of-the-way paths is less excusable than to follow the well-trodden ones" (CSM III, 91). This synoptic criticism is very similar to one about Galileo's *Two New Sciences* (1638) in a Letter to Mersenne of October 1638: "He has not investigated matters in an orderly way and has merely sought explanations for some particular effects, without going into the primary causes in nature; hence his *building* lacks a foundation. Now the closer his style of philosophizing gets to the truth, the easier it is to recognize its faults, just as it is easier to tell when those who sometimes take the right *road* go astray than it is to point out aberrations in the case of those who never begin to follow it" (CSM III, 124–25; emphasis added). Here Descartes' metaphors of the building and the path have become quite overt in their intention, or perhaps one could say, their latent meanings have risen to the surface. He equates a building with an ordered model of acquired knowledge and a path with the style or activity of philosophizing.

Descartes himself was in *two minds* (so to speak) about the manner in which to present his thoughts to the reading public in his first published work *Dis-*

course on the Method. His worry about this is expressed to several correspondents at this time; whether to proceed in the customary fashion, from topic to topic in an ordered, systematic whole, or to initiate his readers into his train of thought stage by stage in a gradual unfolding. He wrote to Mersenne in February 1637: "I was afraid that weak minds might avidly embrace the doubts and scruples which I would have had to propound and afterwards be unable to follow as fully the arguments by which I would have endeavoured to remove them. Thus I would have set them on a false path and been unable to bring them back" (CSM III, 53). He wrote to Vatier in a similar vein in February 1638 on his reasons for the "shocking" format of the proofs given in the *Discourse:* "First, believing that I could deduce them in due order from the first principles of my metaphysics, I wanted to ignore other kinds of proofs; secondly, I wanted to see whether the simple exposition of truth would be sufficient to carry conviction without engaging in any disputes or refutations of contrary opinions" (CSM III, 87). Our previous discussion of Descartes' confrontation with skepticism has shown that he was quite deliberate in not countering each and every skeptical trope with an equal-weighted trope—this is the standard skeptical practice of *isosthenia,* "engaging in disputes or refutations," which Descartes has rejected. His "shocking" and "strange" procedure is to encourage the reader to follow the philosopher's thinking along a single path, from the most basic and evident insights and thus, little by little, to more complex truths.

Such a "groundbreaking" procedure—in the literal sense of razing an extant edifice in order to begin building anew—is not without its own dangers and obstacles. And moreover what is disclosed in this process, if not unexpected, will most likely be entirely mysterious. From the point of view of one setting out to accomplish this task, it is as if he were alone and in the dark, searching for the path.[17]

> Like a man who walks alone in the dark, I resolved to proceed so slowly, and to use such circumspection in all things, that even if I made but little progress I should at least be sure not to fall. Nor would I begin rejecting completely any of the opinions which may have slipped into my mind without having been introduced there by reason, until I had first spent enough time in planning the work I was undertaking and in seeking the true method of attaining knowledge of everything within my mental abilities. (CSM I, 119).

Another significant occurrence of this dual metaphor in the *Discourse* is at the point where the author is about to introduce his provisional moral code, again an entirely practical concern. Having adopted the position incurred by methodical doubt, although he may be obliged to remain indecisive on intellectual matters, he cannot be indecisive in the practical "business" of conducting his own life. "Now before starting to rebuild your house, it is not enough simply to pull it down, to make provision for materials and architects (or else train yourself in architecture), and to have carefully drawn up the plans." This is a clearcut reference to his avowed intent to demolish the accepted scheme of scientific knowledge in order to rebuild it according to a coherent design. "You must also provide yourself with some other place where you can live comfortably while building is in progress" (CSM I, 122). As he remarks on numerous occasions, he is not adverse to employing a probabilistic model of decision-making in practical affairs. If his first maxim is to obey the laws and customs of his country, his second maxim is to be as firm and decisive in his actions as possible, that is, to consistently maintain a definite course of action, even if this should turn out to have been improper or incorrect. "In this respect, I would be imitating a traveller who, upon finding himself lost in a forest, should not wander about turning this way and that, and still less stay in one place, but should keep walking as straight as he can in one direction, . . . for in this way, even if he does not go exactly where he wishes, he will at least end up in a place where he is likely to be better off than in the middle of the forest" (CSM I, 123).

The usage of the building and path images before the *Meditations* is thus more than the employment of mere figures of speech. He returns to the building metaphor again and again to characterize both his own uncritically accepted youthful opinions, taken as a body of spurious knowledge, and to denigrate the so-called scientific edifice of others' theories, pieced together from what is at hand—something the French perhaps would call *bricolage*.[18] He refers again and again to being lost on a path, or not being on the right path, where wandering about in an arbitrary manner can lead one to expect the same sort of results one would have if a building were constructed in this fashion. In this respect the two images merge: he is not opposed to building per se, as long as it is done in the right order, and as long as one does not confuse it with following a path. On the other hand, he repeatedly enjoins those who wish to pursue philosophy to follow the right path, as long as they do not convert this process into a static edifice. It is with this understanding of the fundamental incompatibility of these two formats that the dual rhetorical trope points to a profound philosophical issue, the distinction between *ordo rationarum* and *ordo essendi*. If these latter methodological concepts have not been fully explicated before the *Meditations,* the building and path metaphors serve as a preliminary sketch of this already accepted dichotomy.

Let us return then to the opening lines of the *Meditations*, more fully aware of the mature import of references to buildings or edifices and to paths or roads. Having been struck by the falseness of many youthful opinions and the dubiousness of the whole edifice of alleged *scientiae* based on them, it is necessary once (and not more than once) to raze this edifice to the ground. Only if the ground has been cleared will it be possible to build again, to build a coherent and well-ordered *scientia* which is stable and long lasting. There is no point in renovating any extant edifice, as his work in the *Rules* and the *Discourse* made apparent, since the basic principles or foundations of these buildings are completely undermined without the prior benefit of a proper method. At this point, let us interpolate Husserl's comments on Descartes' enterprise and his own choice of imagery in characterizing this groundbreaking philosophical ambition. "In a bold, even extravagant, elevation of the meaning of universality, begun by Descartes, this new philosophy seeks nothing less than to encompass, in the unity of a theoretical system, all meaningful questions in a rigorous scientific manner. . . . Growing from generation to generation and forever, this one edifice of definitive, theoretically inter-related truths was to solve all conceivable problems—problems of fact and of reason, problems of temporality and eternity" (Crisis, 8–9).

Descartes' specific contributions to this entirely new structure, one which is grounded on indubitable principles, have been the *Treatise on Man* (physiology), and the three essays appended to the *Discourse:* Optics, Geometry, and Meteorology. The experimental results and the verifiable theorems contained in these works have been made possible by the radical method first outlined in the *Rules* and Part Two of the *Discourse.* But in order to explain how he has arrived at these first principles and what constitutes their primacy, he has now decided not to adopt the format evinced in these earlier topical treatises. Rather, this "showing the way" to his radical point of departure will take the form of meditations, of which a precursor is found in Part Four of the *Discourse.* These intellectual exercises should encourage the reader to follow along with him in his discovery of these foundational principles; a process which contrasts with the construction of scientific theories based on these principles. The opening lines of the "Second Meditation" highlight this other format of presentation: "So serious are the doubts into which I have been thrown as a result of yesterday's meditation that . . . it feels as if I have fallen unexpectedly into a deep whirlpool which tumbles me around so that I can neither stand on the bottom nor swim up to the top. Nevertheless, I will make an effort and once more attempt the same path which I started on yesterday" (CSM II, 16).

The meditation format is one with which Descartes' readers will have been quite familiar; in religious works of the period, they took the form of Devotions. Several scholars have pointed to the great popularity and influence of Ignatius Loyola's *Spiritual Devotions,* a work which Descartes knew well from his Jesuit school days. One feature of this format which lends itself to philosophical purposes is that, unlike scholastic compendia of topics, in order to fully assimilate later stages, one must already have comprehended earlier stages, as well as the fact that they unfold in this particular sequence. It is as though one were traversing an entirely unknown terrain (another often used metaphor) and attempting to draw a map of one's course and environs. It is only possible to situate some new feature within the context of one's journey if all the previous features have been carefully marked out and if one has kept track of one's position relative to these features. To jump from point to point, i.e., from topic to topic in a textbook, is to completely lose one's bearings. Thus the author solicits his readers to begin again, to make as many attempts as necessary, in order to follow the meditator's train of thought with complete confidence.

Husserl characterizes his own chosen format of exposition in similar terms: "[I will] attempt to show, to those willing to understand, one of the paths I have actually taken; as a path actually taken, it offers itself as one that can at any time be taken again. Indeed, it is a path which at every step allows just this self-evidence to be renewed and tested as apodictic, i.e., the self-evidence of a path capable of being taken repeatedly at will and capable of being followed further at will in repeatedly verifiable experiences and cognitions" (Crisis, 120–21).

Less than a year before the publication of the *Meditations*, in a letter to Mersenne of Christmas 1640, Descartes has fully worked out the conceptual distinction between *ordo essendi* and *ordo cognoscendi* (or *rationarum*), though this distinction is not stated explicitly anywhere in the text. In fact, it is in response to Mersenne's "Second Objections" that Descartes first publicly declares his twofold notion of demonstration, something that until then has only been implicit in his use of the building and path metaphors. "It should be noted that throughout the work the order I follow is not the order of the subject matter, but the order of the reasoning. . . . I reason in an orderly way from what is easier to what is harder, making what deductions I can, now on one subject, now on another. This is the right way, in my opinion, to find and explain the truth" (CSM III, 163). On this pivotal issue, Martial Gueroult comments:

> From the perspective of the *ratio essendi*, [the progress] arrives at the supreme reality from which all others are derived, the principle of deduction that, following the order of synthesis, climbs back down the ladder of beings beginning with their cause and with respect to their relations of mutual dependency. From the perspective of the *ratio cognoscendi* . . . the fundamental problem, the problem of the foundation of science as valid objective knowledge, seems completely resolved.[19]

One of the most common complaints that Descartes will have against his detractors is that they extract some statement, e.g., about a thinking substance, from its place in the order of reasons and thus distort or even falsify its status as a temporarily secured truth. A specific statement has epistemic weight only insofar as it is an integral component of the grand unified argument formed by all six Meditations taken together. If an objector demands that a specific claim be considered on its own merits, irrespective of its ordered position, he has not understood the initial necessary condition, as prescribed in the "First Meditation," to consider as false all those preconceived notions which make up a faulty and groundless edifice. Prompted by Mersenne's remarks in the "Second Objections," Descartes attempts to forestall further misinterpretations by spelling this out.

> As for the method of demonstration, this divides into two varieties: . . . Analysis shows the *true way* by means of which the thing in question was discovered methodically and as it were a priori, so that if the reader is willing *to follow it* and give sufficient attention to all points, he will make the thing his own and understand it just as perfectly as if he had discovered it for himself. . . . Synthesis, by contrast, employs a directly opposite method where the search is, as it were, a posteriori. . . . It demonstrates the conclusion clearly and employs a long series of definitions, postulates, axioms, theorems and problems, so that if anyone denies one of the conclusions it can be shown at once that it is contained in what has gone before. (CSM II, 110–11)

For the benefit of such readers who cannot follow the analytic method, he appends to the "Second Replies" a short treatise written in the synthetic method or, as he also phrases it, "arranged in geometrical fashion."[20] This latter phrase harkens back to the geometrical arrangement of inferences in the *Rules*, where mathematical truths were held to be immune to doubt. Most famously, this dictum regarding the "user-friendly" aspect of the geometrical method was taken very seriously indeed by Spinoza in the *Ethics*.

Cottingham is surely correct when he expands on the peculiar meaning of *a priori* and *a posteriori* in this passage. Their usage does not seem to correspond with the modern, post-Leibnizian sense, where *a priori* truths are those known independently of experience; nor with the mediaeval Thomistic sense, where *a priori* reasoning proceeds from cause to effect. "What Descartes may mean when he says that analysis proceeds *as it were* a priori (*tanquam a priori*) is that it starts from what is epistemically prior, i.e., from what is prior in the order of discovery followed by the meditator" (CSM II, 110 note). The Cartesian use of the term *tanquam* to characterize the two types of method, analysis and synthesis, further underscores the as-if or as-it-were feature of methodical doubt, the pretense of the *malign genie*, and so forth. It is to E. M. Curley's credit, however, that he is not content to accept what Descartes says these terms are used for, as though they were stipulative definitions, but instead unpacks their textual elaboration. "The essential task of the analytic method is to bring [reflective] knowledge to consciousness, to turn the unclear and indistinct ideas of common sense into the clear and distinct ideas Descartes needs to make his argument demonstrative."[21]

If the *Meditations* is the most fully worked out presentation in the analytic format, the *Principles* is designed to satisfy those readers who demanded an exposition of his philosophy in the synthetic format. Of course, it is also an opportunity for him to publish a more mature version of his theoretical physics first outlined in *The World*, composed between 1630–32, but held back after news of Galileo's condemnation. In the preface to the French edition of the *Principles* (1647), which is dedicated to Princess Elizabeth, Descartes feels obliged to console those who have never studied philosophy: "[There is] the following similarity with what happens when we travel: so long as we turn our back on the place we wish to get to, then the longer and faster we walk the further we get from our destination, so that even if we are subsequently set on the right road we cannot reach our goal as quickly as we would have done had we never walked in the wrong direction" (CSM I, 183). Shortly before the publication of the French edition, in a letter to Princess Elizabeth of September 1646, he responds to her inquiry about his opinion of Machiavelli's *Prince*. He thinks that the Italian author's greatest fault is that he does not distinguish between those who have achieved power by just means and those who have usurped it by unjust means. As such, the author's failure lies at the most fundamental level, that of the political principles which would discriminate between just and unjust methods. His analogy in this instance of political power is precisely the one which Demosthenes used: "If you are building a house on foundations insufficient to support high thick walls, the walls will have to be low and insubstantial; and similarly those who have gained power by crime are usually compelled to continue their course of crime and would be unable to remain in power if they took to virtue" (CSM III, 292).

Before passing on to consider the definitive explication of the building metaphor in the "Seventh Replies," where Descartes identifies his orientation with that of the architect, it is worth mentioning his use of the dual images in *The Search after Truth*. An unpublished manuscript found among his posthumous papers and first printed in 1701, it is generally ascribed to his final years, though there are some internal indications that it was composed just after the publication of the *Meditations*. It is in the form of a dialogue between Eudoxus (Descartes' spokesman), Epistemon (a learned scholar), and Polyander (a simple person of common sense). Eudoxus expresses surprise that not one person is to be found among the learned schoolmen who has the patience to follow the path

Eudoxus has opened for them. "Instead they have nearly all acted like travellers who leave the main path to take a short-cut, only to find themselves lost amongst briars and precipices" (CSM II, 401). Eudoxus is convinced that all can be explained to those who are willing to listen and follow, so that Polyander will most likely benefit from this, while Epistemon will merely counter every claim with its opposite. "Since this knowledge is not enough to satisfy him [Polyander], it must be faulty: I would compare it to a badly constructed house, whose foundations are not firm. I know of no better way to repair it than to knock it all down and build a new one in its place. For I do not wish to be one of those jobbing builders who devote themselves solely to refurbishing old buildings because they consider themselves incapable of undertaking the construction of new ones" (CSM II, 407).

The Cartesian Method Imitates That of an Architect

Descartes certainly considered himself capable not only of demolishing extant faulty edifices in the sciences, but also confident enough to build himself an entirely new structure. If all of his previous uses of the building image indicate only that such faulty edifices must be razed to the ground, it is not till he has been provoked by Bourdin's arrogant mockery of both the meditator's pathfinding and the scientist's building that Descartes will adopt the persona of an architect. Until this juncture, the builder's metaphorical brief has been to demolish, to clear the ground; in the "Seventh Replies," the builder assumes positive duties. If the explicit message in the "Preface to the Reader" has been to meditate along with him, in the "Seventh Replies" there is an explicit statement of the builder's directions. Having attained a clear and distinct understanding of all previously secured propositions, one can also construct a coherent system in which these propositions are interconnected according to valid rules of inference; or, congruent with this imagery, according to correct rules of architecture. "Throughout my writings I have made it clear that my method imitates that of the architect. When an architect wants to build a house which is stable on ground where there is sandy topsoil over underlying rock, or clay or some other firm base, he begins by digging out a set of trenches from which he removes the sand, and anything resting on or mixed in with the sand, so that he can lay his foundations on firm soil" (CSM II, 366).

In one of the most extended philosophical metaphors ever devised, Descartes reviews the arguments from the *Meditations* point by point, relating each to some feature of architectural practice.[22] To begin with, methodical doubt encourages him to reject all that is doubtful, just as he throws out the sand, until he reaches something indubitable, i.e., that a thinking thing exists, which he takes as the bedrock upon which to build. His critic Bourdin is like a bricklayer, who having a grudge against the architect, complains about every aspect of the overall design. The architect explains that, after digging the trenches the topsoil must be removed because it cannot bear the weight of a large building. The sand is unstable because it will shift under a heavy weight or running water, and when this sort of subsidence occurs in mines, the miners attribute it to the action of goblins or demons. But because the bricklayer does not understand the overall design nor the theory of building which extends to any structure, he mocks each separate stage.

The bricklayer (Bourdin) contends that no building could be built over an empty trench, i.e., a philosophy which rests only on the exploration of a new site would be a flimsy structure indeed. He further objects that the architect has thrown out perfectly good blocks of stone and wood with the sand, i.e., standard "blocks" of proof or accepted definitions from the scholastic tradition. He also contends that the architect believes in goblins or demons which may undermine his efforts, an oblique reference to the *malign genie,* the demiurge of the third stage of doubt, whose overthrow reveals the absolute certainty of the cogito. And then, having reached bedrock, the critic objects that this too, the Archimedean point from which to shift the world, is also another stone and should be thrown away. And finally, standing on this bedrock, with the sand, rubble and demons cleared away, the architect begins to assemble his building using both new stones and some of the rejects; to which the bricklayer scolds that this isn't allowed, since all this material has been banished from the start by methodical doubt.

Of all Descartes' critics, Bourdin was the most wrong headed and stubborn in his refusal to understand the very nature of Descartes' radical enterprise. Bourdin takes a gleeful pleasure in repeatedly pointing out that, having passed through the stages of doubt and having dismissed everything as uncertain, the meditator is left with only the cogito as his minimal achievement. In this utterly reduced realm, like a winking point of light in a dark void, one can claim nothing further. Again and again, Descartes reminds Bourdin that the function of methodical doubt is to consider various knowledge claims *as though* they were false, until such time as having reached a clear and distinct perception of something, this intuition will provide a criterion by which other claims, including those previously held, can be evaluated. This is the crux of Bourdin's persistent interruptions of Descartes' theoretical progress after the securing of the cogito; and by analogy, his tut-tuting every time the architect attempts to place another stone at the building's foundations.

Descartes concludes this first response to his own parody of Bourdin's criticisms by making two crucial points. One is that Bourdin has attacked his method and materials *as if* it were not possible to construct such a building, whereas it is a *matter of fact* that the building has already been erected. Bourdin is so blinkered by his own prejudices that he thinks it is impossible to do something which has already been done. Surely the productive criticisms which Descartes encourages should be directed towards flaws in the building itself. The second point is that this is not just any edifice, but "a solid chapel, destined to last for many years to the glory of God." This is an overt reference to the link in the chain of reasons whereby it is divine perfection and infinitude which ensures the veracity of clear and distinct seeing; it might also remind the astute modern reader of the central locale of the "holy chapel" in the first episode of Descartes' dream more than twenty years earlier.

He proceeds to respond to each of Bourdin's exiguous sarcasms by expanding on specific issues already included in the summary of his architectural method. It will serve no good purpose to unpack all of the subsidiary objections, many of which are expressed with such vehemence that one has the impression that, having knocked down his opponent, Descartes is determined to finish him once and for all. However, it is worth underlining several salient points made along the way. It is in this context that he remarks that scepticism is alive and well, and is the first refuge of those who think that they are more gifted than the rest. (CSM II, 374). It is also the only context, aside from his private letters, where he makes the explicit declaration that he has become "the first philosopher ever to overthrow the doubt of the sceptics" (CSM II, 376).

He parodies Bourdin's mockery of his "long odyssey," when the meditator wandered around, exhausted himself, and got stuck on rugged slopes and dense thickets. But this is the very imagery that Descartes himself reverts to near the end of his rebuttal; "on my journey, where I led the mind from knowledge of its own existence to knowledge of the existence of God and to the distinction between mind and body" (CSM II, 375). Couched in this elaborate building analogy are several references to the path and the journey undertaken—but this is not a case of mixed metaphors. In a simplistic fashion one could say that, viewed from the outside, as an accomplished fact, the totality of the results resemble a building; but viewed from the inside, from the viewpoint of the meditator in the ongoing act of philosophizing, the way ahead and behind looks like the itinerary of a journey.

Before considering this final synoptic metaphor, it is relevant to point out the long-lasting effect that the architect of the "Seventh Replies" had on one of his other objectors. Pierre Gassendi, the author of the "Fifth Objections," was quite probably influenced in some way by reading the final version of the published *Meditations*, which contained all the objections and replies. Given his tempering of the extreme skepticism in his *Exercises* (1624), one finds a compromise between excessive doubt and an early version of empiricism in the *Syntagma* (1658). In the section devoted to logic, Gassendi compares the craft of building to several other disciplines: grammar, medicine, and the natural sciences. "A physicist teaching natural science sets before our eyes the outward configuration of nature, or the machine of the world, the heavens, the earth, the things that are found in them, just as if they were the greater and lesser parts of an enormous building, and by resolving them into their smallest elements, he assumes these as his primary particles (*principia*) from which the universe is constructed."[23]

Descartes' lifelong journey will indeed take him to a new world, that is, a new model of the world of scientific knowledge and a new foundation for the systematic acquisition of such knowledge. "It will be enough if I open the way which will enable you to discover them [physical laws] yourselves, when you take the trouble to look for them" (CSM I, 97). The trouble which must be taken is to learn to philosophize in this novel manner, to think through these steps in the order of reasons. "I decided to leave our world wholly for them [the learned] to argue about, and to speak solely of what would happen in a new world" (CSM I, 132). The learned in this world are devoted to their ancient edifices and only argue about minor changes, leaving a faulty structure intact. This new world whose physical laws are described in the Optics, Geometry, Principles, etc. is reached by means of an unprecedented voyage of discovery. This discovery is as revolutionary as Copernicus' cosmology and Columbus' exploration, standards against which later historians will compare the Cartesian overthrow, and its narrative is recounted in the *Meditations*.

Bourdin appropriates Descartes' metaphor of a journey to a new world but only in order to repeatedly mock its results. He is sarcastic and sometimes outright contemptuous of the meditator as a reliable guide, someone who has opened the way to a marvellous new domain which others were too feeble and inept to even have noticed. Bourdin feels shipwrecked on "these shores of renunciation which are so full of terror and darkness" (CSM II, 336). Although his remarks are usually parodic, he correctly equates this philosophical journey with the appropriate methodology for uncovering the ground of certainty when he groups his criticisms under the rubric, "attempt to find a way into the method." In the very same section where Descartes insists that throughout his writings his method has imitated that of the architect, he also refers to the process by which his method has been articulated as a journey (CSM II, 375). In terms of the former image, Bourdin is a stubborn bricklayer, in terms of the latter, he is a foolish and inept sailor. As discussed above, there is no internal conflict between these two images: from the point of view of the philosopher, the unfolding of the order of reasons is a linear progression; from a third-person point of view, the totality of the results achieved by these means resembles a stable building.

The Path of Philosophy Is a Journey of Exploration.

A philosophical enterprise conceived as a long arduous journey is a grand trope which has a long history in principal programmatic statements since the early seventeenth century. It is possible that a large-scale intellectual enterprise could not even be thought of as a journey before the sixteenth century's great voyages of exploration; but in any case, it will only be feasible in this research to trace some of its more prominent forward stations. Although John Locke famously described his own self-appointed task as "an Under-Labourer in clearing Ground a little, and removing some of the Rubbish, that lies in the way to Knowledge," his ambition had grown by the end of Book 1. "In the future part of this Discourse, designing to raise an Edifice uniform, and consistent with it self . . . I hope to erect it on such a Basis, that I shall not need to shore it up with props and buttresses, leaning on borrowed or begged foundations. Or at least, if mine prove a Castle in the Air, I will endeavour it shall be all of a piece and hang together."[24]

If Locke relies on the metaphor of likening the results of philosophical construction to a building, Kant falls back on the metaphor of the philosophical process of discovery as a journey. After he presents the Transcendental Deduction and the Analytic of Principles, he employs this image in order to introduce the ground of the distinction between phenomena and noumena.

> We have now not merely explored the territory of pure understanding, and carefully surveyed every part of it, but have also measured its extent, and assigned to everything its rightful place. This domain is an island, enclosed by nature itself within unalterable limits. It is the land of truth—enchanting name!—surrounded by a wide and stormy ocean, the native home of illusion, where many a fog bank and many a swiftly melting iceberg give the deceptive appearance of farther shores, deluding the adventurous seafarer ever anew with empty hopes and engaging him in enterprises which he can never abandon and yet is unable to carry to completion.[25]

There is a colligation of imagery in this grand metaphor which it is difficult to imagine is *entirely* a Kantian figure of speech, since it so closely parallels Descartes' own usage. This explorer also compares the philosophical quest to a long voyage, the enunciation of its progress to the charting of a new-found land, a new world surrounded by the mists of illusion, and miragelike features which may seduce or tempt those who follow away from the proper path.

Hegel in his *Lectures on the History of Philosophy* is quite explicit in placing this metaphor at the forefront of an early nineteenth-century understanding of Descartes' achievement. "Actually we now first come to the philosophy of the modern world and we begin this with Descartes. With him we truly enter upon an independent philosophy, which knows that it emerges independently out of reason. . . . Here, we may say, we are at home, and like the mariner after a long voyage over the tempestuous sea, we can finally call out, 'Land!' "[26] Nietzsche also was fascinated with the ocean's seemingly limitless extent and called upon fellow 'free-spirits' to cast away the fetters of dogmatic philosophy and launch themselves into uncharted seas.

In any case, as early as 1906 or 1907, with the assimilation of the skeptical impetus and the inauguration of the reduction, Husserl begins to talk about the overall phenomenological enterprise as a voyage of discovery. It's hard to imagine how these several factors could have accidentally generated this grand trope, as though it were no more than a clever figure of speech, a curious metaphor used by a writer rarely given to any sort of literary imagery. It is in these lectures, after all, that one has the first glimpse of the Cartesian way into phenomenology. Before this date there is no discussion of Descartes, no mention of methodical doubt, the transcendental domain of consciousness, or the dual orders of cognitions and things. The lectures of this period make a theme of the train of thought which traverses the various levels of the reduction as the philosopher's "quite personal affair," and one which must be taken up by anyone who seeks to philosophize in this radically new manner. With regard to the apparent world considered purely as a phenomenon, deprived of its tacit positing of actuality, Husserl remarks: "And so we have dropped anchor on the shore of phenomenology, the existence of the objects of which is assured, as the objects of a scientific investigation should be. . . . But we must take new steps, enter onto new considerations, so that we may gain a firm foothold in the new land and not finally run aground on its shore. For this shore has its rocks and over it lie clouds of obscurity which threaten us with stormy gales of scepticism" [IP, 35).

If these lectures have served to demarcate the phenomenological domain as a new-found land, it is not until the *Ideas* that Husserl styles himself an explorer. At the close of Part Three, Chapter Three, he reminds the reader that throughout the previous analyses, phenomenology should always be understood as a beginning science and that only future researches will demonstrate whether or not these results are definitive—an oblique reference to the author's peculiar process of composition, i.e., constant backward glancing reinterpretations which are then assimilated into an even richer forward movement. But one consideration should provide some reassurance to those who follow: that through this movement, one has always striven to faithfully describe exactly what is seen, as it is seen. "Our procedure is that of an explorer journeying through an unknown part of the world and carefully describing what is presented along his unbeaten paths, which will not always be the shortest. Such an explorer can rightfully be filled with the sure confidence that he gives utterance to what must be said . . . even though new explorations will require new descriptions with manifold improvements" (Ideas I, 235).

By the time of the lectures on *Erste Philosophie* (1923/24), Husserl will have become disenchanted with the Cartesian way, though the other ways will remain somewhat inchoate until their definitive formulation in the *Crisis*. If until this date his point of departure had been located in Cartesian methodical doubt, it is a departure from a point in the ongoing journey which opens up the possibility of other routes. This perhaps is why these lectures are often referred to as the history of a *shipwreck*: "It is the path of an experimenting adventurer in thought whose successes are constantly thrown into question in the reflections which accompany the lectures and whose goal is not fixed from the start so that it actually leads elsewhere than initially foreseen."[27] The paradoxical result of Husserl's attempt to take into account all of the advances in his thought since the *Ideas* is that the Cartesian way, with its irreducible foundation in primary principles, is simply not workable. In no other work does he so expose himself to the force of the absolute, to such an extent that the forward movement of his thought is pushed to a virtual limit—"a thought which does not aim at a will to mastery through a system, but one which advances toward the affair with restless abandon."

It is in the context of his most severe criticism of Descartes, that he reached the gate of transcendence but turned away with an ego empty of content, that Husserl again invokes the notion of a journey, but here a journey thwarted, shifted unwittingly off course. "The proper sense of the discovery Descartes could not seize for himself. Behind the apparent triviality of his well-known phrase *ego cogito, ego sum*, there open up in fact depths all too dark and deep. It was with Descartes like Columbus, who discovered the new continent, but knew nothing of it, merely believing to have discovered a new sea-route to India" (HUS VII, 63). There is a certain irony to this passage, since irrespective of whether this new land is America or India (or Erewhon), one's mapping of the territory itself would be deemed accurate and helpful for entirely autonomous reasons. Descartes chides Mersenne in the "Sixth Objections" for appealing to external authority in countering the assertion that there is a basic intuitable distinction between the essence of a thinking thing and an extended thing. "One witness who has sailed to America and said that he has seen the antipodes deserves more credence than a thousand others who deny their existence merely because they have no knowledge of them" (CSM II, 286).

In the *Crisis*, Husserl draws a curious analogy between the transcendental dimension disclosed by Kant's *Critique* and Helmholtz's fiction of a world of 'plane'-beings who have no experience of depth (this may be more familiar to readers from Abbott's *Flatland*). In this imaginary world, all practical, mundane activities and all reflection on these activities which supports the empirical sciences are carried out in two dimensions. However, the true state of affairs is that there is a third dimension of depth from which the 'picture' of the world-plane is projected. Only if one has an understanding of this "infinitely richer dimension" is one able to grasp the necessary conditions which allow for regularities and connections to be discerned within the plane. Husserl's analysis of Galileo's remodeling of the natural order showed how it was plausible that further developments of the empirical sciences were seen as unqualified successes. But between the patent life of the plane and the latent life of depth there is a great distance, a divide which separates "unclearly arising needs [and] goal-determined plans."

> [Here] the explorer is met by logical ghosts emerging out of the dark, formed in the old familiar and effective conceptual patterns, as paradoxical antinomies, logical absurdities. Thus nowhere is the temptation so great to slide into logical aporetics and disputation, priding oneself on one's scientific discipline, while the actual substratum of the work, the phenomena themselves, is forever lost from view. . . . [I will show] one of the paths I have actually taken; as a path actually taken, it offers itself as one that can at any time be taken again. (Crisis, 120)

This is an unusual conjunction of rhetorical images: an explorer who encounters logical ghosts formed from prejudices, who might derive a false confidence from his scientific method, but who reaffirms the necessity for a proper path to be followed. It is the same conjunction of images which Descartes employs, through his mouth-piece Eudoxus, in *The Search After Truth*. As we have seen earlier, this dialogue carries forward from the *Rules* and the *Discourse* the same dual analogy of science as a building and philosophy as a path, a preview of the more explicit formats, order of essences and order of reasons. Polyander, a man of common sense, has shown uncommon willingness to follow Eudoxus' lead, while Epistemon, a learned scholar, repeatedly halts any progress with his cautions and amendments. He thinks that it is dangerous to proceed too far along Eudoxus' line of thinking, for such general doubts would lead straight to Socratic ignorance or skeptical uncertainty. Eudoxus attempts to reassure Polyander on this score:

> I confess that it would be dangerous for someone who does not know a ford to venture across it without a *guide,* and many have lost their lives in doing so. But you have nothing to fear if you follow me. Indeed, just such fears have prevented most men of letters from acquiring a body of knowledge which was firm and certain

enough to deserve the name of *'science.'* ... I would advise you that these doubts, which alarmed you at the start, are like *phantoms* and empty images which appear at night in the uncertain glimmer of a weak light. (CSM II, 408; emphasis added)

For Husserl to claim that all of the many streams of modern philosophy have their source in the radical insights of Descartes' *Meditations* is far more than a seal of approval for his own new phenomenological enterprise. To declare that subjectivity is the proper domain upon which to found a criterion of certainty, to make the philosopher's own commitment to this unique activity a desideratum for its engagement, and to abandon all previous conceptions as unsuitable for such an endeavor is a summons to an arduous though rewarding adventure. "There are some ideas which make it impossible for us to return to a time prior to their existence, even and especially if we moved beyond them, and subjectivity is one of them. ... Subjectivity was not waiting for philosophers as an unknown America waited for its explorers in the ocean's mist. They constructed it, created it in more than one way."[28]

Husserl's Order of Cognitions and Order of Things

It should now be quite clear that Descartes discriminates between the order of reasons and the order of beings for both philosophical reasons and practical considerations. The *Discourse on the Method,* the *Meditations*, and *The Search After Truth* are written according to the order of reasons; whereas the three essays appended to the *Discourse,* the *Principles of Philosophy*, and *The Passions of the Soul* are written according to the order of topics. It's quite obvious, from his grumbling comments in the "Second Replies," that he was reluctant to recast the principal theses of the *Meditations* in the synthetic or geometrical format, since although they would be easier to follow for the less attentive reader, it would distort the very notion of intuitive certainty demanded by the difficult process interwoven in the chain of reasons. It is less obvious that Husserl also endorsed the same discrimination and that one or another text engages either a meditative format or a systematic, expository format. Where Descartes usually captions a passage or prefaces a text with the warning to read it one way or the other, even where he is not explicit, one can make a good guess based on his appeal to the building or path image.

Husserl is much more subtle, or at least less explicit, about this distinction; however, most of his writings fall into one format or the other, with a few strange hybrid exceptions. Aside from the *Cartesian Meditations*, which patently employs the meditative format in homage to Descartes' original, the studies on

Thing and Space (TS; HUS XVI), the *Analyses of Passive Synthesis* (HUS XI), the *Phenomenology of Intersubjectivity* (HUS XIII–XV), and *Inner-Time Consciousness* (Time; HUS X), amongst others, are also written in Husserl's own meditative format. Whereas the *Logical Investigations, Formal and Transcendental Logic, Experience and Judgement,* and much of the three books of the *Ideas* are written in a systematic presentation. It is one of the peculiar and distracting features of the three-volume *Ideas* that the text moves back and forth between one and the other style. It is our contention that some of the extreme difficulties the reader encounters here are the result of the systematic exposition breaking off in favor of an analytic meditation and then reappearing, sometimes much later, under a different heading; thus, for example, the 'synthetic' exposition of the intentional correlates noesis and noema is interrupted again and again. It's little wonder that Husserl was dissatisfied with the overall shape of the three volumes, requesting his assistants to recompose it several times, and virtually abandoning the second and third Books after twelve years.

Dorion Cairns, a pioneer in his English translations and commentaries on Husserl's writings in the 1960s, remarked in his memoirs that Husserl devoted a great deal of work to daily meditations. He would only interrupt this work when the desire came over him to write a book, and then he would write "like someone in a trance." "When I go back to what I have written in an earlier meditation," he told Cairns, "I always go back to that which is most obscure to me and I wrestle with that problem. I never go on and leave a problem unsolved and that is why I shall never write a [systematic] philosophy. My work is not that of building but of digging, of digging in that which is most obscure and of uncovering problems which have not been seen or if seen have not been solved."[29]

The process of daily meditation on a particular theme involved this resolute carrying forward of a train of thought, reaching an impasse, backing up, and then going forward again—a cycle of "endless corrections and revisions" repeated again and again, just as Husserl cautions that the reduction must be activated again and again at will. One of the Husserl Archive editors comments on the enormous quantity of *Nachlass* manuscripts and Husserl's near inability to prepare material for publication. "It may have resulted from the analytical style of his way of practicing philosophy and from the difficulty of systematizing the abundance of particular analyses into a coherent whole."[30] The exceptional difficulties which any commentator faces when attempting to ascribe to Husserl a definitive statement on a specific topic are largely the result of trying to "freeze" a complex, multilayered meditative artefact which was always in motion. "Large parts of the publications Husserl produced in his lifetime . . . look like purely momentary states of rest, or 'condensations,' of a thought movement that was constantly in flux."[31]

Husserl was aware of the tension between two such divergent manners of exposition as early as the *Logical Investigations*, where it is quite clear that he discriminates between the "stepwise ordering of things" which have "a systematic interconnection," on the one hand; and "a secure investigation" which proceeds in a "zig-zag manner," on the other—a metaphor suitable to characterize following a path.

> Systematic clarification, whether in pure logic or any other discipline, would in itself seem to require a stepwise following out of the ordering of things, of the systematic interconnection in the science to be clarified. Our investigation can, however, only proceed securely, if it repeatedly breaks with such systematic sequence, if it removes conceptual obscurities which threaten the course of investigation *before* the natural sequence of subject-matters can lead up to such concepts. We search, as it were, in zig-zag fashion, a metaphor all the more apt since the close interdependence of our various epistemological concepts leads us back again and again to our original analyses, where the new confirms the old, and the old the new. (LI, 261)

Before looking at the complex "interweaving" of analytic meditation and systematic exposition in the three books of *Ideas*, we should be clear about Husserl's careful separation of the two orders and the advantages which attach to each. In the inaugural issue of the journal *Logos* for 1910/11, Husserl published the article "Philosophy as Rigorous Science," an article whose title alone has generated some consternation. His use of the term "science," especially science as foundation, in this piece has been much commented on and much criticized by "postmodern" writers who object to the notion of a single dominant discourse, one which extracritically validates theoretical method in other disciplines. They favor instead a framework of multiple perspectives, each of which complements the others, none of which is reducible to a more primitive, pretheoretical discipline. Their target in many cases has been some version (usually a rather excessive or overly zealous version) of Logical Positivism, whose phantom progeny they discern in any discipline which claims nonrelative validity for its conclusions. However, the notion of science in Husserl's writings should be carefully weighed in terms of his own severe censures. He strongly condemns the philosophical tendency to "naturalize" consciousness, to treat the human mind as entirely a component or product of the natural world, a treatment which he discerns throughout the work of many empirical psychologists. Secondly, "science" (*Wissenschaft*) in the German tradition means organized or systematic knowledge of any kind, one kind of which is systematic knowledge of the natural world; and this is why, in embracing a *mathesis universalis,* Husserl is arguing for a universal and *a priori* discipline of knowledge. And finally, in the second half of the *Logos* article, he counterposes phenomenology as the primordial "scientific" discipline with "worldview" social theories which espoused a culturally dependent philosophical relativism.

The most recent English editor of "Philosophy as Rigorous Science" prefaces the text with the remark that Husserl disassociates himself from the German Idealist interpretations of science as a systematic field of inquiry "in order to emphasize the foundational, *indeed Cartesian*, interpretation of system where the *order of reasons* is essential to the content of the doctrines themselves." Husserl encourages his readers to reflect that the true vocation of philosophy is "to teach us how to carry on the eternal work of humanity," and this is achieved by "rational insights gained by creative spirits" (HSW, 160, emphasis added). Philosophy, however, is not an imperfect or defective science; rather, as it now stands, it is an incomplete science, because the limitless horizon of problems which drive the pursuit of knowledge onward expands with every new step forward; and there are various defects, especially with regard to the concept of logical grounds, in the doctrines which have been advanced, "in the systematic ordering of proofs and theories." But what could be the meaning of a complete system towards which phenomenology strives, a rigorous science which could remedy those defects and clarify its purposes?

> Is it to be a philosophical "system" in the traditional sense, like a Minerva springing forth complete and full-panoplied from the head of some creative genius, only in later times to be kept along with other such Minervas in the silent museum of history? Or is it to be a philosophical system of doctrine that . . . really begins from the ground up with a foundation free from doubt and rises up like any skillful construction, wherein stone is set upon stone, each as solid as the other, in accord with directive insights? On this question minds must part company and paths must diverge. (HSW, 167)

One philosopher Husserl does keep company with is Descartes, whose vision in the "Seventh Replies" of the overall production according to "directive insights'" is that of an architect overseeing the construction of a vast edifice, with solid foundations free from doubt. Husserl moves on to recapitulate his criticisms of the naturalism of a scientific endeavor whose goal is to render philosophy in its own image. This rendering takes place on at least two fronts: the attempt to make a natural phenomenon of consciousness, including intentionally immanent data; and the attempt to naturalize ideas and all other absolute ideals and norms. This new naturalized philosophy believes that it has already attained the status of an exact science, and looks down with disdain on all other philosophical enterprises. They stand in relation to this arrogant philosophical tyrant "like the muddy natural philosophy of the Renaissance to the youthful exact mechanics of Galileo, or like alchemy in relation to the exact chemistry of Lavoisier" (HSW, 171). But all natural science, says Husserl, is naïve in one preeminent respect—the nature that it seeks to investigate is simply there, every scientific judgement participates in the tacit existential positing of the world's being, in its acceptance of the world as already given. But it is inappropriate to treat consciousness in this manner; consciousness is not itself given as just another part of the natural world, it is the being who gives sense to its experiences of the world and of other subjects. The naïveté of the empirical psychologists, in their attempt to ground logical laws on the factual character of mental processes, consists in accepting the correspondence of immanent conscious contents with the 'objects' and causal laws which its experiences disclose.

Husserl say that it is within the methodical disposition and connection of experiences, in the interplay or interweaving of experience and thought which has its own logical laws, that valid and invalid experiences are distinguished. If theory of knowledge explores the problems of the relation between consciousness and worldly being, it must concentrate on being as the correlate of consciousness, as an intentional phenomenon. This phenomenological exploration must be directed toward the meaning of consciousness, as well as toward the different ways in which it intends the objective, that which "lies over against it." All types of consciousness, according to their teleological order under the title of knowledge (*sub specie scientatis*) and according to the cognitive functions that correspond to the object categories, must permit being studied "in their essential connection and in their relation back to the forms of consciousness of givenness belonging to them" (HSW, 173). Nature in the significant sense under discussion here is, first, the spatio-temporal world of bodies, and second, the psychical world of individual being. In principle, only corporeal being can be apprehended in a number of direct experiences (perceptions) as individually identical; only natural realities can be experienced by many subjects as the same realities and determined as such by all subjects according to their "nature." This is one sense of 'nature' to which one sense of ordering belongs. "They stand there as temporal unities of enduring or changing properties, and . . . as incorporated in the totality of one corporeal world that binds them all together, with its one space and its one time. They are what they are only in this unity; only in the *causal relation or connection* with each other do they retain their individual identity (substance) and this they retain as that which carries 'real properties' " (HSW, 179).

This sense of the concept "nature" is the proper subject matter of a philosophically oriented natural science which seeks the systematic knowledge of this world-unity as the normative description of causal regularities, transformations, and stabilities manifest in these connections. On the other hand, the psychical or mental domain is divided into "monads without windows"—Leibniz's phrase, taken up again in the Fifth *Cartesian Meditation*—which are in communication with other monads only through empathy. Unlike physical nature, the "nature" of the mind is in principle not a unity which could be experienced in a number of separate perceptions as individually identical, not even in perceptions of the same subject. Here there is no distinction between appearance and being: "if nature is a being that appears in appearances, still appearances themselves . . . do not constitute a being which itself appears by means of appearances lying behind it" (HSW, 179). From the phenomenological point of view, there is, strictly speaking, only one nature, the one that appears in the appearance of things and that includes the appearance or phenomena of nature in the first sense. In another context, Husserl speaks of a complete reversal of being after the reduction—the being of transcendental consciousness is first in the order of cognitions, the being of the world is second.

In contrast with the systematic investigation of the natural order of worldly beings, Husserl counterposes a phenomenological investigation of the interweaving of thoughts about those worldly beings. The term "interweaving" should be reserved exclusively for the multistranded, multilayered lattice structure revealed by an analysis of the *constitution* of intentional 'objects.' The meticulously detailed analyses in *Ideas First Book* Parts Three and Four of single-rayed and many-rayed thetic 'acts,' the noematic core and its layers, sensuous *hylé* and formative *morphé*, and so forth, are all tracings of this complex pattern of interweaving. A phenomenon is not a substantial unity and has no real properties; it knows of no real parts, no real changes, and no causality. Nor does a psychical phenomenon have a temporal unity, it comes and goes, retaining no enduring identical being. It is simply not experienced as something that appears, rather it is a "vital experience" or what he later calls "living through"; here Husserl's German apparatus allows him to distinguish *Erlebnisse* (lived experience) from *Erfahrung* (outer experience) which retain their original roots, *Leben* or "life"' and *Fahrt* or "path." "Everything psychical which is thus "experienced" is then . . . *ordered in an overall connection*, in a 'monadic' unity of consciousness, a unity that in itself has nothing at all to do with nature" (HSW, 179–80).

Since the principal orientation of "Philosophy as Rigorous Science" is toward the legitimate basis of a *mathesis universalis* or systematic conception of a genuine philosophical project, the separateness of the two orders of thought and being may be obscured. The connections between natural things fall under the categories of substance, property, parts of wholes, change of state, and causality—none of these categories pertain to the 'objects' of thought considered strictly as intentional correlates. The key term in the earlier quotation is *real* relations which hold between worldly things and the *reell* relations which hold between the parts or components of a phenomenon. The *monadic* unity of consciousness endorses one dimension of a Leibnizian "formal atom" or simple substance, that it has no real parts, it cannot be actually divided, but it does have a complex description. It is organized in a hierarchy of levels of constitution, dominated by the unique character, the transcendental ego, which determines it as this individual.[32] As such, the order of cognitive components considered as dependent moments of the whole formed by the "total act" are generative, that is, a componential analysis can be done for the units and relations necessary for the production of a specific perception or memory or phantasy. Husserl does not broach this constitutive dimension of intentional 'objects' in this article.

The topic of constitution does, however, become a principal strand of exposition in *Ideas First Book*, though the reader must postpone fulfillment of the meaning of these passages until the very end of *Ideas Third Book*. In the first text Husserl says that no real being is necessary to the being of consciousness itself. Consciousness and real being are not two coordinate *kinds* of being which are sometimes, given the right circumstances, related to or connected with one another. Only things which are of the same kind, whose proper essences have a similar sense, can become connected in a legitimate manner, that is, can be considered as proper parts of a whole. Mental processes which are immanent to consciousness comprise absolute being, whereas the causal processes of worldly things pertain to transcendent being—thus a "veritable abyss" yawns between consciousness and reality. Consciousness considered in its pure sense must be thought of as a "self-contained complex of being," that is, an ordered arrangement of absolute being into which nothing can penetrate and out of which nothing can escape. On the other hand, the whole world of spatio-temporal things, from the phenomenological perspective, is a merely intentional being, in the derivative sense that it has being only *for* consciousness. The world then is an acceptance phenomenon in that it is tacitly posited in all experiences; to make any claim for the world having being beyond that is nonsense. "Thus the sense commonly expressed in speaking of being is reversed. The being which is first for us is second in itself; i.e., it is what it is, only 'in relation' to the first. But it is not as though there were a blind regularity such that the *ordo et connexio rerum* necessarily conformed to the *ordo et connexio idearum*" (Ideas I, 112–13). The lack of correspondence between order of reality and order of cognitions approximates the same diremption which Descartes perceives between the two orders once the method of universal doubt has put the spatio-temporal world out of play.

The occurrence of these two Latin phrases seems quite odd and is left unremarked by Husserl. It is usually the case that where Husserl employs such

Latinate terminology he makes reference to a source, for example, Augustine or Descartes or Brentano. In this instance a clue is provided in the previous section where he characterizes the immanent being of consciousness as *nulla 're' indiget ad exsitendum*, "no other thing is needed for existence"; a reminder of Descartes' statement in the "Third Meditation" that no really existent thing is necessary for the 'reality' of a thought. There is a good chance that here Husserl had in mind Descartes' distinction between order of reasons (or ideas) and order of things (or beings). In any case, this speculation is not a scholarly gloss on the origin or inspiration for the Husserlian distinction, rather it concerns a pair of Cartesian terms perfectly comparable with Husserl's terms, complex system of ideas and complex system of beings. "It is the task of transcendental phenomenology to make clear the connections between true being and knowing and thus in general to explore the correlations between act, sign and object" (HUS XXIV, 427).

In the last few pages of *Ideas Third Book* (which perhaps dates from as late as 1925), Husserl returns to the issue of the relation between phenomenological analysis of constitution of an object's objectivity and the systematic science of objective beings. The goal of such an analysis is perfect clarity, "clarification must follow precisely the stages of the constitution of the exemplary object of intuition in question" (Ideas III, 88). This process involves two dimensions or orientations: first, to make a concept clear and distinct by recourse to an intuition which fulfills its expectations; and second, the 'object' as a meant unity (the noema) must be brought into accord with perfect self-givenness. This latter course indicates that every 'object' of an intuition can be near or far from its adequate grasp: "There is for all objects an intuitive nearness and an intuitive distance, a cropping up into the bright light, which permits analysis of an inner wealth of definite moments and a sinking back into darkness, in which all becomes indistinct" (Ideas III, 89). Husserl's words here clearly signify the operation of attentional regard, which he routinely characterizes as a spotlight—one's gaze wanders over the objects in a visual field, one thing after another coming into prominence and then fading away into the background. But in terms of reflection performed within the phenomenological reduction, it also connotes Descartes' "light of reason" which provides the opening or clearing in which truth manifests itself.

The general task of transcendental phenomenology is the most all-embracing ideal, "to embrace the world of ideas in systematic completeness," that is, the complex order of cognitions. It must then coordinate all the possible conceptual essences in general with the words and signs which express them in their purest form. A complete and exhaustive "scientific" comprehension of these essence types would comprise a complex system of material ontologies, that is, the complex order of beings. "Only the phenomenologist will be competent to perform the deepest clarifications with regard to the essences building themselves up in systematically constituted layers and thus to prepare the grounding of the ontologies of which we have so great a lack" (Ideas III, 90). Therefore, in a profound sense which will not be fully revealed until a clarification of the phenomenological reduction is achieved, Husserl's task for foundational philosophy is to organize and categorize the connections between the order of cognitions and the order of beings.

The course of our twofold investigation into the development of Descartes' and Husserl's projects will itself follow the complex interweaving of a number of thematic concerns and thus trace the very sort of explanatory pathway extolled by Husserl himself in this passage from the *Crisis*:

> The understanding of the beginnings is to be gained fully only by starting with science as given in its present-day form, looking back at its development. But in the absence of an understanding of the beginnings, the development is mute as a development of meaning. Thus we have no other choice than to proceed forward and backward in a *zig-zag pattern*; the one must help the other in an interplay. Relative clarification on one side brings some elucidation on the other, which in turn casts light back on the former. In this sort of historical consideration and critique, then, which begins with Galileo (and immediately afterwards with Descartes) and must follow the temporal order, we nevertheless have constantly to make *historical leaps* which are thus not digressions but necessities. (Crisis, 58; emphasis added)

4

SIMPLE AND COMPLEX NATURES
AND PART-WHOLE THEORY

Through the course of our researches into the structural developments of Descartes' and Husserl's philosophical enterprises, we should now have a sufficient perspective to discern a wide-ranging parallel in their treatment and orientation. In addition to an overt congruence in the backgrounds to which they react, i.e., skepticism and relativism in the empirical derivation of logical laws, there is a more hidden congruence in the radical direction which their overturning takes; some aspects of this will be studied in upcoming chapters. We can speculate that one of the reasons why there is such an interesting congruence in their motives and their vision of the great task of a rationally grounded philosophy is the fact that they share an abstract framework of ontological terms. Descartes' vocabulary of simples and composites and Husserl's vocabulary of parts and wholes are scattered throughout their writings and are primitive concepts which they repeatedly rely upon. The fact that they share comparable vocabularies of the simplest "elements" is an unavoidable consequence of their having undertaken similar analyses at the ontological level. As such, these analyses are genetically prior to their theories of knowledge formation, clear and distinct seeing, and the function of methodical suspension (epoché). During the course of their investigations of specific topics, Descartes and Husserl consistently fall back on formal and abstract definitions and distinctions which function as primitive terms and axioms.

These analyses are prior in that they occupy—and would always have to occupy—the same first place in the taxonomy of a universal science of rationally ordered principles. It is not merely the case that an explication of a formal ontology would have to occur at a primordial stage, but that Descartes' and Husserl's formal ontologies are also functionally equivalent, i.e., in terms of their place in the theoretical frameworks into which they are fitted. Profound implications of their use of these ontological categories reemerge at similar points in later topical analyses, for example, the components of thought processes, the function of judgement in language, the nature of mind-body interconnection, and so forth.

For Descartes, the only textual commitment to an explicit ontological scheme, a descriptive template for what sorts of things there are, occurs in Rule XII of the *Rules*, a brief supplement in Rule XIII, and its expansion in chapter 2, part 4, of Arnauld and Nicole's *Port-Royal Logic*[1]—the theory of simple and complex natures. For Husserl, the first comprehensive statement[2] of the theory of parts and wholes occurs in Investigation III of the *Logical Investigations*, though it is taken up again in *Ideas First Book* and *Experience and Judgement*. Husserl himself was well aware that part-whole theory was usually overlooked or dismissed in favor of the other investigations. William Kneale, coauthor of the magisterial *Development of Logic* (Oxford, 1962), on a visit to Freiburg in 1928, was informed by Husserl that Investigation III was the best starting point for the study of his writings in phenomenology.[3]

The theme of this present research is the intrinsic convergence, i.e., the structural parallel at this genetically prior level, of these two ontological schemas. To begin with, we can eliminate what this theoretical connection is not concerned to establish. It is not an attempt to demonstrate that Descartes' concept of simple and complex natures had an influence on Husserl in his formulation of part-whole theory. Nor is it an attempt to uncover a startling precursor three centuries earlier, in the way that some might say that the phenomenological concept of intentionality has its origin in the late scholastic, medieval notion of "intentional inexistence"—an interesting historical footnote, but no more.

Rather, our thesis is, first, that the theory of simple-complex natures stands in relation to the maturation of Descartes' entire philosophical project in approximately the same way that part-whole theory stands to Husserl's evolving phenomenological enterprise; second, that each is a sketch of a formal ontology of the world which is an essential preliminary grounding for subsequent epistemological enquiries made about that world; and third, that just as the lawful interrelation of simple and complex will inform a pivotal stage in the certain foundation of the cogito in the natural world for Descartes, so also key features of the part-whole schema will be reintroduced by Husserl to explicate the relation between soul and body after the reduction has revealed a world of essences.

If Husserl's formalization and conceptual analysis of part-whole relations was a groundbreaking theoretical advance, Descartes' rough sketch of these "primitive terms" was very much rooted (at least at this early period before

1627) in the accepted scholastic framework of the late sixteenth and early seventeenth centuries. Recent studies by Jean-Luc Marion, on two fronts, have well documented both the source and the character of Descartes' initial concept of substance in Aristotle's *Metaphysics*[4] and the essential continuity of Rule XII's foundation with its later adumbration in the *Meditations* and the *Principles*.[5] However, neither of these valuable studies devotes any attention to the internal relations established by the eight theorems, especially to these crucial notions: necessary and contingent connection, the origination and construction of these "natures," and their role in the formation of judgements and numerical concepts.

Dennis Sepper's study[6] of Descartes' intellectual interests before the composition of the *Rules* has illuminated some aspects of this work as the resolution of specific problems in the field of cognitive functions, particularly imagination and memory. From his early correspondence, it is apparent that he devoted some study to works on the art of memory, those of Raymond Lull, Agrippa, and Schenkel, among others.[7] In the demonstration of a geometrical postulate, for example, one first grasps the truth of one premise in an adequate intuition, and then proceeds to the next premise (or link in a chain of reasons), which is also secured in this manner, and so forth. Although the relational necessity between these premises may also be intuited, the mind's holding-in-grasp of the truths of these premises is not itself an act of adequate cognition. The condition of having established an inference (or chain of reasons) in demonstration depends on another cognitive faculty, memory, which is open to failure in ways in which the intellect is not.

The elaboration of corporeal images in imagination—what later psychologists will refer to as the process of visualization in mathematical construction—assists in the extraction of that thing, through the process of variation of instances, toward which intuition is brought to bear. Such corporeal images may then also assist in citing or place-holding in memory all those premises which have been secured. But such images only assist, they do not alone secure the accurate transition from point to point in memory, since only one point at a time can be called up from memory and made the 'content' of an intuition. Another way to state this problem is that: having grasped the truth of x, y, and z, and having understood their necessary connection, in the attending to z as the conclusion intuited now, why is it this x that is called up as having been secured, and not some other, say, w? There is nothing intrinsic to z qua intuited truth which points it backward, so to speak, to x merely as an intuited truth which bears a necessary connection to *something*.

In the *Private Thoughts* of 1618–19, the young Descartes already had an insight into a novel way out of this dilemma, in stark contrast to the prevalent doctrine of mnemonic technique.

On reading through Schenkel's profitable trifles . . . I readily thought that everything I have discovered had been embraced by imagination. It occurs by the leading back [*reductio*] of things to causes; when all those things are finally led back to a single one, there will be no need of memory from any science. For whoever understands causes will easily form anew in the brain the altogether vanished phantasms by the impression of the cause. This is the true art of memory and it is plain contrary to the art of that sorry fellow. Not because his art lacks effect, but because it requires the whole space [*chartam*] that ought to be occupied by better things and consists in an order that is not right; the [right] order is that the images be formed from one another as interdependent. He omits this . . . which is the key to the whole mystery. (AT X, 230)

The realization of the problem and the initial glimmer of an answer in 1618/ 19 was to reach fuller theoretical clarification a decade later. In Rule III of the *Rules*, Descartes claims that there are only two actions (or operations) of the intellect whereby one is able to arrive at certain knowledge: intuition and deduction. Intuition is "the indubitable conception of a clear and attentive mind which proceeds solely from the light of reason." Deduction is "the inferring from true and known principles through a continuous and uninterrupted movement of thought in which each individual proposition is clearly intuited." And here one encounters the problem of how discrete cognitions of intuited truths are sequenced or enchained as necessarily following from each other. "Immediate self-evidence is not required for deduction, as it is for intuition; deduction in a sense gets its certainty from memory" (CSM I, 14–15). It is this "in a sense" which requires further elucidation and returns our attention to "the key to the whole mystery." "The main secret of my method [is] in order to distinguish the simplest things from those that are complicated and to set them out in an orderly manner, we should attend to what is most simple in each series of things in which we have directly deduced some truths from others, and should observe how all the rest are more, or less, or equally removed from the simplest" (CSM I, 21).

He goes on to say that this is the most useful rule in the whole treatise for it shows that everything can be arranged serially in various groups, insofar as some things can be known *on the basis* of others; i.e., that some things are *founded* on others in a certain and regular manner. It may seem paradoxical that he qualifies this by saying that such an arrangement is not made by reference to an ontological genus, in the Aristotelian categories of substance and accident. But this is not so, since his main taxonomy of "things insofar as they are known" will be articulated entirely in terms of the ontological structures disclosed through necessary regularities in consciousness. Given this proviso, to consider things in the order which corresponds to our knowledge of them, it is entirely in keeping with the foregoing examination that Sepper remarks, apropos of the algebraic schema in Rules XV—XVIII: "what this amounts to is a formalization of the ontology and epistemology of resemblances to which Descartes held in his private cogitations of 1619–21."[8]

We are on the verge of Descartes' exposition of simple and complex natures, but how far are we from an understanding of the motives and rationale which led Husserl to part-whole theory? Is it possible that the proposed structural parallel in their ontological schemas is at least partly the result of a congruence in their approach to this problematic?

One of Husserl's main concerns before the *Logical Investigations,* aside from his confrontation with empirical psychology of logic, had been an attempt to provide a coherent nonpsychological account of number and the arithmetical operations. Having initially trained in mathematics in the 1870s, Husserl must have been impressed by the lack of general rational procedures by which mathematicians went about their work. "At critical points [it] depended upon the blind (even when accurate) instincts and tact of individual mathematicians—who often held quite divergent theories about the techniques by which they nevertheless obtained identical results."[9] Employing Brentano's notion of intentionality in the phenomenal realm and the novel concept of aggregate, Husserl began his research into the conditions and status of objective knowledge for number and numerical operations.

In the first part of *The Philosophy of Arithmetic* (1891), he contends that one can have a concrete intuition of 'objects' which, as mere contents of presentations, can be given immediately and all at the same time, up to a limit of about twelve 'objects.'[10] Where the content of an intuition is no more than the 'object,' the content of a concept is a second-order content whose 'object' is the original intuition. By disregarding (or abstracting from) specific parts of a concrete intuition, one can have direct cognition of an abstract moment (dependent part) which cannot comprise the entire content of an intuition in isolation. It is by means of abstract and general concepts that the identity, or rather identifiability, of those things in some grouping are understood to be the same sort of thing; and thus comprise just this group and not some other.

Problems begin to occur when the numbers at issue are greater than twelve, for there is no feasible way in which more than twelve 'objects' could be given in a concrete intuition. So-called inauthentic concepts of larger numbers must somehow be ultimately founded on intuitions, but through another mode of cognition; and as concepts, their content is different from the merely concrete. Husserl's answer is that, "in the intuition of a sensible group there must be immediately comprehensible signs in which this group character can be recognized. . . . The name and concept of a group can then be immediately associated with these signs"[11] which Husserl also refers to as "figural moments" and "Gestalt qualities." One should bear in mind that this work and other collateral studies were undertaken at the same time as Ehrenfel's work, "On Gestalt Qualities" (1890).[12] In this paper, he postulated that there were mental states and processes which exhibited two distinct features: that the conscious experience of some wholes' parts was greater than the mere summation of those parts when experienced discretely; and that this specific feature remains unchanged when the complex of parts upon which it is built undergoes certain determinate kinds of displacement. Ehrenfel's illustration of these two features of gestalts was derived from the perception of tones in a musical melody; an analysis which bears a striking resemblance to Husserl's research, as early as 1893, on the consciousness of internal time (Time, 141–55).[13]

It is these *signs* which are immediately apprehended, and as figural moments they are complexes of relational features held by members of the group, not given *tout court* by each and every member qua member. The symbolic character of this gestalt is superadded, just like any other gestalt, when this group comes together in just this way, and is never reducible to the mere summation of all the individual members. This symbolic aspect allows for the conceptual manipulation of very large numbers without ever "losing track" of their ultimate foundation in concrete intuitions.

The system of signs which permit the solution of problems and equations with unknowns are the numerals, which have three essential properties. (1) The signs are perceptible or sensible items, whether written or spoken (or today, computer-coded). (2) They comprise a recursive function, i.e., there is a rule whereby any other numerical item can be generated. (3) One or more of the earlier signs, below twelve, must be correlated with an authentic concept of number.[14] In his overview of Husserl's writings between the early 1890s and 1901, Dallas Willard concludes: "Further examination . . . will show that it not only provides a general statement of the problem of the possibility or objectivity of knowledge as this was conceived by Husserl, but also lays down the framework of a solution to it by initiating the treatment of the cognitive act as a complex whole exhibiting necessary connections between its parts as well as in relation to other acts—necessary connections which are moreover treated as open to rational insight."[15]

It is to this sign-aspect of mathematical and geometrical cognition that Descartes will appeal in his resolution of the problem of how deductive thinking can maintain its grasp on previously secured intuitions. It is this signitive function to which he refers in Rule XII, after considering knowledge with respect to the knowing subject's faculties, as "abbreviated representations"; something like astronomers' "imaginary circles" which they use to describe celestial phenomena

(CSM I, 43). These are figures or schemata which synopsize all the particular cases to which they could be applied *and* provide a focal point which can itself be the entire content of an intuition. L. J. Beck, in the course of a rather prosaic account of simple natures, makes this rather startling and incisive remark:

> There are, Descartes seems to be saying, certain simple natures which *symbolize in letters* the language of reality, an alphabet or, as Leibniz was later to name it, a *characteristica universalis*. The simple natures are then characteristics recognizable in all bodies and in all minds, or all existents whether corporeal or spiritual. They are universal, as is clear from the examples, but yet in some sense they have ontological status, they are simple entities which are the fundamental constituents or elements of all bodies, of all minds, of all that exists.[16]

It is their double-sidedness as symbolic terms and as ontological constituents which permits simple natures to be recategorized later, in Theorem 8 of Rule XII, as features of judgments made about them, but they show up at this later juncture in a variety of guises: linguistic signification, part-whole relations, and geometrical-numerical concepts. Unfortunately, Descartes never reached the promised place in the composition of the *Rules* where a fuller explication of this symbolic function could have been presented. William Shea, however, in *The Magic of Numbers and Motion,* has cogently argued for the notion that these "abbreviated representations" or "symbolic letters" are the seeds for Cartesian algebraic geometry.[17]

Rule XII opens with a discussion of the objects of knowledge considered from the point of view of the knowing subject's faculties. First, insofar as the external senses are all parts of the body, sensory perception is passive, in the same way in which wax takes an imprint from a seal. Second, when an external sense organ is stimulated by an object, the figure is conveyed to another part of the body, the common sense, without any real entity being also conveyed. Third, the common sense in its turn functions like a seal, imprinting in the imagination or memory, as if in wax, the same figures or ideas which came from the external senses. Fourth, the motive power, i.e., the nerves and neural "fluids," has its origin in the brain where the corporeal imagination (and memory) are located; these latter move the nerves in various ways, just as the common sense is moved by the external senses. And fifth, the true power through which we know things is purely spiritual, one single power, which conjoins with the common sense, imagination and memory in the production of factual knowledge about the physical world.

> When we consider things in the order that corresponds to our knowledge of them, our view of them must be different than what it would be if we were speaking of them in accordance with how they exist in reality. If, for example, we consider some

body which has extension and shape, we shall indeed admit that, with respect to the *thing itself*, it is one single and simple entity. For viewed in that way, it cannot be said to be a composite made up of corporiety, extension and shape, since these *constituents* have never existed in isolation from each other. Yet with respect to our *intellect*, we call it a composite made up of these three natures, because we understood each of them *separately* before we were in a position to judge that the three of them are encountered at the *same time* in one and the *same subject* [i.e., subject of thought, the 'object']. (CSM I, 44; emphasis added)

Descartes here (and elsewhere) is at some pains to make a theoretical distinction between, on the one hand, the dependence (on some other thing) of some aspects of a thing as it is merely presented, or already given to consciousness; and on the other hand, the independence of those aspects one stage further in cognition, i.e., when one conceptualizes how it is that those aspects could be given as being about that thing. It is with this passage that Descartes introduces the eight propositions (or theorems) which comprise the ontological schema of simple and complex natures.

D1. A simple nature is that thing which can be known so clearly and distinctly that it cannot be divided by the mind into other things which are more distinctly known, e.g., shape, extension and motion. A composite nature is made up of such simples and is often seized in experience as one complete thing before we are able to isolate its simples in intellect.

D2. A simple can be: intellectual if it is seized upon by means of an innate light and without the aid of any corporeal image, e.g., knowledge, doubt, ignorance, volition; material if it is seized upon as being present only in bodies, e.g., shape, extension, motion; or common to both intellectual and material, e.g., existence, unity, duration, logical axioms.

D3. A simple is self-evident and never contains any falsity, such that if one makes a judgement about it then one must already have adequate knowledge of it, even if one imagines there is more beyond what has been grasped.

D4. These simples can be conjoined in either a necessary or a contingent manner: necessary when one simple is somehow implied in the concept of another simple, such that one cannot conceive either of them distinctly if they are judged to be separate; contingent when one simple is not directly implied in the concept of another, such that each can be conceived distinctly whether they are separated or not.

D5. It is not possible to understand anything more than those simple natures and composites formed from their conjunction; but it is possible to have knowledge of a composite without having knowledge of all the simples which make up that composite.

D6. Knowledge of composites is gained either through experience or through construction: experience comprises whatever is perceived by the senses, learned from others, or from introspection. The intellect can never be deceived by any experience provided that the intuition of an object corresponds exactly to the way in which it is seized upon. A composite can be constructed either from simples or other composites taken from different domains (sense, imagination, memory) and judgments expressed on their account, and as such it is possible to be deceived.

D7. Composites are formed in three ways: through impulse, conjecture, or deduction—through impulse when, in judgments about things, such judgments are not based on good reasons but merely internal or external influence; through conjecture when an observed relation between known things leads one to judge that the same relation holds with an unknown thing; or through deduction when each of the things judged about is clearly intuited and the connection between them is also intuited as necessary.

D8. In the formation of composites of many different kinds (or species, e.g., substantive, causal, or propositional), deduction can only be the derivation of things from words, or causes from effects (or the converse), or a whole from parts, or parts from other parts, or several of these at once. In the latter case of parts and wholes, this composition occurs formally in geometrical and numerical concepts.

Intuition as the pure operation of the cognitive power can grasp only simples, whether taken one at a time or several at once where conjoined through a necessary relation. As the content of an intuition, a simple is always grasped with clarity and distinctness, that is, the whole of its nature is contained in the grasping and nothing else is contained with it. This does not imply that other simples cannot be grasped along with that intuited simple. If another simple is implied by—or cannot be conceived as graspable without entailing that a prior simple has been grasped—then the latter is dependent on the former and a proposition exhibiting this dependency is called analytic. If one simple is conjoined with another but without being implied by it—such that it can be conceived as graspable without entailing a prior simple—then the latter is independent of the former and a proposition exhibiting this is called synthetic.

In the process of deduction, where cognition "tracks" previously secured intuitions, each later term in the sequence, when it is an implication of (dependent on) the immediate prior term could be said to be *founded* on that intuition secured by the prior term. Where a later term in the sequence is founded on some prior intuition, but as the consequence of some other term which is itself founded on that prior intuition, the later intuition is relatively dependent on that prior founding intuition. Where the first term is itself not founded but only founding with respect to successive intuitions, e.g., the cogito, the natural light, etc. it could be said to be absolutely independent (see CSM I, 22).

Descartes will much later, in a letter of 1643 to Princess Elizabeth, refer to this sort of absolute simple as, "primitive notions which are, as it were, the patterns on the basis of which we form all our other conceptions. There are very few such notions [extension, thought, and their union] . . . each of them can be understood only through itself' (CSM III, 218). Though this would be an interpolation of Descartes' taxonomy, one might find it helpful to consider these primitive notions or absolute simples as second-order concepts or, in Husserl's terms, regional categories of being. The remark that such self-founding ideas are innate patterns according to which other concepts are generated has profound ramifications for an understanding of Cartesian theory of knowledge as a type of phenomenological enquiry.

The conclusion of a deductive sequence is a composite (D7), not just another simple in the chain of reasons, since it cannot include all of the intuitions in the propositional form, but must synopsize or "abbreviate" the necessary connections which held between all of the intuited simples. Thus one can have certain knowledge of a composite without having, at that moment when the conclusion is cognized, knowledge of all the simples which compose the composite (D5). Though of course, one must have had, at earlier moments in the chain, certain knowledge of each simple as it was secured in intuition. Remarks about "impulse" and "conjecture" in the formation of composites pertain to the psychical and affective conditions *under which* composites are cognized; whereas remarks about "deduction" pertain to the logical conditions *by means of which* composites are cognized (D7).

All of the above observations pertain to intellective simples, intellective with respect not only to the mode in which they are cognized (intuition), but also with respect to their content (abstract). This is another way of stating the conjunction of D3 and the second clause of D6: a simple is self-evident, such that judgements made about it always imply that one has adequate knowledge of it and the intuition of an object corresponds to the mode in which it is grasped. Material simples are grasped in various cognitive modes (imagination, memory, perception) but as belonging only to material bodies and thus whose correspondent cognitive mode is perception alone. The analysis of the materiality of the piece of wax in the "Second Meditation" is an exemplary instance of the use of this principle. Insofar as the cognitive power is conjoined with imagination and memory, it must employ corporeal images, i.e., visual or audible phantasies, and as such may be liable to noncorrespondent cognition, hence fallible.

But irrespective of the cognitive mode in which material simples are grasped, they also bear relations of dependence and independence with regard to other simples or composites, that is, they are either separable or nonseparable in understanding. An absolute self-founding simple is extension, in the sense that an extended thing must have shape, motility, and color. That some thing has these properties is founded on its being extended, though not the converse. One could not claim that in order for some body to be extended it has to have this shape or be in motion or at rest. A material composite is composed of material simples, each bearing founded relations with its conjoint simples; as a material thing its correspondent mode of cognition is perception.

It is possible to enumerate, not deduce, all those instances of that material thing, such that through the process of abstraction—defined here as attention to only those dependent simples which are invariant—one grasps the *general* concept of that sort of thing, e.g., "book," "heart," "brain," etc. (on universals, see CSM I, 212). Clarity and distinctness in the perception of a material thing are achieved when the intellect grasps that all and only those simples which are given in the perception are adequate for experience to always pick out just this composite and not any other (D1). The simples which are common to the intellective and the material domains will be taken up later in our discussion of Descartes' use of simple-complex natures in his explanation of the union of mind and body in the "Sixth Meditation."

Intellective, material and common simples, and composites formed from them, are all categories of simple-complex in the ideational content of various cognitive modes; in short, they are universal concepts of simples and composites. But simples can also be considered as propositions with respect to the signitive content of judgments made about them, as well as numbers, measure and magnitude. The only comprehensive and straight-forward manner in which to account for the *Rules'* treatment of simple-complex natures in such different guises is that the relations of simples to simples, their conjunction in necessary or contingent fashion, their formation into composites, etc. comprise a formal ontology of parts and wholes.[18] It cannot be denied, however, that Descartes never explicitly discusses this, perhaps due to the incomplete and fragmentary character of the later Rules (after XIV), though perforce also due to the unavoidable fact that the logical basis of sign functions was not a conceptual schema available in the early seventeenth century.

But this is not mere retrospective wishful thinking. A glimpse or a foreshadowing of this formal ontology is provided by proposition D8, which occurs twice before lacunae in the text, but which was taken up by Arnauld in chapter 2, part 4, of the *Port Royal Logic* (CSM I, 77–78). It is in this context that all of the ways in which simples are conjoined with simples, in all of the various spheres of theoretical enquiry, are subsumed under the relations of parts and wholes. The attentive and methodical reader who has adhered to the "technique" advocated throughout the enumeration of the twelve preceding rules is left with this thought-provoking statement: "In order to extend the scope of [these problems] . . . we must note that the word 'part' has to be taken in a very wide sense, as signifying everything that goes to make up a thing—its modes, its extremities, its accidents, its properties, and in general all its attributes." Where Descartes and Arnauld break off, Husserl will begin his discussion of formal ontology: "We interpret the word 'part' in the widest sense: we may call anything a 'part' that can be distinguished in an object, or objectively phrased, that is 'present' in it. Everything is a part that is an object's real possession, not only in the sense of being a real thing, but also in the sense of being something really in something, that truly helps to make it up" (LI, 437).

Let us return to the first clause of proposition D8, which states that deduction can proceed from things to words, or derive words from things. As early as Rule III, simples are referred to as "propositions," or to be exact, specific simples can also be classified as propositions about abstract ideas, some of which can be further classified as absolute or primitive notions, e.g., logical axioms. Propositional simples can also be combined to form composites, that is, in the subject-predicate format, where the predicate is not an analytic *implicatum* of the subject.

Descartes has very little to say on this topic in the *Rules*, apart from a brief excursus on expression and denoting in Rule XIV (CSM I, 61). With respect to nonanalytic propositions, i.e., those not available to clear and distinct cognition of intellective simples, he remarks that one should employ the terms with the help of the imagination. For when the intellect attends adequately to what the word denotes, the corporeal images in the imagination direct the intellect toward the other features of the thing which are not conveyed by the term, i.e., those contingent simples and composites formed from them. It would be more accurate to say that (a) the *expression* of a proposition is conveyed in verbal or graphic signs which, solely in terms of their verbal or graphic features, are arbitrary and graspable only by linguistic convention (CSM I, 81); (b) the *content* of a proposition is not itself either a simple or a composite, but what the parts of the content denote are indeed simples and composites; and (c) as such, the *meaning* of what the content denotes is clearly and distinctly conveyed by its correspondent intuitions.

For a more general context in which to situate these remarks about language, one must turn to a letter to Mersenne of November 1629, a short time after the *Rules* had been abandoned. In response to an unknown author's project for a new language, which mainly comprised some sort of Esperanto-polyglot dictionary, Descartes argues that the discovery of such a "universal" language presupposes a well-grounded philosophy. "For without that philosophy it is impossible to number and order all the thoughts of men or even to separate them out into clear and simple thoughts, which in my opinion is the great secret for acquiring sound knowledge [*science*]. If someone were to explain correctly what are the simple ideas in the human imagination out of which all human thoughts are compounded . . . I would dare to hope for a universal language very easy to learn, to speak and to write" (CSM III, 13). It is the compounding of simple ideas on the basis of these innate patterns (see above), spoken of here with respect to primitive notions, that would lead to a general schema of rules governing those arrangements. This task was only hinted at by Descartes, but was expanded in the most systematic fashion by Arnauld and Nicole in the *Port Royal Grammar* (1660) and *Logic* (1662). At the close of Investigation IV, "The Idea of Pure Grammar," Husserl endorses the "undoubted soundness" of a universal grammar as conceived by seventeenth- and eighteenth-century rationalists and "takes up the cudgels for the old doctrine of a *grammaire generale et raisonné*" (LI, 525).

The theory of simple and complex natures is brought to bear on the concept of number in Rule XIV. The sort of differences which obtain between two or more extensions can be explained in terms of dimension, unity, and shape. By dimension he means any mode or aspect of a thing which can be measured; thus length, breadth, and depth, but also weight and speed, lest this concept be restricted to spatial dimensions. "Division into several equal parts, whether it be a real or merely intellectual division is, strictly speaking, the dimension in terms of which we count things. The mode which gives rise to number is strictly speaking a species of dimension. . . . If we consider the order of *parts* in relation to the *whole*, we are then said to be counting; if on the other hand, we regard the *whole* as being divided into *parts*, we are measuring it" (CSM I, 62; emphasis added). With regard to unity (which, along with shape, is a "common" simple), all of the things which are to be considered in the problem must either share a specifiable unit of measure, e.g., two or more lengths, or any other magnitude may be specified as that to which a unit of measure may be assigned, e.g., length of a line, speed of an object, etc.

Descartes stipulates that there are only two kinds of things which are thus compared with each other—magnitudes and multitudes (CSM translates "sets"). There are two kinds of figure, that is, the third "common" simple in comparisons of extension: the two examples of "sets" which he gives clearly indicate that they are *ordered* arrangements of discrete units, and that means independent parts (or wholes) which are grouped into greater wholes. The concept of magnitude is illustrated by figures which clearly indicate that they are to be considered as wholes whose constituent parts are exclusively dependent. By following Rule VII, "we can easily survey in our mind the individual parts which we have ordered, because in relations of this kind the parts are related to one another with respect to themselves alone and not by way of an intermediary third term, as is the case with measures" (CSM I, 65).

It is not to our purpose to trace the undercurrent of this theory of simple-complex natures as it reappears through the *Discourse, Meditations,* and *Principles*—a reassessment of its ontological significance admirably demonstrated by Jean-Luc Marion.[19] But the continued relevance of Descartes' formal ontology for his philosophical project is reasserted in an exemplary fashion in his discussion in the Sixth Meditation of the way in which mind and body are united. Having defined the essence of mind as thinking and the essence of body as extension, he states that one might consider the human body as "a kind of machine," like a clock, whose actions could be explained in an entirely mechanistic manner. But the human being is a composite, this mind united with this body; a human being whose mind is indivisible (not composed of parts) and whose body is divisible (composed of parts).

> Although the whole mind seems to be united to the whole body, I recognize that if [a part] of the body is cut off, nothing has thereby been taken away from the mind. As for the faculties of willing, of understanding, of sensory perception and so on, these cannot be termed *parts* of the mind, since it is *one and the same* mind that wills and understands and has sensory perceptions. . . . The mind is not immediately affected by all *parts* of the body, but only by the brain, or perhaps just one small part of the brain, namely the part which is said to contain the common sense. (CSM II, 59; emphasis added)

It is the common sense which integrates the apprehensions of material simples and composites through the external senses and makes them available to the mind, which can then formulate common natures, that is, common to the material and intellective domains. The composite formed from an immaterial simple (the mind) and an entirely material composite (the body) can itself be made a theme of an analysis of the cognition of any composite made up of intuitively graspable simples and of material simples which are subject to error in their cognition. An ontological analysis of the mind-body whole is called for, similar to Rule XII's analysis of the physical thing before and after it is turned into a concept, and this is signaled by the word "seems"; the whole mind *seems* to be united with the whole body. That the meditator *seems* to see, to hear, and to be warmed provoked him into thinking about what that seemingness consists in—and so too here. One can indeed have an intellective simple idea of the mind, but the mind itself is not a simple idea, it is an immaterial simple thing. And what one can rightfully say about ideas and about things partly depends on where, in the process of reasoning, one comes to have knowledge of one or the other. Descartes has already warned the reader not to confuse or misplace the two formats, order of reasons and order of essences, and it is in ignorance of this that readers will have problems with the interaction of mind and body.[20]

Every time the brain, or just the pineal gland, is in a given state, it presents the same signals to the mind, even though other parts of the body may be in different conditions at the time, he continues. But what these signals present are not isolated, unconnected sensory simples; they usually present organized or patterned sense data to which the mind can apply abbreviated or synoptic figures (as shown above in Rule XIV). One of the outstanding "figures" of such organized sense impression is our experience of a human being. A specific grouping of visible lines can convey to us more than a mere scatter of marks on a piece of paper; the words are animated by the sense of the story. In a similar fashion, the complex appearance of a human being, including his or her verbal and non-verbal behaviour, is animated by the human spirit; only the mind can 'breathe life into' this sort of thing. In our experience, that is, in terms of the order of beings, we are presented with a human as a mindful body, one whole which is a mind united with a body.

It can be argued that Descartes circumvents the alleged problem of interaction, in much the same fashion as the contentious issue of circularity in the proof of God's existence, because he has been at some pains to discriminate the frameworks which comprise simples and composites; that is, according to the manner in which we come to understand them and the way in which they exist in themselves. With respect to how they are in themselves, the mind is simple, single and immaterial; the body is an extended composite of material simples and composites; the human being is a composite of both an immaterial simple and an extended composite. But this is *not* how we come to understand a human being qua human. If he is not as explicit as one could wish in the "Sixth Meditation," his position is quite clear in the "Fifth Replies": "In fact I have never seen or perceived that human bodies think; all I have seen is that there are human beings, who possess both thought and a body" (CSM II, 299).

Serious conceptual confusions arise in an appreciation of Descartes' formulation of mind-body union if one mistakes the essence of mind and the essence of body as exclusively determining the essence of their union in the human being as a mindful body. This mistake begins with a misreading of the famous statement: "I have a clear and distinct idea of myself, insofar as I am simply a thinking, non-extended thing; and . . . I have a distinct idea of body, insofar as this is simply an extended, non-thinking thing. And accordingly, it is certain that I am really distinct from my body and can exist without it" (CSM II, 54). It is easy and natural to read this "I" as this person, the meditator, instead of from the somewhat unnatural (i.e., methodically reduced) standpoint, as this mind which has uncovered these essential features through an elaborate process of abstraction.

This discursive abstraction is reiterated in the further statement that "I am not merely present in my body as a pilot is present in a ship, but that I am very closely joined and, as it were, intermingled [*permixtio*] with it, so that I and the body form a unit" (CSM II, 56). It should be very clear from the last clause that "I" refers to the mind alone, which with the body forms a unit. Reading the mind alone for "I" in the above two passages gives a much different picture than reading person or human being for that same "I." It is rare in the "Sixth Meditation" for Descartes to talk about this "unit," the human being. Virtually the entire discussion is taken up with the essential natures of the two things which make up the unit. One hint, that is only fulfilled much later, is that it is, "quite certain that my body, or rather my whole self, insofar as I am a combination of body and mind, can be affected by the various beneficial or harmful bodies which surround it" (CSM II, 56).

This last phrase points the reader to a much later work, *The Passions of the Soul* (1649), which explicitly discusses the "whole self." As a natural scientist, Descartes made great efforts to explain the interaction of psychical and physical events at an hypothesized brain site, the pineal gland. But irrespective of the success or failure of this mechanistic account,[21] he provides a profound, if sometimes cryptic, explanation of how mind and body can coexist in one whole self. It is a distorted and unjustified caricature of so-called Cartesian dualism to reduce the latter explanation to the former hypothesis. For commentators to observe that there are serious deficiencies in the causal account of actual psychophysical interactions, especially in the domain of sensory perception, is one thing; to insist that an adequate description of the mindful body is liable to the same sort of problems, is another issue. Recent studies by a number of scholars[22] have done much to correct this pervasive misconstrual and to point the reader of the "Sixth Meditation" straight to Part One, section 30, of *The Passions*.

In this later text, Descartes wants to first carefully delimit the actions of the mind from the passions in the most general sense. Mental actions are, properly speaking, predicated only of volitions which the mind undertakes with respect to its thoughts. The passions, on the other hand, are of three sorts: sense perceptions, bodily sensations, and the emotions. Sense perceptions refer to things outside the body which produce certain movements in the external sense organs and hence correspondent movements in the brain. Bodily sensations, such as hunger, thirst, pain, etc., are not predicated of things outside the body; their essential characteristics are not to be found in objects, although of course, sensations may be caused by the presence or absence of those objects. The passions in the proper sense are the emotions, such as anger, sadness, joy, and so forth, whose essential characteristics are predicated entirely of the soul. There is an *auto-affectivity* to the emotions, comparable to the self-evidentiality of the cogito, which is indicative not of the mental nor of the physical domains alone, but of the person as a mindful body. "We cannot be misled . . . regarding the passions [emotions] in that they are so close and so internal to our soul that it cannot possibly feel them unless they are truly as it feels them to be" (CSM I, 388).

If sense perceptions, which are unreliable and excluded by the first stage of methodical doubt, were the only kind of passion, then it would be valid to conclude that the mind is conjoined with only one part of the extended body, whether the pineal gland or any other site. But that gland is in fact a functional part of a whole extended body whose boundaries and conditions are discovered through bodily sensations and emotional affects. In terms of the whole person, the mind is intermingled with (*permixtio*) the whole body as its (the person's) own extension. According to the order of reasons, as developed through the *Meditations*, clear and distinct knowledge of the essence of mind and the essence of body reveal a real distinction between the two, such that they can be conceived as existing independently of each other. But according to the order of essences, clear and distinct knowledge of the whole person reveals that the whole mind and the whole body are related as interdependent parts which contribute to a functionally greater whole (see CSM I, 339).

> The passions proper [the emotions] reveal that the entity formed by the mind's pervading its own body can form a single whole, a unity whose distinctive benefits and harms are not reducible to those of its contributing constitutive substances. The passions show that the mind is not only permixed with the body but that, taken together, mind and body form a whole with interlocked functions, directed to the well-being of that whole. The we who is served by the passions is not only the machine organism, but the combined mind-and-body, taken as a composite whole.[23]

The issue here, with regard to simple-complex natures, is to understand how the mind-body union of a person is experienced through apprehensions of various "common" natures which partake of both the material and immaterial domains. In other words, to experience a human being qua person is to understand that he or she is corporeal, living, and conscious. Serious and irrefragable problems arise when a univocal and unilateral conceptual schema, i.e., physical versus psychical, is brought to bear on a unified mindful body. Entirely physicalistic and reductionist accounts of mind-body union can never adequately "build in" consciousness and hence are prone to dismiss it as epiphenomenal, a product of an imperfect explanatory hypothesis which further empirical research can remedy. On the other hand, entirely immaterialist or antiphysicalist accounts, though less common, are inevitably faced with the enigma of the soul's insertion in a shared socio-historical world whose linguistic meanings, for example, are the result of intersubjective production.

Let us return to our second point of departure and follow another explorer's lead in the ontological domain. The process by which Husserl came to formulate a general theory of parts and wholes has been outlined above with reference to the kind of cognition that takes place in mathematical 'visualization.' It should not be assumed that Investigation III is the *fons et origo* of all latter-day part-whole theory. Husserl was certainly aware of, and sometimes commented on, earlier theoretical work, especially Carl Stumpf's "Uber den psychologischen Ursprung der Raumvorstellung" (1873), Twardowski's "Zur Lehre vom Inhalt und Gegenstand der Vorstellungen" (1894), and Meinong's "Beitrage zur Theorie der physischen Analyse" (1893). However, Husserl's all too brief, highly condensed work stands far above these and later theories, partly because he successfully avoids internal problems, but mainly because this framework has such an extensive scope over other domains, e.g., semantic analysis, aesthetics, cognitive psychology, and so forth. Barry Smith can quite confidently declare that Investigation III is, "for all its inadequacies, the single most important contribution to realist (Aristotelian) ontology in the modern period."[24]

Husserl begins by introducing two pairs of terms: part and whole, dependent and independent; it is their permutations which exhibit such powerful logical scope. Every intentional 'object,' i.e., everything considered as the 'content' of a cognitive act, can be related to another as part to whole, whole to part, or as parts of one whole. It is the way in which parts are related to parts or in which parts compose wholes that reveals whether they are dependent or independent. An independent whole is a complex 'object,' i.e., divisible into parts, which can exist alone in that it does not require the existence of any other 'object.' A dependent whole is also a complex 'object' insofar as it is divisible into parts, but cannot exist alone; it requires some greater whole of which it is a part.[25]

An independent part (piece) is an 'object' or content of thought which makes up a whole or other complex 'object,' which qua part can stand on its own, e.g., the handle of a teacup. A dependent part (moment) is an 'object' which makes up a whole or other complex 'object,' but which cannot stand on its own, e.g., the teacup's color or shape. With regard to material things whose wholes are concrete, parts and wholes are said to stand or exist on their own (or not) as the 'objects' of cognition; one should say perhaps that they can (or cannot) be made the content of presentations. This further points to the crucial phenomenological distinction between 'objective' and 'objectual,' and the collateral paired terms 'real' and 'reell'; the two first terms pertaining to the thing itself, the two second terms to the phenomenal content.

The great power and scope of this schema, which has inspired so many later workers in the field, lies in Husserl's essential insight into the purely formal *a priori* character of the relations which hold between any sort of part and any sort of whole. These *a priori* regularities have such heuristic scope due to the critical distinction between dependence and independence, a distinction grounded in the definition of foundation. Throughout his discussion, Husserl takes the term 'object' in the widest possible sense (too wide, in fact, for some critics) to include both mind-independent objects existing in the outer world—which is what he does not talk about—and the intentional 'objects' which are present to consciousness, the proper domain of a phenomenological enquiry. Within this domain, a further distinction is made between the psychical act and its content, essential parts of the intentionality of consciousness. An even more refined partition is made later, with respect to the content alone, among its 'object,' its material, and its essence.

The psychical act which presents a concrete 'object,' e.g., the appearing apple, is immediate and independent since it does not need, i.e., require foundation in, any other presentations. Whereas the act which apprehends an abstract content, e.g., redness or roundness, is mediate and dependent since it does require the presentation of a concrete 'object.' Concrete 'objects' can be either wholes, which one thinks of as individual, self-subsistent things, or parts of wholes; as such, independent concrete parts are called 'pieces.' Abstract contents are not thought of as individuals which can exist on their own, though through the process of ideation they can be thought of in terms of universals which are instanced in specific 'objects'; as dependent parts they are called 'moments.' The skin, seeds, pulp, etc. of an apple are pieces of the whole apple, that is, parts in the sense that the whole apple requires their presence, but independent in the sense that they can exist apart from (sic) the whole; though of course that apple no longer exists when so pieced. On the other hand, the redness and roundness of the apple are moments of the whole, since being red and being round as such cannot exist without something whose color and shape they are. This does not imply that they cannot be thought of separately, since of course the 'concept' redness or roundness can be conceived apart from any red or round 'object.' Let it also be noted that a piece of that whole apple, whether just the skin or a segment, can also have both pieces and moments.

At first glance, this might seem to be an elaboration of the notions of primary and secondary qualities, and moreover not to be terribly illuminating. But Husserl's concern is not merely with simple and complex concrete things. The formal character of the theory and its *a priori* laws of essence mean that such ordered structural relations, as outlined above, hold also within other

cognitive domains and higher-order objectivities. These latter comprise, for example, the perceptual field of consciousness, mathematical and geometrical
constructions, propositional meanings, complex highly organized individuals
(human beings), classes of individuals, and masses or collectives of nonindividuals
(or "dividuals," to borrow Jonathan Lowe's term). The fact that an apple always
appears within a field of other coperceived objects, and stands out due to the
advertence of attention, also indicates a relation of essential dependence between
the whole apple and the whole perceptual field. It also indicates that a group of
apples (or, more clearly, a group of dots) organized in a specific manner, though
entirely separate from each other, will always be perceived as forming a determinate figural shape or gestalt; and thus that the gestalt is dependent on a certain
ordered relation between all of its constituent moments.

Of great interest here is the recension of linguistic meaning in light of these
formal features: "[these] yield the necessary foundation for the essential categories of meaning on which . . . a large number of a priori laws of meaning
rest. . . . These laws, which govern the sphere of complex meanings, and whose
role it is to divide sense from nonsense, are not yet the so-called laws of logic
in the pregnant sense of this term: they provide pure logic with the possible
meaning forms." (LI, 493). Husserl first distinguishes the expression of a statement as composed of sensuous (audible) parts from its meaning. An investigation of the former is a matter for descriptive psycho-physiology (later codified
in phonology[26]), but he does hint at some key aspects of the sensuous manifestation of language: stressed *versus* unstressed contents and the manner in which
such contents are blended (LI, 450–53). Meaning, however, only pertains to an
expression in virtue of the mental acts which give it sense. It would be incorrect
to think that Husserl wants to reduce meaning to the mental acts which find their
"voice" in the speaker's utterance. For he does mark the crucial dichotomy
between what an expression intimates, i.e., what it indicates about the speaker's
mental and emotional states, and the 'objectivity' to which the statement refers
by way of its meaning.

A statement is composed of parts, bound together by syntactical rules, which
can be either independently or dependently meaningful. Singular terms and
complete sentences, the linguistic substrate for the statement, are independently
meaningful, that is, a singular term can "constitute the full, entire meaning of a
concrete act of meaning." Whereas other kinds of parts, e.g., connectives, prepo-
sitions, adverbs, etc., are only dependently meaningful, since they require other
terms to complete a content which can be made the 'object' of a presentation.
The *a priori* laws which govern the combination of independent and dependent
contents partially determine the sense (or nonsense) of the whole statement of
which they are parts, insofar as these laws are in accord with the given syntax

of the language. But they cannot of themselves determine the validity or absurdity of such lawfully formed combinations. Thus the statement, "That thing is a round square," is syntactically correct, i.e., it has not violated any of the rules for sentence formation, and yet it cannot be made the meaningful content of a presentation. Because intentionality as such is composed of both the mental act and its content, an intuition of the content as such-and-such can be compatible with another content only insofar as these intuitions are in accord with purely formal logical laws.

An intuition, as the fulfilled content of an intention which grasps the 'object' precisely in the manner in which it is given (cf. D6) can be directed not only toward the concrete, singular 'object'—whether in perception, phantasy, or memory—but also toward abstract, universal 'objects' which function as species for which particulars are either individuals (independent components) or moments (dependent components). It is in terms of universal propositions that Husserl formulates *a priori* laws pertaining to the conjoining of such contents in either a necessary or contingent connection (cf. D4). An analytic proposition is one whose truth is completely independent of the specific content of their 'objects' and of any possible existential assertion. A synthetic proposition, on the other hand, is one whose truth is indeed dependent on the specific contents of their 'objects,' which may be necessarily connected, but which also may be empirical specifications, i.e., with factual delineations. This Husserlian distinction is a more sophisticated version of, but still comparable with, that made by Descartes with regard to the formal relations between the 'abstract' components of analytic and synthetic statements.

This is by no means a complete survey of part-whole relations in the realm of propositional meaning, but a broad overview of the main constituent features. David Bell comments after his critical survey of the principals of part-whole theory: "What, as it were, breathes life into this situation are the mental acts, and in particular the moments of those acts called their act-matters, which are the source of all intentionality."[27] The verbal image "breathes life" is poignant and thought provoking and, strange to say, has its literal fulfilment when we turn to Husserl's explication of the way in which mind and body are conjoined in the human person. It is not to our purpose to trace the complex reticulations of parts and wholes through various topical analyses, nor to explore the more recent research into a well-developed, mature part-whole theory.[28] This conceptual schema does reemerge, however, in an unusual, even unexpected manner in his discussion of the psycho-physical constitution of the mindful body.[29]

> The thoroughly intuitive unity presenting itself when we grasp a person *as such* . . . is the unity of the *expression* and the *expressed* that belongs to the essence of all

comprehensive unities. This body-spirit unity is not the only one of this kind. . . . The book with its paper pages, its cover, etc., is a thing. To this book there does not append a second thing, the sense; but instead the latter, in *animating* it, penetrates the physical whole in a certain way. . . . The spiritual sense is, by animating the sensuous appearances, fused with them in a certain way instead of just being bound with them side by side. (Ideas II, 248–49; emphasis added)

This analogy between a text and its sense, and the mind-body unity picks up on the previous distinction between the expression of a statement and what is expressed through it; as well as the tangential notion of fusion or blending (LI, 450–53), whereby abstract parts are capable of mutually interpenetrating throughout the whole. Some of the phrases which Husserl uses in this passage should now be familiar to the reader and remind one of Descartes' remarks on both linguistic expression and denotation and the permixture of the whole soul in the body. The Cartesian notion of linguistic meaning is closely interwoven with his conception of the representative function of ideas—the audible or visible sign of a word causally produces a specific configuration in the "nervous spirits" (i.e., a specific brain state) which is interpreted by the mind to signify the ideative content which the word intends. This cognitive process is no more an inference than is the judgement that the moving figures under cloaks which he sees out of his windows are human beings because clothes are a sign of human apparel.

Though Husserl's analogy above first points toward the cultural sphere, i.e., works of the human spirit such as texts and pictures, it also indicates a fundamental mode of apperception, an experiential attitude, in which what appears to the senses is not merely a neutral phenomenon, but is already a signification of the appearing thing's value. The experience of a book, a painting, a hammer, etc. is not given merely as a perceptual grasping of its physical qualities to which a grasping of its meaning or value is added as a surplus or "appendix." Rather, it is given in one comprehensive (literally, "grasping-with") experience of the thing as already animated with its sense. This also holds for nonperceptual intuitions of nonconcrete, spiritual 'objectivities,' e.g., the remembered or phantasized sensuous tones of a melody. A similar, though more complex and reflexive apperception takes place in the experience of another human being; it is reflexive in that a human being is not only sense-endowed but also sense-giving, for example, in writing the book, painting the picture, making the hammer, etc.

The apperception of another human being is accomplished through the medium of her appearing, phenomenal body but is directed as well, in the same intentional act, towards her spirit as that which animates the whole being, in the person's actions, speech, movements, and so forth. The apperception of a human being is not that of one thing (the body) conjoined with another thing (the spirit), but of a whole thing whose every bodily movement is imbued with spirit. The ambiguity of the word "sense" here is highly significant; with respect to the human being, "sense" connotes the meaning conveyed by the mindful body whose referent is the body alone; and it connotes the sentient, i.e., the sense-endowed aspect of just this certain kind of being.

> The physical unity of the body there, which changes in such and such a way or is at rest, is *articulated* in multiple ways. . . . And the articulation is one of *sense*, which means it is not of a kind that is to be found within the physical attitude as if every physical partition, every distinction of physical properties would receive significance. . . . Rather the apprehension of a thing as a [human being] is precisely such as to animate multiple, though distinguishable, moments of the appearing corporeal objectivity and to give to the individual sense a psychic content. (Ideas II, 253)

Note the embedded terms "partition" and "moment," part-whole terms which have decisive repercussions when Husserl comes to argue against parallelism and interactionism. A transition is effected here comparable to that in the fifth *Cartesian Meditation,* from the apperception of a human as a mindful body to the transference of this apperception to one's own person, via the operation of empathy. Although this would take us into the domain of the intersubjective constitution of the social world, and thus away from the specific focus of this research, it is worth touching on this crucial juncture in Husserl's later work. In brief, the apperception of the other as a mindful body embraces also the coapperception of implicit but essential features of the other as a being like myself. And this means that my mindful body is an 'object' for the other, within the horizon of other coperceived use-objects and value-objects, in just the same way in which the other was constituted for me. This knowledge of myself, as co-apperceived by the other through empathy, is completely different from knowledge of the self gained through introspection; only through the former can one take one's place in the socio-cultural world.

In general, the lived-body is a two-sided reality (Ideas II, 297) when abstracted from the fact that it is a mere thing, explicable and definable in light of its physical nature. It is constituted by the sensing or sensitive body and the volitional or freely moving body. The soul also has two facets or aspects: one as physically conditioned and thus dependent on the materially conceived body-as-object; the other as spiritually conditioned and thus independent of material determinations. There are thus two poles towards which these paired realities can be oriented: physical nature and spiritual nature (one pole), and the lived-body and its spirit (the other pole). Insofar as the lived-body and its spirit are turned toward, that is, made the theme of "scientific" enquiry in physical nature its relations to this "primary" environing world are explicable in terms of "natural" regularities, e.g., causal laws, temporal bounds, etc. But insofar as they are turned towards the spiritual environing world, comprised of created and valued 'objects,' the meaning of the lived-body and its spirit are explicable only as "things" which confer meaning and value.

> The theoretical object, *human being* . . . which is included in the theoretical positing of nature, is specifically something other than the theoretical object, *human person.* The human being as an object of nature is not a subject, a person, though to every such object a person *corresponds*; so we can also say that every one of them 'involves' a person, an ego-subject, which however is never a component part of nature, contained as a reality in nature, but instead is something that is *expressed* in the environing object, "human body." (Ideas II, 301; emphasis added)

This is a crucial passage and synopsizes many of the points made earlier about both Descartes' and Husserl's conceptual schemas. Note especially the harmonious phrases in this statement: for Descartes, the mind is permixed with one immediate portion of extension, its own body; and for Husserl, the ego-subject is expressed in an environing object, the lived-body. A profound misconception can take place when the spirit as the expressed and the lived-body as expression are articulated in the same order of discourse. We should no more take the sensuous perceptions of a word or a text for the meaning of that word or text, than we should conflate the physical, living body with the mindful presence which "breathes life" into it. The mindful body *takes part in*, but is not *a part of*, physical nature, though it is instanced in the "closest fitting" environing object, its own body.

This is exactly parallel with Descartes' notion that the simple, immaterial mind effects and is effected by the extended, material world due to the fact that it does take part in that world through a specific portion of extension, its own body, that is, the mind's most immediate environment. It is also reminiscent of Descartes' complaint that a correct understanding of mind-body connection presupposes that one has already clearly and distinctly grasped the difference between order of reasons and order of essences. According to the former, so vividly displayed in the "Sixth Meditation," one can arrive at definitions of mind and body which construe them as disparate and isolated. But according to the latter, one can reemploy these hard-won insights to realize that, as these things are in themselves, they are not disparate parts but distinct kinds of parts of one whole; and not isolated, except *post facto,* since they are always given to consciousness as intimately conjoined in the real human person.

In the last sections of *Ideas Second Book* (302–16) and in Appendix III of the *Crisis* (315–34), Husserl focuses on the concepts of dependence and independence in order to refute parallelism and interactionism as solutions to the alleged Cartesian mind-body problem. On Husserl's reading, psycho-physical parallelism claims that for every conscious experience there corresponds an organic brain state, and that regularities which govern the succession of bodily sensations, perceptual events, etc. as given in experience are isomorphic with those which determine the brain states. As such, any given conscious experience is dependent on its coordinate brain state. However, this model tacitly presupposes a psycho-physical world of "windowless" monads; once the concept of empathy is introduced we recognize that other persons' consciousness of us is an essential component of how we understand ourselves.

In fact, our awareness of other lived-bodies as objects in the natural world includes the analogical awareness that they are also subjects of their own experiences. This intersubjective *empathy* cannot be a component in a psycho-physical parallel model since it is not determined by any correlative brain state, for the simple reason that no state of my brain could comprise or "contain" an awareness of another's awareness of me. Moreover, the changes in the brain are contingent events in that they operate according to natural laws which could be otherwise. But with respect to the retention of experiences, linked according to *a priori* temporal succession with specific impressions, what is conditioned is only the content of the experiences or sensations, not the necessary linkage itself.

"On such grounds, it seems to me, one can radically refute parallelism and the refutation thereby has a completely different style than the usual ones which . . . head directly for interactionism, as if the question of parallelism versus interactionism were a radical and exhaustive one" (Crisis, 308). Husserl's rejection of parallelism in arguments for an uncritical conception of mind-body dualism relies on earlier arguments he brought against a psychological derivation of logical laws, namely, conflation of the factual psychical conditions under which a logical law is cognized with the 'ideal' nontemporal content of such laws. Another feasible interpretation of the grounds for Husserl's claim that psycho-physical parallelism fails to adequately account for mind-body union pertains to our conclusions in the last chapter about the "relations" between the complex system of ideas and the complex system of beings. What possible grounds could we postulate for holding that there is a connection between the order of thoughts and the order of beings? If the connections within the first sphere are causal and within the second are motivational, there is no reason for thinking that the connection between the two orders is either causal or motivational. There must be some other supracausal "bridging" principle and the only intelligible candidate is (or has been) a supreme being who sets things up this way. But for Husserl the phenomenologist, God is a spurious transcendence who can never be the 'object' of any kind of intuition whatsoever; whereas human beings do indeed have intuitions of self and others. So the stark choices which parallelism presents us with are either (a) an account which contravenes our basic intuitions about mindful bodies combined with the postulation of a transcendent being to justify our knowledge; or (b) an account which accords with our basic intuitions combined with a transcendent being knowledge of whom it would be impossible to justify.

On the other front, Husserl's dismissal of interactionism is to some extent, at least in its discursive setting, an echo of Descartes' resolution in *The Passions*, in terms of the auto-affectivity of bodily sensations and the emotions. "Surely not only are the sensuous sensations in the stricter sense determined by the body, but so are the sensuous feelings as well, and the lived experience of instincts. Surely a good part of individuality also belongs here, namely the sensuous dispositions with their individual habitus" (Crisis, 308). A third and novel way through these two specious models for mind-body union is provided by a radical rethinking of the individual located both spatially and temporally within the world horizon. A particular thing in the natural sense has its essence in the manner revealed by intuition as a thing with some determinate spatio-temporal properties; once adequately grasped, it is known with certainty. But an individual, a human person in the spiritual sense, does not have its own essence in advance, it is always underway and is not at all graspable in purely 'objective' terms. Rather, because of its subjective, meaning-conferring character, oriented towards the not yet given of all its possible determinations, it has an open essence. The problematic of the relation between mind and body can be made the theme of another phenomenological enquiry—the nature of personal identity over time. Remarks on the necessary linkage of contents in memory, the constitution of an intersubjective world of socio-cultural artefacts already constructed, point in this direction. No acceptable solution to the problem of personal identity can be given if one has already accepted either parallelism or interactionism as a sufficient explanation for the soul's insertion in and exchange with the natural world.

CARTESIAN IDEAS
DOUBTFUL MATTERS AND ACTS OF DOUBTING

> Here is a little-studied aspect of Cartesianism: that of knowing how the soul pos-
> sesses its own ideas. There have been many arguments as to whether clarity and
> distinctness were sufficient signs of truth and in what case divine veracity had to
> lend them its guarantee. . . . The nature of the act in which the I grasps its ideas and
> itself has been less extensively investigated.[1]

Although Gaston Berger made this observation more than sixty years ago,
this little-studied aspect has not been accorded more study. If anything,
Berger's remark has been virtually ignored and the "many arguments" have gone
on proliferating. Until quite recently, Anglo-American scholarship on Cartesian
ideas, including the "class" of ideas which are the focus of methodical doubt,
has been almost exclusively devoted to explicating a problematic which the
scholarship itself generated. From the earlier period of Russell, Ryle, and Austin
to the more recent work of Hintikka, Gewirth, and Kenny,[2] discussions of the
method of doubt, the matter which is called into doubt, and the certitude of the
cogito are almost unrecognizable as being about Descartes' own arguments.
These highly influential "versions" of what Descartes "really meant" by such-
and-such, or what he could only have meant if his argument were to work,
seemed to have pursued an agenda of their own device. This is *not* to imply that
they have not generated valuable and provocative insights within their own field
of discourse.

Partly in response to a different tradition, recent interpretative efforts by
Edwin Curley, Marjorie Grene, and Gary Hatfield[3] (among others) have provided
a much-needed corrective to this prevalent influence. To a greater or lesser

degree, this remedial, almost rehabilitative research owes an enormous debt of gratitude to the singular achievement of Martial Gueroult's *Descartes selon l'Ordre des Raisons* (1953; 2d ed., 1968).[4] It could be argued that any serious reader who devotes his attention to this extraordinary exegesis of the *Meditations* would be incapable of coming away with his view of Descartes unchanged; Gueroult's reading has decidedly effected the shape of the present research. From another perspective, Baker and Morris' research in *Descartes' Dualism* shows that a thorough and meticulous examination of the original texts will not support the numerous interpretations foisted upon him by commentators determined to find the culprit at the source of those metaphysical views which they find so deeply repugnant.

Of the many English-language scholars of Descartes, L. J. Beck, more than thirty years ago, is one whose commentary is entirely resonant with the French research of that period, especially in his emphasis on reading the *Meditations* according to Descartes' own injunction to follow the order of reasons: "M. Gueroult in his magisterial work . . . distinguishes two techniques for the historian of philosophy: 'la critique (probleme des sources, des variations, des evolutions, etc.)' and 'l'analyse des structures.' . . . No student of Descartes can neglect this magnificent analysis. . . . I would accept the 'analyse des structures' as the primordial task of this study."[5] Marjorie Grene makes a comparable observation about previous Anglo-American discussions of Cartesian topics such as doubt and the cogito and acknowledges her own debt to Gueroult's revaluative procedure. In light of this, she points out two fundamental errors in the standard interpretation of Cartesian ideas: the confusion or conflation of a judgment with the act of judging; and the fact that the *Meditations* follows an order of reasons.

> [First] if we are to understand Descartes' argument we must keep this distinction in mind: for both in the Fourth Meditation and in the Second (in the hats and cloaks passage) it is the *mental act of judging* he is concerned with rather than *judgements* as surrogate for logicians' propositions or linguists' sentences. . . . [Second] when we take judgements as the sole locus of truth, we overlook altogether the nature of Cartesian method. Descartes' method was . . . "a new way of ideas." It was a way of ideas, and it was new. The unit of knowledge, and especially of the path to knowledge—the path of analysis—is what its discoverer earlier called an *intuition* and later a *clear and distinct idea*.[6]

Our previous discussion in chapter 2 showed that one of the main complaints which Descartes had against the skeptics and neoskeptics was their inability (or unwillingness) to discriminate between the act of judging and the judgment, between the *positing* of the judgment and what the judgment was *about*. This complaint was echoed by Husserl's charge that the empirical psychologicians persistently confused the factual contingent origin of logical rules with the necessary *a priori* character of the logical rules themselves. Chapter 3 highlighted the methodological disparity of the order of reasons and the order of essences, a disparity the nonobservance of which, Descartes repeatedly emphasized, will permit or even encourage readers to misunderstand the presentation of arguments in the *Meditations,* and hence generate some of the objections which his contemporaries brought against him.

Descartes was certainly aware of an ambiguity in the word "idea," an ambiguity which could permit a lack of clarity and distinctness in the very idea of "idea" itself. He thus cautions the reader in the preface: " 'Idea' can be taken materially, as an operation of the intellect, in which case it cannot be said to be more perfect than me. Alternatively, it can be taken objectively, as the thing represented by that operation" (CSM II, 7). This caution is directed towards a passage in the "Third Meditation" where he is considering the various possible sources of his ideas, whether innate or otherwise. "Insofar as the ideas are considered simply as modes of thought, there is no recognizable inequality among them. . . . But insofar as different ideas are considered as images which represent different things, it is clear that they differ widely" (CSM II, 27–28). Let us quickly point out that here the distinction is being made, not with respect to ideas as images (which is a further distinction within all idea-contents), but with respect to ideas of any sort as representative. In his "Replies to the First Objections," it is to this passage that Descartes refers in his explicit discrimination of "the determination of an act of the intellect by means of an object [from] the object's being in the intellect in the way in which its objects are normally there" (CSM II, 74–75).

The expansion of the technical sense of 'objective' reality of an idea as the way in which the intellect's 'objects' are normally there points to a decidedly phenomenological account of the intellective domain, i.e., strictly in terms of these 'objects' being presented to consciousness. Editors of the *Meditations* usually footnote this passage in the "Third Meditation" with reference to the scholastic definitions of 'objective,' 'formal,' and 'eminent' reality. Although it is probably the case that Descartes utilized his scholastic training to intercalate a conceptual distinction which is required in this context, the context itself is entirely novel. The *Meditations* is the first working out of an account of certain knowledge as the product of the immanent "contents" of consciousness, without presupposing an external or underlying reality towards which consciousness has an as yet unknown relation. However, these highly refined scholastic terms have to undergo some sort of transformation. Perhaps then this 'objective' reality should be bracketed: both graphically in the use of single quote marks and thematically, that is, as that which has undergone a phenomenological epoché or suspension. This is precisely the groundbreaking stage achieved by the highest level of doubt and what is achieved within it will take on a novel sense.

Husserl acknowledges this self-founding domain of the phenomena as the point of departure in Descartes for a strictly phenomenological investigation. In his meditations on Descartes' *Meditations*, Husserl reconfirms the radicalness of this conception of philosophy's enterprise, a radicalness which demands an "absolute universal criticism." Descartes' uncompromising adherence to the method of doubt in order to abstain from all positions which already presuppose an existent world "out there," produces "a universe of absolute freedom from prejudice." Adherence to this principle restricts his meditative investigation to the phenomenal "contents" of consciousness which must be taken precisely as given without recourse to a post-theoretically justified world beyond the contents given. Another way to put this is that Descartes cannot rely on what he will only demonstrate in the "Sixth Meditation," the existence of material things in the natural world, in order to facilitate adequate conceptual distinctions in the "Second Meditation." Husserl claims that this abiding with the mere presentedness of thoughts (*cogitationes*) opens up for Descartes a protoconception, a foreshadowing of the intentionality of consciousness, in terms of the two correlative sides of the cogito: the cognitive 'act' and its 'object.'

> On the one hand, descriptions of the intentional object as such, with regard to the deter-minations attributed to it in the modes of consciousness concerned, attributed furthermore with corresponding modalities . . . (for example, the modalities of being). . . . This line of description is called *noematic*. Its counterpart is *noetic* description, which concerns the modes of the cogito itself, the modes of consciousness (e.g., perception, recollection, retention), with the modal differences inherent in them (e.g., differences in clarity and distinctness). (CM, 35–36)

This is not such a highly contentious reading (though the paired terms "noetic" and "noematic" may seem to suggest this) as to find no clear support[7] in what Descartes discloses about the character of ideas after a universal abstention has been carried through: "The nature of an idea is such that it requires no formal reality except what it derives from my thought, of which it is a mode. . . . The mode of being by which a thing exists 'objectively' in the intellect [is] by way of an idea" (CSM II, 28–29). The elision in the quotation occurs where Descartes appeals to the primary notion that there must be "at least as much" formal reality in the cause of the idea as there is 'objective' reality in the idea from which it is derived (of which, more later). Husserl would, of course, continue to suspend any affirmation of such an unwarranted assumption and demand that the analysis operate entirely within the suspension.

Descartes' essential insight into the two-sidedness of thinking, the cognitive act and the 'object' of that act, pertains to the entire domain of conscious activity. This domain is much "wider" than doubting as such, for it also embraces wishing, fearing, willing, and so forth: "what is doubting if not thinking in a certain kind of way?" (CSM II, 415). All of the disclosures made with respect to ideas in general apply as well to doubting as a particular mode of thinking, most specifically to the distinction between act and 'object.' The act-feature of a cognitive mode may seem to be more "obvious" in the domain of memory and imagination, since in these two domains there is a spontaneity in the engaging of a particular memory or phantasy, a directedness in how the content, the sequence of 'objects,' is played out. The act-feature in sensory perception may seem to be less "obvious" due to the essential and invariant fact that the sensed 'objects' always override any seeming directedness towards them. In one sense, the connectedness of sensed 'objects,' whether spatially arrayed or temporally sequenced, is an entirely contingent matter insofar as these objects are elements of the naturally occurring world and could be arranged otherwise. In another sense, the fact that these contents always override any directedness towards them is itself a necessary connection—sensory perception as such could not be otherwise.

This "overriding" takes the form of either fulfillment or frustration of the perceptual act, i.e., the idea one has of some thing is either adequate or inadequate to all of the features discerned in its 'object.' The act-feature in the perceptual mode is just this, namely, the recognition that only in cases of fulfillment of the perceived content has the intentional directedness the perceptual act brought about elicited evidence for which the fulfillment is an indication of certainty. Descartes would perhaps formulate this in terms of clear and distinct seeing: the clarity and distinctness of an idea is the result of the ideative content being grasped by consciousness in just that mode where the ideative act could only bring forth ("illumine") just this 'object' and no more than this 'object.' Nor can this adequation of ideative act with ideated 'object' have been otherwise, hence it is *beyond doubt*.

To the extent that the term "idea" is open to ambiguity, so also is the term "doubt," though this is not spelled out in such a clear-cut, easy to footnote manner. One might choose to illustrate this ambiguity by pointing to the equivocation in the use of the word "doubtful." For example, one could say, "He is doubtful about the project," where the subject is the one full of doubt. But one could also say, "He thinks that it is a doubtful project," where it seems that the project itself is full of doubt. Of course, it is trivial to reflect that no insentient thing can be full of doubt (or fear or desire); rather, the sense of this is that the project inspires doubts in someone. One question here could be, *what* is it about the project that inspires doubt? The answer might implicate design flaws, financial constraints, lack of viability, and so forth. But another question could be, how is the inspiring of doubt in the subject manifest? What is it about the subject's attitude or orientation to the project which characterizes the attitude as doubt, and not fear or desire? Any plausible answer would have to account for features of the subject's considerative *act* and not just the content of that which the subject considers doubtful.

Although the reader or commentator could grumble, with some justification, that Descartes does make terms such as "idea," "mode," and others do too much work, he usually emphasizes the fact that ambiguities are inherent in their use and that this use embraces more than one sense. He was reluctant to introduce novel technical terms, one of the characteristics of scholastic textbook philosophy which he vigorously criticized. He relies almost entirely on standard literary Latin and French in order to make some very complex distinctions.[8] It is, of course, one of the great ironies of the early modern period that his groundbreaking overturn of the philosophical enterprise accomplished far more than all of the technical apparatus of the previous scholastic disputations combined.

In any case, although separate terms might have allowed the reader to pick out more easily which sense was relevant in a specific context, he almost always qualifies the term in some way which sufficiently discriminates it from other senses and is consistent with other qualified uses of the term in other contexts. With respect to the ambiguity in the term "idea," as we have seen, Descartes distinguishes two senses: in the material sense it is an operation of the intellect, in the objective sense it is the thing represented by that operation. The remark in the preface points forward to the pivotal role of "idea" in the elucidation of a necessary distinction *before* his proof of God's existence in the "Third Meditation." The conceptual distinction made there has only been possible by following the order of reasons through the various stages of doubt and the isolation of the self-evident character of the cogito. He expands on this distinction in his "Replies to the First Objections," where it is obvious that his critic (Caterus) does not discriminate *within* the realm of ideas but only between an idea and the thing itself. This is one of the rare circumstances where Descartes does indeed rely on a scholastic apparatus, but here it is done in order to give the terms a radically new slant. Brentano will rely on an explicitly neo-Aristotelian interpretation of the "intentional in-existence" of an idea in order to make a very similar point—about the intentionality of consciousness.[9] In a number of lectures and texts, Brentano clearly distinguishes the two-sidedness of Cartesian mental phenomena and identifies this with the 'act' and 'object' correlates of the intentional structure[10]; though he is severely critical of Descartes' further attempts to build a theory of judgement on this. In the past decade, phenomenologically inspired

Descartes scholars deserve the credit, not for uncovering a nascent conception of intentionality in the "Third Meditation," but for balancing the conflicting and sometimes ambiguous remarks which Descartes makes regarding the 'material' and 'objective' senses of "idea."

Several recent articles have been devoted to an exposition of the tangled skein of Cartesian theory of ideas.[11] In order to avoid the repeated use of two rather awkward phrases, Vere Chappell, for instance, designates $idea_m$ as "idea in the material sense," and $idea_o$ as "idea in the objective sense." An $idea_m$ is a mental *act* or event; an $idea_o$ is something towards which the mind is directed, that is, a mental object. A given $idea_m$ is that in virtue of which just this $idea_o$ is picked out and not some other $idea_o$. Chappell also distinguishes two further senses of "idea" which should be mentioned, though they are not essential to our analysis here. A third sense is that of a "corporeal image," usually spoken of in discussions of imagination and memory. And a fourth sense is that of an "innate idea," where this refers to the source or origin of an idea and is thus not a mental act or content but a cognitive faculty.

To further complicate matters, Descartes' use of "material" is ambiguous: on the one hand it is distinguished from the "formal" aspect of an idea, on the other, from the 'objective' aspect. Does this mean that there are three terms in the Cartesian doctrine of ideas? Richard Aquila provides a clear exposition of the way in which these terms might be related and draws a valuable lesson for an understanding of the first proof for God's existence. The distinction between "material" and "formal" is between two different ways in which one might regard an operation of the understanding; either with respect to its feature of occurrence to some person, at some time, or with respect to its representation of some particular object or kind of object. So *this* distinction between 'material' and 'formal' applies only to ideas taken in their "active" sense, as cognitive operations. Aquila uses another set of subscripts to capture this twofold distinction: $material_1$ versus 'objective,' and $material_2$ versus "formal." To distinguish between ideas in the $material_2$ sense and in the formal sense "commits us to the existence of operations of the intellect as occurrences which are regarded as at least occasionally present in the understanding." To distinguish between ideas in the $material_1$ sense and in the 'objective' sense "appears to require the further admission that something may exist in the understanding in addition to its own operations"—namely the ideative content towards which the operation is directed.

Thus two quite different things might be signified by the 'objective' reality of an idea: in addition to whatever feature an idea possesses in virtue of which it is an idea of one thing rather than another, it might also be said to have the feature of being about the very object of that cognitive act. This would indicate that an idea in the 'objective' sense is the 'thing' which is represented by means *of* a particular operation of the intellect; "this implies that objects may exist 'in' the understanding in something much stronger than the sense that there are acts in the understanding which refer to those objects." Aquila argues that Descartes needs this notion of 'something stronger' in order to make his argument for God's existence work on the basis of a discrimination within the realm of ideas.

> Descartes could not have supposed his proof to have any force at all unless he had already been prepared to suppose that an infinitely perfect nature does at least exist in the understanding which contemplates it in something more than the sense that there exist mental acts by which such a nature is contemplated.... In order to be able to infer that this particular amount of perfection is infinitely great, we must also assume that an idea of infinite perfection is itself of infinite perfection and we must assume that it is so in something more than the sense that it is an idea which merely represents infinite perfection.[12]

Irrespective of the success or failure of Descartes' first proof for God's existence and its reliance on the doctrine of ideas, we must have a clear understanding of what it means for an act-idea to be an operation of the intellect. For this purpose, it is essential that we situate the intellect and its operations within its original Cartesian framework. This will also be helpful in allowing us to discriminate a further ambiguity in the term "act" or "activity." This larger framework is succinctly articulated in *Principles,* Part One, section 32: "All the modes of thinking that we experience within ourselves can be brought under two general headings: perception, or the operation of the intellect; and volition, or the operation of the will. Sensory perception, imagination and pure understanding are simply various [sub-]modes of perception; desire, aversion, assertion, denial and doubt are various [sub-]modes of willing" (CSM I, 204).

A number of exegetical comments are called for here: first, perception is the exemplary mode of the intellect and must be clearly distinguished from sensory perception (with which operation alone it is usually identified). Several commentators have remarked on the inexplicable absence of memory from the first grouping, since Descartes does include it in similar taxonomies in other contexts. Second, pure understanding is the clear and distinct seeing at work in the piece of wax instance in the "Second Meditation" and is the mature version of the intuition of the *Rules* and the *Discourse.* The above extract has interpolated [sub-]modes with respect to these two general operations; this is not an attempt to improve on Descartes' classification (or its English translation). Rather, it is a purely heuristic device to distinguish modes *tout court* from specific modes, since in the strict sense one cannot have a mode of a mode. Further, another ambiguity in the analysis of ideas should also be underlined, in this case with regard to the term "act." In the narrow sense, only volitions can be properly termed acts of the mind; but in the broad sense, every thought includes an act component, that is, an idea in the material sense. These two senses of "act" will be quite clearly revealed in, and are essential for an understanding of, phase five of methodical doubt.

Descartes makes explicit use of the dual sense of idea, and elaborates the intrinsic relation of one with the other, in the "Third Meditation": "The nature of an idea is such that of itself it requires no *formal reality* except what it derives from my thought of which it is a mode [Fr.: a manner or way of thinking]. But in order for a given idea to *contain* such and such *objective reality*, it must surely derive it from some cause which *contains* at least as much formal reality as there is objective reality in the idea. . . . The *mode of being* by which a thing exists objectively in the intellect [is] by way of an idea" (CSM II, 28–29; emphasis added).

This discrimination of formal from objective reality and the delimitation of the manner in which an idea can possess a reality of its own, not just having a label attached to it ("in the mind," "outside the mind")—this extraction one from the other is made entirely from the standpoint of the purely phenomenal domain established by universal doubt. This radical rethinking of the idea of an "idea" is succinctly formulated in an almost aphoristic fashion in his replies to Caterus' criticisms. "An idea is the thing which is thought insofar as it has objective being in the intellect . . . ; objective being simply means being in the intellect in the way in which 'objects' are normally there" (CSM II, 74). This is a highly unusual sense of the term 'object,' and it is small wonder that Caterus, Bourdin, and Descartes' other critics had genuine difficulty in grasping it. They would quite "naturally" assume that Descartes was drawing comparisons between an idea as a representation and the actual thing itself. Any such assumed comparisons, however, would inevitably have had to cope with the skeptical tropes designed to destabilize any postulated standard by means of which an epistemic comparison could be evaluated. The fact that he is making an essential distinction between two aspects of an idea, its act and its content, entirely within the phenomenal domain is precisely what will allow him to make a claim about the certainty of the cogito without appealing to some other criterion for comparison.

There are at least two unfortunate by-products of Descartes' use of the term 'objective' to distinguish the content of an idea, that towards which the act-idea is directed. One is that it easily misleads the reader into thinking that Descartes is here referring to the actual thing itself, e.g., the sun in the sky. The other by-product of his persistent attention to the idea-content is to draw interpreters towards an almost exclusive concern with epistemological problems about the connections between ordered arrangements of ideas, for example, the demonstration of the cogito through the stages of methodical doubt, the two proofs for the existence of God, and so forth. In effect, this is to ignore any possible descriptive analysis of the mutual dependency of act and content in one cogitatum and the interconnections between act-ideas through many cogitata, unified in the ongoing stream of one consciousness.

Let us return for a moment to one intermediate conclusion which Chappell draws here: "To be conscious is to be conscious *of* something; consciousness must have an object. . . . The precise object of consciousness . . . is not the conscious event, not the thought or idea$_m$ but rather the idea$_o$ that necessarily is associated with it. . . . It is thoughts, and hence ideas$_m$ by which consciousness is carried in the Cartesian mind: they are its indispensable *vehicles* even if not its specific targets."[13] The meaning of "vehicles" here relies on an equivocal sense of "contains" in the previous passage where Descartes discusses the 'objective' reality contained in the idea-content. It may seem strange to contemporary readers for him to qualify this containment with "at least as much" in the context: "There must be at least as much formal reality [in the cause of an idea] as there is objective reality in the idea." One might be tempted to interject that reality is not something which admits of degrees; some thing either is real or is not real, not more or less real. But we have to be willing to accommodate this novel sense of "reality" in much the same way that we were open to a revision of the meaning of 'object' in the 'objective' sense of idea. There is a clue to this novel sense of reality in the Axioms appended to the "Second Replies": "There are various degrees of reality or being: a substance has more reality than an accident or a mode; an infinite substance has more reality than a finite substance. Hence there is more objective reality in the idea of a substance than in the idea of an accident; and there is more objective reality in the idea of an infinite substance than in the idea of a finite substance" (CSM II, 117).

It seems to be the case that this sense of reality implies at most a two-termed relation, namely, that between ontological independence and nonindependence. This interpretation rests on Descartes' maintenance of the ontological schema of simple and complex natures first outlined in Rule XII of the *Rules* and covered in detail in the last chapter. Whether physical, abstract, or propositional, some simples are dependent on the existence (or holding true) of some greater whole of which they are parts. For example, being colored, shaped, etc. are dependent on some thing of which they are the properties; this thing itself is not dependent for its existence on some other thing. In the intuitive understanding of some thing, one is able to abstract such properties and, in considering or adverting to each property separately, to make of this simple a single 'object' of thought.[14] Within the phenomenal domain of consciousness, Descartes draws a parallel between the relations among ideas in the 'objective' sense, according to which they are said to be consistent or inconsistent, *and* the predicative attribution of properties to things (or features to ideas), according to which an idea is said to be adequate or inadequate.

The complex framework of ambiguous senses of "idea," "mode," and "reality" permits what is most distinctive about the Cartesian project—the founding of evidential certainty entirely within the "subjective" world of the meditator. But so far we have only seen this in light of two-termed relations deliminable within the cogitata *qua* cogitata. After all, that they are disclosed as grounds for evidential certainty is the product of a specific act-idea—the setting forth of the cogito.

> This is not the whole story, however. For representation . . . is not merely a two-termed relation between a mental state and an object of thought, with a thinker attached, as it were, by a different relation to the mental state. Representation is rather a three-termed relation with the thinker as one of its terms. The thinker's (or the mind's) role in representation itself is just as essential as that of the representing state, and its link to the represented object is no less intimate and direct. The mind, or myself, Descartes says, is what the objects of my thoughts are represented *to*. My mental acts serve to represent things, but they represent them *to me*.[15]

Given Chappell's interim conclusion, quoted before, and his explicit reference here to the third term in what can only be described as the Cartesian intentionality of consciousness, it is odd that Chappell never draws attention to the parallel with a phenomenological analysis of this same theme. It seems odd especially since this is virtually the same observation which Husserl makes with regard to the same point of departure in Descartes:

> Accordingly we have, in the Cartesian manner of speaking, the three headings, *ego—cogito—cogitata*: the ego-pole (and what is peculiar to its identity), the subjective, as appearance tied together synthetically, and the object-poles. . . . [These are] different aspects of the general notion of intentionality: direction towards something, appearance of something, and something (an objective something) as the unity in its appearances toward which the intention of the, ego-pole, through these appearances is directed. Although these headings are inseparable from one another, one must pursue them one at a time and in an order *opposite* to that suggested by the Cartesian approach. (Crisis, 171–72)

It is not to our purpose here to clarify the oppositeness of this opposite path which Husserl takes from the Cartesian point of departure. But it is crucial to make sense of Husserl's claim[16] that a genuine notion of intentionality is to be found in Descartes' theory of ideas *without distorting the very terms and relations with which Descartes explicates consciousness.* One of the essential features of the intentionality of consciousness is that it objectifies, makes an 'object' for consciousness whatever it is that consciousness is turned towards. "The forms or corporeal impressions which must be in the brain for us to imagine anything are not thoughts; but when the mind imagines or turns toward those impressions, its operation is a thought" (CSM III, 180). This turning-toward is the activity of the mind (in the broad sense) which embraces the specific act-character of thinking. "As to the fact that there can be nothing in the mind, insofar as it is a thinking thing, of which it is not aware, this seems to me to be self-evident. For there is nothing that we can understand to be in the mind, regarded in this way, that is not a thought or dependent on a thought. If it were not a thought or dependent on a thought it would not belong to the mind qua thinking thing; and we cannot have any thought of which we are not aware at the very moment that it is in us" (CSM II, 171). Consider the example which Descartes uses in his discussion of a perceived object and the idea which one has of it—the sun in the sky (CSM II, 27). Let us bring into this scenario another celestial object, the moon, in order to better draw out all the distinctions made thus far. The moon itself and the sun itself differ in a number of respects such that a perceiver can univocally pick out one and not the other. The actual differences between the two celestial bodies cannot alone account for the difference between my idea of the sun and my idea of the moon. It is not necessary that there even be some thing "out there" for me to have an idea, which qua idea can be distinguished from some other idea. My idea of a griffin is clearly distinct from my idea of a unicorn, but certainly not in virtue of the ideas being about two actual things "out there," since there aren't any such things.

It is also possible to have more than one idea-object of some thing, e.g., the sun seen by the naked eye and the astronomical construct, though they both pick out the same thing. How then can one claim to know that the sun or the moon exists and not the griffin? Not merely by resorting to the fact that one can *see* the former and not the latter. "This seeing does not affect the mind except insofar as it is an idea. . . . Now the only reason why we can use this idea as a basis for the judgement that the sky exists is that every idea must have a really existing cause of its objective reality; and in this case we judge that the cause is the sky itself" (CSM II, 117). But in other cases, the cause of the idea-object is not a thing "out there"—this in no way diminishes its 'objective' reality as an immanent content of consciousness.

"In just this case" here serves to highlight that one cannot resolve the issue of the ontological status of the cause of an idea merely by inspecting the ideative content. One must in addition attend to the act-feature by means of which the idea is given as an 'object' of thought. "In just this case," one can turn toward the sun in the sky in a way in which one cannot turn towards a griffin. That we have different idea-objects of the sun in the sky and that we know that they are ideas of one and the same thing—this knowledge cannot be the result of an appeal to some resemblance between the actual sun itself and my idea of it, for this is exactly what is called into question by the various stages of doubt.

> We cannot have any knowledge of things except by the ideas we conceive of them; and consequently that we must not judge of them except in accordance with those ideas, and we must even think that whatever conflicts with these ideas is absolutely impossible and involves a contradiction. . . . I do not deny that there can be in the soul or the body many properties of which I have no idea; I deny only that there are any which are inconsistent with the ideas of them that I do have, including the idea that I have of their distinctness. (CSM III, 202–3)

Internal consistency among one's ideas qua 'objects' of thought is one criterion by means of which some predicates (those items dependent on an 'object') can either be included or excluded in the intellective grasping of a given idea; that is, included when the idea is clear and distinct, excluded when the idea is obscure and confused. However, at this stage in the order of reasons, one cannot make further appeal to any coherence with respect to how (or if) the idea corresponds with an alleged thing itself. Before the proof of God's infinitude and benevolence, it is not necessary to prove that the world could not be an illusion generated by a "malign demon." Given that the world's existence is bracketed by the highest level of doubt, it is only necessary to demonstrate that different operations of the intellect can be distinguished on the basis of the formal and eminent reality of their causes. It is this separability within the realm of the way things *seem to be* that permits determination of some predicates as inconsistent with other predicates.

The idea-objects "chimera," "triangle," "piece of wax," etc., are not discriminable merely in terms of the properties which these 'objects' endorse, but must take account of the manner in which they are conceived. And that means the specific mode of cognition (the "class" of act-ideas perceiving, imagining, remembering) which is the sole contributive cause of their being perceptual ideas, imaginative ideas, etc. At this stage then, the correlation of cognitive modality and modalized content serves to exclude only adventitious ideas, those which are not innate or purely fictitious. The intellective mode as a "class" of act-idea has its own formal and eminent reality, in the same sense, but not with the same origin that alleged things "out there" have. "Just as the objective mode of being belongs to ideas by their very nature, so the formal mode of being belongs to the causes of ideas . . . by their very nature" (CSM II, 29). The various cognitive modes and their modalized contents are minimally separable by the "real" causal character of act-ideas as cognitive acts.

If one views the Cartesian theory of certain knowledge from the point established by the "Fifth Meditation" in which clear and distinct understanding has been guaranteed by God's existence then one would not need to look backward to an earlier stage for any other condition-setting criteria. But this standpoint has not yet been secured in the "Second" or "Third Meditation"—the formal and eminent reality of the ultimate cause hovers further down the meditator's path. One need look no further for the "real" causal character of the cognitive act than the first secured certainty—the cogito. "This proposition, 'I am, I exist,' is necessarily true whenever it is *put forward* by me or conceived in my mind" (CSM II, 17). It is the "putting forward" which signifies the cognitive act, here the primordial cognitive act as the first certainty. It is an essential component in the unifying intentional consciousness which is directed towards that which is seized through the act in its most significant content—thinking thing. "When the intellect puts forward something for affirmation or denial" (CSM II, 40), the will is inclined in such a way that one does not feel determined by any external force. Numerous other instances underscore the active position-taking of the cogito. But by far the greatest interpretative effort has been expended on the proposition and that which it signifies, *res cogitans*, and far too little attention has been paid to the putting forward—the topic for an analysis (Gueroult's "l'analyse des structures") of the act-features of Cartesian ideas.

In order to gain a better insight into the genesis of a Cartesian-inspired phenomenology, what we need is a detailed analysis of the phases into the cognitive act of doubting to complement an already well-established analysis of the stages to which methodical doubt is directed. The meditator is able to progress from sensory illusions through dreaming delusions and finally to the hypothesis of systematic deception due to the fact that he has a rigorous cognitive procedure which he adheres to despite the various temptations and seductions he encounters on the way. It is this meditative practice which makes sense of his ability to withstand the inclination to abandon his efforts and sink back into his earlier, comfortable beliefs. It would be mistaken to think of this "ability" as exclusively a kind of psychological stubbornness (though Descartes was a very single-minded person), rather it pertains to another dimension of the methodological expedient with which he began his investigation. Perhaps it might be helpful to think of these cognitive phases in the act of doubting in a manner similar to Loyola's *Spiritual Exercises*; these required a situation of peace and quiet, focusing on a specific verse from Scripture, repeating it several times, and then concentrating on a visual scene to secure its remembrance.

In any case, irrespective of how one goes about visualizing the different steps in Descartes' meditative practice, a fuller understanding of the act-features of doubting will help to secure the cogency of his later claims about "higher-order" and more controversial items of philosophical debate. Husserl explicitly focuses on the act-feature (noesis) of all positings as a valuable area of analytic scrutiny: "We wish to examine the structures which belong to the 'higher' spheres of consciousness in which *a number of noeses are built up on one another in the unity of a concrete mental process* and in which, accordingly, the *noematic correlates* are likewise founded. Thus the eidetic law, confirmed in every case, states that there can be *no noetic moment without a noematic moment specifically belonging to it*" (Ideas I, 226). In our study of Descartes' stepwise progress towards a science of securely founded intuitions, we will have to bear in mind that nowhere does he overtly call attention to these phases in the concrete mental process of doubting.

Doubt is an Act of Positing As-If False

What is it about idea-objects which would incline the meditator, in a pretheoretical manner, i.e., before the inception of universal doubt, even to consider that they might resemble things out there? Why even think of it as an issue of resemblance or correspondence as opposed to some other as yet undetermined relation? Wherein consists the 'objective' reality of the idea-object in virtue of which other ideas are consistent or inconsistent? Descartes has rejected "sensible species" and other physical-analogue models for the transmission of sensual and perceptual content. My idea of a tree is not itself green, leafy, and branching; the "at least as much" reality which the idea-object contains has an as-if *(quasi)* or as-it-were *(tanquam)* character. "There can be no ideas which are not as it were *[tanquam]* of things; if it is true that cold is nothing but the absence of heat, the idea which represents it to me as something real and positive deserves to be called false" (CSM II, 30). But if the idea-object represents something as if it were real and positive then it has this minimal objective reality which can then serve to indicate some formal or eminent cause. "Every clear and distinct perception is undoubtedly something (real and positive) and hence cannot come from nothing" (CSM II, 43).

Whether this representing takes the form of a proposition, a judgment, a desire, etc.—and thus implicates divergent cognitive modes—is an issue for the conceptual analysis of the idea-objects. But irrespective of their modes, each of these is a positing or a holding-forth, specifically a positing of an as-if character.[17] That is, it holds-forth in the "mind's eye" an idea as if it were something real and true, or as if it were *unreal and false*. To be directed towards an idea-object as if it were unreal and false is to *doubt* that 'object,' to find that idea (or all ideas!) doubtful. But doubting is not thinking about a divergent *kind* of 'object,' it is not just being directed towards the contents of one's thoughts of which some are unreal and false—"doubting [is] thinking in a certain kind of way" (CSM II, 415). What exhibits or shows forth doubting as a specific mode, in the broad sense, of thinking? One must turn to the faculty of willing and its active character, in the narrow sense, for an answer.

In addition to intellective or pure thinking, Descartes distinguishes other modes of thinking: "Thus when I will, or am afraid, or affirm, or deny, there is always a particular thing which I take as the object of my thought, but my thought includes something more than the likeness of that thing" (CSM II, 26). What is this "something more" included (i.e., in the way that act-ideas contain 'objects') in the 'object' of my thought (i.e., the 'objective' reality of an idea-object) that is not to be found merely in the allegedly objective character of whatever my thought turns towards? The "something more" is to make the positing act-idea directed toward the as-if idea-object into an idea-object itself and then to modalize this in a certain manner.[18] The idea-object of any given thought is not modalized in the same manner when it is an act of will as when it is an act of desire. For the purpose of this analysis, the surplus in the cognitive mode of doubting is to regard the act-idea of a thought as itself an idea-object which is then considered as if it were unreal and false. It is to step back, so to speak, in the putting forward of the quasi-reality of an idea (or all ideas) and their hypothetical substruction, in which one adopts a quasi-positional stance on the positing regard itself. This is the essence of the Cartesian epoché, the "bracketing" of the world achieved at the highest level of universal doubt.

Descartes explicitly introduces the topic of doubt with this as-if qualification: "Anything which admits of the slightest doubt I will set aside just *as if* I had found it to be wholly false" (CSM II, 16). And in the "Fourth Meditation": "The mere fact that I found that all my previous beliefs were in some sense open to doubt was enough to turn my absolutely confident belief in their truth into the supposition that they were wholly false" (CSM II, 41). A perfect choice of terms, for what is supposition but *sub-posito*, a modalized form of positing or holding-forth.[19] In his critics' intractable wrangling with the depth and scope of methodical doubt, this is one complaint which Descartes constantly has to rectify: that he has not taken the world *to be* false or not to exist, but has considered the world and worldly sense data *as if* it were false. One path then to an understanding of what methodical doubt means as a supposition is to eschew analysis and interpretation of what doubt is about, what is taken as doubtful, and to turn our attention instead to the as-if positing as revealed in the act-features specific to doubting. Our analysis of the theory of ideas has hopefully made clear that a comprehensive understanding of methodical doubt is not to be found only in what can be doubted (since anything can be doubted), or under what circumstances some thing is doubtful (since these can be varied at will), but in the specific modalized features, which we shall call "phases," of the cognitive act of doubting.

The well-known stages of methodical doubt are initiated by skeptical queries and problems directed toward those opinions and beliefs which the meditator had once taken to be genuine knowledge: First, my sensory knowledge of external objects sometimes deceives me; this impels me to consider all such knowledge *as if* it were false and its objects unreal. Second, it is sometimes the case (for example, while dreaming) that what appears to me may have an unknown, undetermined relation to an external world; this impels me to consider any purported relation to that world *as if* it were false and its relational connection as unreal. Third, it is possible that it is always the case that beliefs about the world, which include my own body and its purported relation to other bodies, may be the result of a systematic deception; this impels me to consider the notion of an external world as an hypothesis and the worldly things my ideas are about *as if* they were false.[20]

The little-studied phases of methodical doubt are cognitive act-features which characterize considering something as-if or treating something as-if, and "something" here comprises whatever comes within the scope of reflection on first-order thoughts. As such, these phases are essential features, specifically temporal "moments" (dependent parts), of doubting as one of the principal cognitive modes. They cannot be considered as act-features of the general activity of consciousness, for which other position-takings (desiring, fearing, and so forth) have a divergent "class" of act-ideas pertinent to the manner in which the respective "class" of idea-objects is cognized. With respect to the intrinsic act-features of methodical doubt considered as a "class" of act-ideas, we can discriminate six distinct phases: (1) abandoning prejudices, (2) detachment from the senses, (3) abstention from judgment, (4) clear and distinct seeing, (5) an act of will, and (6) attentional regard. In order to illuminate the internal relations and sequences among these phases, it will be necessary to examine a number of Cartesian texts and extract those remarks directed explicitly toward ideas in their "material" or active sense. It may then be possible to provide an answer to Berger's question as to "how the soul possesses its own ideas, . . . the nature of the act in which the I grasps its own ideas," at least with regard to ideas which are taken as doubtful.

The Six Phases of the Cognitive Exercise of Doubting

1. *Abandoning prejudices.* This theme is present in Descartes' thinking from the earliest period, from his first confrontation with the problematic of initiating an entirely radical refounding of the scientific enterprise. The dual sense of "radical" (*radix*, from the Latin, "root") can be seen in the repeated uses of the phrase "uprooting from my mind" all unexamined opinions; and its complement, "starting again from the root," the point from which any source springs. One must bring one's previous beliefs into the "natural light" for what they really are when divorced from solid foundations—prejudices, that is, prejudgments made before the establishment of a coherent standard which permits the appraisal of competing claims made about perceptual reports. As a theme the abandonment of prejudices is found throughout Descartes' principal works: from its earliest occurrence in the *Rules*, "We reject all such merely probable cognition" (CSM I, 10); from the *Discourse*, "the simple resolution to abandon all the opinions one has hitherto accepted"; "I had to uproot from my mind all the wrong opinions I had previously accepted" (CSM I, 118, 22); from the *Meditations*, "These proofs . . . require a mind which is completely free from preconceived opinions and which can easily detach itself from involvement with the senses" (CSM II, 5); and from the *Principles*, "There are many preconceived opinions that keep us from knowledge of the truth" (CSM I, 193).

On the one hand, the overcoming of prejudices is one of the purposes for which a universal science strives, that is, in order to found a comprehensive system of certain knowledge, free from the merely probable, the dubious, and the confused. On the other hand, abandoning prejudices is one of the preconditions for bringing methodical doubt into play. One particular scholastic precept, namely that nothing is in the intellect which was not first in the senses, is enough to make doubt seem spurious. It is sometimes unclear whether Descartes arrives at a clear and distinct idea of methodical doubt as a principle after freeing himself from prejudices or whether these prejudices are exposed as such after the operation of methodical doubt. "The usefulness of such extensive doubt is not apparent at first sight, its greatest benefit lies in freeing us from all our preconceived opinions and providing the easiest route by which the mind may be led away from the senses" (CSM II, 9). In resolving the issue of how it is that one could understand the efficacy of methodical doubt in vitiating prejudices, he has recourse to the "natural light" which God has bestowed on human minds: "Since God has given each of us a [natural] light to distinguish truth from falsehood, I should not have thought myself obliged to rest content with the opinions of others" (CSM I, 124). "Thus I gradually freed myself from many errors which may obscure our natural light and make us less capable of heeding reason" (CSM I, 116). So in this sense, the natural light is that "divine spark" which is capable both of exposing our beliefs and opinions as ill-founded *and* is requisite for the procedural decision to abandon those beliefs and search for more certain knowledge. "Someone who is stuffed full of opinions and taken up with any number of preconceptions finds it difficult to submit himself exclusively to the natural light" (CSM II, 417).

Abandoning prejudices, in addition to its function as a thematic concern for a radical first philosophy, can itself be taken as a specific positional attitude within the disclosure of the ground made ready for building again. As a specific cognitive *act*, it is the first order of business in the *Meditations*, i.e., it is the primordial act in the unfolding of the chain of reasons which leads link by link to greater epistemic security. After setting the stage and resolving on this course "once in his life," in the second paragraph, he states that it is not necessary, not even feasible, to show that all his opinions are false. He considers that he should withhold his assent from any opinions which are not completely certain just as if they were false. "So for the purpose of rejecting all my opinions, it will be enough if I find in each of them at least some reason for doubt."

2. *Detachment from the senses.* If prejudices are unfounded beliefs based on spurious evidence—"I will suppose then, that everything I see is spurious" (CSM II, 16)—the second phase in methodical doubt requires detachment from the senses as the most likely source of sensory illusions and deceptions. In the *Discourse*, this second phase is not clearly demarcated from the abandonment of prejudices, though it is tacitly included in the summary of his search for truth at the start of Part Four (CSM I, 127). His outline includes the following chain of reasons: (a) because our senses sometimes deceive us, one should suppose that nothing really is such as our senses lead us to imagine; (b) since it is possible to make mistakes in reasoning, one should no longer accept as sound arguments previously taken as demonstrative proofs; (c) since thoughts similar to those experienced while awake occur during dreams, without any of them being true, one should pretend that all such thoughts are no more true than the illusions of my dreams.

Detachment from the senses is explicitly indicated in the *Meditations* and the *Principles* as a distinct phase in the elaboration of methodical doubt, one which is subsequent to freeing from prejudices. "These proofs . . . require a mind which is completely free from preconceived opinions and which can easily detach itself from involvement with the senses" (CSM II, 5); "freeing us from all our preconceived opinions and providing the easiest route by which the mind may be lead away from the senses" (CSM II, 9). "If I were not overwhelmed by preconceived opinions and if the images of things perceived by the senses did not besiege my thought on every side ..." (CSM II, 47). And in regard to arguments for the existence of God, "they are clearer in themselves than any of the demonstrations of geometers; in my view, they are obscure only to those who cannot withdraw their minds from their senses" (CSM III, 53).

This second phase of detachment from the senses has both a ground and a purpose, just as in the previous phase of abandoning prejudices. The grounds upon which detachment from the senses is requisite are that sensory perceptions may be deceptive; if there is the least cause for doubt in that domain, one should withhold or suspend judgement about claims whose origin is that domain. The purpose of detachment is to place oneself in a position where that which is not doubtful may make itself apparent. It is important to understand these two conjoint phrases as a pretense or fiction which Descartes employs in an as-if manner, a manner similar to that in which twentieth-century analytic philosophers employ thought experiments. It is necessary to detach the mind from the senses, because in the later dualistic conception, the body and the mind are so intermingled that the nature and extent of mind is obscured in an unknown manner. One would be unable to clearly and distinctly grasp the nature of the mind without first having divorced oneself from sensory influences.

Let us reiterate the meditator's previous statement that one of the preconceived opinions now rejected is that there is nothing in the intellect which was not first in the senses. To discover whether this opinion has the least ground for doubt should not lead one to dispute this opinion by counterposing another opinion; this procedure would fall back on the skeptical technique of *isosthenia* which Descartes also rejects—he rejects it because it's another prejudice. Rather, his procedure is to suppose that the senses are simply not accessible for the kind of inquiry being carried out at this stage in the chain of reasons. What remains then in the intellect after abandoning prejudices and detaching from the senses? If one were to consider this scholastic maxim as an hypothesis—if there is something (an idea) in the intellect, then it must first have been in the senses— and then deny that there are any senses to appeal to, does this entail that ideas in the intellect are false, or that there are no intellective ideas at all?

In fact, the opinions and beliefs which he has rejected all have this epistemic characteristic: "Whatever I have up till now accepted as most true I have acquired either from the senses or through the senses." There is no point in arguing against this, employing other demonstrations which are equally liable to this weakness; rather the next link activates another phase of the pretense which is dramatically brought into force in the opening lines of the "Third Meditation": "I will now shut my eyes, stop my ears, and withdraw all my senses. I will eliminate from my thoughts all images of bodily things. . . . I will regard [them] as vacuous, false and worthless" (CSM II, 24). This startling statement underscores the notion that it is not the thought-contents which are the "subject" matter of this cognitive exercise, but the reflective attitude towards whatever enters consciousness; and this attitude is decisively that of positing as if.

3. *Abstention from Judgement.* It is after the two-part withdrawal from prejudices and sensory pressures, and consequent on the state of mind which results from this, that Descartes finds himself in a position to abstain from affirming or denying those things (if any) which remain. Attaining this position makes it feasible to neither affirm nor deny that which is presented to one's positing regard *and* compels one to carry out this abstention as the optimal procedure for achieving certainty. This third phase is clearly marked out as such in the *Meditations* and the *Principles*, but unlike the two phases of withdrawal and detachment above, abstention is not made explicit in the *Rules* and the *Discourse*. This lack of thematic focus is largely due to the fact that the highest stage of doubt, which suspends the purported existence of the world, depends on the unique epistemic power of the malign demon hypothesis, one that was not available until the *Meditations*.

In the synopsis in the *Discourse*, Part Four, regarding the chain of reasons which leads to methodical doubt as a procedure, abstention does not figure as a separate phase. Instead, after rejecting prejudices, impugning sensory perceptions, and then finding his dreams liable to the illusion of being just like wakeful realities, he will pretend that all other position-takings are equally prone to error—and thus to consider them as if they were false. His resolve at this point is to accept nothing as true and real which is not conceived clearly and distinctly, and this truth, about the acceptance of this criterion, is assured by the perfection and beneficence of God (CSM I, 130). There is a considerable difference between assuming something to be false, insofar as it does not attain to a clear and distinct intuition, and suspending or bracketing (in the skeptical epoché) the truth or falseness of something in order for such an intuition to be brought into play. There are two important points to be made about the omission of abstention from judgment in the *Discourse*: one is that the most pervasive and corrosive stage of doubt awaits the entrance of the malign demon; the other is that here mathematical truths are exempt from this pretense, whereas in the *Meditations,* they too succumb to the contagion of hyperbolic doubt.[21]

After recalling the time "some years ago" when he composed the *Discourse*, in the next paragraph he states that, "reason *now* leads me to think that I should *hold back* my assent from opinions which are not completely certain and indubitable just as carefully as I do from those which are patently false" (CSM II, 12; emphasis added). And later, prior to the "persuasive reason" which clear and distinct intuition will provide, he states that "I am indifferent as to whether I should assert or deny either alternative, or indeed refrain from making any judgement on the matter" (CSM II, 41). And this achievement of an abstentive position is also assured by our God-given freedom of will: "It is surely no imperfection in God that he has given me the freedom to assent or not to assent in those cases where he did not endow my intellect with a clear and distinct perception" (CSM II, 42). This conditional notion of freedom is picked up again in the *Principles*: "We have free will enabling us to withhold our assent in doubtful matters and hence avoid error" (CSM I, 194). Husserl also will underline this volitional condition within the transition from the natural standpoint to that of the first phenomenological reduction: "The attempt to doubt universally belongs to the realm of our perfect freedom: we can attempt to doubt anything whatever, no matter how firmly convinced of it. . . . This changing of value is a matter in which we are perfectly free and it stands over against all cognitive position-takings" (Ideas I, 58–59). This fullest or perfect freedom as the fundamental condition for withholding assent and denial is emphatically distinguished from the cognitive act of will which is exercised on the basis of clear and distinct seeing (see the fifth section below).

In contrast to the many standard skeptical techniques which Descartes rejects, such as counterposing arguments, forcing the opponent into a regress, and so forth, there is one which he adopts—the epoché or suspension. This withholding of judgment was, of course, the procedural terminus for the ancient skeptics, though the practical result of acknowledging the appropriateness of the epoché was tranquillity or quietude. Descartes also placed great store in achieving peace of mind as the highest stage of wisdom (CSM I, 149), but in his case this was the fortunate consequence of having attained certainty in his scientific endeavours. Abstention from judgment is the hinge in a comparative analysis of Cartesian methodical doubt and the phenomenological reduction. In the course of his historical tracing of the Cartesian path, it is at this interpretative point that Husserl parts company with Descartes and thus makes the skeptical epoché into a new starting point. Where Descartes seeks to secure the closure of abstention by recourse to a proof for God, Husserl maintains the epoché in order to disclose the structures of consciousness.[22]

Abstention may seem to be a rather peculiar form of cognitive activity, if anything it seems to signify a lack of activity in the way that abandoning and detaching, though privative, do not. But this is to take the meaning of this cognitive phase in the sense of a volition, a sense which none of the other phases warrant. Abstention is indeed a specific positional regard, almost always qualified in terms of affirming or denying a judgment, and hence taken with respect to an idea-object of an act of will. Abstention from affirming or denying brings forward or discloses the 'objects' of thought, and the act of will which follows overcomes this hesitancy in asserting one or the other; it is the first step in gaining a secure grasp on what one would claim to know as true or false. "Now all that the intellect does is to enable me to perceive (without affirming or denying anything) the ideas which are subjects for possible judgements" (CSM II, 39). Adhering to an abstentive attitude prevents one from inclining toward affirmation or denial as the result of some "blind impulse"—blind in that it is not open to clear and distinct seeing—which would bestow no greater epistemic weight on an option than if it were the product of pure chance.

4. *Clear and distinct seeing.* Once one has acknowledged prejudices as prejudgments made without grounded evidence, detached oneself from the senses as the probable source for the spuriousness of such evidence, and abstained from assenting to or denying any other judgements—only then can clear and distinct seeing come into play. It is this cognitive phase which will permit a warranted assent or denial, according to a criterion which discriminates only one possible idea-object as the adequate grasping of a specific act-idea. In an exemplary manner, this is what happens in the "piece of wax" episode in the "Second Meditation": the invariant "nature" of the wax is adequately seized in a clear and distinct seeing by means of the intellect alone, the "sharp edge of the mind."

The concept of clear and distinct seeing has a thematic continuity throughout Descartes' writings. It appears as early as Rule III of the *Rules* in the guise of intuition "of a clear and attentive mind, which is so easy and distinct that there can be no room for doubt about what we are understanding . . . [i.e.] intuition is the indubitable conception of a clear and attentive mind which proceeds solely from the light of reason" (CSM I, 14). Note that even here, in its earliest formulation, this cognitive operation explicitly excludes the minimal ground for doubt and includes a reference to attention (see phase six below). One should not overlook the fact that intuition in the *Rules* is a less mature, less complex operation than the pure intellective seeing of the *Meditations*, yet even in the earlier text it already contains some of the crucial conceptual features found in the latter version.

Clarity and distinctness appear in the *Discourse* immediately after the summary of the chain of reasons at the start of Part Four mentioned above. "I decided that I could take it as a general rule that the things we conceive very clearly and very distinctly are all true; only there is some difficulty in recognizing which are the things that we distinctly conceive" (CSM I, 127). Prior to that it forms the key feature of the first of his practical "moral maxims" (CSM I, 120). Although clarity and distinctness may be enough for moral or practical certainty, it is not sufficient by itself to insure metaphysical certainty, that is, the guarantee that the grounds which would permit minimal doubt are impossible. Since this guarantee is not available without the proof of God's existence, this rule about conceiving clearly and distinctly is itself only secured by the intuition of perfection and infinitude in God's "nature."

This phase is set forth in "geometrical fashion" in the Postulates appended to the "Second Replies," where Descartes asks the reader to review all the examples of clear and distinct seeing in the *Meditations*: "I ask them to conclude that it is quite irrational to cast doubt on the clear and distinct perceptions of the pure intellect merely because of preconceived opinions based on the senses, or because of mere hypotheses which contain an element of the unknown" (CSM II, 116). Each of the subordinate clauses in this passage excludes the "infection" of minimal doubt; first, from the fact that prejudices and sense-based beliefs have been neutralized by the first two phases; second, due to the premise that any new hypothesis inserted during a regress is still suspended through abstention. The paired terms clarity and distinctness receive a precise "synthetic" exposition[23] in *Principles* Part One, section 45:

A perception which can serve as the basis for a certain and indubitable judgement needs to be not merely clear but also distinct. I call a perception 'clear' when it is *present* and accessible to the *attentive* mind—just as we say that we see something clearly when it is present to the eye's gaze and stimulates it with a sufficient degree of strength and accessibility. I call a perception 'distinct' if, as well as being clear, it is so sharply *separated* from all other perceptions that it *contains* within itself only what is clear. (CSM I, 207–8; emphasis added)

Perception (in the widest sense) as the exemplary mode of the pure intellect is here being compared to sensory perception in order to better draw out the meaning of clarity and distinctness. As other contexts make evident, this operation is itself clarified and made distinct in the perception of simple natures. When insight is turned in that direction, for instance, in the sensory perception of a malleable, textured, colored piece of wax, any one concrete simple is present to (i.e., an idea-object of) the visual regard in such a manner (i.e., according to its own cognitive mode) as to call forth a perceptual simple in terms of the formal reality of its cause. Furthermore, when no other concrete simple is present with this idea-object then the act-idea of the visual regard contains (in the way all mental acts contain contents) no more then just this idea-object. Obscurity and confusion are the opposites of clarity and distinctness and to emphasize the act-feature of intellective regard, i.e., the advertence of the attentive mind, these act-ideas can themselves be made the content of a further reflective regard. The significance of the passage below about the transparency of reflection cannot be over-estimated.

We must distinguish between the subject-matter, or the thing itself which we assent to, and the formal reason which induces the will to give its assent [phase five]: it is only in respect of the reason that transparent clarity is required. As for the subject-matter, no one has ever denied that it may be obscure—indeed obscurity itself. When I judge that obscurity must be removed from our conceptions to enable us to assent to them without any danger of going wrong, this *very obscurity is the subject concerning which I form a clear judgement*. It should also be noted that the transparency which can induce our will to give its assent is of two kinds: the first comes from the natural light, while the second comes from divine grace. (CSM II, 105; emphasis added)

Now Descartes is the first to admit that issues of divine grace are best left to theologians and this is not one of the subject matters to which his attention as a philosopher is directed. But it is certainly directed towards the natural light which itself is God-given and which illumines the simple fact that what secures clarity and distinctness in intellective seeing as the criteria for certainty is God's infinitude and perfection. Nevertheless, the choice of terms here cannot be ignored: the formal reason (act-idea) requires transparency with respect to its subject-matter (idea-object) which can itself be either clear and distinct or confused and obscure. One can adopt a position (in the purely ideative sense, of course) in which one can clearly and distinctly see through the clear and distinct (or confused and obscure) seeing of any given idea-object as the effect in virtue of which the idea contains just this 'objective' reality. But the formal reality of this operant condition which renders transparency perspicacious is not to be found within the immanent domain of consciousness; one must have recourse to something beyond. Or so at least Descartes' scheme demands.

Since there is no direct consciousness of anything except what is enclosed within immanence, a strategy must be found for explaining the possibility of ever reaching the object of true cognition. That strategy is to infer one's way out of the prison of subjective appearances by means of a transcendental guarantee [God], who himself must be verified by means of a proof. With this guarantee in hand, the tacit judgement that ideas really do correspond to objects can be saved, with the qualification that such judgements are justified only within the limits of clear and distinct perceptions.[24]

5. *Act of will.* We return here to the strict sense of act discussed in an earlier context where an ambiguity in the term "idea"was first introduced. In the broad sense, an act-feature indicates the specific positing regard in thought, i.e., "idea" in the material sense, in virtue of which any mode of thinking may be characterized

as having both a class of act-ideas and a correlative class of idea-objects. But *Principles* Part One, section 32 also distinguishes volition as another primary mode, along with the intellect, namely the operation of the will which comprises desire, aversion, assertion, denial, and doubt (CSM I, 204). Section 33 endorses the notion of abstention as long as what is perceived, and hence what is a subject-matter for judgment, is not resolved in a clear and distinct manner. Section 34 clearly indicates that an act of will is genetically posterior to clear and distinct seeing which has been activated with regard to all idea-objects which are held in suspense. "In order to make a judgement, the intellect is of course required. . . . But the will is also required so that, once something is perceived in some manner, our assent may then be given" (CSM I, 204). And section 43 builds in the notion of a divine guarantee of clear and distinct seeing according to which an act of will affirms just that perception which is real and positive and whose judgement is true. "It is certain . . . that we will never mistake the false for the true provided we give our assent only to what we clearly and distinctly perceive. I say that this is certain because God is not a deceiver, and so the faculty of perception which he has given us cannot incline to falsehood; and the same goes for the faculty of assent [volition], provided its scope is limited to what is clearly perceived" (CSM I, 207).

So much for the synthetic presentation, according to the order of topics, of the faculty of volition.[25] Where does it appear in the order of reasons as presented in the *Meditations*? If our analyses of the phases of methodical doubt are correct then this phase can only form a secure link in the chain of reasons once the previous phases have been activated. Indeed this step-by-step linkage has been true of phase three (abstention) and phase four (clear and distinct seeing). The "Third Meditation" opens with a taxonomy of those things which the meditator knows at that point to be true of himself as a thinking thing: "that is, a thing that doubts, affirms, denies, understands a few things, is ignorant of many things, is willing, is unwilling, and also which imagines and has sensory perceptions" (CSM II, 24).

The meditator has already discovered the meaning of some of these self-assigned features; but nothing so far has been disclosed about the meaning of willing and unwilling. The "Third Meditation" endorses the procedure of abstention from judgement, illuminates the criterion of clarity and distinctness, establishes the difference between formal and objective reality of an idea, and then demonstrates the existence of God as a surety for the criterion. Only then in the "Fourth Meditation" does volition come into its own, as the second of two concurrent causes (or principles) which, in conjunction with the first intellect, are requisite for affirming the truth of judgments. "The will consists simply in our ability to do or not to do something (that is, to affirm or deny, to pursue or avoid); or rather, it consists simply in the fact that when the intellect puts forward something . . . our inclinations are such that we do not feel that we are determined by any external force" (CSM II, 40). In other words, forces or causes which are external to the purely immanent data of consciousness, such as "blind impulse," "prejudices," and so forth, have been eliminated by the successive phases of doubting. It is essential, however, to recognize that it is always possible for one to be deceived or misled and hence to incline towards something for no good reason. Since human beings are imperfect and limited in their understanding, the scope of the will is always greater than the scope of the intellect, that is, one can always imagine something which cannot be made the content of a clear and distinct idea. Insofar as one is not inclined to either affirm or deny a judgment about things which fall under the will alone, one is merely *indifferent* (in Descartes' terms), and this is "the lowest grade of freedom." But in actively affirming that which is given in a clear and distinct idea or in adhering to that which one considers to be morally good, one fully exercises human freedom. The sequence of this linkage is made quite explicit in the next passage: "A great light in the intellect was followed by a great inclination in the will"; and further, "it is clear by the natural light that the perception of the intellect should always precede the determination of the will" (CSM II, 41).

6. *Attentional Regard.* The concept of attention, like that of act, thinking, and mode, has both a broad sense in which it appears in a variety of contexts in Descartes' works, and a strict sense in which it signifies a definite phase in the stepwise procedure of methodical doubt. In the broad sense, attention has the straight-forward connotation of mental effort, studied focus on a theme; it is what Descartes calls for on the part of the reader of the *Meditations*. In the strict sense, as the final phase in carrying through the cognitive exercise of doubting, attention signifies the gathering together of the previous five phases and the securing of each interlinked intuition; if this is done properly, then the whole intricate process does not have to be carried out again and again. Like the abandonment of prejudices, but unlike abstention and an act of will, attention in the broad sense appears in numerous places throughout the *Rules*. Attention is a positive, steadfast mental regard which goes hand in hand with intuition, "the indubitable conception of a clear and attentive mind which proceeds solely from the light of reason" (CSM I, 14). In conjunction with deduction, these two operations comprise a method, that is, "reliable rules which are easy to apply, and such that if one follows them exactly, one will never take what is false to be true or fruitlessly expend one's mental effort" (CSM I, 16). Attention as the devotion of one's mental efforts takes the form of concentration in the summary

of Rule V: "The whole method consists entirely in the ordering and arranging of the objects on which we must concentrate our mind's eye if we are to discover some truth" (CSM I, 20). However, this focal regard takes on a procedural character in Rule Seven where all the component intuitions in a deduction must be surveyed in a continuous sweep of thought. This is taken up again in the summary of Rule XI, which thus gives an inkling of the sort of cognition required in order to understand the whole of the *Meditations* as a complex of chains of reasons.

This broad sense of attention appears in numerous places in the *Meditations*, often phrased in a privative manner, that is, in terms of a mental condition when attention has been dissipated. "If one concentrates carefully, all this is quite evident by the natural light. But when I relax my concentration . . . I am aware of a certain weakness in me, in that I am unable to keep my attention fixed on one and the same item of knowledge at all times; but by attentive and repeated meditation I am nevertheless able to make myself remember it" (CSM II, 32, 43). Devoting one's mental efforts to the *Meditations* as cognitive exercises is exhausting, even for the most unprejudiced, sense-detached reader. The author cautions those who want to follow him on this path to "a new world" to read one Meditation each day and then to reread them with an enhanced focal regard, paying attention in a new way to what is accomplished by adhering to an order of reasons. The proper destination can only be reached in this manner, but if one should fall by the wayside, an appeal to the footholds already secured will put one back on the right track.

Husserl also would concede that these procedures require the utmost attentional effort. Holding the bracketed world in front of one's thematic regard through the maintenance of an abstentive posture demands "strenuous labours."[26] In the transition from the natural attitude, the proper procedure for the reduction would in some sense guarantee that it would hold in place throughout further analyses. "I can let my mind wander away from [these things] in a knowing of them which involves no conceptual thinking and which changes into a clear intuiting only with the advertence of attention" (Ideas I, 52). This is highly reminiscent of Descartes' comment in a closing statement at the end of Part One of the *Principles*: "Our mind is unable to keep its attention on things without some degree of difficulty and fatigue; and it is hardest of all for it to attend to what is not present to the senses or even to the imagination" (CSM I, 220).

For Descartes, the carrying through of the procedure of methodical doubt is not to be abandoned after one had arrived at the principle of clear and distinct seeing in the cognition of certain truths, nor is it essential to repeat all of the steps in order to return to the indubitable fulcral point of the cogito. Having attained attentional regard as the final phase, all of the previous steps are retained within it. In some sense, all of the prior links in the chain of reasons forged through an adequate intuition, are recapitulated in this attentive holding-in-regard. The synoptic or recapitulative characteristic of attention is crucially important for Descartes when he attempts to answer Arnauld's charge of circularity against the second proof of God's existence. "We are sure that God exists because we attend to the arguments which prove this; but subsequently it is enough for us to remember that we perceived something clearly in order for us to be certain that it is true" (CSM II, 171). A human being, imperfect and easily distracted, cannot persistently maintain an attentive grasp on an intuitive truth, and hence must have the capacity to fall back on what one knew to have been securely understood. However, as we showed in our discussion of Descartes' analysis of mathematical cognition, it is necessary that further higher-order claims have a foundation not just in the content of singular intuitions, but in the manner in which these intuitions are interlinked. With respect to positive statements made on the basis of metaphysical principles, this interlinking takes the form of deduction or inference. With respect to the procedure of methodical doubt, this interlinking in a manner which can be relied upon to obviate unforeseen deceptions and prejudices is the stepwise process of working through the phases of doubting. In a letter to Mesland of 1644, Descartes synopsizes the last four phases of doubt:

> I agree with you when you say that we can *suspend our judgement*; but I tried to explain in what manner this can be done. For it seems to me certain that a *great light in the intellect* is followed by a *great inclination in the will*; so that if we see *very clearly* that a thing is good for us, it is very difficult . . . to stop the *course of our desire*. But the nature of the soul is such that it hardly *attends* for more than a moment to a single thing. . . . Since we cannot always attend perfectly to what we ought to do, it is a good action to pay *attention* and thus ensure that our will follows so promptly the light of our understanding that there is no longer any indifference at all. (CSM III, 233–34; emphasis added)

The metaphorical sense of "light" in Descartes' appeal to "the light of reason" or "divine light" is particularly evident in the way in which attention is a matter of focal regard. At each stage in the stepwise achievement of another link in the argument, the meditator is in danger of straying from the path, of succumbing to the darkness and obscurity which lies on all sides and behind. "But this is an arduous undertaking, and a kind of laziness brings me back to normal life. . . . In the same way, I happily slide back into my old opinions and dread being shaken out of them . . . and that I shall have to toil not in the light, but amid the inextricable darkness of the problems I have now raised" (CSM II, 15).[27] This issue of being enlightened is also true for whatever is held within an attentional regard, lest it slip away from the clarity and distinctness which marks out an object of intuition. It is with very similar sentiments that Husserl describes the phenomenological concept of attention, which he says is usually compared to a spotlight. "The object of attention, in the specific sense, lies in the cone of more or less bright light; but it can also move into the penumbra and into the completely dark region. Though the metaphor is far from adequate to differentiate all the modes which can be fixed thus. . ." (Ideas I, 224).

Summary of the phases of doubt. First, it is the natural light, source of God-given eternal truths, which reveals that prejudices must be abandoned before one can begin to know where to look for a certain foundation for knowledge. Second, one must detach oneself from the world of the senses in order that one is not predisposed to locate this "where" in the world of extended things. Third, one must abstain from affirming or denying judgments based on sense-derived ideas, since these may be "infected" by this-worldly instabilities (such as illusions), from which one has just withdrawn and detached. Fourth, the stability and epistemic centrality established thereby allows one to clearly and distinctly grasp, in intellective seeing, whatever resists the destabilizing and decentering influence of the uncertain, of anything which is open to the least suspicion of doubt. Fifth, by an act of will, in our fullest freedom, one endorses all that which has been clearly and distinctly seen, or can be posited as such; one endorses also, as the source of this freedom, the perfection and infinitude of God. And finally, by holding in steadfast mental regard all the previous phases and their necessary connectedness, one not only retains the certainty of every prior intuition which forms a link in the chain or reasons, but also recapitulates these cognitive "moments" whenever a new concern calls forth the argumentative certainty which this chain endows.

These detailed analyses comprise an attempt to answer the question initially proffered by Gaston Berger: what is the nature of the mental act in which the soul grasps its ideas? In order to clear the ground for assaying an answer, it has been necessary to carefully untangle the dual sense of "idea" and to show that it is legitimate to discuss ideas as cognitive acts. Further, it has been our task to show that doubting is a distinct mode of thinking identified by an as-if positing of idea-objects. In a manner parallel to the necessary connections between idea-objects in their 'objective' reality, there are also necessary connections between act-ideas solely in terms of their "active" features. In conclusion, these latter connections have an ordered sequence of decisive phases which proceed from the banishment of all previously assumed beliefs about the world and the self to the certain, indubitable foundation upon which all conceivable knowledge claims are grounded.

6

METHODICAL DOUBT AND THE
PHENOMENOLOGICAL REDUCTION

In these investigations into the dimensions of convergence and divergence between Descartes and Husserl, one should pause here for a reconnaissance of
secured territory and future areas of inquiry. One should pause here because the
juncture of Cartesian doubt and the phenomenological reduction is an explicit
congruence of interest repeatedly acknowledged by Husserl himself and by
Husserlian commentators. It has been our contention all along that Descartes'
and Husserl's overall projects trace complementary trajectories—that is, both
before the methodological inception of epoché and after its purging (or reducing) of the world has been accomplished. We have argued that for both thinkers
it was through the study of mathematics that they came to realize the problem
of the rational stepwise securing of mathematical cognition in adequate intuition. This impelled Descartes on a course toward algebraic geometry whose
ontological ground was laid in the schema of simple and complex natures; and
stimulated Husserl in the articulation of a formal ontology of parts and wholes.

Descartes confronted the most fundamental problem posed by skepticism—
how it is possible to have certain knowledge of the natural world—by assuming
the skeptics' position and pushing it to the limit in order to overturn any possible
skepticism. Husserl's other great philosophical effort in his early period was
directed towards empirical psychology and its attempts to validate logical laws.
This was a position which Husserl characterized as an "absurd skepticism," that
is, a theoretical stance which denied the very possibility of theory in general, and
which he thoroughly refuted by revealing its internal contradictions. One of the
primary argumentative engines in this overthrow relied on a crucial conceptual
distinction between the act of judging and the judgment itself; or in more comprehensive terms, between the psychical act and its intentional correlate. We

have already shown that this fundamental phenomenological distinction, first disclosed by Brentano within the intentional structure of consciousness, was prefigured by Descartes in his discrimination of two senses of "idea," i.e., act-idea and idea-object. This dual notion is essential for Descartes to make sense of the "objective reality of an idea," the feature which characterizes the ontological status of constituents of the subjective domain.

In addition to Husserl's repeated insistence on the importance of the Cartesian point of departure, there is another reason to pause here, and that is the abundance, even superfluity, of commentaries on this avowed influence. With one exception,[1] these exegetes take for granted the accuracy, or at least relevance, of Husserl's references to Descartes' method of doubt and rarely seem willing to unpack what Descartes actually said—what was the Cartesian insight which so inspired Husserl? In other words, commentators report, explicate, and criticize what Husserl says about his relation to Descartes, but are not very illuminating about the relation between the two thinkers. In this regard, such analyses are often excruciatingly accurate about Husserl's interpretation of the significance of Descartes' project, but unenlightening about what is significant in Descartes' position. It seems that here we have an opportunity to remain faithful to the phenomenological method with regard to Husserl's Descartes as a theme, that is, to discriminate what Husserl says about Descartes and what is said in this saying. Husserl can rightfully claim, for instance, that the Cartesian way is "already given" in the philosophical tradition—it is something found as built into the natural-scientific attitude (for which, see below)—but this claim cannot remain as an unexamined given for us in this research.

Although there are numerous and diverse interpretations of Descartes' method of doubt, at least there is one well-defined textual locus in which it is deployed, the first two Meditations. Such is not the case with the phenomenological reduction which, like most of Husserl's other central concepts and strategies, underwent continuous revision and expansion. From its first appearance in the *Idea of Phenomenology* (1906), through *Ideas First Book* (1913), the lectures on *First Philosophy* (1923/24), the lectures on *Phenomenological Psychology* (1925), the *Cartesian Meditations* (1929), to the *Crisis of European Sciences* (1936), the reduction takes on many different guises and employs a burgeoning, almost bewildering, terminology. There is no one univocal definition or explanation of the phenomenological reduction, though to be sure, there are aspects of its orientation which remain unchanged.[2] It is simply not feasible to trace its chronological development, nor would that be, in any case, strictly relevant to our purpose. Neither would this purpose be served by an investigation of the consequences of the reduction as such, except insofar as it takes its point of departure from Descartes. Thus we will focus our attention on the Cartesian motivated reduction in its most mature version, in the *Cartesian Meditations*, and only then turn to Husserl's own criticisms of this way into phenomenology, in the *Crisis of European Sciences.*

Both Descartes and Husserl are strongly motivated to provide a basis for the autonomy of reason in *prima philosophia*, part of the original full title of Descartes' *Meditations* and of Husserl's lecture courses of 1923/24. That they would both formulate this in terms of an "all-embracing, universal science" is not a solecism, given their antipathy to then current natural-scientific theories. Descartes rejected the notion that any philosophy worthy of the name could be founded on the neo-Aristotelian or scholastic model of scientific inquiry, though he readily admitted that any Galilean-type physical science could be generated from, or at least be compatible with, his metaphysical first principles (CSM III, 41, 124).

Husserl rejected the possibility that a genuine science of consciousness could be developed from empirical psychology and anthropology. If anything, he averred, their findings would always be corrigible if they did not take account of the *a priori* foundation of the very realm of being which they were investigating. Whether it be "classical" natural science, a psycho-physiological model or (today) a neurological schema, such models are concerned with contingent matters-of-fact, which could be otherwise, in actual instances of cognition (even if multiplied billions of times), and not with the formal *a priori* character of that which is cognized, which is always the one truth (e.g., in mathematical axioms) grasped on many occasions. This science of consciousness is directed towards those structures of knowledge formation which *could not be otherwise*, and the articulation of those essential structures in universal principles. The natural-scientific model presupposes the general validity of such principles in order to construct arguments which have evidential, as opposed to merely probable, weight.

As early as the *Logical Investigations* (1900), Husserl had recognized the need for an entirely new methodological principle with which to begin philosophizing in a manner freed from the philosophical tradition and the natural-scientific model of explanation if one were to return to a point where *prima philosophia* could take its start. In the Introduction to Volume Two, he formulated his discernment of this pressing need in the following manner:

An epistemological investigation that can seriously claim to be "scientific" must . . . satisfy the principle of freedom from presuppositions. This principle, we think, only seeks to express the strict exclusion of all statements not permitting of a comprehensive phenomenological realization. . . . From the beginning, as at all later stages, its "scientific" statements involve not the slightest reference to real existence: no metaphysical, scientific and, above all, no psychological assertions can therefore occur among its premises. (LI, 263–65)

This brief characterization, in the third sentence, of the investigative domain sought for is a prefiguring of the phenomenological world of essences disclosed by the reduction. But the crucial technique, epoché or suspension, which brings forth 'eidetic' statements of this sort, was not discovered until 1905–6. Husserl's mature education in ancient skepticism occurs through his intensive reading of Raoul Richter's *Der Skeptizismus in der Philosophie* (1904) and Albert Goedeckmeyer's *Geschichte des griechischen Skeptizismus* (1905).[3] It is only after this date that the term epoché enters his working vocabulary, first in the lecture course of 1906–7, published as *The Idea of Phenomenology*.

This date also coincides with a profound personal crisis[4] with distinctive skeptical overtones. In a little-known personal diary, Husserl reflected on his rereading of his earlier work in mathematics and allied disciplines a decade before. "How immature, how naive and almost childlike that work appeared to me!" While laboring over projects in mathematics, he was "tormented by those incredibly strange realms": pure logic and consciousness. He had come to relinquish those aborted efforts and, wracked by doubt and unclarity, sought a deeper understanding of the philosophical foundations for a valid claim to an achievement of knowledge. Since this document has not previously been brought into the context of the inauguration of the notion of epoché and since it is a powerful declaration of intent in its own right, a crucial passage is here quoted at some length.

> Without getting clear on the general outlines of the sense, essence, methods and main points of a critique of reason, without having thought out, outlined, formulated and justified a general sketch of such a critique, I cannot live truly and sincerely. I have had enough of the torments of unclarity, of tottering back and forth in doubt. I have come to an inner stability. I know that this concerns high, even the highest matters. . . . I will, *I must*, approach these sublime goals, through self-sacrificing labour and purely disinterested absorption in the work. I am fighting for my life, and because of this have confidence that I shall be able to make progress. . . . Only one thing will fulfil me: I must come to clarity! Otherwise I cannot live. I cannot endure life without believing that I shall attain it—that I myself can, with clear eyes, actually look into the promised land. (Early, 494)

This account finds a quite similar parallel in Descartes' "discovery" of the heuristic value of skeptical doubt, though it is not possible to trace this to any particular skeptical author. As Stephen Gaukroger and others have observed, there is no real notice taken of doubt, and definitely not as a methodological principle, before the *Discourse* (1637). At the end of Part Three (CSM I, 126), he famously refers to two distinct phases in his previous life. For nine years, after the revelatory dream of November 1619, he roamed the world, "a spectator rather than an actor in all the comedies that are played out there." A further eight years elapsed since something happened which instilled in him a resolve to abandon those worldly pursuits and devote himself to philosophical reflection. This crucial juncture in the winter of 1628–29 has left little documentary evidence but we know that it coincided with his abandonment of the *Rules* and his strange encounter with the mysterious Chandoux.[5]

At the home of the papal nuncio, a number of learned men had been invited to hear a lecture by this itinerant savant on "the new philosophy." Everyone except Descartes was favourably impressed by what apparently was a sustained and clever attack on neo-Aristotelian scholastic philosophy using skeptical tropes to demolish its prime tenets. It seems that Descartes fell into a "brown funk" and could not be roused to give his opinion for some time. Eventually, to everyone's astonishment, the young cavalier held forth at some length on the utter groundlessness and abundant sophistry in the peroration which they had just heard. He showed that Chandoux wanted to accept probability as the standard of truth, that opposite conclusions were at least as probable, and that every skeptical trope could be countered with another, turning every truth into a falsehood. Cardinal Berulle was very impressed with this impromptu speech and persuaded Descartes to organize and publish his arguments on this matter—these were the seeds which bore fruit in the *Discourse on the Method*.

It is unfortunate that due to a lack of primary, corroborative testimony, this decisive episode is ignored or dismissed in a few sentences by most twentieth-century Descartes scholars. However, R. H. Popkin has forcibly argued[6] that the meeting with Chandoux was "a microcosm of the plight of the whole learned world," and the instigation for Descartes' philosophical search for a certain foundation for knowledge in the sciences. It is our contention that this episode synopsizes two aspects of this turning point. First, it highlights a sort of philosophical disgust that anyone adroit enough with skeptical tropes could turn any statement on its head, and hence inspire a repugnance towards skepticism per se. And second, it signals Descartes' abandonment of the mathematical research he had already undertaken as being irremediably undermined by its lack of proper metaphysical foundations.

Thus there are several substantive parallels in the philosophical motivations for Descartes and Husserl: (1) disenchantment with, even rejection of, previous mathematical investigations; (2) a skeptical and/or personal crisis directed at the very heart of their own philosophical enterprise; (3) the resolve to ground a *mathesis universalis* on irreducible first principles; (4) the discovery of the methodological technique of epoché or suspension, but detached from its allegedly inevitable telos—"Nothing is certain." These complementary motivations will impel both Descartes and Husserl towards intrinsically congruent conclusions:

(5) that a criterion for certain knowledge can be found entirely within the sub-jective or intentional domain: for Descartes this is the clarity and distinctness of an adequately grasped simple idea, for Husserl this is the self-givenness of that which appears in the appearance; (6) that this criterion is allowed to stand forth through a distinction internal to the cogitatum qua cogitatum, that between the psychical act and its 'objective' correlate; and (7) that what makes possible the reflective cognition of (5) and (6) is the transcendental ego, which is not to be confused with an empirical or mundane ego.[7]

With regard to this last point, it will be shown that it is a serious, if almost unavoidable, error to equate the ego in the Cartesian "ego cogito" with the mind in the "Sixth Meditation," the mind which with the body forms a substantial union. In this connection, Descartes explicitly refers to a consciousness which is *transparent* to an already unified and unifying ego (CSM II, 105)—the notion of transparent insight is crucial to both thinkers, as we shall see. The focus of this present study is on the transition from (4) to (5), from the technique of suspension to the criteria of certain judgment; this is accomplished through a methodical procedure which has an epistemological origin and metaphysical repercussions. Such an interpretative uncovering cannot be achieved by follow-ing only Husserl's analysis and critique of the Cartesian epoché, but must allow Descartes' own arguments to inform a complete account of the phenomenologi-cal reduction's originary impetus.

One initial problem which faces the Husserlian researcher is how many reductions there are and what they are called.[8] That there is more than one reduction is without question—references to "a further reduction" are common, whatever the textual source. Any reduction is usually characterized as total and universal, though some are enacted once and for all, others are brought in and out of play as the occasion demands. Throughout the period of the *Cartesian Meditations* and *Phenomenological Psychology,* Husserl had focused his atten-tion on two ways into phenomenology: the Cartesian and the psychological. By the time of the *Crisis*, earlier glimmers, even brief sketches of a third way, sometimes referred to as "logical" or "ontological," had reached fruition and detailed elaboration.[9] Here the third way from the lifeworld shares equally large attention with the way from psychology, completely overshadowing the previous favorite (the Cartesian) now relegated to the stature of an historically ground-breaking, but abortive and misleading, attempt to disclose the "nature" of the subjective domain. It is not to our purpose to explore the other two ways except insofar as they help to explain Husserl's disenchantment with Descartes and the consequent criticisms which he brings against the Cartesian epoché.

In any case, what first appears to be a bewildering variety of reductions, at least in terms of what they are called, becomes much more straight-forward when they are situated within the three different ways. Thus in *The Crisis of European Sciences,* Part IIIA, "The Way from the Lifeworld," the reductions are designated (1) objective-science, (2) transcendental, and (3) intersubjective (Crisis, 172, 79). In Part IIIB, "The Way from Psychology," they are (1) psychological, (2) transcendental, and (3) intersubjective (Crisis, 256, 59). "The Cartesian Way," discussed in a brief section of Part II, distinguishes only two: (1) natural-sciences, or just plain science, and (2) transcendental, with no third stage (Crisis, 78–80). This last grouping should not be taken to indicate that Husserl claims that Descartes himself enacted a transcendental epoché, but that one can enact such an epoché from the reduced Cartesian standpoint. This two-stage reduction is indicative of the later Husserl's disavowal of the Cartesian path, for in the *Cartesian Meditations,* the first two paths do indeed lead to the third, meticulously unfolded in Husserl's "Fifth Meditation." Another well-known reduction, the "eidetic," has not been ignored in this outline, but is postponed until a proper context makes its significance relevant.

Several points should be readily noticeable: that each way begins with a "bracketing" of that theoretical field which it has made thematic; that each then proceeds to a transcendental reflection which reveals the necessary condition (within the subject) for the possibility of knowledge achievements; and that each returns to the pregiven world as one shared by other sense-giving and sentient beings. Only the Cartesian way falls short, in that by making a "leap" directly to the hypothesis of a nonempirical or supramundane ego, it arrives "empty of content" (Crisis, 155). Where does one go from here, since our guide Descartes has disappeared? Back to the beginning, remaining true to the injunction that one must always be an absolute beginner and take nothing for granted.

In *First Philosophy* (1923/24), Husserl looks both backwards to *Ideas First Book* (1913) and forward to the *Cartesian Meditations* (1929) in historically situating Descartes' project in terms of the skeptical legacy. For Husserl, the Greek skeptics, Plato, and Descartes are the "three great beginners in the entire history of Western philosophy" (HUS VII, 7). As we saw in chapter 2, Husserl was greatly concerned with the skeptical undercurrents of nineteenth-century empirical psychology, proponents of which remained oblivious to the "hidden truth," the "eternal significance" of the original skeptical challenge. This challenge proceeded on two fronts, though from completely divergent and incompatible epistemological standpoints (hence its enigmatic "naturalness"). On the one hand, skeptics argued vehemently for the relativity and instability of subjective appearances, while restricting all presumed knowing to the sensory realm; as such, they questioned the natural thesis of the true being of the experienced world. On the other hand, they rejected as unintelligible a reflective thesis that there was a hidden, underlying reality behind these appearances and thus rejected the notion that the search for certain knowledge meant discovering a criterion of correspondence between the hidden and the apparent reality.

> For the first time the naive pre-givenness of the world becomes problematic, and from there the world itself according to the possibility in principle of its cognition and according to the fundamental sense of its being-in-itself. In other words, for the first time the real world-whole, and in consequence the whole of possible objectivity in general, becomes transcendentally considered as the object of possible knowledge, possible consciousness in general. It becomes considered in relation to subjectivity. (HUS VII, 59)

The skeptical challenge turned the very concept of objectivity into a problem which could not be accounted for by any theory whose truth condition for assertions, including those about the intelligibility of objective being, rested on a hypothetical correspondence between an adequate cognition and an unknown reality. The counterposition camouflaged in this charge of *petitio principii* was the radical insight that the criterion for certain knowledge was not to be found in an external bridging theorem but in an internal fulfilling (of evidence) procedure. Until the time of Descartes, skepticism was an entirely negative force, since it focused on where the criterion was not to be found—it was a "hydra ever growing new heads." Its progeny were more truculent and garrulous than ever by the early seventeenth century, nourished on theologians' ambivalence regarding the standard for correct doctrinal interpretation. "Modernity begins with Descartes because he first sought to theoretically satisfy the indubitable truth that lay at the basis of the skeptical arguments. He was the first to make theoretically his own the universal field of being, the very one which the extreme skeptical negations presupposed, and turn the argument back on them, namely on their own certain knowing subjectivity" (HUS VII, 61).

Descartes famously begins this overturn by stating that since he has found to be false much of what he took to be true and that what he has built out of these alleged truths is highly dubious, it is time to demolish everything. He will thus interrogate all of his cherished opinions and beliefs to see whether they can withstand skeptical queries. Not only is he willing to grapple with any of the available skeptical arguments which might impugn these opinions, he even adds one of his own making, the fiction of the evil genius. Before considering his technique of withholding assent, it is as well to pause here and examine his starting point on this long and arduous journey. What many commentators on Cartesian doubt neglect to point out is that, in addition to the philosophical thesis that what he has accepted until now has been acquired either from or through the senses, he has tacitly accepted the natural thesis of the world's objective being. All of his various opinions, though purged via the stages of methodical doubt, are still governed by an all-inclusive higher-order conviction in the objective reality of the world as it is given in appearances.

Let us clarify this point of departure for the phenomenological reduction in its Cartesian setting in the hope that thus, in this case anyway, we can have some idea of where it can be heading. No matter which stage in Husserl's writings one focuses on, he explicitly situates this starting point in Descartes' method of universal doubt, and more specifically in the attempt to doubt. There is a crucial distinction made here by Husserl and then employed diligently in further reflections which find a *prima facie* equivalent in a distinction made by Descartes, ignorance of which led several of his critics in the wrong direction. To attempt to doubt everything, to put oneself in a position where anything that admits of the least doubt is considered as though it were entirely false is not to consider everything as indeed false; it is not to negate or deny the (being of) the world. This is clearly stated in the first paragraph of the "Second Meditation": "Anything which admits of the slightest doubt I will set aside just *as if* I had found it to be wholly false" (CSM II, 16). Since this is such a pivotal and commonly mistaken statement, let us quote the original Latin: "removendo scilicet illud omne quod vel minimum dubitationis admittit, nihilo secius *quam si* omnino falsam esse comperissem" (AT VII, 24).

The as-if character of doubting as a mode of cognition (what Husserl calls a modification of the originary positing) is clearly indicated by the use of *quam si* in this passage and was prefigured at the end of the "First Meditation," where the meditator says that he will "deceive myself by pretending *[esse fingam]* for a time that these former opinions are utterly false and imaginary." In the "Seventh Replies," Descartes was thoroughly exasperated by Bourdin's relentless misquoting of his original statements, attributing to him claims which he never made, and remarks that overlooking the notion of "pretense" completely changes the purpose and scope of doubting. "Now my critic has ignored most of this passage [and] . . . what is more, for the word 'pretend' he has substituted 'maintain and believe,' and indeed 'believe' to the extent of taking the 'opposite of what is doubtful' and affirming it as true" (CSM II, 356). Although the original sense of *fingere* is "to form or shape," in classical Latin its broader connotations embraced the notions of "suppose, consider, imagine." However, Descartes has quite precise terms for each of these notions, and *fingere* is reserved for "pretend or invent"; its past participle is *fictum* from whence the English "fiction." This may seem a curious etymological digression, but it is in fact essential to one of the strands of the principal theme of this chapter—that Cartesian doubt is not a world-denial or negation, but a procedural requirement to establish the threshold of immunity to being put out of play through the epoché. One critic (and great admirer) of Descartes who places acute emphasis on doubt as denial and rejection, instead of on *suspension* of that which is considered doubtful, is Husserl himself.[10]

In the standard philosophical vocabulary of the late sixteenth and early seventeenth century, the Latin word for the Greek *epoché* was *suspensio*, for example, in Pierre Gassendi's neoskeptical empiricism and translations of Sextus Empiricus; the French was *suspendre* or *surseance*, for example, in Montaigne's immensely popular *Essays*. It is no accident or puzzling oversight that, aside from one later emendation in the French text, there is no occurrence of the term *suspensio* in the *Meditations*. It is a common assumption that since the overall message (or purpose) of skeptical epoché is there, the precise concept which is its vehicle must also be found in the text—but this is not obviously the case. The one exception to his studied avoidance of the term is on the last page of the "First Meditation," where Descartes remarks that if it is not (so far) in my power to know any truth, "I shall at least do what is in my power, that is resolutely guard against assenting to any falsehoods" (AT VII, 23). The French translation of this passage slightly expands on what is legitimately within his power before expressing his resolve to carry on: "à tout le moins il est en ma puissance de *suspendre* mon jugement" (AT IX, 18). It seems likely that the only other occurrence of this term in Descartes' entire *oeuvre* is much later in the *Principles*, Part I, section 39: "dont nous ne pouvions douter pendant une *suspension* si générale" (AT IX(B), 41).[11]

Let us note, in passing, that although Husserl usually employs "epoché" and "reduction" in a synonymous fashion, such that it is easy to read one for the other in any given passage, it is possible to tentatively discriminate between these two terms. Epoché signifies the initial moment (dependent part) of "bracketing," the putting-in-place of brackets in order to take out of play what is contained in the brackets; it is thus the necessary higher-order "act" which initiates the reduction.[12] Husserl's original term for this is *Einklammerung*, a technical mathematical operation which places a number in brackets |1|, such that it has neither positive nor negative value; if no value is indicated for an unbracketed number, the value is always assumed to be positive, +1. The analogy here is then quite obvious: one always assumes a positive "value" for the natural thesis of the world, viz. that it does indeed exist "outside" our consciousness of it. This mathematical analogy will be of some help when we come to consider the meaning of the eidetic reduction. A brief overview of the interrelations between these moments reveals that the first stage of the reduction places brackets around some apparent thing, e.g., this table t1, so that it no longer has a presumptive thetic value, |t1|; the second stage operates through the technique of free variation and transforms the bracketed concrete 'object' into a variable, $|x_{t1}|$; the third stage seeks to discern the invariable within all the invariant occurrences, that is, to disclose the *essence* of "table," |e$_{tl}$|, still deprived of any presuppositions about its existence independent of a possible consciousness.

Searching for our own point of departure from which to come to grips with the necessity of the points of departure which Descartes and Husserl have blazoned as distinctively their own, we could not do better than to follow the order of reasons which they both enjoin, and thus proceed little by little from the simple to the more complex. One who is about to begin to philosophize, finds himself or herself already living in a natural world; what this means can be made clear by "simple meditations which can best be carried out in the first person singular" (Ideas I, 51); "Philosophy (wisdom) is the philosopher's quite personal affair. It must arise as *his* wisdom . . . a knowledge for which he can answer from the beginning, and at each step, by virtue of his own absolute insights" (CM, 2). Surrounded by things, persons, values, traditions, customs, and a corpus of received opinions about all of these things, what underscores their appearance is an unexamined belief, a naive acceptance, in the being of the world just as it is given in one's natural living. For those who are motivated to philosophize, that is, for those who have already stepped back from this living and made of it a possible theme of inquiry, the skeptical challenge transforms the inquiry into a problematic. It specifically disassociates any query about the world in itself being answered by an appeal to the ways in which worldly things appear to the questioner. No certain answers are forthcoming, only probable or practical rules-of-thumb which are at least preferable to remaining in an aporia, baffled about how to carry on.

But does the philosopher not have, as a matter of fact, a theoretical model, namely the natural sciences, which would provide guidance in ascertaining what sort of evidence a belief must have in order to at least qualify as possible knowledge; and moreover provide a formal procedure which permits the interlinking of belief statements in a valid manner? Descartes does indeed agree that there is such a theoretical model, that the *Principles* are designed in the "geometrical fashion," but that this has to be purified of prejudices and preconceptions in order to be founded again on a more solid basis. On several occasions he argues that specific results of his physiological investigations into the workings of the human body support his epistemological claims, for example, in his theory of visual perception; in addition, he argues that his general metaphysical principles issue directly in his conception of natural physical laws. Husserl, on the other hand, is not going to acquiesce in an established model of scientific theory-building and instead argues that the "matter-of-factness" of natural scientific theory is itself already given as another worldly objectivity, thus making it open to standard skeptical criticisms. Another way to articulate their diametrically opposed attitudes is to say that Descartes revolted against the unscientific approach to issues of legitimate knowledge, whereas Husserl rejected any pro-scientific attitude to the 'nature' of consciousness as mistaken from the very beginning.

Descartes was repulsed by the pseudoscientific character of then-current studies in the art of memory, anatomy, optics, and the false sciences (such as alchemy and astrology), so disparaged in Part One of the *Discourse* (CSM I, 113–15). His previous works *The World (or Treatise on Light)* and the *Treatise of Man,* composed between 1629 and 1633, explicitly endorse Galileo's model of the cosmos and his mathematical method of demonstration; only Galileo's condemnation prevented Descartes from attempting to secure their publication. In contrast, Husserl revolts against the natural-scientific model itself as one which is not suitable for investigations into the nature and structure of consciousness, an orientation most notoriously displayed in psychologists' efforts to derive logical laws from empirical facts about human psychical constitution. For Husserl, Galileo's (and Descartes') mathematical objectivization of nature was the source of a false theoretical equilibration between descriptive statements about psychical states of affairs and explanatory statements in scientific language about the alleged "origin and validity" of those states of affairs.

Husserl thus argues from an orientation which is opposed to Descartes' attitude toward science; for the phenomenologist, the natural sciences are already given to the philosopher's reflection as knowledge achievements which have to be accounted for in terms of the scientist's cognitive ability to reach these "ideal" objects. This can only be accomplished in an incorrigible manner by the elaboration of a formal *a priori* science of consciousness. C. W. Harvey is quite right in saying that Husserl does not always "distinguish sharply enough between the positing theses of the natural attitude and the positing theses of the natural scientific attitude."[13] But Husserl at least once overtly makes this distinction, in the *Crisis of European Sciences* (140–45) in the course of one of his numerous redactions of the stages or steps in the phenomenological reduction. Nevertheless, Pierre Thevanez, in an otherwise stimulating and provocative article, goes too far in his *précis* of their respective orientations toward natural science.

> Descartes defined his ambition in reference to an uncertain science and philosophy, and his reform aimed initially at making a clean slate, then at remaking science *ab ovo.* It was a question of assuring the basis of an unshakeable certitude of a corner-stone for the edifice of future science. . . . Husserl, on the other hand, found himself in the presence of a secure science, a completed science, in possession of its practical usefulness and its uncontested results. . . . The crisis of science did not touch its results but only its foundations and its meaning.[14]

It is then my decision, as the philosopher engaged in this activity, to no longer acquiesce in the tacit presupposition that the world exists as an absolute datum. The philosopher does so in the complete freedom to withhold his assent: "the attempt to doubt universally belongs to the realm of our perfect freedom." If this attempt does not have universal scope, it undercuts its own radical ambition, since insofar as it only counters particular skeptical tropes, it leaves the general thesis of the world's being intact. Husserl synopsizes the general thesis thus: one finds the actual world as a "factually existent actuality and also accepts it as it presents itself to me as factually existing. No doubt about or rejection of data *belonging to the natural world* alters in any respect *the general positing* which characterizes the natural attitude" (Ideas I, 57).

Descartes also acknowledges that the first two stages of doubt—illusions of sensory experience and delusions of dreaming states—are processes in the accepted natural world, that when stricken out are not enough to overcome the criterion which excludes a minimum of uncertainty. Even if these errors are corrected, the objective status of the source of the errors is left unresolved; only the fiction of the evil genius can cast doubt on the being of the world itself, the only feasible source for illusions and delusions. Descartes thus indicts the prime suspect: "What is my reason for thinking that [ideas] resemble these things? Nature has apparently taught me to think this . . . [that is] a spontaneous impulse leads me to believe it, not that its truth has been revealed to me by some natural light" (CSM II, 26).

Descartes' discussion throughout the first three Meditations of the preconceived opinions with which he began his inquiry are hold-overs from his pretheoretical (or prereflective) starting point within naive experience. Each of them is taken up, according to the order of reasons, and then examined from the purified position secured through the establishment of the first certain truth, the cogito. Nevertheless, these opinions and beliefs (which Gassendi chided him for retaining) have not been purged or vaporized by hyperbolic doubt. Insofar as they were constituents of his pretheoretical worldly knowledge, they were inexplicit and unthematic; but methodical doubt serves to make them thematic and to explicate their origin in the natural standpoint. "Whereas Cartesian epoché is prompted by the defect of the teaching of nature, Husserl's epoché thematizes the very naturalness of the natural attitude."[15] "We can now proceed with the potential and inexplicit positing precisely as we can with the explicit judgment positing. One procedure, possible at any time, is the attempt to doubt universally which Descartes carried out for an entirely different purpose with a view toward bringing out a sphere of absolutely indubitable being. We start from here, but at the same time emphasize that the attempt to doubt universally shall serve us only as a methodic expedient" (Ideas I, 58).

Here "methodic expedient" functions as an express route for the way into phenomenology, one which will be derogated later in favor of more incremental approaches. Where the first divergence occurred at Descartes' presumptive and Husserl's nonpresumptive attitudes toward natural science, here a second divergence erupts, that is, with regard to the fact that this attempt to doubt effects an "annulment" of positing per se. For Husserl, this does not mean a change of a positing into a counterpositing, a rendering of the positing as merely possible, undecided, or doubtful—"Rather it is something wholly peculiar." Descartes, in contrast, employs as a "methodic expedient" a type of skeptical *isosthenia*: allowing the counter-positing to assume an equal-weighted claim in order then to withhold assent from either claim. He achieves this by turning his will in "the completely opposite direction until the weight of preconceived opinion is counterbalanced and the distorting influence of habit no longer prevents my judgment from perceiving things correctly" (CSM II, 15).

Bourdin in the "Seventh Objections," as was his habit, misinterpreted this statement and declared that Descartes should thus have felt compelled to assent to the opposite, since if doubt had shown that p was false, then surely not-p was true. To which Descartes responded that "I did not mean that I should regard either side as true, or set this principle up as the basis of a system of certain knowledge" (CSM II, 313). Bourdin misses precisely the *quasi*-positional character of universal doubt which modifies not the belief qua belief, whose eventual truth-status will ultimately be resolved, but instead modifies (puts out of play) the presumed conditions under which one can know that the belief is true or false. Nevertheless, this is not the criticism which Husserl introduces here, for the second divergence revolves around the two-sidedness of the phenomenological epoché. In terms of its act-character, the putting-out-of-action remains in place as a permanent modification of conscious regard; and in terms of its 'objective,' what has been stricken out remains held in the suspension. Let us call these two aspects, the parenthetic act (of the epoché as moment) and the thesis within the parenthesis.

In what we have continued to refer to as the quasi-positing of doubt, i.e., considering in the mode of *as-if* false, the positing indicates the directedness towards something which is intrinsic to the intentional structure of consciousness (cf. Ideas I, 72). However, as pointed out in chapter 5, this is not another mode of cognition in the same way that imagination, memory, and perception are modes. Whether or not my memory or phantasy of x adequately represents the remembered or phantasized x, it still *seems* to me that my memory or phantasy of x is such-and-such; my conscious intending can itself be put out of action. The as-if feature serves to contrast this type of directedness from all acts of positing, and that means to posit the being of an 'object' precisely in the manner of the 'objective' reality of an idea. In other words, the intentional 'object' of conscious regard cannot be given as dubious in the way that it can be given as imaginary or memorial. As such, universal doubt is a reflective act of consciousness which takes other cognitive acts as idea-objects, including the inexplicit aspect of the idea-object which brings with it the object itself as existent; "our understanding of other things always involves understanding them *as if* they were existing things" (CSM II, 83).

What is it then that is put out of action or stricken out when one adopts this quasi-positional attitude, considering some thing as if it were false? Not the reality of the idea, for that is made the 'object' of a higher order act; Husserl remarks that the phrase "putting out of action" is literally apropos here, since it relates to the act-feature. What would allow the cogitatum to remain while the mode of the cogitatio is altered? Only that it no longer brings with it the general thesis of the objective in-itself of the world towards which all positings are allegedly oriented. Just as the act-phrase is better suited to the noetic aspect of consciousness, so the "metaphor" of parenthesis is more suited to the objectual or noematic domain (Ideas I, 60). This then is Husserl's clearest terminological expansion of the sense of phenomenological epoché: "The positing undergoes a modification: while it in itself remains what it is, we so to speak, "put it out of action," we "exclude it," we "parenthesize it." It is *still there*, like the parenthesized in the parentheses, like the excluded outside the context of inclusion. We can also say: the positing is a mental process, but we make no use of it. . . . [It is] a specifically peculiar mode of consciousness" (Ideas I, 59; cf. 113).

The etymological meaning of parenthesis is "place beside with": the thesis of the world's being remains "beside with" the alteration which it undergoes in the epoché.[16] The being of the world precisely as it is given to consciousness and thus all those appearances which are or could be illusory, doubtful, etc., are considered as indicative of just those manners of givenness in which appearing things appear. A clear-headed understanding of this is absolutely vital for an appreciation of the fundamental orientation of phenomenology in general. That a stick looks bent in water, that the contents of dreams seem like veridical experiences, and so forth, are not problems to be overcome by a theory of knowledge, but indicators of the way (the "how") in which things could not possibly be given otherwise. Efforts to correct or adjust for their not appearing in manners which are self-evidentially certain is to import a theoretical preconception about the relation between phenomena and the things themselves which could only be justified by an appeal to an unknowable reality.

Later in the *Crisis*, Husserl chides Descartes for the fact that he takes it for granted that the phenomena point to a realm of the in-itself, though it can deceive us, and that there must be a rational method for dispelling this deception. Descartes hopes to achieve this through the purging of methodical doubt, but should not this taken-for-grantedness and this reconciliation itself be bracketed through the epoché? Despite his radical, groundbreaking procedure, Descartes has a goal in advance,[17] before his meditations began, in virtue of which methodical doubt and the isolation of the cogito are means to that end. "I see that without any effort I have now finally got back to where I wanted" (CSM II, 22). True radicalism "is not achieved by merely deciding on the epoché, on the radical withholding of [judgment on] all that is pregiven, on all prior validities of what is in the world; *the epoché must seriously be and remain in effect*" (Crisis, 79).

The converse aspect of this second divergence in terms of modification of the reflective act-mode which would maintain the thesis within brackets, i.e., transforming acceptance of the world's being into an acceptance-phenomenon, is that the modification cannot be relinquished. Descartes acknowledges the issue of the persistence of universal doubt and considers its avoidance a prime concern. If anything, he thought that to maintain such skepticism beyond its necessary employment would lead to hyperbolic doubt which was counterproductive and would obviate efforts to establish practical results in the sciences. The reason why universal doubt does not have to remain in force is due largely to the fact that, since the cogito has been secured in certain intuition, it provides a fulcral point from which to return to the natural world.

Having established this exemplary first truth and the mode of its adequate grasping in insightful attention, the memory of this securing and all its subsequent enchained truths prevents doubt from re-infecting one's newly acquired knowledge. "So long as we attend to a truth which we perceive very clearly, we cannot doubt it. But when, as often happens, we are not attending to any truth in this way, then even though we remember that we have previously perceived many things very clearly, nevertheless there will be nothing which we may not justly doubt as long as we do not know that whatever we clearly perceive is true" (CSM II, 309; cf. II, 100, 171).

The significance of the cogito as first truth in the order of reasons is to disclose an epistemic criterion within the purified domain of 'objective' being in order to then be able to employ it in proving the validity of other nonobjective claims made about the relation between the posited as such and a "reality" to which it makes reference. Since this relation holds between the formal cause of the idea and its 'objective' being in the intellect, further knowing is open to possible doubt which can only be corrected by recourse to the prior criterion. The disparity in Descartes' and Husserl's respective notions of evidence points both to the potential inadequacy of Cartesian evidence—which he indeed recognized in searching for a further guarantee in divine veracity—upon which Husserl's notion of apodicticity supervenes *and* also points to the necessity of the phenomenological reduction remaining in force throughout every subsequent analysis.

> Any evidence is a grasping of something itself that is, or is thus, a grasping in the mode "it itself," with full certainty of its being, a certainty that accordingly excludes every doubt. But it does not follow that full certainty excludes the conceivability that what is evident could subsequently *become doubtful.* . . . An *apodictic* evidence, however, is not merely certainty of the [states of] affairs evident in it; rather it discloses itself, to a critical reflection, as having the *signal peculiarity* of being at the same time the *absolute unimaginableness* (inconceivability) of their non-being, and thus excluding in advance every doubt as 'objectless,' empty. (CM. 15–16; emphasis altered)

Persistence of Previous Formal Ontological Schemas

Lest it seem that these conjunctures are nothing but a rhizome of divergences, we can point to one critically overlooked continuity: the persistence of a prior convergence on the formal ontological level.[18] The simple-complex schema first articulated in Rule XII is consistently appealed to by the meditator throughout the stages of methodical doubt. In a similar way, Husserl makes repeated use of part-whole theory in his unpacking of the reduction, and does so not as a reconstruction of Descartes' course but as a procedure which he explicitly discriminates from that course. A succinct synopsis[19] of Descartes' continual reliance on simple-complex natures through the process of doubt may be helpful.

The process of universal doubt moves from the complex to the simple and is accomplished according to the order of reasons. Not only do the senses sometimes deceive us, but all sensory perceptions may perhaps be only the contents of dreams. Dreams are imaginary only because they arbitrarily combine simpler (but not purely simple) components, but these components can only be taken as real since they are taken as the simplest and thus escape the possible artificiality of composition. However, these elements are actually composites themselves (e.g., eyes, heads, hands, etc.) and since it is conceivable that they are imaginary, they are thus open to being doubted. It is thus necessary to proceed to the ontological level of the elements of those elements (shape, number, quantity, etc.) that are entirely simple and hence escape the arbitrariness of composition. These are not open to being doubted since any cognitive grasp of shape, number, or quantity must be given in a clear and distinct seeing, and such ideas are by their very nature given with evidential certainty.

Analysis of ideas in the stepwise manner advocated by the meditator considers the presumed origin of those ideas, although it has not yet uncovered the 'objective' reality intrinsic to ideas. Descartes has already made an important dichotomy in this respect between adventitious and artificial ideas, on the one hand, which are composites and have an admixture of external qualities; and simple ideas, on the other, which can be either sensible or intellective. All those ideas which are irreducible or simple natures, whether they are intellective or sensible, are necessarily indubitable, since they cannot be artificial. These are the first notions, or immediate givens, which Descartes will later argue are innate and revealed by the natural light. At this point in the chain of reasons, only the simple intellective natures are retained in his explication of the objective reality of ideas. After reviewing the features of sense deception in Appendix VI of the original *Crisis* (HUS VI, 403–5), Husserl allows that even if all appearances are only a dream, even if no experience corresponds with "reality" as such, the status of mathematical propositions cannot be invalidated. Since there seems to be no ground to doubt the validity of *a priori* knowledge, the problem emerges when the philosopher or scientist wants to employ mathematical knowledge as the basis for judgments about the necessary form of regularities in nature.

For Husserl, the universal depriving of acceptance of the general thesis does not leave us confronting nothing. On the contrary, we gain possession of something through the epoché: "my pure living" and the subjective processes which comprise this, i.e., the universe of phenomena and the pure ego for whom these exist (CM, 20). This purified or reduced ego is not a piece (independent part) of the world, nor is the world or any worldly thing a piece of my ego, found in my consciousness as a really inherent part of it, as a complex of data of sensations or a complex of acts (CM, 26). The proper task of reflection is to explicate what can be found in the original subjective process, now altered in such a manner that it exposes the intentional structure of all such prereflective processes. Thus reduced, the ego is fully aware that the experience of an objectual perception includes all of its constituent moments (dependent parts) which are prefigured in the horizon of not-yet-given but expected perceptions. These comprise both the moments of the perceiving act itself and the moments of the perceived 'object' (CM, 26).

A transcendental descriptive analysis can start with nothing other than the ego cogito, which is parallel to the disclosure of the empirical ego in all its concrete fullness. But it must not confuse one inquiry with the other and begin with a physicalistic or reductionist account of sensation. If the analyst does so, then "In advance . . . one misinterprets conscious life as a complex of data of external and (at best) internal sensuousness; then one lets form-qualities *[gestalts]* take care of combining such data into wholes." To avoid the inevitable problem of an atomistic version of immaterial contents, one then fallaciously inserts "the theory that the forms or configurations are founded on these data necessarily and the wholes are therefore prior in themselves to the parts" (CM, 38). In contrast to this, phenomenological inquiry into consciousness concerns two aspects (the noetic and the noematic) which belong together inseparably and which are present in all conscious acts combined according to a unique process, that of synthesis. Synthetic structures of possible combinations give unity to single cogitations in themselves as concrete wholes and in relation to one another, i.e., as founded moments of the basic form of all possible syntheses, internal time consciousness.

The Cartesian Hinge and the Husserlian Hinge: The Gate into Phenomenology

We are at a fulcral point in Descartes' and Husserl's arguments from which many other points of divergence will emerge: the theme of the cogito as *res cogitans* versus the cogitatum qua cogitatum; the transcendence of God and the natural light which also must be bracketed; the empirical ego and its "shadow" versus the genuine transcendental ego, and so forth. As we have seen, there is arguably some notion of intentionality in Descartes' "Third Meditation," and as we shall see, a glimpse of the transcendental ego, but he touches on these notions in the way that he remarks that a finite mind may grasp the infinite (CSM II, 81); in other words, he grasps (*prendre*) a simple idea, but does not completely understand (*comprendre*) this ego.

Throughout Husserl's writings on the Cartesian point of departure, there are references to a "threshold" or "gate"[20]—a gate is a transition point which gives on to a way or path. Husserl has meditated along with Descartes until the end of the "Second Meditation," from the explication of the method of universal doubt to the disclosure of the cogito, after which there is little if any direct commentary in Husserl's lectures. The opening of the "Third Meditation" is a *hinge* in the entire structure of the *Meditations* as it follows the order of reasons, a hinge which occurs within an overall coherent framework.[21] Beyond this juncture Descartes begins a return journey, recapitulating what has been lost through methodical doubt by means of what has been gained through the double guarantee of divine veracity, at one terminus, and clear and distinct seeing at the other. The point in Husserl's own founding of the phenomenological project which approximates this Cartesian juncture, also follows the order of cognitions and signals a hinge, though not in the sense of a refolding upon itself, rather in the sense of a continuous unfolding.

What happens here at these two hinge-points? Why does one hinge pivot (so to speak) on the other? The answer to this will also lead eventually to an answer to one of the questions we began with—why does Husserl abandon the Cartesian way into phenomenology? The name of the gate upon which the hinge pivots is *transcendence*: before this gate Descartes balked, beyond this gate lies the domain of transcendental phenomenology. Moreover, beyond this gate many of Husserl's students (and current critics) will not venture. Much of the very recent rapprochement between the two "traditions" of analytic and continental philosophy is centered around Husserl's work before this turning point, as though it were not conceivable that problems generated *before* this gate can only be resolved *after* it has been crossed. In any case, Descartes "stands on the threshold of the greatest of all discoveries . . . yet he does not grasp its proper sense, the sense namely of transcendental subjectivity, and so he does not pass through the gateway that leads into genuine transcendental philosophy" (CM, 24–25; cf. FTL, 227). This acknowledgement is later reworked by Husserl in these startling terms: "The original Cartesian motif [is] that of pressing forward through the hell of an unsurpassable, quasi-skeptical epoché toward the gates of the heaven of an absolutely rational philosophy" (Crisis, 77)—this extraordinary statement will need to be unpacked in the last chapter.

If the notion of transcendence can be clarified here, our study will also be able to press forward to a rational understanding of why this one path is so inextricably linked to the Cartesian starting point and at the same time leads off in an entirely unexpected direction. Within the confines of the current topical study, we can only begin to make clear a highly charged and profound problematic—but if we begin in the right way at least this beginning won't have to be engaged again. In all phenomena, strictly as "showing-forth," some thing is given to consciousness and always given in some determinate manner, i.e., in the "how" of its givenness. The exact delineation of the intentional structure of consciousness allows one to discriminate the psychical act from its 'object' insofar as its 'object' is immanent to consciousness, irrespective of course as to whether or not there is some actual object "out there." The unknowable mind-independent object is a spurious transcendence, a new sense of transcendence first delimited by Husserl in the lectures of 1905/6 and not the notion which is under phenomenological investigation. For something to be an *object* is (literally) for it to lie or be thrown "over against" consciousness, and insofar as it is an intentional 'object,' it does so (or is so) in an absolutely unique manner.

The way in which an 'object' is included in consciousness is not the way in which an object is a real part of the world. Nor on the other hand, is it included in the way in which psychical acts are moments of a unitary consciousness, which are not only unable to exist without the mind's existence, but are immanent to the ongoing stream of my conscious living. Transcendence consists in the 'object' being nonreally included in consciousness, inasmuch as any worldly object participates only in the reduced sense of the world as acceptance-phenomenon and the purified ego bears within itself the world as an accepted sense. The way in which an intentional 'object' exists is "a being-in of a completely unique kind: not a being in consciousness as a really intrinsic component part, but rather a being in it ideally as something intentional, something appearing . . . a being-in-it as its immanent objective sense" (CM, 42; cf. TS, 37–46). This quotation should evoke a strong resonance with Descartes' definition of the objective reality of an idea: "The idea [is] never outside the intellect, and in this sense 'objective being' simply means being in the intellect in the way in which objects are normally there" (CSM II, 74).

Though a phenomenological reading of the Cartesian idea does accord well with an interpretation of this link in the "Third Meditation" as a version of protointentionality, it would be misleading to construe it as indicative of a hitherto unheard of transcendental turn. In the context of the "Third Meditation," an ambiguity in the sense of "idea" is cleared up: "objective reality" is introduced to distinguish it from the "formal reality" of an idea, i.e., the cause of the idea as such. If anything, the only genuine transcendence (sic) in Descartes would pertain to the ultimate cause of an idea, a cause which in the case of the ideas of infinity and perfection can only exist outside the mind. This principle of causality would perforce be excluded by the reduction as another belief founded on the general thesis of the world's being, specifically the belief that mental events are causally related to worldly objects in the way in which worldly objects are related to one another. Husserl's criticism here is that no philosophical or scientific investigation can ever establish the validity of this belief since it misconstrues the essential "nature" of consciousness as ground for the appearance of the world itself.

A collateral distinction is made with respect to the ego in the formula "ego—cogito—cogitatum." To construe the cogitatum (idea) as a 'real part' of the mind is to obliterate its necessarily transcendent character, which then leads one to consider the object in itself "outside" the mind as the genuine transcendence—an absurd notion[22]—and the totality of psychic life as the only immanence. This compression into one intramental term of psychical acts and their 'objects,' i.e., the nonobservance of the heterogeneous status of the two sides of intentionality, leads one in the converse direction towards a notion of the ego as factually and contingently determined. This ego, the one which Husserl identifies as the Cartesian meditator, does "bear within himself" the world as an accepted sense. This sense is first tacitly accepted in the natural attitude, then called into question by universal doubt, and then purified through the filter of clear and distinct seeing.

This identification generates an immense problematic: for the ego, defined by Descartes as *res cogitans*, a thinking thing, is a substance and though "really distinct" from *res extensa*, it nevertheless appears again as another thing in the natural world. As such, it is accessible to a type of perception, *inspectio mentis*, which is of the same order as all other 'objective' experiences; though to be sure, it is not of the same specious insight as Hume's "looking within oneself." The ego secured through the Cartesian epoché has a certainty which attaches to an empirical fact; in this case (granted) to an indubitable fact, first in the order of reasons. For Husserl, it is not first in the order of cognitions revealed by the phenomenological reduction since the *ground* for the worldliness of any worldly thing cannot itself appear as an object in the world but must be genetically prior in the sense that it is presupposed as the condition for anything worldly appearing at all. "This world, with all its objects derives its whole sense and its existential status, which it has for me, from me myself, from me as the transcendental ego, the ego who comes to the fore only with the transcendental epoché" (CM, 26).

From Husserl's point of view, there is a conflation in Descartes' thesis between, on the one hand, the mundane or empirical ego, united with the body in a substantial union which can only be explained by recourse to psychophysical causality; and on the other hand, the transcendental ego as the ground condition according to which that which appears, as a substance, as causally related, as part of a whole, and so forth, can appear at all. This is why, despite Husserl's unwavering respect for Descartes, he can still censure him for being "the progenitor of the psychologism which saturates the whole of modern philosophy" (HUS VII, 338); or "the father of transcendental realism, an absurd position" (CM, 24). Baker and Morris have argued convincingly, in contrast to this standard reading, that any attempt to construe the Cartesian "primary notion" of the union of mind and body on a causal interaction account is doomed to failure. "It is ironic that one common criticism of Descartes' Dualism points to the a priori impossibility of his *explaining* mind-body interaction. That is precisely his *doctrine*, not a *problem* for it. It is part of what he meant to be understood, not something that he would have preferred to pass unnoticed."[23]

Thus far Husserl's critique of Descartes' purified psychical ego has taken our inquiry; but how accurate an assessment is this of Descartes' own explication of the nature of the ego in ego cogito? It definitely accords well with a standard line of interpretation, but on the issue of transcendental experience, Gaston Berger once remarked, "One cannot say that Descartes was ignorant of this domain if one believes the words he puts in the mouth of Polyandre in the final lines of what has reached us of *The Search After Truth*: 'There are so many things contained in the idea of a thinking thing that entire days would be needed to unfold them.' "[24] Berger leaves the discussion with this provocative *aperçu* (as did Polyandre before him); but an emphasis should be placed on the word "idea," for an idea of a thinking thing is not the same as a thinking thing *as a thing*, even if this is defined as the "nature" of the ego. Gueroult emphasizes the difference between these two notions, a distinction which then allows the ego's "universal condition" to stand forth, a condition which precisely implicates transcendence. "The fact that the cogito finds in its characteristic of most simple and most general ultimate nature the deep justification of certainty that we are constrained to give to it, proves that the reality it entails is not that of my personal concrete self, but that of my thinking self in general, as universal condition of all possible knowledge."[25]

As for Polyandre, if he had devoted more days, i.e., meditative exercises, to the task of explicating the nature of the soul or mind, he might have uncovered all of those attributes of the ego which, though previously unknown, could be truly predicated of that which is certainly known, namely that the principal attribute of the mind is thought. Only insofar as the mind is *really* united with the body in the individual person is it a substance, a thing unlike the bodily thing. However, in respect to the *idea* of the mind, i.e., the objective reality of its idea, it is *modally* distinct from the idea of body. Husserl's criticisms regarding this unfortunate "reification" of the mind are, strictly speaking, only pertinent to the mind as a self-subsistent substance: "Consciousness . . . is not a psychical experience, not a network of psychical experiences, not a thing, not an appendage (state or action) to a natural object. Who will save us from the reification of consciousness? He would be the saviour of philosophy, indeed the creator of philosophy." (1905 MS).[26] Descartes himself strongly objected to Hobbes' surreptitious replacement of the original notion of abstract being with "concrete words" (CSM II, 123). As an abstract being, the mind's autonomy is only endorsed by the possibility of its being conceived clearly and distinctly as a whole separable from every other whole, and the result of a process of "stripping away" all the attributes that do not properly belong to it. As a concrete being, however, the mindful body is always what is given to our understanding before the process of abstraction begins.

In this regard, the ego even as an abstract being is indeed a residue or a remnant of doubt's purging, the focus of another charge which Husserl will direct at Descartes.[27] However, on Descartes' own injunction (CSM II, 78), one must not confuse the question whether (*quod*) something is a substance with the question of what (*quid*) that substance is. In the case of a complete and simple thing, such as the mind prior to abstraction, to know this thing *to be* a substance is not to know the substance itself. A complete thing is "nothing more than a substance endowed with forms or attributes that are sufficient to let me know that it is a substance" (CSM II, 78). But though this is also necessary for knowing *what* that thing is, it is not sufficient for that purpose. This is attained by a process of elimination in which those properties which could not possibly belong to the mind's essence are excluded, but unknown attributes not thus disqualified are not excluded (CSM III, 236). The cogito then should not be equated with "a simple act of self-consciousness, of psychological origin, within the power of anybody whatever. It affirms only a *pure intellect*, an essence detached from everything that would mask it from natural consciousness, and which is affirmable as actual only insofar as it is perceived as the sine qua non condition of the possibility of all knowledge."[28] Nevertheless, with regard to an explication of those unknown attributes which can be truly predicated of the transcendental ego, this was a task which Descartes left unfolded; an installment of *The Search After Truth* which has disappeared forever. The fullest investigation of the ego revealed by the successive reductions is the "enormous labor" of constitutive analysis, and since the phenomenology of self-constitution coincides with phenomenology as a whole (CM, 68), only this process will disclose "an entirely new realm of being."

The Transcendental Reduction and Its Policy of Eminent Domain

After the point of convergence in the isolation and anchorage of the cogito as the fulcrum from which to shift the natural standpoint, a second divergence has emerged in the description of the essential "nature" of the ego. For Descartes, this is a substance, a thinking thing, really distinct from the body to which it is wholly united. For Husserl, such a description pertains only to the empirical, mundane ego which participates in the spatio-temporal world and is governed by psycho-physical causal laws. This is not the domain which phenomenology investigates, for to construe consciousness as another object in the world is to completely close off any feasible explanation for how it is possible for the world whole to appear to a subject. The true sense of the ego, in the formula "ego— cogito—cogitatum," will only be revealed through a further reduction, the transcendental epoché. "Descartes does not make clear to himself that the ego, his ego deprived of its worldly character through the epoché . . . cannot possibly turn up as subject matter in the world, since everything that is of the world derives its meaning precisely from these functions" (Crisis, 82).

In the "inexhaustible depths" of this entirely new domain of subjectivity, Descartes unwittingly substituted the psychological ego for the transcendental ego and misunderstood the distinctive character of the *cogitationes* which are the only indubitable 'objects' given to this ego. Phenomenological inquiry will shift the weight of criterial evidence from the Cartesian ego to the manifold of *cogitationes* (CM, 31). Investigation of the two topics, ego and cogitata, leads in two directions, each with a reciprocal influence on the other in terms of constitutive features uncovered by intentional analysis. Before pursuing our own line of inquiry on the first topic regarding discrepancies between Husserl's account of Descartes' ego and Descartes' own cautionary remarks on its potential misconstrual, let us examine the notion of "idea" as a separate field of sense. For Husserl, turning to the cogitata qua cogitata is specifically the work of intentional analysis which discriminates the psychical 'object' as such (noema) and the psychical act or mode of the cogito (noesis) (CM, 36–37; Crisis, 170–72). From the point of departure in the Cartesian cogito, "a hidden double meaning of Descartes' ideas will become evident: there arises two possible ways of taking these ideas, developing them, and setting scientific tasks; whereas for Descartes, only one of those was obvious from the start. Thus the sense of his presentations is factually (i.e., as his own sense) unambiguous" (Crisis, 78). There is a twofold criticism here, only one aspect of which the *Crisis* elaborates: first, that Descartes does not distinguish within the notion of "idea" between ideative act and its object; and second, the sense of "idea" which he does work with is that of an "image" or "picture." Husserl attributes one or both of these "superficial" notions to Descartes' "hidden, unclarified prejudice" in favor of the scholastic tradition (CM, 24; Crisis, 75). Without a doubt, this remark refers ultimately to Descartes' use of terms such as "objective" and "formal reality" of an idea; all too eager objections to this crypto-scholasticism were already familiar to him after the publication of the *Meditations*.

It is, however, rather alarming to read that (half of) the problem is an unambiguous misconstrual of the 'nature' of an idea when Descartes had explicitly warned the reader on this point. "There is an ambiguity here in the word 'idea.' 'Idea' can be taken materially, as an operation of the intellect. . . . Alternatively, it can be taken objectively, as the thing represented by that operation" (CSM II, 7). Chapter 5 developed in some detail an interpretation of the Cartesian "idea" as composed of two interdependent moments: the cognitive act and its purely immanent 'object.' His choice of scholastic terms may have been somewhat unhappy, but he is quite explicit about the meaning of 'objective' reality of an idea. "An idea is the thing which is thought insofar as it has 'objective' being in the intellect; . . . 'objective' being simply means being in the intellect in the way in which 'objects' are normally there" (CSM II, 74).[29] Husserl's reading, however, is not so perverse as not to recognize that in Descartes' reflection on the cognitive mode in which the certainty of the ego stands forth, he has broached the notion of intentionality, though "to be sure, there is no question of a true presentation and treatment of the subject of intentionality" (Crisis, 83).

Fair enough; there isn't a full-blown concept of intentionality in the "Third Meditation," and analyses of the cogitata stop short of the point where they alone, in their self-givenness, would have provided an index of the sort of evidential certitude which consciousness alone requires. But is this enough to disqualify Descartes' interpretation of ideas as being a "hidden prejudice"?

The obverse side of Husserl's twofold criticism is his claim that the univocal sense of the Cartesian "idea" is that of an "image" or "picture." After summarizing the stages of methodical doubt in the "First Meditation," via sense deception, madness, and dreams, Husserl remarks:

> Now here one says the senses deceive. That means, properly, the imagination which produces complex *images* out of the data of sensation, deceives us. Or, the *pictures* in our soul, as it were, do not portray actuality, they conform to no original, neither these complex imaginings, nor the simple elements, colours and other general sense data. All that belongs to myself, and to the extent it is what I take it to be just as I sense it or as a complex *image*, I obviously do not deceive myself. (HUS VI, 402; emphasis added)

Descartes does indeed begin the process of doubt with common-sense notions (including the commonsense notion of 'idea'!), each of which is discovered to be susceptible to the skeptical purge. The reason for this is that such common-sense notions are all composite ideas; the cognitive power when conjoined with imagination (or memory) produces images or likenesses which, insofar as they are not simples, are liable to falsity. That there are intellective "ideas," e.g., number, magnitude, logical axioms, etc., may be called into doubt by the fiction of the evil genius; but if there are such "ideas," then what they convey in a clear and distinct seeing cannot be false. The ideated number given in a mathematical intuition is adequately given itself; there is no ontological need for any sort of mediate representation by an image. Descartes repeatedly distinguishes between the strict sense of "idea" as that which is seized by the pure intellect alone and the loose sense of "idea" as an image formed by composition in imagination, memory, etc. (CSM II, 113, 117, 273).

Although one may provisionally agree with Husserl's typification of scholastic ideas as images which succumb to universal doubt, he inadvertently identifies his own reading of the univocal Cartesian idea with Descartes' equivocal sense of idea. "The discussion about inner-psychic geometrical and other images seem to yield the result that all a priori knowledge can primarily attain an apodicticity which has to do with images as inner-psychic events" (HUS VI, 404). If Descartes' notion of idea were entirely image-based, then one consequence is that he would indeed be stranded with a spurious notion of transcendence (even if only a glimpse); no transcendent object could ever be given to consciousness by means of an image or picture. In the course of an otherwise balanced article on this topic, John Burkey never questions Husserl's construal of Descartes' ideas as images and says that, insofar as Descartes borrowed the terms "objective" and "formal reality" from the scholastics, "he insufferably compromises his radicalness"[30]—and this is a completely inaccurate assessment.

We seem to have made a great conceptual leap forward—from the universally doubted world, the world bracketed by the epoché, to the transcendental ego, the *a priori* condition for the possibility of the world's appearance. These worldly appearances are now no longer considered merely as that which appears through the appearing, but that *towards which* anything must make its appearance—the world is a phenomenon *for me*. Only the thing gives itself, in some mode of presentation, but it is consciousness for which what appears is given. The Latin origin of *donare, donatio*, and its many cognates demanded an accusative and a dative 'object': one gives some thing to some one. This tripartite structure, ego—cogito—cogitatum, is one which Husserl traces from its original formulation in the Cartesian cogito.

Thus for Descartes, although the self-evidentiality of the cogito would indeed be apodictic in Husserl's sense, i.e., it is impossible that it could be otherwise, this sort of evidentiality does not extend to any other ideas, even those seen clearly and distinctly. *That* some thing is clearly and distinctly perceived to be x, and that this x is known to have just this essential nature (e.g., the piece of wax), does not entail that *when* this x is not cognized in this manner, it could not now be otherwise. It only strictly entails that it *was* this x, presented in an adequate intuition which, if it becomes a link in a chain of reasons preserved in memory, has "a derivative sort of certainty." That the cogito has this originary certainty is one issue: the criterion of clarity and distinctness is inferred from the cognitive mode (not its 'object,' which here is unique) of purely intellective seeing in which the cogito is grasped; this criterion cannot itself be secured through transparency in its cognition, but is guaranteed by something transcendent, namely God. It is a gross error of interpretation, which invites the charge of circularity, to think that it is somehow divine veracity which underwrites (insures the insurer) the content of all intellective insights, once the manner in which such insights are to be achieved has been demonstrated. For Descartes, one could say, the truth of God's essence, revealed through analysis of the ideas of infinity and perfection, and *then* God's existence as necessarily implied by this, are indeed apodictic—it is not conceivable that God could be otherwise. This is indeed true in both senses of the true nature of his being: that he could not *not be* (quod), and that he could not *be otherwise* (quid).

For Husserl to carry forward this second-order security would be to bankrupt his enterprise, to remove the parenthesis from the thesis. God, as the phenomenologist might have said, is a transcendent being which properly belongs to the domain of theological discussion. But as far as philosophical speculation, he belongs to the same sort (well, a peculiar sort) of spurious transcendence to which the thing-in-itself belongs. One could say that God as a being who is independent, self-subsistent (and omnipotent, etc.) and not directly available to any possible experience (which excludes any proof by cause and effect, etc.) is a patent nonsense.[31] The transcendent God has already been bracketed by the first reduction and is as much a "faithful" (?) phenomenon as the world is an acceptance phenomenon. "The theological principle which might perhaps be rationally supposed could not be assumed as something transcendent in the sense in which the world is something transcendent for . . . that would involve a counter-sensical circularity" (Ideas I, 116). This would make the phenomenologist open to a charge of circularity in the way that Descartes was alleged to commit circular reasoning, though for a different purpose.

Since an entirely worldly God is evidently impossible and since God cannot be taken as being immanent in consciousness the way mental processes are, then there must be modes within the absolute stream of consciousness according to which transcendencies other than that of physical realities can be made known. It is not at all clear what such cognitive modes could be, nor what would be the kind of intuitions directed toward God, nor what ordering and unitary rule such intuitions would have to conform to in order to implicate a divine transcendence. However, "the idea of god is a necessary *limiting concept* in epistemological considerations, and an indispensable *index* to the construction of certain limiting concepts which not even the philosophizing atheist can do without" (Ideas I, 187, note 17). Husserl thus "passes over" whatever could be considered as a rational motive for the postulation of a divine being. The phenomenological reduction is extended to include this absolute, transcendent being since the field proper to phenomenological investigation is pure consciousness. (Ideas I, 134).

But our discussion of Husserl's criticisms of the various stages in Descartes' initial disclosure of the purely subjective domain must remain faithful to a reconstruction of Descartes' own original insights, irrespective of the originality of phenomenological insights which they inspired. Husserl concurs in the standard objection of circularity in the proof of God's existence: "Descartes loses his way here, in the attempt to demonstrate the right of evidence and its trans-subjective scope, in an early seen and much bemoaned circle. He infers *in the same way* the necessary existence of God from the last specific character of the human pure ego—that God cannot deceive us within the criteria of evidence" (HUS VII, 65). Husserl takes this same position again fifteen years later: "He had not noticed the circle in which he was involved when he presupposed, in his proof of the existence of god, the possibility of inferences transcending the ego, when this possibility, after all, was supposed to be established only through this proof" (Crisis, 90; cf. CM, 82–83). Our citation of Husserl's critique has highlighted the phrase "in the same way"; for Descartes does *not* infer or demonstrate the criterion of evidence in clear and distinct seeing in the same fashion as the (first) proof of God's existence, and thence the essential guarantee of the non-transient holding true of insight into this criterion.

Charges of Circularity in Reasoning for the Existence of God and of Other Egos

We thus arrive at the fourth alleged divergence: that for Descartes there are two ultimate poles which secure certain knowledge of the material world, the cogito and God's infinitude and beneficence; that for Husserl, there is only one principle of principles, that which confers the genuine right of evidence. "Every originary presentive intuition is a legitimizing source of cognition, that everything originarily offered to us in intuition is to be accepted simply as what it is presented as being, but also only within the limits in which it is presented there" (Ideas I, 44). We have no reservations about the profound and revolutionary consequences of this metatheoretical statement, our concern is rather that Husserl himself, sometime later, was to grapple with a puzzle or paradox generated partly by the exclusiveness of this principle. There is one thing that seemingly cannot by its very essence be presented "only within the limits"—and that is another ego as a self-contained subject in the world.

Thus our query here has a twofold approach: can the charge of circularity against Descartes' argument for God's existence be legitimately sustained beyond any reasonable doubt? That is, is this objection against his position infected with a minimal element of doubt and should it thus be rejected as another prejudice? And on the other front, to what extent does Husserl's own project eventually open his position to a charge of circular reasoning, even if this also is just as much a misinterpretation and misreading sponsored by hidden prejudices? Why is Descartes so brusque, for instance, in dismissing Arnauld's charge of reasoning in a circle (CSM II, 150, 171)? It is curious that he is at some pains to answer questions and elucidate problems posed by a thinker whom he much admired (that in itself, a rare occurrence), but on this issue, Descartes simply says that he has adequately dealt with it elsewhere, in the "Second Replies" (CSM II, 100–103). At this earlier passage, he refers to a distinction between the sort of evident insight attained in the momentary act (attentive regard) of clearly and distinctly seeing and the derivative certainty which attaches to the memory of those evidential insights.[32]

If anything, a better indication of a possible answer to Arnauld occurs in the context of a reply about the "greater than ordinary certainty" with which the mind alone can be known. "We commonly judge that the *order* in which things are mutually related in our *perception of them* corresponds to the order in which they are related *in actual reality*"; but the process of doubt excludes this *thesis* insofar as he supposes himself to be ignorant of God (CSM II, 159). Here is the key to unlock the circle: it is only at a certain point in the order of reasons (which is the only permissible method here) that the demonstration of God's existence from the essential truth of the 'objective' reality of ideas can legitimate a determinate relation between the order of reasons and the order of beings. This second-order demonstration is in sharp contrast to what the proof for God's existence does not do, that is, to retroactively justify a previous point in the chain of reasons, i.e., the criterion of certain evidence.

It is simply not within the scope of this chapter to rehearse the standard formulation of the circularity indictment nor the standard, if reluctant and regretful, acquiescence on the part of most commentators. There have been vigorous challenges mounted in Descartes' defense against this charge, most notably by Harry Frankfurt, Edwin Curley, and Martial Gueroult;[33] and we concur with Curley's provisional finding, that though Descartes' project for a defense of reason and a foundation for the sciences may not eventually succeed, this is not because his reasoning is circular but because his arguments for God's existence are just not good enough. However, we concur with this assessment on the basis of different, though compatible, analyses which have their framework within two intersecting orders. "[These are] the reciprocal independence of the series of the cogito and the series of god and their criss-crossing at a given point. We encounter a nature that reveals itself to our intuition as a foundation finding a point of support in itself, and not in us, imposing itself on me, *in spite of myself*, irresistibly testifying about its objective validity by getting me to touch the Other directly within myself."[34]

Let us now recapture two of our guiding Cartesian motifs: the cogito is first in the order of reasons, revealed in a self-evident and transparent intuition; and God is first in the order of being, a unique being the idea of whom is demonstrated as the necessary formal cause of the 'objective' reality of the ideas of infinity and perfection. The relation between these two orders, having been suspended through the universal epoché, is now reestablished through the criterion of clear and distinct seeing as that of the correspondence between idea and ideated, foremost in the case of the idea of God and of God himself. And what is the status of the world as such after the phenomenological epoché has rendered it merely the intentional correlate of any possible consciousness? "The sense commonly expressed in speaking of being is reversed. The being which is first for us is second in itself; i.e., it is what it is only in relation to the first. But it is not as though there were a blind regularity such that the *ordo et connexio rerum* necessarily conformed to the *ordo et connexio idearum*" (Ideas I, 112). The instructive resonance of this passage with Descartes' two-termed priority according to the order of reasons and the order of beings finds an even more striking echo in the last pages of the full text of the *Crisis*, twenty-five years later: "In respect of knowledge, for us men, our own being goes before that of the world; but this does not mean that this same thing holds in respect to the actuality of being." This last clause the editor/translator expands as, "man's objective being (as subject in the world) comes first in the order of knowing but not in the order of being" (Crisis, 262, note 6). Husserl then goes on to reiterate his claim that the process of reaching this domain is achieved through bracketing all worldly beliefs and remarks that consciousness is "a strictly self-contained domain, yet without any boundaries separating it from other regions. For anything which could limit it would have to share a community of essence with it."

This remark is connected with a passage from *Ideas First Book* which famously devotes little attention to what would later become such an important theme. One could make a "conceptual leap" from the above point to the final page of the *Cartesian Meditations*: "The intrinsically first being, the being that precedes and bears every worldly objectivity, is transcendental *inter*-subjectivity: the universe of monads, which effects its *communion* in various forms" (CM, 156). Although it is only in this later period that his published writings show him grappling with the issue of intersubjectivity, it is now known that he had been working with this incipient problem as early as 1905, roughly the same time as the inception of the phenomenological epoché itself.[35] Simply stated, how is it possible that within this absolute domain, this "island of consciousness," into which nothing can penetrate, other egos as subjects of their own psychical acts could be constituted? The question is not, how can they be represented or pictured as thinking beings, but rather how can they be intuitively given in the originary sense. It seems that transcendental phenomenology, rigorously pursued to its limits, leads inescapably to an intractable solipsism (CM, 89).

It is to Husserl's immense credit that what is first proposed as an objection from outside the discipline of phenomenology is transformed into an essential problematic within phenomenological investigation. His extraordinary arguments to dissolve this "illusion" or to resolve this "paradox"[36] receive detailed exposition in the Fifth *Cartesian Meditation*. As was the case with Descartes' alleged circle and its potential refutation, so here too, it is not to our purpose to trace the complex lines of thoughts which lead to this illusion, nor those which dispel it.[37] Rather it is to indicate that one purported divergence has collapsed under the weight of convergent requirements.

Whereas Descartes transcends the cogito by means of God, Husserl transcends the ego by the alter ego. . . . One may wonder whether Husserl escaped what might be called the "Husserlian circle" any better than Descartes escaped his own famous "circle." In the same way that Descartes can be criticized for basing all truth on the divine truth and this on the idea of infinity, we may question whether Husserl succeeded in getting the originary ego, in which the alter ego is constituted, back "into" intersubjectivity.[38]

In order to close our account with two balanced books (so to speak), we have to return to the setting out of different stages of reduction and pick up the thread of the eidetic reduction. However, we have not yet quite succeeded in extricating our analyses from the labyrinth of the many-named reductions. Due partly to Husserl's own use of phrases like "stepwise" and "graded" or "layered" reductions, it may seem that these are performed within one another—a steady, relentless etiolation of the point of departure until it winks out, like a once luminous point-source. C. W. Harvey's clever metaphor about the "branches" of the several reductions, in shape something like a decision tree, makes their interrelation much clearer. Differentiated acts of epoché are used to suspend judgments and beliefs based upon separate regions of knowledge, e.g., material objects, linguistic states-of-affairs, the formal sciences, and so forth. A layered or graded reduction would take place within a branched act of epoché and therein proceed deeper into the constitutive origins of that region.[39]

This is perhaps most obviously the case with the eidetic reduction, whose subject matter Husserl takes to be the science aimed at by the entire phenomenological method. That is, just as there are empirical sciences of matters of fact, so there are eidetic sciences of a priori truths. The first reduction which brackets the general thesis of the objective being of the 'external' world reveals only momentary particulars, "a ceaseless flux of never-returning phenomena" (CM, 49), "a realm of a Heraclitean flux" (Ideas I, 168). The transcendental reduction has uncovered the absolute ground for the possibility of knowledge in the genetic priority of transcendental consciousness. The world of the former natural attitude is transcendent to any consciousness, but it is still the one world, the actual world now deprived of its actuality-character. Over against every empirical science of actualities lies an a priori science of possibilities: the former is concerned with valid laws of nature which express factual regularities, each of which could be different; the latter is concerned with ideal laws which express universal states of affairs that could not be otherwise, i.e., the necessity which pertains to apodictic evidence.

The institution of a priori sciences is accomplished through the eidetic reduction which proceeds in several stages, the formulation of which Husserl returned to again and again (Ideas I, 156–61; EJ, 340–48; CM, 69–72). We will postpone detailed exposition of this topic since it forms the main part of a later chapter on "Intuition and Seeing of Essences"; however, a brief overview is called for in the current context. For every given intentional 'object,' this appearing thing here and now, presenting first one and then other sides, there attaches a horizon of determinate other sides not yet given, but which are coposited as possibilities. Some other as yet unspecified aspects cannot be given in further perceptions if this thing is to remain just this and not some other thing. For instance, having seen five square, flat sides of a cube, if the sixth side turns out to be curved, the original 'object' was not a cube after all. What is it about the essence of a cube that allows one in advance to extend the copositing of other sides in just that determinate manner, such that some eventualities are fulfillments and others are frustrations?

Through the technique of free variation in phantasy, the universal kind is able to be actively seen as the pervasively identical or invariable x which is found in every particular when it is construed solely as a possibility—though here this one possibility is the actual thing. One can then "run-through" the particular variables and discern the *en epi pollon* (one in many), such that this perceived thing is then the mere exemplification of the *eidos* or essence. "What can be varied . . . bears in itself a necessary structure, an eidos, and therewith *necessary laws* which determine what must necessarily belong to an object in order that it can be an object of *this kind*" (EJ, 352). The essential truths given through these laws are called *a priori* by reason of the type of validity which they govern: they precede all factual occurrences, that is, everything arising from experience. Every experienced actuality is subject to the unconditional proviso that it must conform to the *a priori* conditions of possible experience and cognitions directed towards such experience. The one formal discipline to which Husserl here explicitly appealed was mathematics, especially geometry because it dealt with essences of shape and volume. Mathematical cognition was one of eidetic insight: the 'eidos' triangle was seized or grasped as the invariant 'object' which remained unchanged in any imagined triangle. Husserl discerned the advent of such a pure *mathesis* in Galilean (and Cartesian) physics through the application of a geometry of nature. "The possibility emerges of producing constructively and univocally, through an a priori, all-encompassing systematic method, all possibly conceivable ideal shapes" (Crisis, 27)—in other words, a pure eidetics. In the seventeenth century, for the first time, lies the foundation for "the sure prospect of an infinity of truths for one of the great regions of experience, truths that are valid in unconditional necessity for everything of this region that is experienceable" (Ideas III, 37).

How far are we now, at the end of an exposition of Husserl's reductions, from Descartes' conception of the goals of his own project? Husserl says that he has been guided by the idea of philosophy as an all-embracing science, which he now realizes must be grounded in an eidetic discipline in order for the actualization of first philosophy to take place (CM, 72). Descartes asserts in the "Preface to the Reader" that the *Meditations* will deal with "the foundations of first philosophy in its entirety," and that the only order which could be followed to achieve this is that of the "geometrical style" (CSM II, 8), i.e., the order of reasons. Wherein consists the peculiar character of this order of reasons? "The true way by means of which the thing in question was discovered methodically and as it were a priori, so that if the reader is willing to follow it and give sufficient attention to all points, he will make the thing his own and understand it just as perfectly as if he had discovered it for himself" (CSM II, 110). Surely the primary notions employed by geometers are clear and distinct enough that no further demonstration is needed to convince one of the truths asserted, provided one correctly follows the rules of inference. In metaphysics, however, such is not the case and great effort is needed to reach this level of evidence in the understanding of primary notions. "Admittedly they are *by their nature* [=essence] as evident as, or even *more evident than*, the primary notions which geometers study" (CSM II, 111). But these primary notions are often in conflict with preconceived opinions derived from the senses which cloud our mind and render things obscure.

Here then is Descartes' motivation for methodical doubt and the suspension of all beliefs: to clear the ground and demonstrate the necessary conditions for the clarity and distinctness of any intellective cognition (of simple truths) and thus to show that they attain at least as much self-evidential certainty as the 'objects' of mathematical intuition. This attainment of a criterial objective goes a long way towards fulfilling Descartes' initial vision, in Rule IV of the *Rules*, about an all-embracing general science, "which explains all the points that can be raised concerning order and measure irrespective of the subject matter and this science should be termed *mathesis universalis . . .* for it covers everything that entitles *those other sciences* to be called branches of mathematics" (CSM I, 19).

In summary, the Cartesian point of departure is a way into phenomenology because for the first time the purely subjective domain of the knowing subject is thematized as the ground for an investigation of what can count as certain knowledge. In stark contrast to the medieval schoolmen, Descartes is not in search of some theory of correspondence or resemblance between appearances and an underlying reality. The very notion that there is such a theory is an unexamined assumption and any candidate for such a theory can always be called into question by the skeptical problematic of the criterion. Descartes' method of universal doubt employed as a fiction revealed the presumptive nature of theory construction and showed that the only feasible candidate for a criterion of evidence was the clarity and distinctness in which the cogito disclosed itself. Husserl's principle of principles regarding the originary self-givenness of all presentative intuitions is a radicalization and extension of this Cartesian criterion within the phenomenological reduced sphere of consciousness. The various stages of the reduction revolve around an entirely unnatural suspension of the natural attitude, which saturates all philosophical activity, and must be renewed again and again. In this process, the transcendental ego is shown to be the necessary condition for the possibility of the world-whole and worldly things to appear.

The first divergence between Descartes and Husserl pertains to their attitudes to science: where the former accepts the mathematical model of the natural sciences as one that philosophy should emulate, the latter brackets the natural-scientific model as another knowledge construction founded on the natural thesis of the world's being. The second divergence pertains to the nature of the self: where the former identifies the ego as *res cogitans*, a thinking thing within a world of things, the latter argues that the empirical ego is subtended by the transcendental ego. But a misreading on Husserl's part fails to show that, for Descartes, the *idea* of the ego is indeed an abstraction, modally distinct from the mind as substance, and as such there is a glimpse, though not carried through, of the transcendental ego. The third alleged divergence regarded the 'being' of an idea: for Descartes, the formal and objective reality of an idea comprised an intentional structure between act and content; for Husserl, an idea is the intentional correlate of all cognitive acts, an irreal component of consciousness.

This alleged discrepancy conceals a convergence, however, since Husserl's criticisms that Cartesian ideas are univocal and unambiguous and that they are images or pictures are simply inaccurate. The fourth divergence regarding the dual poles from which a chain of reasons can establish a fulcral point for the demonstration of evidential knowledge also conceals a parallel. As much as Descartes is guilty or not of circularity in arguing from God as first truth in the order of being and the cogito as first in the order of reasons, so Husserl is committed to arguing from the transcendental ego to the essential structures of the lifeworld, within which other ego-subjects are either objects constituted by the one originary ego or subjects which bestow the sense of being-an-ego as one among many. The final congruity is to be found in their respective notions of the universal science which can be built on these foundations: for Descartes, his metaphysics are the surest guarantee of the validity of theoretical physics; and for Husserl, the eidetic reduction leads to an *a priori* science of essences.[40]

There is a standard line of interpretation on Descartes' main concerns, a line which still holds sway, colored by undisclosed "hidden longings" within the post-Cartesian tradition. So also there is a standard line of interpretation regarding Husserl's "Descartes"; not about his avowed point of departure in Descartes' attempt to doubt, but about all those Cartesian claims which Husserl allegedly departed from. Husserl remarked that Descartes had remained too true to the original skeptical impetus and not radical enough in his overthrow of that position. It is hoped that our research has shown that Husserl remained far truer to Cartesianism, precisely in those places where the influence is inexplicit, and less radical than a faithful reading of Descartes' project according to the order of reasons would reveal. This last comment readily acknowledges that Descartes is often silent, or at best highly cryptic, at those places where a truly radical investigation could have extended. Nevertheless, many commentators "fill in the blanks" with very dubious estimates which are often unsupported and sometimes contradicted by Descartes' own assertions.

It would never be sufficient for a proper understanding of the phenomenological reduction to show that it was improperly founded on a mistaken Cartesian epoché. "The precise nature of Husserl's neo-Cartesianism is thus hard to specify. To the extent that Husserl's view of his relation to Descartes is correct, his claim as a neo-Cartesian depends upon the distinction between motif and doctrine. To the extent that his view of the relation is incorrect . . . Husserl's claim can be ironically supported in some measure."[41] The meaning-realm which the reduction discloses would still retain all of its objective validity irrespective of its aetiology. On the other hand, any demonstration that a reduction can be securely anchored on a rightly understood Cartesian metaphysical doubt would do nothing to further its own ambition anyway. This then is the principal reason why Husserl abandons the Cartesian way into phenomenology, without derogating the revolutionary character of Descartes' original insight. Instead it has hopefully been shown that it is due to Husserl's letting slip from his grasp the genuine sense of Descartes' method that the reduction itself is permitted, or even encouraged.

INTUITION AS SEEING WITH THE MIND'S EYE

Since the demise of neo-Kantianism in the late nineteenth century, the concept of intuition has gone out of favour among Western philosophers, but perhaps for the wrong reasons. If those who objected to its use in philosophical discourse, for example by Henri Bergson, had been correct in identifying to what they imagined intuition to refer, then perhaps they would have been justified in jettisoning the concept itself. However, a wide-ranging implication of the present research is that such critiques, for the most part formulated by early proponents of the language-analytic model, incorrectly equated intuition with a mysterious, ineffable mental faculty—a sort of "sixth sense" super-added to the other five—and hence brought a rich and complex terminological development to a premature closure. Aside from the avowedly Kant-influenced Ernst Cassirer in *Philosophy of Symbolic Forms* (1923–29), the last great exponent of a systematic philosophical project which relies centrally on the original significance of intuition is Husserl.

But there have been other philosophical enterprises which relied on the same basic notion of unmediated knowledge, though expressed in a different and perhaps more acceptable terminology. A strong case has been put forward recently by J. Hintikka, C. O. Hill, and D. W. Smith,[1] among others, that Bertrand Russell's notion of *acquaintance* is parallel to Husserl's notion of intuition, i.e., that authentic presentation is equivalent to knowledge by acquaintance, and inauthentic presentation to knowledge by description.[2] Hintikka also observes that Russell's 1913 work *Theory of Knowledge* (held back due to Wittgenstein's criticisms and not published until 1984) advances an "excellent counterpart to Husserl's categorial intuition," that is, acquaintance of *logical forms*. "The upshot would have been to turn Russell's work in logic and in the foundations of mathematics into a counterpart of Husserl's enterprise of phenomenological reduction . . . in the realm of essences."

C. O. Hill astutely observes[3] that what Russell and other early analytic philosophers found objectionable about Husserl's early work was what they took to be the meaning of the term *Vorstellung*, usually translated "idea." Since there was already a sympathetic reception for Frege's theories, and since Frege disparaged *Vorstellung* (in one sense) as an entirely subjective and superfluous aspect of consciousness, governed by the psychological laws of association, Russell and others were inherently suspicious of any account of consciousness which accorded primacy to anything like "ideas." Husserl's account, as early as *The Philosophy of Arithmetic*, granted just such epistemic primacy to *Vorstellung*, but he meant something much different than what Frege took him to mean. To further complicate matters, Frege had discriminated an objective sense to *Vorstellung*, with respect to the logical, nonsensible aspect, but abandoned it in favor of "object" and "concept." It would take us too far afield to trace the complex interplay of accusation and counter-accusation between these three logicians. Suffice it to say that Russell credited Brentano with an important influence on his own work in theory of knowledge and may have been more receptive to Husserl's work if not for this disastrous misidentification.

In support of the richness of Husserl's concept of intuition, D. W. Smith has developed an intriguing theoretical model of acquaintance from a brief earlier sketch in his work with R. McIntyre.[4] Their earlier work isolated one of the most significant omissions from Husserl's basic theory of intentionality, namely, that determination of the perceptual 'object' cannot depend on analysis of the intentional 'meaning' (*noematic sinn*) alone. According to Smith and McIntyre, what Husserl's account lacks is some sort of frame for *contextual* influences, indices which make reference to the perceiver and the object in his/her perceptual environs. Smith and McIntyre propose a *pragmatics* of intentionality to complement an expanded version of Husserlian semantics; and this is what Smith provides in *The Circle of Acquaintance*. This juncture in our investigation is an appropriate place to synopsize Smith's basic theorems,[5] since as we shall see in Descartes' and Husserl's notions of intuition, the skeleton of Smith's model can serve as a useful template with which to keep track of a highly diverse dual set of terms, each of which undergoes correction and revision.

1. *Acquainting* experiences or awareness include (a) perception of physical objects (events); (b) inner awareness, in consciousness, of oneself and of one's experiences; (c) empathic perception of others as persons.
2. A person is *acquainted* with an object if and only if he or she is having an acquainting experience of, or intentionally related to, the object.

3. An acquainting experience is a *self-evident cognitive* experience.
4. An acquainting experience or awareness is an *indexical* presentation or awareness, e.g., of "this" or "you" or "I."
5. Acquaintance is an *indexical* intentional relation, i.e., . . . to an object in the subject's *presence*, or in *contextual relation* to the acquainting experience.

With this clearly articulated template in mind, we can proceed to trace the maturation of Descartes' notion of intuition from the *Rules* to the *Meditations*, before moving on to untangle the complex strands in the correction and revision of Husserl's notion of intuition. As with a number of other central concepts in late scholasticism, such as the theory of ideas, the notion of intuition undergoes an elaboration and refinement in Descartes' hands. The extent of the transformation of core concepts between late scholastic thinking and Descartes' "new world" vision is the subject of much current debate. Gary Hatfield makes a strong, even convincing case, that the Cartesian faculty model of the intellect fits squarely with the doctrine espoused by Suarez, Toletus, Rubius, and the Coimbran commentators. As such, the thesis that intuition alone can guarantee knowledge of true being is intimately tied up with arguments for the immortality of the human soul and the validity of innate ideas; the latter two doctrines, of course, are also held by Descartes. However, "Descartes' theory diverged sharply from that of the Aristotelians. He designated external sense perception, imagination, memory, and pure intellection as modes of a single power of perception (i.e., as operations of the intellect, considered generally)."[6]

In any case, this refinement is not quite so obvious in his early work in the *Rules* as it is later in the *Meditations*, where clear and distinct seeing definitely signals a departure from his earlier version. Here intuition or intellective insight takes on a richer and more complex role in the account of the achievement of scientific knowledge. This enrichment is in some measure due to his having overcome problems in the physiology of visual perception at various stages, from the *Rules* to *The World* and then in the *Optics*. In the *Discourse*, Descartes explicitly warns the reader about his novel use of the term "intuition" and that he shall be obliged to give it a different meaning than the ordinary one. The "ordinary" meaning upon which he thought his readers could rely was that of a rational power of insight, endowed by divine order, and which could become clouded through the obscure and confused ideas of the senses. It is part of Descartes' general plan for the renovation of the sciences to firmly anchor the cognitive power of the intellect within "the light of nature." He begins in an exemplary, even standard fashion by invoking the unitary cognitive operation of intuition in conjunction with the stepwise cognitive operation of deduction. In contrast with the demonstration of a process of reasoning which leads to a conclusion, what is the cognitive operation of intuition directed toward? Rule III states that there are only two "actions of the intellect" by means of which one is able to attain indubitable knowledge: intuition and deduction.

> By intuition I do not mean [a] the fluctuating testimony of the senses or [b] the deceptive judgment of the imagination as it botches things together, but [c] the conception of a clear and attentive mind, which is so easy and distinct that there can be no room for doubt about what we are understanding. . . . Intuition is [d] the indubitable conception of a clear and attentive mind which proceeds solely from the light of reason. . . . Thus everyone can mentally intuit [e] that he exists, that he is thinking, that a triangle is bounded by just three lines, and a sphere by a single surface, and the like. (CSM I, 14)

This is a highly compact and elliptical passage, the *locus classicus* for the Cartesian definition of intuition and also the germ for many fruitful notions in the *Meditations*. Descartes is here concerned to eliminate (a) sensory perception and (b) imagination from contention as eligible sources for indubitable knowledge. The rationale for excluding (a) and (b) is not provided until Theorem D5 of the first part of Rule XII (CSM I, 42). There we learn that the "cognitive power" through which we know anything in the strict sense is "purely spiritual." When conjoined with "figures" supplied by the sense organs, it produces sensory perceptions in the mind. When conjoined with retained or invented images, it produces remembered or imagined thoughts. Only when this power acts on its own can the mind be properly said to understand. This basic operation is a precursor to the principle which underlies the operation of the pure intellect in the piece of wax exercise in the "Second Meditation."

The first positive indication of the meaning of intuition is in clause (c) which characterizes intuition as the conception (in the broadest sense) of "a clear and attentive mind," of which the intuited content is "easy and distinct," such that the intellectual operation excludes minimal doubt. Readers of the *Meditations* will be predisposed to regard "clear and distinct" as binomial terms which unequivocally demarcate seeing as a mode of certain cognition; here these two terms have not yet taken on their more precise later signification. However, "attentive" is a common term in the *Rules* and should not be construed exclusively as pertaining to a particular psychological state of the subject. As chapter 5 showed, attention is in fact the final phase in the process of methodical doubt, and as such "attentive," though admittedly ambiguous, pertains to the epistemic status of the knower.

The term "easy" is not so simple to explicate; one can hazard the speculation that it refers to the direct (i.e., unmediated) access to the intuited 'object.'

Where clause (d) seems to be a mere periphrasis of the former clause, it is rather an alternative formulation since it interpolates a new partial *definiens* in the second clause. Where the minimal doubt condition in (c) was used to qualify intuition as an indubitable conception, we now have the (so far) mysterious phrase, "which proceeds solely from the light of reason." Finally the author provides some examples of intuition in (e); note well at this point that the instances cited pertain to a subject's mental states or to mathematical-geometrical 'objects' and that they are all propositional, i.e., that a state of affairs obtains. But what can the inclusion of the phrase "the light of reason" add to our understanding of the operation of the intellect?

"The light of reason," or "the natural light," is a recurrent motif throughout Descartes' writings, from the *Rules* to *The Passions of the Soul*. Perhaps its most obvious import is to provide Descartes with a legitimating source for the faculty (or, more properly, the operation) of intuition in every human being—this source is God himself. In a letter to Mersenne of 1639, regarding the natural instinct towards bodily preservation and the purely intellectual instinct, he explicitly equates the natural light and mental vision (CSM III, 140). In his replies to Hobbes, he states that "a light in the intellect means transparent clarity of cognition" (CSM II, 135), a notion upon which he had expanded earlier in the "Second Replies." Here he says that we must distinguish between the thing itself which we assent to, and the formal reason which induces the will to give its assent. It is only in respect of the formal reason that transparent clarity is required, and this comes from one of two sources, the natural light or divine grace. (CSM II, 105). In *Principles,* Part One, section 30, these several strands of thought come together: "The light of nature, *or the faculty of knowledge* which God gave us can never encompass any object which is not true insofar as it is indeed encompassed by this faculty, that is, insofar as it is clearly and distinctly perceived" (CSM I, 203).

Thus it is no surprise that after the caution about using Latin words with a novel meaning (a strictly parenthetical remark), he continues from "and the like" to connect intuition with deduction. "The self-evidence and certainty of intuition is required not only for apprehending *single propositions*, but also for any train of reasoning whatever." The example which he adduces is the identity of the sum of two arithmetical operations, each of which has to be intuited with certainty and then the necessary equivalence of the two intuitions also intuited with certainty. There follows this definition of Cartesian deduction:

> The inference of something as following necessarily from some other propositions which are known with certainty. . . . Very many facts which are not self-evident are known with certainty, provided they are inferred from true and known principles

through a continuous and uninterrupted movement of thought in which each individual proposition is clearly intuited. . . . Hence we are distinguishing mental intuition from certain deduction on the grounds that we are aware of a movement or a sort of sequence in the latter but not in the former and also because immediate self-evidence is not required for deduction as it is for intuition; deduction in a sense gets its certainty from memory. (CSM I, 15)

We have briefly touched upon the relation of intuition and deduction in chapter 4 in connection with Descartes' attempt to resolve the problem of how the certainty which attaches to discrete cognitions can be maintained across "a continuous movement of thought." In the demonstration of a mathematical postulate, one first grasps the truth of one premise in an adequate intuition and then proceeds to the next premise, which is also secured in this manner, and so forth. Although the relational necessity between these premises must also be intuited, the mind's holding-in-grasp of the certainty of these premises is not itself an act of immediate (i.e., direct) cognition. The epistemic condition of having established an inference in a demonstration depends on another mental faculty (memory) which is open to fallibility in ways in which the intellect is not. This is why he says that "deduction *in a sense* gets its certainty from memory"—the italicised phrase highlights his reservation. Is it possible to eliminate memory's inherent fallibility in moving from cognition to cognition, i.e., giving up its grasp on the secure intuition of a single proposition?

Strictly speaking, this proviso attached to deduction in the passage from the *Rules* is misleading and inaccurate, due perhaps to the uneven strata of composition.[7] Rule VII is devoted to an exposition of the concept of enumeration and Rule IX takes up a more specific definition of deduction and its attendant intuitions based on the careful discrimination of deduction from enumeration of which it is said that "*its* certainty in a sense depends on memory" (CSM I, 37). Some of the argumentative problems which are alleged to emerge when one considers that the pseudo-certainty of memory is derivative of *deduction* disappear when this dependence is recalibrated in terms of *enumeration*. An enumeration of either all the links in a chain of reasons *or* all the members of a given class must be sufficient, but need not be complete or distinct. It must be sufficient insofar as it determines all the possible instances which fall under the topic (or concept).

It is worth pursuing Descartes' discussion of deduction since it leads directly to two rules which elucidate characteristic features of those things which are intuited with certainty and self-evidence. The summary of Rule V states that the whole method consists in the right ordering and arranging of those objects upon which our 'mind's eye' (intellect) must focus its attention. This order is followed if one first reduces complicated and obscure propositions step by step to simpler ones, and then starting with the intuition of the simplest ones, ascends through the same steps to knowledge of the rest, i.e., the original complex propositions and their corollaries. Rule VI states that in order to distinguish the simple from the complex and to arrange them in an orderly manner, one should attend to what is most simple in each series of things (i.e., chain of reasons) in which some truths have been directly deduced from others. Then one should observe how other truths are more or less or equally removed from these simplest truths. Descartes says that "this is the main secret of my method; and there is no more useful rule in this whole treatise" (CSM I, 20–21).

The young Descartes is convinced that the "seeds of truth" contained in mathematical propositions are also concealed in other related disciplines, that there is a unified science (*mathesis universalis*) for which these exemplary propositions are more "its outer garments than its inner parts." Rules V through XII are an elucidation of the systematic structure of these "inner parts" and the concomitant technique for extending analysis beyond the ordinary mathematical operations. The initial development of this unified science reached its culmination in the second half of Rule XII with the formal-ontological schema of simple and complex natures. The meaning of a simple nature is central to an understanding of what constitutes the proper 'object' of an intuition.

"The secret of the technique consists entirely in our attentively noting in all things that which is absolute in the highest degree." Some thing is called "absolute" if it contains "a pure and simple nature"—in other words, if it is the basis upon which other things are known in a deductive sequence , and no other thing can be the basis for it. For some thing to be the epistemic basis for another thing does not pertain to mathematical simples alone. Though the type of inference which allows for the clarification of founding relations between relative levels of simple natures is different for abstract simples than for material simples, the latter type of "inference" is possible through the process of elimination. Lest it seem that physical objects have been excluded from the field of intuitive contents, he refers to this in Rule VI, well before its detailed unpacking in Theorem D2 of the second part of Rule XII.[8]

"There are very few pure and simple natures which we can intuit straight off and per se (independently of any others) either in our sensory experience or by means of a light innate within us" (CSM I, 22). *However*, the concept of intuition endorsed by the *Rules* excludes material composites, i.e., middle-sized physical things, since the intellectual process which decomposes them is liable to "lose track of" the ordered arrangement of intuited material simples. The decomposition through inference of a sequence of abstract simples is thus not corrigible since the ordered structures between these simples are themselves open to intuition as necessary relations. Some scholars have objected to what they see as a latent confusion in Descartes' description of the subject's condition vis-à-vis intuition and deduction. The objection is that Descartes conflates the psychological conditions under which intuition can in fact take place with the epistemic conditions without which an intuition could not take place. The use of phrases such as "the sharp edge of the mind," "careful concentration," the cultivation of "good study habits," and so forth, would decidedly lend themselves to such a psychological interpretation. However, in Rule IX he discusses "two special mental faculties" which are acquired skills and which are indeed dependent on contingent circumstances. These two skills are "Perspicacity in the distinct intuition of particular things and discernment in the methodical deduction of one thing from another" (CSM I, 33). It is through practice in these two skills that one becomes adept at employing the two principal operations of the understanding.[9] If anything, it is his cavalier use of the term "faculty" which leads some scholars to problems of exegesis; thus, where it does make sense to speak of cultivating a faculty such that it improves success at a cognitive operation (or function), it doesn't make sense to speak of a gradient in the function itself— either intuition reaches its 'object' or it doesn't.

Perhaps the summary of Rule XI can also be understood as addressing the practical concerns of these two faculties taken together. "*It is useful* to run through them [simple propositions] in a continuous and completely uninterrupted train of thought, to reflect on their relations to one another, and to form a distinct and, as far as possible, simultaneous conception of several of them" (CSM I, 37). The postulation of a sort of *synchronous cognition* is an attempt to avoid the problem of derivative certainty connected with the memory's holding-in-grasp of intuited truths. In order for deductive inferences to qualify as certain, though not self-evident, 'objects' of knowledge they must "present themselves simultaneously." This may seem an insuperable criterion for what is a sequence of interconnected links in a chain. But he points out that one does not have to examine every link in a chain in order to know with certainty that they are all connected—hold the chain up, so to speak, and if it doesn't fall apart, it must be securely interlinked. Descartes' answer as to how a synchronous runthrough of discrete intuitions and their necessary relations is possible is ingenious; it is through "abbreviated representations," e.g., astronomers' imaginary circles. As discussed in detail in chapter 4, this is the symbolic groundwork for his invention of algebraic geometry and parallels Husserl's insight into the gestalt-figural 'objects' of suprasensuous numerical cognition.

One of Richard Rorty's criticisms[10] of the Cartesian concept of intuition is that Descartes attributes intuition to a separable mental faculty to which one must have some sort of special access. Granted that Descartes does sometimes speak of intuition in this manner, but where this occurs it's always expressed within his *enumeration* of the notion of human knowledge. He signals the end of this enumeration at the start of Rule XII with the phrases "complete enumeration" and "sufficient explan[ation]" (CSM I, 39–40). After this, it is possible to discuss what an adequate intuition of the concept of intuition itself would be. In this context, he speaks of one single power (*vis cognitiva*) which conjoined with various types of corporeal images yields four functions. These functions are discriminable through a continuous movement of thought and are intimately implied by each other just as much as several geometrical properties of a triangle are ascertainable via an adequate intuition of the concept "triangle." Descartes' perspicacious and discerning study of the nature of human intelligence, which includes its division into four faculties, has placed him in a better position to have a certain and self-evident grasp of the meaning of "intuition."

Let us recall that the first five remarks of Rule XII are devoted to knowledge of things considered from the point of view of the knowing subject.[11] In the second section, eight theorems are directed towards the possible 'objects' of knowledge and are designed to answer these questions: "What presents itself to us spontaneously? How can one thing be known on the basis of something else? What conclusions can be drawn from each of these?" These queries are not answered until the very end of Rule XII, with the passage which opens "a problem is to be counted as perfectly understood only if we have a *distinct perception* of these three points" (CSM I, 55). Note that a complete analysis of the enumeration of the current field of investigation, and here this is knowledge *tout court*, is given as the 'object' of a cognition which qualifies as an intuition. It is completely inaccurate to claim that Descartes confuses the psychological, contingent conditions under which topics in science or factors in scientific cognition are to be enumerated according to practical rules (since he admits that their order can be arbitrary), with the epistemic criteria whereby any given function of the mind can be certainly and self-evidently demarcated insofar as the function itself satisfies the condition of being the possible 'object' of an intuition.

The fifth remark of the first group specifics that there is one single power, purely and distinctly spiritual, which when conjoined with corporeally inspired images produces what an enumeration considers to be four faculties. But "according to its *different functions*, then, the same power *is called* either pure intellect or imagination or memory or sense perception" (CSM I, 42). Granted the intellect's success in reaching the 'object' of cognition when this content is an abstract simple (or irreal entity), such as a logical axiom, or where the content is the psychical state of the subject, given in a certain and self-evidential awareness, what of the material simples, i.e., the constituents of physical things?

When the cognitive power is conjoined with sensory perceptions of a physical thing, "the idea of that thing must be formed as distinctly as possible in the imagination. In order to do this properly, the thing itself which this idea is to represent should be displayed to the external senses" (CSM I, 43). This crucial passage in the transitional paragraph between the five remarks about the knowing subject and the eight theorems about the object of knowledge cannot be over-emphasized. It marks the point of departure from a proto-phenomenological account of Cartesian intuition in the *Rules* and Husserl's primitive, irreducible notion of intuition in the *Logical Investigations*.

In summary, Descartes' early notion of intuition as an operation of the understanding has the following essential characteristics:

(i)   it is certain, i.e., does not admit even minimal doubt;
(ii) it is self-evident, i.e., presents itself as absolute or self-founding;
(iii) it is instantaneous, i.e., given in one temporal "moment."[12]

In terms of the intuitive content, possible 'objects' of intuition are

(iv) abstract simples, i.e., mathematical or logical truths;
(v)   material simples, e.g., a color, a shape, a sound, etc.; and relations which hold between material simples;
(vi) material composites, each of whose constituent simples and their complete interrelations have been adequately intuited;
(vii) one's own mental states, and this includes propositional attitudes about instances of (iv)–(vi), i.e., "that p is the case."

Husserl's Early Concept of Intuition in the Logical Investigations

Though Descartes would not have had to contend with any reluctance on the part of his critics regarding his use of the term *intuitus*, though its range may have been open to dispute, such was not to be the fate of Husserl's use of the German equivalent, *Anschauung*. This term was first introduced into German philosophical discourse in the eighteenth century for the purpose of rendering the Latin term *intuitus* and its cognates and was systematically employed by Kant in his major works. Husserl's use of this term, however, cannot be traced to late scholastic terminology, any more than can the term "intentionality"[13]; its distinctively modern usage has its origin no earlier than the seventeenth century—and that means Descartes and John Locke.[14] Jaako Hintikka summarizes his own research into the etymology of intuition and its relevance for understanding Husserl's writings:

Husserl makes heavy use of a term whose primary function is to call attention to what is immediately given to us in experience. This term is intuition (*anschauung*). Unfortunately it is one of the least clearly understood terms in philosophical language. Its semantical history makes it particularly prone to misunderstandings. . . . It is thus a serious mistake to attribute to Husserl a view of intuition as a separate source of truth or certainty. Intuition is not a separate epistemological consultant, it is a generic term for whatever any privileged consultant tells me. An expression like "immediate intuitive truth" is for Husserl a pleonasm.[15]

As we have pointed out above, it is quite plausible to interpret what Descartes has to say about intuition in the *Rules* as pertaining to a faculty model of the mind, and hence to construe intuition as "a separate source of truth." However, as with a number of other central Cartesian terms, e.g., substance, idea, science, etc., this one also is ambiguous. The fifth remark of the first group in Rule XII clearly indicates another reading of intuition as a discriminable function of a unitary cognitive power, in virtue of which specific features of its act-character and its ideative content can be delimited. One can arguably criticize Descartes for not highlighting this ambiguity, either here or later in the *Meditations*, but one should not fault him when the reader fails to discern the ambiguity and subsumes all statements about intuition under a faculty model.

One of Husserl's earliest critics, Moritz Schlick, accused Husserl of something similar to a facultative interpretation of intuition, of espousing an epistemological theory which relied on a mysterious and privileged mental insight. Schlick claimed that such a private insight was only available to those who had already acquiesced to the cogency of the phenomenological project. Husserl's *Ideas,* "asserts the existence of a peculiar intuition, that is *not a real psychical act*, and that if someone fails to find *such an experience which does not fall within the domain of psychology*, this indicates that he has not understood the doctrine, that he has not yet penetrated to the correct attitude of experience and thought, for this requires 'peculiar, strenuous studies.' "

This passage from Schlick's *General Theory of Knowledge*[16] is quoted by Husserl himself in the foreword to Volume Two, Part Two, of the 1920 edition of the *Logical Investigations* and though the attack is directed towards *Ideas First Book* (1913), it is equally culpable as a misconstrual of Husserl's term in the 1900 work. If this was one of the first such remarks castigating Husserl for his resort to an almost hermetic doctrine of privileged access via intuition and the reduction, it was not to be the last, for such disparagement of the foundations of his transcendental idealism persists today. Husserl's response to this charge was particularly acerbic and reminds one of Descartes' barely controlled vexation in the face of Bourdin's "Seventh Objections." "The total impossibility that

I should have been able to utter *so insane an assertion* as that attributed to me by Schlick . . . and the falsity of the rest of his exposition of the meaning of phenomenology, must be plain to anyone familiar with *this meaning*" (LI, 663; emphasis added). Though this counterobjection to Schlick's cursory dismissal and Hintikka's defense of the cogency of Husserl's usage are strictly relevant to the later Husserl's mature reworking of fundamental phenomenological concepts such as intuition, in this specific instance, eidetic intuition or seeing of essences is only an enriched and more complex version of the same basic notion in the 1900 work.

Intuition is such a primitive term in Husserl's early work that it never receives an unequivocal definition in the manner in which so many other terms are carefully circumscribed. It is possible, however, to tease out a definition which will provide signposts for delimiting characteristics of its cognitive operation and those things which are open to intuition. Clues to such indicative features are scattered throughout the six investigations, most of which employ an equally primitive term, "presentation."[17] Chapter Six of the Fifth Investigation synopsizes thirteen (!) ambiguities in regard to this term[18] of which one is directly counterposed with intuition. "To mere thinking 'presentation' is opposed; plainly this means the intuition which gives fulfilment, and adequate fulfilment, to the mere meaning intention. . . . What we intuit stands before our eyes in perception or imagination just as we intended it in our thought. To present something to oneself means therefore to achieve a corresponding intuition of what one merely thought of or what one meant but only at best very inadequately intuited" (LI, 65).

This passage should strike a chord with the reader regarding Descartes' remark that all conscious activity is thinking, but only some thoughts are ideas (CSM II, 113). For Husserl, if some thing is presented to the mind, then that thing is open to further qualification as the possible 'object' of an intuition. What could count as a possible 'object' of an intuitive presentation? With regard to external things, Husserl says that this occurs in perception, imagination, and representation, i.e., memory or picture-consciousness, but only insofar as the 'grasp' of understanding is coupled with an interpretation; and this latter means that the sense of the thing is given along with the thing itself. This "sense" should not be confused with the meaning of a word or a sign, though it is convergent with its intentional "meaning" on a lower cognitive level—of this relation, more later.

Nor should the meaning of this "sense" be extracted from corporeal sensations, since deprived of any meaning-giving character, all experiences are merely lived through. Unthinking sensations do not count as signs of the properties of an object and their combination does not count as a sign of the object itself;

though this would be an accurate, partial description of animal consciousness. It is not the case that the mind first looks at its sensations, then turns them into perceptual objects, then bases an interpretation on them; such sequential, layered discrimination only takes place in reflection on the process of understanding. In their original, naive givenness, sensations are "components of our presentative experience, *parts* of its descriptive content, but are not at all its objects. . . . Sense-contents provide, as it were, the analogical building-stuff for the content of the object presented by their means" (LI, 309–10). Although Husserl's formal ontological framework of parts and wholes is far more sophisticated than Descartes' simple and complex natures, this statement is roughly compatible with Theorem D5 of Rule XII, which states that it is possible to have knowledge of a composite without having knowledge of all the simples which make up that composite; though it's not possible to understand anything more than those simple natures and composites formed from their conjunction.

Phenomenological analysis reveals the ambiguity latent in empiricist discussions of the "location" in subjective/objective terms of so-called secondary qualities. The same words (color, shape, sound) whose central motif is sensation are applied to the apparent determinations of things, on the one hand, and to the presentative aspects of our perceptions, on the other. But there is an *a priori* opposition between the two: "Sensations, *animated* by interpretations, present objective determinations in corresponding percepts of things, but they are not themselves these objective determinations. . . . The apparent objects of external intuition are *meant unities*, not ideas or complexes of ideas in the Lockean sense of these terms" (LI, 356). Properties taken as attributive aspects of an object are clearly inseparable from their concrete basis in the object itself. Insofar as an object's properties are given as the contents of an intentional act, they cannot exist independently of the object to which they are attributed, but each such property qua content can be independently meant. The intention does not segregate essentially dependent parts into independent pieces, but rather refers to those moments as meant elements of the whole perceptual object. Thus, "not every meaning is an *intuitive beholding*, and not every intuition an adequate beholding of its object, *embracing* that object perfectly and exhaustively in itself." This is very similar to Descartes' remarks concerning the distinction between the intellect's grasp (*prendre*) and its comprehension (*comprendre*): that is, between an intuition of a simple nature conveyed in the *idea* of some thing, in contrast with intuitions of all the simples which completely comprise the truly assertible *ideata* which the singularly grasped idea could possibly pick out.

Such an enriching or enlarging of cognitive grasp into all-embracing comprehension is a direct function of the *fulfillment* of an intuitive presentation. In the First Investigation, Husserl signaled the "long, difficult analyses" which would be needed to clarify the relations between cognitive grasp of meaning-intention (signitive) and the straight-forward presentation of an intentional content (intuitive). "The draft it [the former] makes on intuition is as-it-were cashed" (LI, 294). This *totalizing act*[19] in which a fusion takes place between a meaning-intention and its intuitive "substance" shows that the discrimination of essential dependent parts of such intentions is not exhausted by the moments of "act" and "matter"; "The work of intuition . . . contributes to the intended act, when authentically fulfilled, a genuinely novel element, to which the name 'fullness' may be given" (LI, 722).

The intentional content of any psychical act directed towards an individual person, perhaps a loved one, can be given through various sensuous "matters," some of which are only signitive. The word written on a card, the name spoken, initial letters traced on a frosted window—are not themselves intuitions of this person, the way mediate pictorial intuitions are so presented, e.g., a photograph, a drawing, etc. Rather their significance (i.e., sense-endowed aspect) is fulfilled only if there is some possible intuition, sensuous or nonsensuous, to which all 'matters' univocally pertain, i.e., *in propria persona,* in her remembered face, her phantasized face. "Fullness is . . . a characteristic moment of presentations alongside of quality and matter, a positive constituent *only* in the case of intuitive presentations, a privation in the case of signitive. . . . The ideal of fullness would accordingly be reached in a presentation which would embrace its object, entire and whole, in its phenomenological content" (LI, 729).

Thus we learn that a presentation can have a sensuous 'matter' (as a *reell* part of its intentional content), given in perception without being an intuition, specifically when it is a presentation of a sign qua sign. Can a presentation not given in perception, where the object does not appear *in propria persona,* be accurately termed an intuition? Yes, insofar as it is given in imagination or recollection, though of course, such phenomenological consideration entails moving from the domain of "outer" perception to "inner" perception. "Inner intuition need not be actual internal perception or other internal experience [*erfahrung*] e.g., recollection; its purposes are as well or even better served by any free fictions of inner imagination provided they have enough intuitive clarity" (LI, 607).

Lest one mistakenly construe such internal perception as introspection or as some sort of concomitant reflexive perception parasitic on the original perception, Husserl has already carefully disqualified these spurious notions from an authentic phenomenological notion. Every perception in the broadest sense can be characterized by the intention of grasping its 'object' as if it were present, as if it were given *in propria persona.* To this intention, outer perception corresponds with complete perfection and thus achieves adequacy if the object given in the percept is itself actually present. It should be clear and evident, asserts Husserl, that "adequate perception can only be 'inner' perception, that it can only be trained upon experiences simultaneously given and belonging to a single experience with itself. This holds, precisely stated, only for experiences in the *purely phenomenological sense*" (LI, 542–43).

Let us recapitulate a few steps in our untangling of the basic features of intuition before making a final assay at the meaning of straight-forward intuition, which will then put us in a position to make a coherent estimate of higher-order (categorial) intuition. Husserl has carefully delimited one ambiguity, among many others, in the sense of presentation from "mere thought," i.e., empty intending, in the manner in which one can say, "You look, but you don't *see*." In the case of mere thought, innumerable objects may be present in one's visual field, but none is intended, none can be intended as the such-and-such, until the advertence of attention. All phenomenological analyses presuppose that the 'object' as a real (*reell*) part of an intentional content stands out against a background of unattended 'objects.' Descartes touches on this notion in his brief remarks about ideas which are confused and obscure before they are brought to clarity and distinctness through intellective insight. It is a matter of psychological verification that certain empirical contingent conditions are operant in attending to something, but the essential necessity which pertains to the epistemic requirement that some thing stand out as the focus of attentive regard is a phenomenological desideratum. That is why attention in phase five of Cartesian methodical doubt is not a psychological stipulation for the holding-in-place of previously secured intuitions. For Descartes, this is achieved by the "sharp edge of the mind" (*acies mentis*), "the pure mental gaze"; for Husserl, this cognitive insight is directed specifically towards the 'object' adequately given in a presentative mode insofar as it is a real (*reell*) part of the intentional content.

A passage in the Fifth Investigation provides an exact demarcation of what can function as the intuitive content (*Gehalt*) of a straight-forward intuition and is a preliminary disclosure of what will later be developed into the phenomenological reduction: "Phenomenological intuition . . . fundamentally *excludes* all psychological apperception and real (*reale*) assertion of existence, all positings of psycho-physical nature with its actual things, bodies and persons. . . . This *exclusion* is achieved eo ipso, since the phenomenological inspection of essence, in its turning of immanent ideation upon our inner intuitions, only turns its ideating gaze on what is proper to the real (*reellen*) or intentional being of the experiences inspected" (LI,607). In summary, for Husserl's early notion, something is an 'object' of an intuition under these conditions:

(i)   it is adequately, and not emptily, intended;

(ii)   it is a real (*reell*) part of the intentional content;

(iii) it is given in inner or outer "perception," in a variety of cognitive modes insofar as each mode determines its own manner of givenness;

(iv)   it can function as the fulfilment of a meaning-intention which itself is not intuitive but signitive;

(v)   it is not *re*presentative of some originary presentation upon which such representative acts are founded;

(vi)   it is the 'object' of a founding not a founded act, except in the case where the founded acts occur as identities-in-manifold, i.e., categorial intuition of species.

All of the above target features, except (vi), can be characterized as sensuous perceptions which have a straight-forward (*schlichter*) intuitive basis; but Husserl also makes a case for a supersensuous perception which has a categorial intuitive basis. He first mentions this at the opening of the Second Investigation, though it is not until the Sixth that he brings reflective analyses to bear on the topic. In the Second Investigation, he states that the cognitive act in which we mean (or intend) the individual is essentially different from the act in which we mean the species of which the individual is an instance. In either case, the same concrete thing makes its appearance, but in the former case the appearance provides the basis for an individual reference whereby we intend this one thing here (*todi ti*), this feature or this part of the thing. In the latter case, it provides the basis for a conception directed toward the species, where what is meant or intended is the ideative content, e.g., the color red as such (LI, 339–40).

In the Sixth Investigation, acts of categorial intuition are explicitly described as being necessarily founded upon lower-order acts and ultimately on acts of sensuous intuition. Descartes' reference to the signitive characteristics of that which is represented to the mind as "the outer garments of its inner parts," is echoed by Husserl's own sartorial metaphors: "the meaning which *clings to* the words fits itself into what it means, its thought intention finds in the latter its fulfilling intuition" (LI, 676); "the expression seems to be *applied to* the thing and to *clothe* it like a garment" (LI, 688). Lower-order acts of sensuous intuition of aspects of a single thing are synthesized as being of one and the same thing since they are fulfillments of partial expectations given via the original intuitions. Thus we know, using Husserl's example, that the pattern in the carpet continues beyond what is given in the immediate visual field, and this is confirmed or disconfirmed by further intuitions. But to some sensuous intuitions, a signitive function may not be copresented, e.g., in seeing the marks of an alien script, though to be sure, a signification must necessarily be available for someone. Husserl makes the ingenious suggestion that some such cognition probably underscores the wordless process of scientific discovery: "we observe here how trains of thought sweep on to a large extent without bondage to appropriate words, set off by a flood of intuitive imagery or by their own associative inter-connections" (LI, 716). This is not far removed from Descartes' prescriptions regarding the enumeration of examples in mathematical research and their sub-sequent run-through in a continuous movement of thought which "sweeps" on to its conclusion.

There are other syntheses of identification besides the grasp of the unity-in-manifold of various aspects of a single thing. Two further processes are dis-cussed under the heading of suprasensuous intuition, the first of which concerns the logical categories according to which identifiable semantic meanings which fulfill lower-order intuitions are interconnected in a propositional format. Such interconnections, for which logical terms such as being, unity, plurality, number, ground, etc. correspond, are not themselves the 'objects' of straight-forward intuition, but arise through reflection upon certain intuitive acts, and so fall within the sphere of inner sense or inner perception (LI, 782). Just as the sen-sible object stands to sensory perception, so the state-of-affairs stands to the "becoming aware" in which it is given and for which a proposition is its expres-sion. But with respect to these founded acts, it is not in these acts as 'objects,' but in the 'objects' of these acts, that we have the abstractive basis which enables us to realize the concepts for the logical categories.

This preliminary exposition of the intuitive basis for cognition of logical categories is essential for Husserl's postulation of the categorial intuition of species.[20] A backward reference to previous analyses of acts of sensuous intu-ition directed toward a *single object* reminds us that even here there is a continu-ous synthesis of fulfillment through separable intuitions of aspects (pieces and moments) which are meant of one and the same object. But the unity of identification is not the same as the unity of an act of identification; in this case, an identification is performed, but no identity is meant. Only when we employ this perceptual series to found a new act, and when we articulate our percepts and relate their objects to each other, does the unity holding among these per-cepts provide a purchase for a consciousness of identity. Herein, the identity is made objective, the moments of coincidence serve as representative content for a new percept, founded upon these lower-order percepts (LI, 790–91). This new type of percept is categorial intuition and its unique representative content is the species meant by means of or through all its particular instances.

Whereas in the synthesis of aspects of a single thing, the separable intuitive acts are merely serried or iterated, in the higher-order categorial act, a collection of 'objects' is given as the representative content via categorial forms such as "and," "or," and "is." This content is unique but is not the result of an abstraction from all underlying, founded contents, though there is an abstraction (in the sense of exclusion) from the quality or act-feature, and the interpretative sense. In the signitive identification of the species-sense, the identity of the meant 'objects' is not *lived through*, but is merely *thought of*, that is, it is a concept. In contrast to this, in the case of the intuited 'objects,' the identity is indeed perceived or imagined and is only given in experience where adequation is complete. "The mental bond which establishes the synthesis, is therefore a bond of thought or meaning (*meinung*) and is as such more or less fulfilled" (LI, 809). The categorial moment binds together what is *essential* to all of the underlying sensuous acts, and connects their intentional *materials*. The identity of the essence is not the immediate form of unity among the sensuous contents but is the unity of consciousness based upon repeated cognitions of the same 'object'—there is thus a unitary conscious act, given in an intuition, of an essence as such.

Descartes' Mature Notion of Intellective Insight

Descartes' mature notion of intuition in the *Meditations* is termed clear and distinct seeing, or the clear and distinct perception of the understanding alone. He employs a number of interchangeable phrases for this, but for the sake of brevity and to avoid equivocation, let us refer to it henceforth as "intellective seeing." It is our contention that this mature, enriched notion of intuition is only possible after Descartes' philosophical researches have satisfied conditions, or overcome problems, which the earlier dual operations of intuition and deduction are too impoverished to explain. There are (at least) four developments between *The World* (1633) and the *Meditations* (1641) which permit, if not impel, Descartes' elaboration of intellective seeing. (1) The construal of ideas as signs which signify a sensory percept caused by a physical object, in a manner similar to the way in which words signify their referents; (2) the complete rejection of an imagistic or pictorial model of ideas as mediate entities in favor of a direct realist account; (3) the method of systematic doubt in the "First" and "Second Meditations" permits the formulation of an entirely new theory of the internal relations among ideas; (4) clarity and distinctness are defined as criteria of evidence for the assertion of propositions based on certain knowledge.

One of the less-remarked passages where he speaks of the relation between ideas and 'objects,' and what it means for the mind to have an idea of an 'object,' is on the first page of *The World:* "Now if words, which *signify* nothing except by human convention, suffice to make us think of things to which they bear no resemblance, then why could nature not also have established some *sign* which would make us have the sensation of light, even if the sign contained nothing in itself which is similar to this sensation? . . . It is our mind which *represents* to us the idea of light each time our eye is affected by the action which *signifies* it" (CSM I, 81; emphasis added).

He returns to this dual parallel—word is to sign as meaning is to signified, and idea is to sign as 'object' is to signified—in the *Optics*, "We should recall that our mind can be stimulated by many things other than images; by signs and words, for example, which in no way resemble the things they signify." Even if one persists in the belief that objects causally transmit "images" to the brain of the perceiver, this belief is still not sufficient to support the further claim that such images are *simulacra* (or actual likenesses) of the original. "In no case does an image have to *resemble* the object it represents in all respects, for otherwise there would be no distinction between the object and its image. It is enough that the image resembles its object in a few respects" (CSM I, 165). The example which he uses to illustrate the phrase "in a few respects" is of an engraving with its recognizable arrangement of lines, shapes, and proportions. These are all geometrical features of the perceived object, and recognizable as being about some thing because of the underlying, all-pervasive geometrical structure of nature itself.

It is important to stress here that ideas per se are not themselves signs of things, as though knowing were merely "reading off" sensations produced in the sensory organs. This would be to conflate a physiological description with an epistemological explanation, something Descartes is always careful to keep apart. Physical objects causally produce motions in the sense-organs, and hence the brain, which the mind then interprets. It does so by representing the idea of the object which the corporeal motions signify. "This is the point of the reverse-sign relation: ideas are not signs of things, they are the interpretations of physical motions (of things), the cognitive counterpart of things and their physical features. Interpretation is not signification; it is representation."[21] In further support of this reading one should also compare Descartes' own remarks against Regius in *Comments on a Certain Broadsheet*: "Everything over and above these utterances and pictures [about God] which we think of as being signified by them is represented to us by means of ideas which come to us from no other source than our own faculty of thinking" (CSM I, 305).

In a recent historical survey,[22] Martin Jay gives a well-balanced exposition of both the mechanistic-mathematical account of visual perception and the linguistic-signitive extrapolation of this to the realm of ideas. He points out that it is entirely plausible to argue that these passages in *The World* and the *Optics* are among the earliest instances of a large-scale shift away from a purely visual, imagistic model of human consciousness toward a sign-based model of what it means for a mind to be conscious of some thing. Here, as in other cases of interpretation of Cartesian texts, one is confronted with two unreconciled, though not incompatible, explanations for one and the same investigative topic. It is to Descartes' immense credit that he attempts to overthrow virtually every main principle of neo-Aristotelian, scholastic theory of knowledge and assays this with an absolute minimum of technical vocabulary. It is no small wonder that, in part due to his texts' great brevity and density, contemporary and current scholars grumble at consequent ambiguities. But one should not *succumb* to these ambiguities, despite the temptations, and mistake them for equivocations or confused thinking.

Clarity and distinctness have served to characterize intuition as early as Rule III of the *Rules* (CSM I, 14) and are repeatedly cited as such in the *Discourse*, where these two terms first appear in his cardinal epistemic rule: "to include nothing more in my judgments than what presented itself to my mind so clearly and so distinctly that I had no occasion to doubt it" (CSM I, 120; cf. I, 127, 130, 131). However, it is not until the *Meditations* that clarity and distinctness are explicated as criteria of the evidential givenness of ideas and the certainty of judgments based on them.[23] The ground is prepared for such an explication as the result of the purging of false beliefs and prejudices through methodical doubt in the "First" and "Second Meditations." It is from the reduced standpoint achieved at the opening of the "Third Meditation" that a genuinely novel model of ideas emerges. More than this, the reduced world of the meditator leaves him with only his thoughts—*cogito ergo cogitata*.

Not all thoughts are ideas, and not all ideas are clear and distinct. In a letter to Gibieuf of 1642, Descartes states that "the soul is always thinking . . . that whatever constitutes the nature of a thing always belongs to it as long as it exists" (CSM III, 203). And since thinking is the principal attribute of the soul, whether awake or asleep, there is always some mental activity, even though no trace of this activity remains in the memory. Insofar as any thought is occurrent, one cannot but be immediately aware of it (CSM II, 113, 171); a thought is already given to the mind before the mind "turns toward it," i.e., fixes its attention thereon. The consequence of this is that no unattended thought can be an idea, and he sometimes seems to intimate that bodily sensations, such as pain and hunger, also cannot properly be construed as ideas. Or at least, such sensations can never qualify as "perceptions," the ideas of which are both clear *and* distinct, at best they would be clear, as he indicates at *Principles* Part One, sec. 46 (CSM I, 208).

In a passage in the "Sixth Meditation," he observes that if the nerves in the foot are violently disturbed, the motion is communicated to the brain "and there gives the mind a sign [*ibi menti signum*] for having a certain sensation, namely the sensation of a pain as occurring in the foot" (CSM II, 60). It might just as feasibly have been instituted by God that the mind was aware of the actual motion of the animal spirits in the brain. In a letter to Arnauld of 1648 (CSM III, 357), Descartes remarks that where infants are directly, though inattentively aware of bodily sensations, adults have the sensation and simultaneously perceive something else about it. They are also able to reflect on the sensation, but since these two thoughts occur together, they appear to be indistinguishable from each other. The implication here, of course, is that the sensation and its reflected ideation are actually distinguishable, though only through a process of abstraction. It is this process of abstraction which allows the meditator to separately consider the thought of warmth in front of the fire from the sensation of being warm.

With respect to the reverse-sign relation discussed above, such an occurrence as a bodily sensation would not qualify as an idea. It could not be said that the mind represents the idea of a painful sensation when the physical motions which signify it take place. Rather, the whole relation collapses—the painful sensation just is that set of violent physical motions which triggers or occasions the sign that it is occurring now. In the *Passions of the Soul*, he carefully delimits bodily sensations, e.g., "hunger, thirst and other natural appetites," from sensory perceptions, on the one hand, and the emotions proper, e.g., "joy, anger and the like," on the other (CSM I, 337–38). Of this third class, he says that they alone are properly predicated of the soul itself.[24]

In virtually all of the cases where Descartes discusses sensations he is referring to what is more commonly called the secondary qualities of an object: "light and colours, sounds, smells, tastes, heat and cold, and other tactile qualities" (CSM II, 30). Cognitions of these sorts of things can indeed be characterized as ideas, though they contain "so little clarity and distinctness" that the objects to which they refer cannot be considered "real and positive." A. W. MacKenzie remarks that "In the case of sensations themselves, it would be misleading to suggest that we mistake their objects, since they have no objects. The only mistake we may be inclined to make in the case of sensations is to take them as having objects—that is, as representing something."[25] Given Descartes' commitment to a mechanistic account of the physiology of perception based on a mathematical model of natural order, it would be more fitting to refer to so-called secondary qualities as *macro-features* of objects which do not represent anything outside the mind, and to so-called primary qualities as *micro-features* which do indeed represent things outside the mind. These fairly neutral terms, micro and macro, allow commentators such as MacKenzie, Peter Markie, and others to classify distinctive group attributes without relying on the historically later terms, primary and secondary. His definitive position on this distinction is carefully and concisely stated at *Principles* Part One, sec. 71: "Sensations . . . do not represent anything located outside our thought. At the same time the mind perceives sizes, shapes, motions and so on, which were presented to it not as sensations but as things, or modes of things, existing (or at least capable of existing) outside our thought" (CSM I, 219). As such our ideas of macro-features can never attain to complete clarity and distinctness, but are always to some degree confused and obscure.

Since he is determined not to accept any of the neo-Aristotelian framework in his account of human knowledge,[26] e.g., form and matter, substance and accident, the four causes, etc., he is certainly not going to discriminate between mind-dependent and mind-independent properties of objects in terms of their qualities, nor of observable alterations in terms of qualitative changes in state. He is quite explicit in demarcating macro from micro phenomena in terms of a corporeal nature which is subtended by a mathematical model of coordinate points in space. In his reflections on his previous scrutiny of the piece of wax, he isolates those modes of things which he had clearly and distinctly perceived: size, shape, position, motion, and then further, substance, duration and number; and those of which his ideas were confused and obscure: colors, sounds, smells, tastes and so forth (CSM II, 30). A more fundamental category of the former group of modes is continuous quantity, whose variable extension can further be analyzed in terms of its parts, to which can be assigned various sizes, shapes, positions, local motions, and durations (CSM II, 44). The meditator's own understanding (i.e., intellective insight) of what constitutes the basis for clear and distinct ideas of sensory perceptions is specified at the cusp of the "Fifth" and "Sixth Meditation." It is possible to achieve certain knowledge of God himself, other purely intellectual natures, and the "whole of that corporeal nature which is the subject-matter of pure mathematics."

There has been a great deal of debate on whether Descartes held a "veil of ideas" theory of sensory perception and what class of ideas is pertinent to this intermediary status. M. D. Wilson argues against John Yolton's direct realist interpretation of the Cartesian account of sensory perception, though she admits that her original position has been mitigated by further considerations. Attributions of a "veil of ideas" theory rest on a few enigmatic passages in the *Meditations*, and the detailed analyses of the three grades of sensory experience in the "Sixth Replies" (CSM II, 294–96). At the end of the "Second Meditation," he reflects on the process whereby he came to understand the true nature of the piece of wax: "when I distinguish the wax from its outward forms; *take the clothes off*, as it were, and consider it naked" (CSM II, 22). In the "Third Meditation," when speaking of the quantifiable micro-features of an object, he says that they are "merely modes of a substance," but the French edition expands on this phrase: "and as it were, the *garments* under which corporeal substance appears to us." But if this phrase may be dismissed as a mere rhetorical flourish, perhaps interpolated by the French translator, there is a passage in the "Sixth Meditation" which seems to be both definitive and unequivocal. Regarding the macro-features of an object and the ideas of them which are presented in my thoughts, "although the ideas were, strictly speaking, *the only immediate objects* of my sensory awareness," there was no reason to think that bodies which caused these ideas were not distinct from the bodies themselves (CSM. II, 52). In this context, the reader should remember the previous explication of the manner in which an 'object' can be said to be in the intellect—the 'objective reality' of an idea. Otherwise, the easiest, most straight forward reading of this statement will take 'object' to be an intermediary entity between the "real" thing and the perception of it.

M. D. Wilson comments on this pivotal statement:

> Descartes may *not* be explicitly making the point . . . that we directly perceive ideas of sense, as opposed to physical things. Rather, he may just be isolating what is 'properly and immediately sensed,' according to terminological assumptions which distinguish what is 'proper to sense' from perception involving active intellectual processes. This reading would help to leave open the question of whether or not *physical objects or bodies* actually are (immediately or directly) perceived, in circumstances that we would count as sense perception.[27]

In his clear-headed and balanced survey of the various positions in this debate, John Yolton draws attention to a vital distinction which Descartes makes about an ambiguity in the term "idea," something which we have repeatedly emphasized in this research. Only if one takes idea in a univocal sense and ignores the dichotomy between (what we have called) an act-idea, as a cognitive operation, and an idea-content, as the form in which an 'object' is present to the mind, is Descartes forced to choose between an indirect realist approach and a disguised version of a neoscholastic imagistic account. In reply to Arnauld's objections about ideas of sensory qualities, Descartes responds (CSM II, 163) that ideas can be construed as either forms of a kind, not composed of any matter and representative; or cognitive operations which have 'formal' as opposed to 'objective' being. If the term "ideas" in the passage from the "Sixth Meditation" is taken in the sense of mental operation or activity, this is no more controversial and no more in line with indirect realism, than to claim that one's own mental states are immanent in consciousness. "If ideas are in fact activities, the temptation to take the content of these activities as an entity may fade. And if . . . the causation of the *esse objectivum* is semantic [i.e., sign-based], this temptation may disappear entirely. The reality of the object in the idea is the *meaning*, the cognitive meaning, of the object. . . . There is a new doctrine: to be in the understanding for physical objects just is *to be understood*."[28]

Although it is not feasible, nor strictly relevant, to sort out this complex issue, one or two comments are called for. According to the order of reasons, advocated by the meditator with respect to his own path towards certain knowledge, previous notions which have fallen away are called up for review in light of further links now secured. The recommendation to follow the order of reasons should be adhered to in the case of this passage about the *alleged* immediate 'objects' of perception. It opens with a point of order: that he will review everything that he previously took to be perceived by the senses and his reasons for thinking this. The meditator will then set out any reasons for calling these beliefs into doubt, adjudicate among these reasons according to more certain criteria established in the foregoing five Meditations, and then finally determine whether they should still be believed.

One of the beliefs which he took to be true of sensory perceptions was that ideas were the immediate objects of awareness. One of the reasons for believing this is that having sensory ideas was involuntary, in virtue of which such ideas seemed more lively and vivid. Another reason was his holding the belief that nothing is in the intellect that was not first present in sensory experience—and this he has already rejected. The passage in question closes with the remark that he had already made up his mind about "how things were," before working out any arguments to prove his belief to be well grounded. But later on many experiences undermined the faith, i.e., nonevidential belief, which he had in the senses. This faith in the deliverance of the senses included the notion that ideas are objectlike entities which mediate between the knower and the thing known. Thus the "veil of ideas" theory is one which he throws out in favor of a more sophisticated representative model.

As well as intellective insight into the nature of a particular thing, e.g., a piece of wax, Descartes sometimes seems to be saying that one also has a clear and distinct insight of the essence of which that thing is an instance. Although one usually assumes an equivalence between the terms "nature" and "essence" of some thing, at least in the case of mind and body, one can discriminate a further application of what clear and distinct ideas extend to: that is, the essence of kinds or classes of things of which individual minds and bodies are exemplifications. This emerges most clearly in *Principles* Part One, sec. 48: "two ultimate classes of things: first intellectual or thinking things, i.e., those which pertain to mind or thinking substance; and secondly, material things, i.e., those which pertain to extended substance or body" (CSM I, 208). Where we might now think of these as universals (or universal concepts), his discussion of what he calls 'universals' at *Principles* Part One, sec. 59 pertains to the nominal relations which instances of some thing have with respect to an essence. Hence cognition of them cannot be said to involve a clear and distinct idea, except perhaps in the manner in which one has certain knowledge of mathematical laws, i.e., insofar as these laws pertain to *a priori* relations which must obtain among the 'objects' of thought. "The five common universals: genus, species, differentia, property, accident . . . arise solely from the fact that we make use of one and the same *idea* for thinking of all individual items which resemble each other: we apply one and the same *term* to all the things which are represented by the idea in question, and this is the universal term" (CSM I, 212).

In his discussion in the introduction of *Ideas First Book* of the eidetic sciences which phenomenology investigates, Husserl divides the domain of material essences, or essences per se, from the formal region which is not coordinate with these essences, but is the empty form of any region whatever. As such, the latter prescribes for material ontologies a formal structure common to them all—this formal structure is articulated in terms of logical categories. "Concepts such as property, relative determination, predicatively formed affair-complex, relationship, identity, equality, aggregate (collection), cardinal number, whole and part, genus and species, and the like, are examples of logical categories" (Ideas I, 212). One is reluctant to impute to Descartes a conflation of cognition via categorial relations with cognition of what is related via those (purely formal) categories. In a letter to Princess Elizabeth of 1643 (CSM III, 218), he attempts to explain the thesis that there are "certain primitive notions which are as it were the *patterns* on the basis of which we form all our other conceptions." The most general of these primitive notions are 'being,' 'number,' and 'duration'; with regard to body alone, the notion of 'extension'; with regard to the soul alone, the notion of 'thought; and with regard to the soul and body together, the notion of their 'union.' He goes on to state that "all human knowledge consists solely in clearly [and distinctly?] distinguishing these notions and attaching each of them only to the things to which it pertains." These primitive notions are quite patently exactly the same as the highest-order simple 'natures,' intellectual, material and common, of Theorem D2 of Rule XII and can be grasped only through intellective insight; "since they are primitive notions, each of them can be understood only through itself."

In addition, this debate on whether Descartes held a "veil of ideas" position on the proper 'objects' of knowledge points to further large scale issues. To the extent that one agrees or disagrees that Descartes holds such a position and the reasons one advances in support of this, to the same extent and roughly for the same reasons, one would hold that Husserl does or does not endorse an exclusively 'object'-oriented explanation of the phenomenological genesis of meaning. And this endorsement applies to both the notion of the signitive apprehension of a sign and the notion of the perceptual presentation of an 'object' qua intentional content. Despite the fact that there is modest agreement on the interpretation of intentional content in the early Husserl, there is profound dissension on the status of his later reworking of this notion under the designation *noema*.[29] Aron Gurwitsch and Dagfinn Follesdall, most notably, have carried out a long, heated debate on this question: are *all* or only *some* noematic contents linguistically mediated; or perhaps, in another wording, are all noematic contents at their base constituted by linguistic determinations? In any case, irrespective of the resolution of these exegetical questions, both Descartes and Husserl considered some form of rational insight as the paramount reflective practice which would lead the investigator toward the genuine principles of a First Philosophy.

> Cartesian meditation is a method of discovery. . . . The cognitive exercises of the *Meditations* are engineered to suspend prejudice through skeptical doubt, to exercise one's intuition through the illumination of the cogito and the proofs of God's existence, and to prepare one for the intuitive apprehension of mind and body as having distinct essences through the exercises of the Second Meditation, which are consolidated in the arguments of the Sixth Meditation. The *Meditations* is successful when it can be laid aside in favour of direct apprehension of the clear but remote principles of First Philosophy.[30]

In terms of the Galilean-Cartesian model of a mathematized natural world, the "order of things" permits a real distinction between micro and macro features of physical objects, the mathematical expression of the inherent structural relations among macro-features (natural laws), and judgments formed on the basis of the same criteria which impart evidential certainty to these laws. He is now at a stage in the order of reasons where he can stipulate his most general epistemic rule: that whatever is clearly and distinctly perceived is true, i.e., every clear and distinct perception is undoubtedly something real and positive. (CSM II, 43). That it is *real* pertains to the 'objective' reality of an idea; that it is positive pertains to the "fact" that such an idea cannot signify nothing, but must signify some thing whose representation it is. The real and positive characteristics of a true 'object' of intellective insight are comprised under the two key terms, "clear" and "distinct," whose most succinct statement occurs at *Principles,* Part One, section 45: "I call a perception 'clear' when it is *present* and accessible to the attentive mind—just as we say that we *see* something clearly when it is present to the eye's gaze. . . . I call a perception 'distinct' if, as well as being clear, it is so *sharply separated* from all other perceptions that it contains within itself only what is clear" (CSM I, 207–8).

For the mature Descartes of the *Meditations*, what then is the proper 'object' of a clear and distinct idea? Our untangling of the various strands of Cartesian ideas leads to the conclusion that the following are open to the "grasp" of intellective insight:

(i)   simple micro-structural properties of composite physical objects; one can only *seem* to have clear and distinct ideas of macro-structural properties;

(ii) primitive notions, i.e., first principles which are innate;

(iii) logical truths which are derivable from primary notions;

(iv) one's own mental states, i.e., cognitive operations;

(v)   essences of kinds or classes of things, e.g., minds and bodies;

(vi) propositions (judgments) about states of affairs, with respect to (i)–(v).

Husserl's Mature Notion of Eidetic Insight

Husserl introduces his "principle of all principles" in *Ideas First Book* in terms of what characterizes the legitimacy of an idea (or presentation) in a formula which nearly approximates Descartes' main epistemic rule. "Every originary presentive intuition is a legitimizing source of cognition, that everything originarily (in its 'personal' actuality) offered to us in intuition is to be accepted simply as what it is *presented as being,* but also only *within the limits* in which it is presented there" (Ideas I, 44). In this statement, one should bear in mind the Cartesian definition of the two criterial marks as "present and accessible to the mind" and "sharply separated" or delimited from all other 'objects.' The phrase "in its personal actuality" refers to just that immediate aspect in which some 'object' appears *in propria persona;* that such an originary givenness of the 'object' means that it is indeed a real *(reell)* part of the intentional content, and that nothing else not thus given shall be considered as pertinent to the cognition of its 'object' being taken as evidentially certain. In other words, the object of an intuition is clear only insofar as it is taken just as it presents itself, and distinct only insofar as its being clearly given is limited by the conditions under which only clearly given things can appear.

Where the early Husserl spoke of straight-forward *(schlichter)* and categorial intuition, the later Husserl speaks of seeing *(einsehen)* or insight *(Einsicht)*, on the one hand, and seeing of essences *(Wesenschauung)* or eidetic intuition, on the other. "Seeing" becomes a *term of art* in the 1905–6 lectures and denominates the most primitive cognitive grasp with which consciousness is apprised.[31] "Seeing" *(schauen, schauende)* and its cognates comprise the dominant motif of these lectures in much the same way as *video* and its cognates do in Descartes' *Meditations*[32]; and this "seeing" motif dominates for reasons which Husserl clearly expresses in his discovery of Cartesian-inspired skeptical doubt. At the first level of the phenomenological orientation, the thesis of the natural attitude is brought to the surface in order to reflect on the status of scientific theories about the world. Under the aegis of a theoretical science, it is uncertain, or at least unclear, how it is possible for cognition to reach its object—the doubts unleashed by the skeptical assault have not yet been overcome. A complete overcoming can only be accomplished through the phenomenological reduction which excludes all that was once posited as transcendental, i.e., all that is allegedly beyond human knowledge's achievement. "If I am in the dark as to how cognition can reach that which is transcendent, not given in itself but 'intended as being outside,' no cognition or science of the transcendent can help to dispel the darkness. What I want is clarity. I want to understand the possibility of that reaching. . . . I want to come face to face with the essence of the possibility of that reaching. I want to make it given to me in an act of 'seeing,' [but] a 'seeing' cannot be demonstrated" (IP, 5).

At the second level, after the inception of radical doubt, a whole new domain of 'objects' of investigation is opened up. The essence of the sort of thinking which makes this domain available is the result of explicit reflection on just that manner in which some 'objects,' irrespective of whether the 'object' of thought points to an actually existent thing, are given to consciousness as pointing beyond their intentional content. The givenness of the cogitata is self-evidential according to the criteria of clarity and distinctness established as preeminent in the case of the indubitable truth of the cogito. But the apodicticity with which the cogito is given is unique, it surpasses the conditions of clarity and distinctness "as long as one is thinking" of some thing. One cannot proceed further in a search for the evidence with which phenomena are presented by attending to this paragon content. One must investigate the manner in which it is possible for anything else to be given as a self-evident 'object' of cognition. This specific manner is denominated *seeing*, the direct and immediate apprehension of that which is given purely in its self-givenness.

At the third level, the question arises; "How far does self-givenness reach? We are once again led somewhat deeper, and in depths lie the obscurities, and in obscurities lie the problems" (IP, 8). At least part of the obscurity rests in an equivocation in the meaning of transcendence and immanence, an ambiguity which unthinkingly can have been transposed from its significance at the naive level of experience into this reduced or "bracketed" level. To continue to think of transcendence as pertaining to whatever it is that the appearance points to beyond itself is to surreptitiously reintroduce the thesis of the actual being of the world. Rather, transcendence and immanence must be reconceptualized in terms of the now obvious elision in the meaning of "appearance" (phenomena): between appearance eo ipso and that which appears in the appearance. There are now two absolute data under phenomenological scrutiny—the givenness of the appearing and the givenness of the 'object' in the appearing.

At the first, naive level, seeing seemed such a simple operation: "The seeing just sees the things *(Sache)*, the things are simply there and in the truly evident seeing, they are there in consciousness." But this being "simply there" obscures the depths which radical skepticism has disclosed, and being in consciousness seems to be a matter of containment, e.g., "in a hull or a vessel." Here, of course, Husserl has parted from the Cartesian path, since for Descartes, though the mind is not in the body the way a pilot is in a vessel, ideas are "modes" of cognition which contain formal and objective reality. For Husserl, in contrast, ideas are constituted in consciousness and it is the laborious and complex task of phenomenological anlysis to trace the stepwise aetiology of the constitution of 'objects' of all sorts within cognitive processes. Every such process, while being enacted, can be made the 'object' of a pure seeing, and is something absolutely given in this seeing, whose being cannot be doubted (IP, 24).Husserl concludes the fourth lecture with this synoptic simile (though the reader may wince at the mention of a "mystical intuition"):

> Thus as little interpretation as possible, but as pure an intuition as possible *(intuitio sine comprehensione)*. In fact, we will hark back to the speech of the mystics when they describe the intellectual seeing which is supposed not to be a discursive knowledge. And the whole trick consists in this—to give free rein to the seeing eye and to bracket the references which go beyond the "seeing" and are entangled with the seeing, along with the entities which are supposedly given and thought along with the "seeing," and finally to bracket what is read into them through the accompanying reflections. The crucial question is: Is the supposed object given in the proper sense? Is it, in the strictest sense, "seen" and grasped, or does the intention go beyond that? (IP, 50–51)

Both Descartes and Husserl disparage introspection as a valid form of intuition into one's own mental states or into the nature of the subject whose states they are.[33] Whatever emphasis they place on sensuous perception as an exemplary form of cognition, one cannot be said to inwardly perceive the percipient mind. (Thus Descartes' rejoinder to Gassendi's remark that one can use the eye to see the eye in a mirror.) However, they both place a high premium on "seeing" as a figurative term to designate clear and distinct apprehension of the 'object' of knowledge. Recent scholarship has pointed out the predominance of visual metaphors in the language with which philosophers, at least until the twentieth century, talk about the most immediate and direct cognitive "grasp." The designation of certain knowing as a kind of "seeing" is still readily apparent in many modern European languages. To the question whether or not you understand my meaning, you might respond that you "see" or "don't see." This construction is paralleled in German: *sehen* is "to see," *verstehen* is "to understand," *nachsehen* is "to check out or confirm," and so forth. Descartes relies heavily on visual terms, especially in the *Meditations*, to convey the notion of clear and distinct understanding. This usage crystallizes in one of his most far-reaching phrases, *videre videor*, "it seems that I see." Why then the derogation of introspection, "looking within," for the truth of consciousness or the nature of the self? Because of the profound difference between the notions of *looking* and *seeing*; and for Husserl, seeing just is understanding an 'object' as it is directly given in experience, and not via some privileged access.[34]

At one time or another, we have all had the experience of walking in the woods, a natural habitat removed from our usual surroundings. Perhaps you are with a friend who, at some point in your walk, halts abruptly and says, "Look over there! Do you see that red squirrel?" You follow his pointing finger and survey the nearest trees but you don't see a red squirrel. "But you're *looking* right at it," your friend might comment. You look again; suddenly a component of your perceptual field resolves itself into a red squirrel; what you had taken to be a chunk of bark is in fact a small, furry creature. You were *looking* at it, but you didn't *see* it. This usage is perfectly captured in the etymological meaning of intro*spection*, retro*spection*, *specta*tor, and so forth; *specto* means "to look at," thus *introspection* would mean "to look within," and this would orient the viewer in the right direction, a notion which Descartes endorses when he talks about attention or the attentive mind. But it is *video,* "seeing," which allows (or elicits) the resolution, the bringing into fullness, of the knowing subject's self within intuitive clarity.[35] So, much later, when Hume looked within for the self and found naught, he was looking in the right place, he just shouldn't have been *looking*.

Six years after these lectures, in the 1911 article "Philosophy as Rigorous Science," Husserl withdraws his earlier comparison of pure intuition with the sort of intuition spoken of by mystics. If anything, he says here, mystification resides in the attempt to exploit phenomenological insights while remaining within the natural attitude. *"The spell of inborn naturalism* also consists in the fact that it makes it so difficult for all of us to see essences or ideas. . . . Intuiting essences conceals no more difficulties or 'mystical' secrets than does perception" (HSW, 181). He goes on to explicitly identify the proper domain of phenomenological investigations as those disclosed by intuitions of the essences of conscious states and processes: perception, imagination, recollection, judgment, emotion, the will. Here he rapidly summarizes some of the main points of the Second Investigation regarding the fulfilment of intentions in intuition, adequate judgments based on valid cognitions, and his criticisms of Locke and Hume's notions of ideas. He is at some pains to stress one of his central theoretical insights: that the physical and the psychical are not the only explanatory frameworks within which philosophy must work. Phenomenology is not concerned with matter-of-fact mental events as occurring in this human being, in these particular circumstances, but with the *a priori* conditions and structural relations without which cognition could not take place. As such, of course, he endorses a Kantian transcendental perspective on the issue of the ultimate ground for the certainty which attaches to human knowledge; unlike Kant, this transcendental ground is discovered within, or on the basis of, the phenomenologically reduced ego.

However, Husserl's mature notion of intuition as seeing or insight into both particulars and essences is not presented in a systematic format until the introduction to *Ideas First Book* (1913), where he begins by addressing an issue not included in the preceding article. Transcendental phenomenology is not a science of matters-of-fact, whether physical or psychical, but an eidetic science of phenomena which can be characterized as *irreal*. The claim that these phenomena are irrealities can only be adequately understood after the phenomenological reduction has bracketed the being (or reality) of the world and all its attendant psycho-physical corollaries. To denominate this transcendentally reduced sphere as an irreal domain is thus an attempt to avoid the standard dichotomy of real and ideal, a contrast which in metaphysical position-taking fails to be exclusive. This early mention by Husserl of a position which entails neither realism nor idealism points forward to the source of a heated debate (which cannot be entered here) on the unique status which phenomenology claims in being a transcendental idealism, but an idealism of an entirely unprecedented nature. "The realism of the *L. U.* was only a stage in the elaboration of phenomenology, and that what is now called the idealism of the *Ideas* had to appear in order to give an ontological value to the data of intuition. The idealism of *Ideas* is an intentional idealism and consequently conceives in a new way the mode of existing and the structure of consciousness, as well as the phenomenal existence of things. This idealism seems to solve the 'enigma of intuition'." [36]

Section 1 of chapter One begins with a programmatic statement regarding sciences of the natural attitude to which object-provinces correspond. To all of their correct statements, there also correspond as basic sources which validate their legitimacy, certain intuitions in which these 'objects' are themselves given as existing. The presentative intuition *(gebende Anschauung)* proper to this level is experience, and that which presents something originarily is intuition:

> To have something real given originarily and 'attentively to perceive' and 'experience' it in an intuiting simpliciter are one and the same. We have originary experience of concrete physical things in 'external perception,' but no longer in memory

or in forward-regarding expectation; we have originary experience of ourselves and of our states of consciousness in so-called internal or self-perception; not, however, of others and of their mental processes in 'empathy.' As belonging to them, we 'view the mental processes of others' on the basis of the perception of their outward manifestation in the organism. This empathic viewing is, more particularly, an intuiting, a presentive act, although no longer an act that is presentive of something originarily. The other and his psychical life are, to be sure, given in consciousness as 'themselves there' and in union with his organism; but they are not, like the latter, given as originary (Ideas I, 6).

This passage has been quoted at some length because it succinctly enumerates all the principal constituent modes in which intuition can legitimately be spoken of, aside from eidetic intuition which brings them all thematically to the fore. This passage also includes reference to an important new mode of intuition, one which is not mentioned in his earlier versions of 1906 and 1911, that of the *empathetic* intuition of others. Further analyses in the introduction, taken up in detail in later sections, elucidate reworkings of the earlier notion of straightforward intuition into nonoriginary and originary intuition, the latter of which is roughly congruent with the sense of *'in propria persona.'* It is worth noting that later revised copies of the printed text of *Ideas First Book* are marked by Husserl to indicate that he had changed his mind, or was at least in some doubt, that one does not have originary intuition of others. Some of the more convoluted arguments in the Fifth Lecture of the *Cartesian Meditations* seem to be dedicated to a position that, through the intersubjective reduction, one may indeed attain an originary presentation of the other him/herself.

Any individual thing, as the 'object' of sciences of matters-of-fact, has a contingent existence, in the sense that with regard to its essence, it could have been otherwise. Even though there are necessary relations (scientific laws) which obtain between things, the fact that (sic) such laws do indeed obtain could be read otherwise; though of course, such an alternate "reading" would express a new set of necessary relations. But the phrase "with regard to its essence" means that it pertains to the sense of anything contingent that it *have an essence*, i.e., its own definitive character and features about which true judgments can be predicated. Everything which belongs to the essence of an individual of some kind (e.g., a musical tone), another individual of the same kind can also have—that each tone is a tone pertains to the essence of tone as such. An intuition of something individual can be transmuted into eidetic seeing (ideation) and the essence presented immediately to consciousness, though this content may be adequate or inadequate to a greater or lesser degree.

At least in the case of physical objects given originarily in perception, intuition of essences is limited by correlative considerations. That is, certain categories of essences can only be given one-sidedly in a momentary intuition, many-sidedly in a sequence of intuitions, but never all-sidedly. Seeing an essence, nevertheless, is indeed consciousness of something, an 'object' in the broad sense proper to formal logic, i.e., any 'object' which is the subject of possible true predications. As an essence itself given in an intuition it can be 'objectivated' in other intentional acts, for instance, it can be thought of vaguely or distinctly, it can be imagined or recollected, and still remain just this same essence. Seeing an essence, in the pregnant sense, is an originarily presentive intuition, grasping the essence in its "personal selfhood" *(in propria persona)*. Husserl remarks here in a footnote that the earlier notion of ideation (categorial intuition) requires a "freer concept" which encompasses every consciousness directed simply and immediately to an essence (Ideas I, 10, note 14). In the *Logical Investigations*, he thought of the 'object' of a categorial intuition largely through analogy with the 'object' of sensuous intuition, which is *as it were* a representation on a higher level. But in the third edition (1920), in line with analyses in the *Ideas*, he remarks that he no longer approves of his own doctrine. He now considers categorial intuition to be a *founded* cognitive act, founded that is on lower level apprehensions of sensuous contents, synthesized through processes of identity and directed towards an ideal 'object.'

There is, however, an ineliminable difference between these two orders of intuition: that directed towards the factually existent and that directed towards an essence. If one seizes with essential insight upon the 'objects' which are thus differentiated then all the "semi-mystical thoughts" attached to them will be removed. The pure essence *(eidos)* can be exemplified through experience, in the paradigmatic case of perception, but can also be exemplified through the 'objects' of mere phantasy. As such, an eidetic intuition can take its point of departure from that which is nonperceptual, that which is imagined *as if* it were an actual instance of the type. "Positing of, and to begin with, intuitive seizing upon essences implies not the slightest of any individual factual existence; pure eidetic truths contain not the slightest assertion about matters of fact" (Ideas I, 11). This thinking in the mode of *as if* involves the methodological technique of "free variation in phantasy" which is re-invoked in greater detail in Part III (Ideas I, 157–60; 260–68), *Experience and Judgement* (EJ, 352–60) and in *Phenomenological Psychology* (PP, 54–65).

The method of variation in phantasy is the necessary propaedeutic for the eidetic reduction, the version of the reduction which distinguishes eidetic intuition (or *Wesenschauung*) from the earlier categorial intuition and provides Husserl with the *point d'appui* for his founding of phenomenology as an eidetic science. The notion (or technique) of variation in phantasy, and hence seeing of essences, has occasionally been misunderstood.[37] The misreading usually goes like this:

you select some item x in your perceptual environs, fix your attention on it, and then imagine (in the sense of invent) other sorts of x, "seeing" whether or not each imagined x can be construed as a genuine instance of the sort at issue. But this reading commits two basic errors: the first is to operate from the natural standpoint in which one has tacitly accepted the actual being of the world; and the second is to confuse contingent, psychological features of one's imaginings with the ideal possibilities of an *a priori* conformity to type. Husserl's mature vision of phenomenology as an eidetic science is connected very closely with his own distinctive concept of a pure, *a priori* cognition, and this concept descends ultimately from his understanding of mathematical intuition.[38]

In his 1929 work, *Formal and Transcendental Logic*, he remarks that "the concept eidos is also given a maximally broad sense, . . . this sense defines the only concept belonging to the ambiguous expression *a priori* that I grant philosophical recognition to" (FTL, 248, note). The most basic feature of *a priori* thinking is that it accomplishes a *liberation from the facts*, the reconfiguring of the fact into *an arbitrary example*. Husserl appeals to the 'objects' of geometry as pure spatial figures: the essence of "triangle" and its essential laws are not tied to imagined or concrete triangles, though the geometer may *start from* any arbitrarily given example in his considerations of triangular possibilities. One would never be able to assert as axiomatic that all the angles of a triangle always equal 180 degrees unless all the intuited instances conformed to an ideal type. The crux of eidetic intuition here consists in seeing the invariable among all the variations; that in the coincidence of intentional contents of innumerable instances, one (or more) things remain unchanged. "This universal essence is the eidos, the *idea* in the Platonic sense, but apprehended purely and free from all metaphysical interpretations, therefore, taken precisely as it becomes given to us in *immediate intuitiveness* in the seeing of ideas which arises in that way" (PP, 54).

At this stage, we are in a position to draw together several strands in Husserl's mature project: the basic sense of intuition, pure phenomenology as an eidetic science, seeing of essences, and the Cartesian notion of *mathesis universalis*. "The insight into the pure eidetic universality permits every imaginable particularization to be known in advance (a priori) as a particularization of its essence, that is, in the consciousness of mere exemplification (as a member of the range of singular, pure possibilities)."[39] It is to the seventeenth-century scientific revolution which instaurated a mathematical model for natural laws, in the work of Galileo, Descartes, and Newton, that Husserl gives the historical credit for initial insights into purely eidetic sciences. Descartes' quest for an all-embracing universal science would necessarily require that it be stripped of all contingent, qualitative determinations, liberated from the facts, if it were to have *a priori* legitimacy in all the domains which fell under its discipline. For Husserl, there is one final theme to which eidetic intuition must be directed. "Immediate seeing, not merely sensuous, experiential seeing, but seeing in the universal sense as an originarily presentive consciousness of any kind whatever, is the ultimate legitimizing source of all rational assertions" (Ideas I, 36). Phenomenology itself is the discipline of such rational assertions about the *a priori* nature of consciousness. Eidetic intuition must be brought to bear on the ramiform possibilities which phenomenological analyses have disclosed among an immense diversity of *a priori* structures of consciousness itself.

Truth Is the Conformity of Thought with Its Object—
But Which 'Object'?

Perhaps one of the most perspicacious ways to show the parallels between Descartes' and Husserl's mature notions of intuition or insight is to compare their positions on the issue of truth. On the rare occasions when Descartes directly addresses the question of truth, he holds the view that truth is the agreement of thought and thing (*adequatio rei et intellectus*), another example of a scholastic maxim which he was usually so careful to avoid. In a letter to Mersenne of 1639, he offers his comments on Lord Herbert of Cherbury's *On Truth* by remarking that the notion of truth is so eminently clear that no one could be ignorant of it. What reason, he asks, could we have for accepting anything which could teach us the *nature* of truth, if we did not know that *it* was true, that is, if we didn't already know what truth meant? The only thing which could teach us the nature of truth is God, through the light of reason; God's essence is such that he would never deceive, not even about the meaning of truth itself. Truth then is a primary notion, not explicable in terms of more simple ideas, but if compelled to "spell it out" for someone, he would reply that "Truth, in the strict sense, denotes the conformity of thought with its object, but when it is attributed to *things outside thought*, it means only that they can be the *objects* of true thoughts, either ours or God's" (CSM III, 139; emphasis added).

At the end of the "Fourth Meditation," he returns to the topic of truth and explains that, "Every clear and distinct perception is undoubtedly something (real and positive) and hence cannot come from nothing, but must necessarily have God as its author" (CSM II, 43). It is not nothing in the sense that the 'object' of an intuition cannot be invented like a chimera, nor can it be the product of a deceptive force, but rather is comprised of elements which really pertain to the thing itself, arranged in a manner which is supported by the principles of the natural order; as a "thing outside thought" it can then be made the 'object' of a true judgment. In the "Replies to Arnauld's Objections," Descartes makes a further distinction between adequate and complete knowledge. "If a piece of knowledge is to be *adequate* it must contain absolutely all of the properties which are in the thing which is the 'object' of knowledge. Hence only God can know that he has adequate knowledge of all things" (CSM II, 155). In contrast with this hypothetical capacity for infinite analysis (which Leibniz was to make much of), the human intellect may in fact possess adequate knowledge about many things but cannot know for certain *that* it has such knowledge, unless God grants "a special revelation of the fact." Descartes astutely points out that it may be the case that one does not need to have wholly adequate knowledge of things, but rather may possess knowledge adequate enough for the thing in question. For example, in order to intuit the real (in contrast with the conceptual) distinction between two things such as the mind and the body, it cannot be necessary that our knowledge of them is wholly adequate, since it is not possible for us to know that such knowledge is adequate. In the case of mind and body, one has to have the intuition that the principal attribute of mind is thought and that of body is extension. One also has to know that this knowledge is adequate enough insofar as other properties which remain unknown (and perhaps unknowable) cannot contravene the initial insight. The truth about the basis of mind-body union can only be revealed by the light of divine grace, not that of reason, and cannot be made completely intelligible since only God has knowledge wholly adequate to its principle.

In sum, for Descartes, truth is the conformity or adequation, expressed in an assenting judgment, of a clear and distinct thought (intuition) with the 'object' of that thought; with respect to things which lie "outside thought," some judgments accurately indicate the real properties of those elements whose causal impact on the neural "spirits" signify to the mind just that thought. True judgments can be made on the ground of intuitions directed toward: (a) the simplest elements of natural things; (b) the relations of dependence and independence which hold between them; (c) primary notions such as mind, body, God, truth, and so forth; (d) rules of inference and deduction which allow the mind to move securely from insight to insight; and (e) one's own mental states which can be truly predicated of the mind alone, such as occurrent perceptions, bodily sensations, and the emotions proper.

In Husserl's earliest consideration about truth, he also endorses the maxim that truth is the conformity of thought with its 'object.' "Where a presentative intention has achieved its last fulfillment, the genuine *adequatio rei et intellectus* has been brought about. The object is actually 'present' or 'given,' and present as just what we have intended it" (LI, 762; cf. 254). By fulfillment, Husserl means a cognitive act in which an empty intention, a vague direction toward, is brought into connection through various syntheses with a correspondent intuition; the intention is confirmed or disconfirmed through the carrying out of the syntheses. The synthetic relations are comprised under a categorial point of view, for example, that of part and whole, dependence and independence, and so forth, a point of view whose intention presupposes both the acts brought into unity and the 'objects' of those acts. It goes without saying that, in light of the reduction's bracketing of the world's existence, such objects can never lie outside thought.

Rudolf Bernet comments that in the Sixth Investigation, "Husserl was not yet able fully to free himself from the old concept of adequation.... In any case, it is perfectly clear that the old problem of the 'bridge' between subjective, cognitive activity and objective thing no longer presents itself for Husserl.... Truth rather concerns the agreement among various intentional acts or their intentional objects. The phenomenological analysis of truth is especially dedicated to formulating the ideal conditions for the possibility of this agreement."[40] In the sections on adequate and inadequate evidence in *Ideas First Book*, Husserl turns his attention to those ideal conditions and makes a radical reassessment of the character of evidence as it pertains to different possibilities of intentional fulfillment; thus he claims that intuition can achieve evidence in the positing of retrospective memory, of empathy with another person, and of an irreal essence. In a later marginal note to this passage he states: "There is an absolute (an adequate) evidence. Adequate truth is not as good an expression [as] *absolute* truth. Still one can also accept it and say: adequation consists of the fact that truth is directed toward the existing . . . affair-complex," or state-of-affairs (Ideas I, 334, note), that is, the 'object' of thought considered strictly as an intentional correlate.

Perhaps the key insight into the profound though subtle difference between Cartesian and Husserlian intuition has to do with the scope and function of the many-layered reductions. The phenomenological reduction deprives the meditator of the pretheoretical ground for maintaining the thesis of the world's existence, and without a transcendent divine being there is no post-theoretical reason for bringing back the world lost through the methodical purge. The transcendental reduction provides the insight that only mundane consciousness would construe itself as a part of the world responsible for the conceptual schema within which the world appears. Transcendental consciousness is now understood as that which could survive the annulment of the world because it is not *a real part* of that world, rather it constitutes the mind in a naturalistic sense. The eidetic reduction refuses to grant the deeply buried presupposition that it is a thinking *thing* (or substance) which has thoughts; instead it focuses on the essences of thoughts and the systematic interconnections between their simplest components and synthetic relations.

Husserl's deviations from Cartesian intuition are the consequences of his transformation of methodical doubt into the progressive layers or branches of phenomenological suspension. The first epoché restricts the scope of evidence to cogitata as the correlate of intentional acts, suspending any positing of real objects as material support for sensory perceptions. Intuition provides its own 'seal' of evidence; what is presented in an intuition is absolute, in the sense that the truth of its givenness is not contingent on the truth of anything else, and is self-founding in the sense that it is the basis without which cognitive acts of a founded or modified character, such as doubting, affirming, and denying, could not take place. The second epoché refocuses the superseded notion of transcendence as the ground for the world's appearing to a higher-order consciousness whose insight is directed toward the constitution of the objectivity of 'objects' in the empirical domain and the synthetic relations which obtain between their interwoven moments. In the final stage of First Philosophy, the eidetic reduction is devoted to intuition of the pure essences which pertain to the regional ontologies of being and the formal principles of an abstract language which can ultimately express the dream of a universal science.

8

THE CONCEPT OF
RADICAL CONVERSION

W/e have followed two paths from our initial points of departure: Descartes'
overthrow of traditional metaphysics through methodical doubt and
Husserl's reinstitution of this doubt in the genesis of phenomenology. These two
paths have traced a zig-zag pattern across a variety of topics, sometimes converging, sometimes diverging. But both these trajectories are plotted against an
otherwise unknown landscape—it is no arbitrary rhetorical choice that both
repeatedly describe their enterprise as the exploration of a new world. Even their
divergences occur as the result of encountering similar salient features in the
landscape, but to which they ascribe different interpretations.

In these closing stages we reconsider a speculation made at the beginning,
but which we can only now hope will have been adequately demonstrated.
Descartes' and Husserl's philosophical projects are parallel for a number of
reasons: they are reacting to similar background problems (primarily skepticism), they abandon the vocabulary and method of their predecessors, adopt a
novel formal ontology, and commit themselves to a grounding of evidence in the
domain of subjective experience. Specific areas where they converge in their
thinking have been uncovered in our discussion of the intentionality of consciousness, the distinction between cognitive act and content, the union of mind
and body as dependent parts of a whole person, universal doubt as a methodical
expedient for disengagement, and intuition as direct cognitive grasp or immediate presentation.

Chapter 8 is a revised version of an article published by *Philosophy & Theology,* vol. 10,
no. 2, (Dec. 1997).

One of the main reasons why their trajectories are structurally isomorphic and reveal so many convergences is due to an overriding initial demand made on the reader to participate actively in the enterprise—and this is a call for radical conversion. One might think that the relation between Descartes and Husserl is obvious and topic-specific, but it isn't—it is subtle and pervasive. Does Husserl talk about radical conversion in the *Cartesian Meditations* because his subject is Descartes' notion of a turning-away which must begin at the foundations? Well, yes of course, this is patently the case. But since 1907 Husserl had already been talking of radical conversion in many other contexts. Descartes speaks of turning away from the old world and turning toward a new world for reasons which underpin his entire project, and Husserl speaks of this turning-with for the same reasons, some of which he cites as his motive for taking Descartes as his point of departure.

Is "conversion" such an anomalous term in philosophical discourse that no other instances could be cited? Is this calling something unique to Descartes' and Husserl's vision of First Philosophy? Wouldn't every philosopher call for the reader to turn with him or her and see things in a new light? Of course, and such "seeing" is no more a special talent or superadded faculty than the achievement of seeing the difference between necessary and sufficient condition; once you have seen the difference you are able to make distinctions unavailable before. It is as though an ill-defined misty patch suddenly resolves into sharply outlined contours and then you recognize the object. Every philosopher wants to convince or persuade the reader on a specific point, and to do so by appeal to rational argument; but this is not a call for *conversion*, which demands that one abandon all previous convictions and commit oneself entirely to a new path.

The most likely reaction when reading the word "conversion" is to think of it in a religious context, in terms of a turning of one's faith. In the Old Testament, the Hebrew word for this is most commonly expressed in the verbal form, literally "to turn in one's tracks," away from one ritual or sect and toward another ritual or sect. Regarding conversion's explicitly religious connotations, "it has been described as a dramatic confrontation in which the Law and the Temple are essential elements. Israel repents its adulterous abandonment of its covenant with God, an infidelity that involves it in a tragic series of misfortunes of which the Exile is the worst. In sorrow it now turns heart-broken to Him and to the faithful practice of the Law."[1] The presumption here is that conversion occurs in an interreligious context.

This notion undergoes a considerable modification in New Testament use of the term *epistrepho* (verbal again, the noun *epistrophe* is unknown in NT), which means "turning toward" Christ as savior and turning away from all things opposed to Christ and his teaching. "Conversion is now described as exclusively concerned with a change in man. God is no longer portrayed as turning to man . . . [for] the incarnation is in every respect the ultimate turning of God to man."[2] Lest it be unthinkingly assumed that conversion occurs only *between* religious faiths or between a nonreligious and a religious viewpoint, it is also characterized as intrinsic to the progress of faith *within* the Christian Church itself, i.e., from one sect to another. Robin Lane Fox cites several famous examples of early Christians who lapsed from belief to nonbelief and remarks: "We do not hear of anyone who left Christianity for simple paganism without any accompanying philosophy: perhaps this silence is significant and a lapse from Christianity did always lead to a favour for some systematic belief."[3] However, religious conversion is but one manifestation of a more fundamental cognitive-affective reorientation of the whole self away from the old and toward the new.

The Latin (and hence Vulgate) *con-verto* is a nearly exact translation of the Greek *epi-strepho*, a key term which Plato employs toward the end of the famous analogy of the cave. Here then is an explicit philosophical usage of the term which predates the New Testament and inaugurates a secular etymology with which Augustine, among others, would have been well aware.

> The true analogy for this indwelling power in the soul and the instrument whereby each of us apprehends is that of an eye that could not be converted to the light from the darkness except by turning the whole body. Even so this organ of knowledge must be turned around from the world of becoming together with the entire soul, like the scene-shifting *periactus* in the theatre, until the soul is able to endure the contemplation of essence and the brightest region of being. . . . There might be an art, an art of the speediest and most effective shifting or conversion of the soul, not an art of producing vision in it, but on the assumption that it possesses vision but does not rightly direct it and does not look where it should, an art of bringing this about.[4]

A. D. Nock cites this passage from the *Republic*, as well as Seneca's *Epistles* (108.17), Aristotle's *Protrepticus*, and Cicero's *De Natura Deorum* (I. 77) in his chapter on "Conversion to Philosophy"[5] before the Christian era. It is worth noting that in all the cases Nock considers, the person in question reorients himself away from a nonphilosophic position toward philosophy per se. Nock argues convincingly that before the fourth century B.C.E., even interreligious conversion must be understood in a highly restricted sense. For the various Greek and Near Eastern cults and their gods, there was no organized, systematic doctrine toward which persons could orient their entire self. It was more a matter of observing specific precepts and rituals, usually in a very narrowly defined time and place, i.e., festivals and precincts. Beyond the sacred precinct, an adherent of Zeus Sabazaos or Phrygian Cybele, for example, would not consider his worldview to be informed by his allegiance, or structured according to his beliefs (with the possible exception of Mithraism). If anything, it is only with the arrival of Plato's Academy, Aristotle and the other competing Schools that one can genuinely speak of a transformative conversion.

The passage from Plato is highly significant in another respect, for it synopsizes a number of salient points already discussed in previous chapters and points directly toward their optimal outcome—a call for radical conversion. The "indwelling power in the soul" is virtually identical with Descartes' formulation of the innate cognitive power (Rule IV) which, when combined with other cognitive operations, produces the four mental functions (or faculties). The "true analogy" for this is the eye which turns from darkness to light; for Descartes, vision is the exemplary mode of intuition which pierces through the darkness thrown up by skeptical doubt and turns back to draw on the natural light of reason. It is necessary that this vision turn away from the "world of becoming"; and this points to Descartes' injunction to withdraw from the world and detach from the senses, in order to endure "the contemplation of essence and the brightest region of being," a description which both Descartes and Husserl employ to characterize the proper field of philosophical inquiry. And finally, Plato asserts that such an intellective vision does not have to be instilled, but only directed to look where it should; and this points to the Cartesian and Husserlian invocation of *video* (seeing) instead of *specto* (looking). Husserl's remark to the effect that the "irreal" objectivity of mathematical entities, toward which categorial intuition is directed, may be construed as referring to a "Platonic realm of being" finds more than a chance touchstone here.

It seems to me that there are two principal dimensions with respect to which one can be converted: the philosophical, which is this-worldly; and the religious, which is other-worldly. It seems to be a highly strained sense of the term to say that one is converted, for example, to a genre of music, a football team, a style of clothing, or a political party.[6] In all such cases, everything else is left intact, only one component of one's worldview has been changed. It is not the case that the worldview itself has been transformed, as a result of which all the components undergo change. In every case of religious conversion which William James examined a century ago both the self and the world are completely transformed.[7] It is very common for the convert to speak of confronting an entirely *new world*, an expression which, as we have seen, both Descartes and Husserl use to describe the domain disclosed by their investigations. Of course, it seems trite to remark that it is hard to conceive how the self could be entirely transformed without its world being also thus affected; on the other hand, it seems strange to imagine what it would be for one's world to be overturned while the self remains as it was.

The most common rhetorical trope used to typify this profound change in self and world is that of *loss and gain*, a trope found often in both philosophical and NT-religious conversion contexts. Perhaps the best known passage is "For those who want to save their life will lose it, and those who lose their life for my sake will save (or find) it. What does it profit them if they gain the whole world, but forfeit themselves?"[8] St. Augustine's experience of conversion occurred during a profound philosophical crisis. While reading St. Paul's Epistles (*Romans* chapter 7 is the best known first-hand account of conversion), he received a summons: "In an instant . . . it was as though the light of confidence flooded into my heart and all the darkness of doubt was dispelled."[9] It is Augustine whom Arnauld quotes to Descartes for a precursor to the *cogito ergo sum*,[10] and it is with Augustine's words that Husserl closes his own meditations: "Do not wish to go out; go back into yourself. Truth dwells in the inner man" (CM, 157).

What would discriminate religious from philosophical conversion? In the former case, the experience of conversion is the realization that the new world is God's creation and the self God's creature. For religious conversion, it is irrelevant how one came to be in a position to be converted, or how the conversion was effected. The most famous example of Christian conversion, St. Paul on the road to Damascus, is also a paradigm for the unpreparedness, even the unwillingness, of the soon to be converted. But in the case of the philosopher, the new world is constructed from the singular, irreducible point of view of the meditator and if, as is the case with Descartes, it shows a necessary role for God's will, this is still only a part of the overall picture. In addition, it is absolutely essential for this sort of conversion that the philosophizing self is able to look backward (so to speak) and point to all the discursive stages which inescapably result in this reorientation. This is the point of presenting the *Meditations* according to the order of reasons which exhibit these discursive stages so that the reader can follow the explorer's trail, and not just survey an already corrected and revised map.

Descartes indicates his awareness of another dimension of conversion when he states that there are two possible authorities for the assurance that one has attained certain knowledge: the natural light (reason) and divine grace, a topic which he says is better left to theologians. The young Descartes would certainly have been familiar with the force of authority in illumination by divine grace. His years at the Jesuit College of La Fleche would have exposed him to the *Ratio Studiorum* and to Ignatius Loyola's *Spiritual Exercises*. The example of

Loyola provided an historical precedent for radical conversion more recent and far more personal than Plato or Augustine. Loyola was canonized in 1611 and the young student, a few years later, would have been dramatically impressed by the attendant ceremonies. Loyola himself had undergone a profound conversion experience while at Manresa, near Barcelona, in 1522. During this time he abandoned his previous career as a proud and idealistic courtier and retreated to a cave for solitude where he mortified his flesh through fasting and penance. His *Spiritual Exercises* are not a record of his own transformation—this was compiled by his faithful disciple de Camara—nor are they in any way a guidebook by which one could be converted. However, they are the direct consequence of his conversion and are designed to be followed, under the direction of a confessor, by a retreatant who desires to gain a deeper knowledge of the foundations of his own faith.[11]

L. J. Beck quite rightly points to the "formal similarity" between this work and Descartes' *Meditations*: both are divided into daily meditations which enjoin solitude and contemplation, both are punctuated with moments for rest, and their persuasive effect is cumulative upon multiple readings. The principal value of his comparison between these two exemplary texts is to clarify their convergent rhetorical purposes, which place a heavy demand on its readers or students to carry out these exercises for themselves. "At the back of Descartes' mind is the idea . . . that philosophy is not a class-room subject of instruction but a special kind of activity; and that accordingly nobody can really begin to understand it except by being induced to indulge in the actual exercise of it, by grappling with the problems under the guidance and help of a more experienced thinker, but nevertheless, in the last resort, thinking the problems out for himself."[12]

Gary Hatfield's recent work admirably shows the close analogy between the *Meditations* as cognitive exercises and then-current spiritual exercises.[13] Loyola's treatise with its basis in an Aristotelian account of cognition, and the works of Eustace de St. Paul in the Augustinian tradition, were both familiar to Descartes. Each emphasized three faculties or powers of the mind (memory, intellect, and will) and the three ways or stages through which the meditator progresses. The scheme of three powers (along with sense perception) had long been endorsed by Descartes, in the *Rules,* the *Discourse*, and of course, as the several "courts of appeal" by which to adjudicate certain knowledge in the *Meditations* itself. The religious sense of the three ways comprised the purgative, in which the body is mortified and one turns away from the senses; the illuminative, in which one becomes aware of one's moral power through Christ's example; and the unitive, in which one seeks to join or merge one's will with the divine will.

Hatfield astutely points out that both the three powers and the three ways are paralleled in Cartesian cognitive exercises. In the "First Meditation," me-

thodical doubt purges the senses of illusions and the memory of delusions (prejudices); in the "Second" and "Third," the meditator's disclosure of the cogito
occurs within the illumination of the natural light; and in the "Fourth," the
meditator seeks to direct his will in accordance with what has been clearly and
distinctly perceived, and this means in accord with God's will. Our analyses of
the phases of methodical doubt in chapter 5 showed just this sequential structure: first, abandon prejudices and withdraw from the senses; second, clear and
distinct seeing via the natural light; third, an affirmation by an act of will regarding that which one has clearly and distinctly seen. Another parallel is that the
discursive force of spiritual or cognitive exercises relies on both argumentation
and exemplification.[14] The process of doubt is presented in an argumentative
form but one grasps the truth of the proposition *"cogito ergo sum"* through
exemplary insight. The doctrine of ideas articulates the necessary features of
'formal' and 'objective' reality and the innate principles with which they are
interconnected, but one insightfully grasps the reality of God prior to the proof
of God's existence. Hatfield observes that "the *Meditations* are not so much a
continuous argument as a set of instructions for uncovering the truths that lie
immanent in the intellect."

Descartes could also be said to subscribe to the moral precepts which were
intrinsic to an ascetic or contemplative approach, especially in a monastic context—poverty, chastity, and obedience. His provisional moral code in Part Three
of the *Discourse* is clearly enunciated along these lines, though in a more secular
setting (CSM I, 122–24). The first maxim is to obey the laws and customs of his
country, including the Catholic religion; the second, regarding constancy, is to
be firm and decisive in all his actions; the third is to always try to master himself
rather than fortune, to change his desires rather than the worldly order; and the
fourth is to devote his whole life to cultivating the faculty of reason.

This moral code may seem little more than the adoption of simple spiritual
guidelines by a solitary thinker, but the analogy to ascetic precepts holds also
with his explicitly philosophical purposes in the *Meditations*. The meditator
endorses *poverty* in discarding all preconceptions and prejudices acquired through
education and tradition; *chastity* in complete disengagement from the world of
the senses; and *obedience* to the rational injunction to abstain from what is open
to minimal doubt and to affirm only what has been seen with evident insight.
Later, we will discover that Husserl also, in his overt likening of the phenomenological orientation to a religious conversion, also employs a rhetoric associated with the ascetic life. Descartes' appeal to figures of speech and analogies
with conversion experiences may not be purely literary but may have autobio-
graphical sources as well. His dream of November 1619 may be seen as an
account of just such a personal transformation, and though *prima facie* this may

seem a mere anecdotal curiosity, it is worth reconsidering this episode in virtue of a similar *point d'appui* twenty years later in the *Meditations*.[15] In a state of "great mental agitation," the young chevalier fell asleep and in his first dream was assailed by several "phantoms" who so terrified him that he had to change course (in the dream town). With "a great weakness" in his right side he had difficulty walking, when a violent wind sprang up which swept him round in a kind of whirlpool. He made a determined effort to reach a college chapel where he intended to pray. He then noticed someone whom he knew, but the strong wind prevented him from making any forward progress. When he awoke, "he felt at once a sharp pain which made him fear that it was the doing of some evil demon [sic] who had wanted to deceive him."

After an interval of two hours, he fell asleep again and at once "another dream" came to him, in which he thought he heard a loud and violent noise like a thunderclap. This so frightened him that he woke up and saw many fiery sparks scattered through the room. His biographer Baillet adds that this (hypnagogic?) phenomenon had happened to him several times before and it was "not very unusual" for him to see these bright flashes in the middle of the night. This time he wanted to perform an experiment, so blinking his eyes, he observed "the quality of the forms which were represented to him." He fell asleep again and had his "third dream" which involved a strange figure in a library and the alternatives symbolized by two books, a dictionary and a poetry anthology (which we have previously interpreted in chapter 3 as indicative of the order of essences and the order of reasons).

It should strike almost any modern reader as odd that the so-called "second dream" consists of nothing more than a loud noise and bright flashes, and that it was not uncommon for him to experience these *while awake*. There have been several, disparate attempts to interpret Descartes' dream[16] but as Freud himself pointed out when queried about this, there is simply not enough associated psychic material to work with, and much of the third dream bears the marks of a highly stylized symbolic reworking. Why bother then to bring the dream into our discussion of radical conversion? Because whatever its latent idiosyncratic meaning, Descartes himself considered it to be an extremely important turning point and one which was intimately linked with the "wonderful discovery" he had just made.

Perhaps the most cogent assessment of these events, leaving aside interminable analyses of symbolic content, is that offered by Steven Gaukroger.[17] The loud noise and flashing lights perhaps indicate the onset of a severe migraine; in addition, it is quite possible that Descartes was suffering a nervous breakdown. Gaukroger quotes an early seventeenth-century medical account of melancholy whose reported symptoms bear a striking resemblance to Descartes' own remarks on his emotional and physical condition, as well as the dream contents. "I suggest that the events of the days surrounding 10 November probably constituted a mental collapse of some kind, and that the thoughts on method that Descartes had been pursuing at the time came to symbolise his recovery from this."

Gaukroger highlights an inconsistency between the Olympica Manuscript and the passage in the *Discourse* which recounts these events seventeen years later. In the former, Baillet reports that Descartes, "in a state of *great mental agitation*, went to bed quite filled with *this mental excitement* and preoccupied with the thought that that very day he had discovered the foundations of a wonderful system of knowledge." The *Discourse* version of these events is decidedly different: "fortunately having *no cares or problems to trouble me*, I stayed all day shut up alone in a stove-heated room, where I was completely free to converse with myself about my own thoughts" (CSM I, 116). In the former account, his mental agitation and enthusiasm is inspired by the wonderful discovery which his dream then articulates or symbolizes. In the much later, cool and detached revision it seems as though the dream inspires a thorough reexamination of his previous scientific researches which then results in the construction of a new method.

Adrien Baillet mentions two references to *mirabilis scientiae fundamenta* in the text of the original manuscript which he faithfully transcribed (AT X, 179), but which of the two episodes came first—dream or discovery? Gaukroger's reading offers a plausible reconciliation of the two accounts: having suffered a complete mental collapse *and* made a marvellous discovery, Descartes later *rationalized* his recovery in terms of the discovery. However, it seems quite odd that in Gaukroger's careful paraphrase of the Olympica Manuscript, he completely omits the dreamer's supposition that the first dream might be the work of an evil genie who wanted to deceive him, and that he then offered a prayer to God to preserve him from all the ills which might be hanging over him as punishment for his sins. These are quite overt images of a conversion experience with religious connotations which are much the same as those reported by Loyola, among others.

It is arguable then that Descartes had an intimate acquaintance with the sort of transformation under review here; certainly in November 1619 and probably again in late 1628, during the Chandoux affair, though this would have been more of an intellectual *volte face*. Our current discussion involves the primary claim that some sort of radical conversion is demanded of the reader of the *Meditations*. And "conversion" here means that the reader is asked to *turn with* the meditator; in so doing to *turn away* from the old world and *turn toward* the new one. For this turning to be "radical" means that it must be carried out at the *root*, at the very basis of any experience whatsoever. In turning away from all one's previous convictions, they must be completely uprooted. In the building metaphor, everything must be demolished, nothing must be reused, in order to start again from the beginning. All one's philosophical baggage must be left behind before one is suitably prepared to embark on this journey. It is not a journey with a preplanned destination, nor one with any recognizable landmarks. In turning toward the path which opens ahead, the stability with which one can eventually reconstruct the itinerary lies in having established at the outset a method of fixing points along the route with utter reliability. The method of universal doubt reveals, through the natural light, the "primary notions" without which one could not have got underway and leads inevitably to those principles of *prima philosophia* which are the roots of the tree of scientific knowledge. Methodical doubt "provides the means for freeing one's attention from sensory ideas in order to attend to an independent source of knowledge: the pure deliverances of the intellect."[18]

In the preceding summary of the Cartesian sense of radical conversion, we have effectively traced its aetiology backwards from its most mature avowal in the *Meditations* to the cryptic dream imagery in the Olympica Manuscript. Running through these textual variations is the persistent theme of an intellectual or cognitive transformation.

> In the fully explicit philosophical sense, cognitive conversion is "the radical clarification and consequently the elimination of an exceedingly stubborn and misleading myth," by which a person spontaneously assumes that "knowing is like looking, that objectivity is seeing what there is to be seen and not seeing what is not there, and that the real is what is out there now to be looked at." But if cognitive conversion eliminates this *myth of naive realism*, it does so because it consists essentially in what Lonergan calls the "discovery of the self-transcendence proper to the human process of coming to know," the recognition and appropriation, in other words, of the radical dynamism and structure of one's own cognitive capacities and operations.[19]

Walter Conn's sophisticated multidisciplinary analysis of the cognitive dimension of conversion experience succinctly captures several central tenets of our argument. This transformation involves the elimination of an epistemic myth whose explication reads very much like the sort of Aristotelian picture of knowledge attainment which Descartes so vigorously attacks. Knowing is *not* like looking, but rather like *seeing* in a certain way; and objectivity is an achievement of knowledge construction, not something already inertly constituted before one's knowing regard turns toward it. In addition, what is real is as much a characteristic of the psychical as the physical and is not simply "out there" in contraposition to an unreal inner domain. All of this Husserl would also wish to reject and transform, repeatedly denominating it "naive realism," whose overturning is fulfilled in a "self-transcendence proper to the human process of coming to know"—an accurate depiction of the subject domain of the transcendental reduction.

It is only after Husserl's skeptical crisis in 1905–6 that one can legitimately speak of him calling for radical conversion on the part of the beginning philosopher. The notion of conversion itself, and the rhetorical tropes attached to it, do not appear in the *Logical Investigations*. The Prolegomena, however, does achieve the aim of demolishing the shaky edifice of empirical psychology in its derivation of logical truths, flawed at the very ground by its inability to discriminate the psychical act of logical judging from the 'content' of the logical judgment itself. The six investigations elaborate novel conceptual apparatuses which are "navigation equipment" necessary for the journey ahead. The announcement of this journey does not take place until shortly before the transcendental turn in the *Ideas*. It is thus not possible to *turn toward* the new field of transcendental experience disclosed by the phenomenological reduction until the way forward is seen to be possible. Having razed psychologism on the island of skepticism and relativism, the mists which hang over the environing waters disperse, and a passage opens to a new world.

In the lectures for those years, he compares the current situation in philosophy with that of the seventeenth century in which it was assumed that there could be only one method for achieving certain knowledge in philosophical enquiries, the same method as that of the natural sciences. But all natural sciences, precisely because they are "natural," take for granted the general thesis of the world's being which they find lying-over-against their inquiries. None of their questions penetrate beyond the naive acceptance of the worldly character of all worldly realities. But what does it mean for something to be "worldly," to be a possible 'object' of cognition? This is the task of a genuine philosophy, one which eschews the naiveté which is "natural," i.e., perfectly consonant with scientific cognition. "Philosophy lies in a wholly new dimension. It needs an entirely new point of departure and an entirely [or radically] new method distinguishing it in principle from any 'natural' science" (IP, 19).

Husserl descries this new point of departure in the Cartesian epoché, a form of systematic doubt which calls into question the very givenness of that which appears, and the new method as that of phenomenological analysis which is yet to be explicated. There is, however, an always present problem: to consider that which supports or that which makes possible all "natural," mundane cognition as something transcendent to consciousness, something which in principle remains wholly inaccessible to consciousness, and then a transformation (*metabasis*) of one into the other seems inevitable. "The *metabasis* is so exceedingly dangerous, partly because the proper sense of the problem is never made clear and remains totally lost in it, and partly because even those who have become clear about it find it hard to remain clear and slip easily, as their thinking proceeds, back into the temptations of the natural modes of thought and judgement as well as into the false and seductive conceptions of the problems which grow on their basis" (IP, 32). Without focusing in these lectures on Cartesian literary imagery, he nonetheless echoes the same sentiments expressed in the "First Meditation," and though it may be unintentional, his style plays on the notions of sin and grace in its use of terms like temptation, seduction and being totally lost.

It seems as though the phenomenological procedure, just like its ancestor Cartesian doubt, is never impervious to the recrudescence of further doubts and aporias, but must overcome each along the way toward a foundation which will permanently secure further inquiries from skeptical assault. It is the unique trait of philosophical conversion then, that it does not banish from the outset the occurrence of further doubts, that it must incessantly begin again. It is "hard labor," it requires "strenuous efforts"; the investigator is *naturally* inclined to fall away from this course, and here 'natural' is also to be taken in the literal sense (see PP, 149). It is thus unlike religious conversion which arrives, or is visited upon the convertant with the unassailable guarantee that this new-found conviction does indeed have a transcendent (i.e., divine) origin. This sort of transformation does not exclude the irruption of temptations and seductions, but all such strayings from the path are known to be illusory and specious. It is a sad fact of fallible "human nature" that we are always subject to them, but a mark of divine benevolence that they are only placed in our way to seduce us from what we already know to be the one and true way.

At the close of the "First Meditation," the thinker is exhausted by the exercise itself and the constant struggle to keep his "habitual opinions" from interfering with the insights gained. "This is an arduous undertaking and a kind of laziness brings me back to normal life. . . . I happily slide back into my old opinions and dread being shaken out of them" (CSM II, 15). We have already indicated Descartes' repeated usage of the image of a difficult, awkward path along which the guide must contend with false trails, unexpected crevasses, and intermittent darkness, where the best option is to remain still, not to rush about in a panic. In this way, one knows that one has at least reached this point in the chain of reasons. L. J. Beck's gloss on this passage echoes Husserl's remarks: "Methodical doubt is a dangerous exercise. It is in no degree astonishing that the *Discourse*, intended for a wide public, does not even hint at the final stages of the hyperbolical doubt. A philosopher with a modicum of moral responsibility does not carelessly provoke the *spiritual crisis* which is the end product of the real experience suggested to us, if that experiment is successful."[20]

This oscillation between the natural and the unnatural attitude, the loss of bearings engendered by the inception of doubt and the reduction, is signaled by the phrases "remain lost," "become clear"—it signals the darkness which engulfs one when entering a new domain. This imagery tacitly plays on the peculiarly philosophical significance of the journey metaphor which we have isolated in the Evangelists' notion of *epistrepho*: to lose the world in order to gain it. This Husserlian transformation is effected on the ground of this world: one loses, strictly speaking, the *sense* of the old world naively taken just as it appears; and gains a new sense of the *same* world, but now purged of prejudices and presuppositions. Let us (again) carefully segregate this notion from the Cartesian rhetoric of loss and gain; for one of the presuppositions which Descartes explicitly accepts and which Husserl rejects is the natural scientific model for philosophical explanation. Thus Descartes will replace prior theoretical constructions with a new model whose subsequent articulation in the *Principles* applies to an entirely new world, and not a new sense of the same world.

This distinctively philosophical significance has perhaps floated beneath the surface of previous discussions, but makes its first overt declaration in *Ideas First Book* (1913). In section 50 of Chapter Two, the author harkens back to the introduction of the phenomenological reduction in sections 31–33 of Chapter One. With respect to the "putting out of action" through the epoché, the whole world with its physical things and living beings is excluded, but the theoretical regard which makes this possible reveals a residuum. "Strictly speaking, we have *not lost* anything but rather have *gained* the whole of absolute being which, rightly understood, contains within itself, "constitutes" within itself, all worldly transcendencies" (Ideas I, 113). In the natural attitude, we simply effect or perform the acts in virtue of which the world is there for us. Through the epoché, instead of living in these acts, instead of effecting these acts, we effect acts of reflection directed toward them. We are now living in acts of the "second degree," acts whose basis is the infinite field of mental processes.

In a textual revision from 1929 of the earlier passage, the author presents a similar exegesis of what remains within the parentheses when the epoché takes place. The phenomenological reduction suspends the following considerations: "Our existential acceptance of the objective world as existing, this sphere of 'immanental' being does indeed lose the sense of being a real stratum in the reality belonging to the world and human being (or beast), which is a reality already presupposing the world. . . . But it is *not simply lost*; rather, when we maintain that attitude of epoché, it *receives* the sense of an absolute sphere of being, an absolutely self-sufficient sphere, *which is, in itself, what it is*" (Ideas I, 65, note 17, emphasis added; cf. also CM, 36).

From the 1931 lectures on "Phenomenology and Anthropology," he brings this loss and gain opposition directly into his discussion of both the Cartesian origin of "scientific" radicalism and the necessary first-person attitude of one who wishes to philosophize in an entirely new way. Here Husserl asserts that all modern philosophy originates in Descartes' *Meditations*, insofar as every genuine beginning of philosophy issues from solitary reflections. In this condition, it is incumbent on me to accept only what is evident to me and pursue the source of this evidence beyond the level at which others regard such claims as "scientifically" grounded. The level at which others cease their questioning coincides with the presumed existence of the 'objective' world. Presumed on the basis of what? My experience of worldly realities? But these experiences are open to illusion; some perceptions are so dubious that the certitude already taken for granted is canceled. What is the status of the evidence with which I accord the being of the world lying-over-against me? In order to answer this, in order to step back and see what constitutes an experience as such, it is an "obligation to practice a universal epoché" (HSW, 317–20).

But what remains after this? Do I who invoke the epoché disappear, am I also put out of action? Husserl adroitly paraphrases Descartes' robust rejoinder to the malign demon: "Let the existence of the world be questionable for me now because it is not yet grounded, let it be subject to the epoché; I who question and practice the epoché, I exist nonetheless." The first level of the reduction places brackets around the mundane, empirical ego and discloses the transcendental ego as logically prior to the world's being. Descartes and his followers "remained blind" to what lay before them and turned back to the "scientifically" grounded world. What lay before them is "a unique entrance to this new realm," one which is reached via the second level of the reduction, which asks what constitutes this transcendental ego. One vital discovery made here is that whatever belongs to the world, including my own worldly being, exists for me only as the intentional content of experiential apperception or self-reflection. This reflection on a "second-order" ego shows that I alone am the absolutely responsible subject for whom other subjects in the world and their worldly ways-of-being have existential validity.

> This absolute position above everything that is or might ever be valid for me, including all its possible content, is necessarily the position of the philosopher. It is the position which the phenomenological reduction assigns to me. I have *lost nothing* of what existed for me in the naive attitude, nothing in particular whose real existence

was shown. In this absolute attitude, *I know the world itself*, and know it now, *for the first time*, for what it always was and had to be by its very essence: a transcendental phenomenon. (Ideas I, 320; emphasis added)

In the lectures to the Sorbonne in 1929 which became known as the *Cartesian Meditations*, Husserl opens his exposition of the eternal significance of this text by citing it explicitly in terms of a radical new science and method. "Their study acted quite directly on the *transformation* of an already developing phenomenology into a new kind of transcendental philosophy. Accordingly, one might almost call transcendental phenomenology a Neo-Cartesianism." In these lectures he is, of course, entirely committed to the Cartesian way into phenomenology, although as early as *Erste Philosophie* (1923/24) he had begun to be disenchanted with this approach and thought of it more as "the history of a shipwreck," a metaphor which itself is an extension of the journey motif. One of the features which makes the *Cartesian Meditations* more accessible, more readable than many of his other works is their lecture format. Here the introduction adroitly plays on the meaning of "radical," showing a skillful speaker's isolation of key terms, called up again and again to reinforce the message. His closing remarks are in the form of a series of queries, the announcement of a *calling* for conversion.

Must not the only fruitful renaissance be the one that reawakens the impulse of [this text]: not to adopt their content, but in *not* doing so, to renew with greater intensity the *radicalness* of their spirit, the *radicalness* of self-responsibility, to make that *radicalness* true for the first time by enhancing it to the last degree, to uncover thereby for the first time the *genuine sense* of the necessary regress to the ego, and consequently to overcome the hidden but already felt naiveté of earlier philosophising? (CM, 6; emphasis added)

Husserl consistently manipulates an ambiguity in the meaning of "radicalness"—that it pertains to the root or basis of any genuine philosophy, and that it is a thorough, even violent, overthrow of previous traditions. However, this surface ambiguity conceals a deeper univocalness, that the only responsible overthrow must begin at the very basis which previous thinking has assumed. We can say that this overthrow is carried out along three axes: the reflecting ego who initiates it, the world transformed thereby, and the "science" which articulates this transformation. At the close of the lectures, Husserl returns to one source of this potential ambiguity regarding the ground upon which this radical change must be predicated. "Philosophy after all demands an elucidation by virtue of the ultimate and most concrete essential necessities; and these are the necessities that satisfy the essential *rootedness* of any objective world in transcendental subjectivity and thus make the world intelligible concretely *as a constituted sense*" (CM, 137). If this passage traces the world-axis of radicality, and the delineation of the transcendental ego the personal-axis, in the closing pages, he picks up on the third axis, that of the *"scientific" description* of the unified ego-world conversion. The path which leads to an absolutely grounded knowledge is the path of universal self-knowledge. Such a path is the continuation of Cartesian meditations conceived as an all-encompassing and self-accountable "science," i.e., *a mathesis universalis*[21] (CM, 156).

The specific contributive senses of this threefold rootedness can be spelled out in phenomenological terms. The new world is uncovered through the reduction which brackets the general thesis of the world's being and thus discloses an entirely new realm of sense. The transcendental ego has universal *a priori* features in virtue of which it is prior to the ground of the world's being; the reflective phenomenological self is usually spoken of as a disinterested observer, "above this life, above these actions." These remote orbital images which occur throughout Husserl's writings signify a peculiarly ascetic orientation towards phenomenology as a vocation, a vertical profundity in keeping with Descartes' avowal of a quasi-monastic attitude towards doing philosophy as a personal calling. This motif will be picked up again in our discussion after its most explicit evocation in the *Crisis*.

The descriptive science of transcendental phenomenology must be without ontological or metaphysical presuppositions, abide by the principle of principles (to only take what is given precisely as it is given), and orient itself towards the ideal of an eidetic discipline concerned with the essential structures of consciousness and its correspondent regions of being. If anything it is this third axis of a rigorous eidetic science which distinguishes philosophical from religious conversion, at least in terms of a metaphysics devoid of theological overtones, as Descartes' or Leibniz's was not. In the religious sense of conversion, there is no need to account for the transformation of ego and world, whereas in the philosophical sense, it is absolutely requisite since making intelligible this radical change constitutes the *raison d'etre* of First Philosophy as a Phenomenology of Reason.

Husserl's exposition of this eidetic science in his lectures on *Erste Philosophie* involves the rehabilitation[22] of the Cartesian notion of a *mathesis universalis*, in terms which emphasize its rootedness in the most fundamental questioning. "First Philosophy is the science of method in general, of knowledge in general, and of possible goals of knowledge in general . . . in which all a priori sciences that have disconnected all types of the contingent . . . show themselves to be *branches* which have developed from *one and the same science. A mathesis universalis* stands above all sciences as a mathematics of knowledge achievements" (HUS VIII, 249). This statement serves to isolate the peculiar systematic endeavor which pertains to the theoretical elucidation of ego and world, and in its distinct concatenation of phrases is closely linked to Descartes' arboreal image in the preface to the *Principles*.

The First Part is devoted to First Philosophy or metaphysics whose essential themes had already been traced in the *Meditations*; the Second and Third, to the physical laws of the heavens and earth; the Fourth, to the physical and chemical laws of animals and humans. "The whole of philosophy is like a tree. The roots are metaphysics [i.e., First Philosophy], the trunk is physics, and the branches emerging from the trunk are all the other sciences" (CSM I, 186). His description of what this unified science embraces harkens back to his formulation of a *mathesis universalis* twenty years earlier in Rule IV: "A general science which explains all the points that can be raised concerning order and measure irrespective of the subject matter" (CSM I, 19). Such a science was also famously the obsessive goal of Leibniz's work on the rational calculus, which he also called *mathematique universelle*. At the end of the Prolegomena, it is Leibniz's model which Husserl cites prior to his own demarcation of the formal, *a priori* theory of theory construction, the necessary form of theory as such, in chapter 11. Although he had abandoned such a working hypothesis in the *Crisis*, it is still considered a vibrant and realizable ambition in *Erste Philosophie* and *Formal and Transcendental Logic*.

Husserl's earliest formulation of *mathesis universalis*, the root notion of the most primordial discipline, focuses on the unity of two disparate dimensions in metaphysical enquiry. "It can be understood as an inter-connection of the things to which our thought experiences (actual or possible) are intentionally directed, or on the other hand, as an inter-connection of truths, in which this unity of things comes to count objectively as being what it is" (LI, 225). This unification then is predicated on the merger of what he later called the *order of beings* and the *order of cognitions* (or in the *Ideas, ordo rerum* and *ordo idearum*). This is, of course, more than a chance echo of Descartes' order of essences and order of reasons, though it is fruitless to speculate on whether Descartes envisaged his universal science as the syncretism of these orders. But for Husserl, this yields the most foundational (or the most abstract) conception of all: the eidos or ideal essence of theory as such. Just as the justification of a concept, i.e., its conditions of possibility, is achieved by returning to its intuitive or deducible essence, so the justification of a given theory demands that one return to the essence of its pure form alone. Categorial (or later, eidetic) insight into the pure form of theory as such reveals formal laws which regulate, in an *a priori* deductive fashion, every specialization of the essence of theory in all its possible kinds.

"We are dealing with systematic theories which have their *roots* in the essence of theory, with an a priori, theoretical, nomological science which deals with the ideal essence of science as such" (LI, 235).

This specific exegetical "zig-zag" which Husserl himself called "backward glancing reinterpretation" leads us back to his repeated attempts in *Erste Philosophie* to find the grounds for such a formal *a priori* theory construction within the purview of phenomenology as a theory of transcendental subjectivity. It is not enough to stipulate the 'objective' grounds as conditions for the possibility of an eidetic science of consciousness without taking account of what it means for consciousness to have its own grounds for thematizing that particular activity. Again and again, Husserl reengages the question: what would be the motive (i.e., subjective ground) for initiating the phenomenological reduction? This motive and its subsequent legitimization cannot be found in the natural attitude which strives to knowingly establish a basis for norms governing practical life and its interests.

Only when these interests have been given up and one has adopted the "unnatural" attitude of a disinterested observer would one then be motivated to proceed towards an absolute and universal foundation. But this seems to skip over entirely the issue of the transition from one attitude to the other. "Only through the *free act* of holding back judgement, of willingly freeing myself from this primordial co-interest [in the natural world] can that attitude . . . come into being. [However,] a particular motivation must release me from this sympathy. . . . What can serve here as a motive?" (HUS VIII, 92). Husserl here points towards the personal decision on the part of the absolute beginner, in his fullest freedom, to realize a complete transformation of both self and world—and that means nothing less than responding to a call for radical conversion.

The root-sense of the radicality (*radix)* of conversion is thus at the root or basis of any genuine philosophical activity. A radical reconception of its task, in the sense of a violent overthrow, can only be accomplished at this level—a fundamental and incontrovertible starting point. Husserl thus shares with Descartes the conviction that a new rethinking of the world must take shape as First Philosophy, a *mathesis* of irreducible principles.

> Consciousness is the *root*, the source of all else that is called being. . . . It is not a unity of multiplicity; it does not refer to something further, from which it could or must have been derived. All other being is precisely unitary and points mediately or immediately back to the absolute flow of consciousness. If the flow of consciousness *is* in accordance with *its* mode of being, then everything else, whatever it might be, *is* also. Nothing further is required. . . . This state of affairs justifies our designating the *root-giving* consciousness as absolute consciousness.[23]

First Philosophy then is the Phenomenology of Transcendental Subjectivity, the absolute consciousness which is always prior to any other psychical activity and the worldly correlate which it otherwise presupposes. Second Philosophy is metaphysics in the Cartesian sense, still tied to the natural thesis of the world's being and the natural sciences as its theoretical paradigm (CM, 139). This does not mean that Second Philosophy is condemned to being some sort of spectral twin to the empirical sciences of psychology, sociology, anthropology, etc. which would certainly undercut the validity of demarcating the third way as phenomenological, descriptive psychology. Rather, the *a priori* structures and logical forms revealed through the eidetics of First Philosophy are presumed to obtain in metaphysical inquiries in Second Philosophy. The Kantian project of a transcendental derivation of *a priori* principles is legitimate only from the first to the second level—it makes no sense to speak of a derivation of such *a priori* features from anywhere else. Beyond (or before) the absolute priority of consciousness to world, there is nothing else. Husserl speaks here of the "irrational fact of the rationality of the world." The ineluctable fact that actuality corresponds with the theoretical and practical ideals of reason is the object and theme of a new metaphysics (HUS VII, 188).

This phrase—"the irrational fact of the rationality of the world"—is extremely resonant, especially in the context of radical conversion. The beginning philosopher, having eschewed all theoretical preconceptions, can never derive his motive for performing the phenomenological reduction, for engaging in philosophical activity, as though it were the conclusion in a dynamic syllogism whose premises were metaphysical principles. Before and above all else, his motive springs from an act of will in his fullest freedom, confronting the radical contingency of this irrationality. However, insofar as his purpose is to extend the horizons of the clearly intuited rational world, he makes of this a necessity, rigorously obeying the principle to take *what* is given only *as* it is given. The philosopher's conversion is thus entirely his own responsibility, open to endless corrections and revisions, and adheres to rational explication. In contrast, one could say, the religious convert, confronted with this irrationality, abdicates responsibility to the divine presence; one has no need of correction since the message (*kerygma*) is already fixed, though one may be ignorant of some parts; and abjures explication in favour of other-worldly salvation.

For the philosopher, it is thus not a matter of *apprising* oneself of the facts in the case, as though it were a puzzle whose answer was hidden somewhere— it is a matter of *surprise* (Socratic wonder) that the world appears just this way and not otherwise. As long as this attitude of surprise is maintained one is less likely to fall into the trap which the world sets for your thought (as Kafka said)—"Look here, it's just as you imagined it would be." Another way to put this: insofar as the philosopher empirically considers the world's connection with mind, it will always be the case that the world looks just like the philosopher's terms describe it to be. This should remind one of Hume's remark that Berkeley's proofs for God are irrefutable but carry no conviction. There isn't anything else against which a "bridging theory" of the mind's knowledge of the world could be adjudicated. What is it about consciousness and the world such that this egregious fulfillment would always come about? One way to answer this question would be to look at the various frameworks in which thinkers articulate their conceptual vocabularies, e.g., Foucault's archaeology of knowledge, or a taxonomy of philosophical discourse. Since it is not possible to ask what the world would be like disengaged from consciousness, another approach to this question would ask: what would consciousness be like disengaged from the world? This disengagement is the phenomenological epoché and the domain disclosed thereby is the only proper subject of a transcendental philosophy.

The transformation of world-meaning is effected by the reduction, the personal transformation of the self is motivated by the philosopher's free action in the face of the world's ineradicable contingency, and the transformation of the descriptive science which accounts for this is the result of sublating (*aufgehoben*) the material ontology of nature for formal eidetic science. For Descartes the engine of universal doubt has to be engaged only once (*semel in vita*); the purgative is so thorough that no further skeptical doubt can creep back in. Perhaps this is why he remarked that one should not indulge in metaphysical speculation more than a few days a year (!). For Husserl, on the other hand, the epoché has to be actualized again and again, never ceasing to start the project anew.

In this sense, he speaks in the *Crisis* of the *vocation* of phenomenology, a term reserved, strictly speaking, for a priestly mission, since it plays on the notion of a call or summons. Another reason is that, in Descartes' scheme of things, God secures the entire validity of the enterprise, from which one cannot fall away, though one may be tempted. In a similar fashion, a religious person would never say that he could be deconverted from faith to atheism, but only reconverted from one faith to another. But for Husserl, there is no transcendental guarantee of the knowledge achievements made possible through the reduction. It is "hard labor" and "strenuous efforts" are needed to maintain what is, after all, a highly unnatural orientation.

The mention of "strenuous efforts" should alert the reader to the peculiarly ascetic character which seems to attach to Husserl's summons to conversion. There is an almost penitential overtone to his references to "the way of the cross of corrections and revisions" (PP, 95)—a very potent rhetorical trope.[24] At once it signifies both the highly idiosyncratic manner in which Husserl practiced phenomenology, i.e., constantly revising previous material and rarely expressing satisfaction with the results, and the fact that he considered this to be an intrinsic, unavoidable burden. "Large parts of the publications Husserl produced in his lifetime . . . look like purely momentary states of rest, or condensations, of a thought movement that was constantly in flux and which can be followed precisely only in the mss."[25] These *Nachlass* are more philosophical monologues than finished treatises and vividly reflect the process of composition: ceaselessly calling into question and criticizing prior statements, tentatively striving forward, and then retracting in order to strike off in another direction. It reflects also his extremely analytic, but nonsystematic style of thinking—no system was envisioned in advance of individual efforts in specific problematics. This distinctive process of correction and revision is comparable to an explorer's charting of new territory; repeated forays make possible the adjustments needed for an accurate map.

The strenuous efforts peculiar to the philosophical explorer seem to call for certain types of self-denial reminiscent of Descartes' quasi-monastic precepts. The sort of reflection attendant on the thematization of pure consciousness disengaged from the world, bracketed by the reduction, are a *sine qua non* for further analyses. "They are necessary in order that, in the face of our *poverty* in which . . . we are vainly *fatiguing* ourselves, it may at last become clear that a transcendental investigation of consciousness cannot signify an investigation of Nature" (Ideas I, 115). "It is a long and thorny way starting from purely logical insights" to arrive at an intuitive understanding of the *a priori* relations of consciousness. "If the right attitude has been won . . . if one has acquired the *courage to obey* the clear eidetic data with a *radical lack of prejudice* . . . then firm results are directly produced" (Ideas I, 212; emphasis added).

The *Cartesian Meditations* even more overtly plays on these ascetic features attaching to the pursuit of phenomenology. Anyone who seriously intends to philosophize must overthrow all that has been uncritically accepted and instead acquire knowledge as entirely one's own achievement. "If I have decided to live with this as my aim . . . I have thereby chosen to begin in *absolute poverty*, with an absolute lack of knowledge" (CM, 2). Obedience to the principle of only taking that which is given precisely as it is given is expressed in this manner: "The realm accessible to transcendental self-experience . . . must be explored, and at first, with simple *devotion* to the evidence inherent in the harmonious flow of such experience" (CM, 29). The description of the disinterested observer, above the naively involved self, elaborates the essential *purity* of this mode of reflection. (CM, 35).

It is in the *Crisis*, however, that the strictures incumbent on the phenomenological orientation receive their most pronounced expression. The philosophical conversion toward this attitude, away from the empirical sciences of nature, reveals not only the truths of this new world-meaning, but also seems to indicate a transformation of the philosophical self. The statement of this attitude is a direct descendant of the 1906 diary entry (see chapter 6), that the pursuit of absolute clarity is "a matter of life and death." "Through the epoché a new way of experiencing, of thinking, of theorizing, is opened to the philosopher; here situated *above* his own natural being and *above* the natural world, he *loses nothing* of their being and their objective truths and likewise nothing at all of the spiritual acquisitions of his world-life or those of the whole historical communal life; he simply *forbids himself* . . . to continue the whole natural performance of his world-life" (Crisis, 152; emphasis added).

One could not wish for a more straight-forward expression of the "vertical profundity" which typifies the German transcendental spirit, the "vertigo of great depths" (in Gilson's phrase) which inspires such utter dedication to an abstract truth. The vocational character of the phenomenologist's attitude does not, however, preclude other practical interests, but instead all such worldly interests— religious, ethical, aesthetic, etc.—become themes for reflection. In this context, Husserl invokes a well-known metaphor, equating religious with philosophical conversion: "the total phenomenological attitude . . . [is] destined in essence to effect, at first, a complete personal transformation, comparable in the beginning to a religious conversion, which then however, over and above this, bears within itself the significance of the greatest existential transformation which is assigned as a task to mankind as such" (Crisis, 137).

It is very easy to misconstrue this passage, to take it to mean that someone converted to phenomenology has some sort of privileged access, denied to one who has not undergone this transformative experience; as though the "seeing" attendant on the epoché was some sort of esoteric "sixth sense." It is not the case of the blind being made to see, or Berkeley's sight-restored patient asked whether he could now identify the visual object as the touched object—here the naively perceived object with the reduced 'object.' Rather, it is a demand to see more clearly and distinctly what was given before in an obscure and confused way. And it is like a religious conversion only "at the beginning"; it is an attitude which can never be taken for granted. There is no divine grace here, by virtue of which one is held or suspended before the splendor of the created world. One has to suspend the old world in order to attain the understanding that the world is entirely the product of sense-giving, creative activity. So perhaps there is at least a light "natural" to humans, a light of reason, within which this revelation can take place.

NOTES

Chapter 1. Introduction

1. Paul Ricoeur, *Husserl: An Analysis of his Phenomenology*, trans. Edward G. Ballard and Lester E. Embree. (Evanston: Northwestern University Press, 1967), ch. 4.

2. Jan Patocka, *Philosophy and Selected Writings*, ed. and trans. Erazim Kohak. (Chicago: University of Chicago Press, 1989), 285–325.

3. John Burkey, "Descartes, Skepticism and Husserl," *Husserl Studies*, 7 (1990); Walter Soffer, "Husserl's Neo-Cartesianism," *Research in Phenomenology*, 11 (1981).

4. Pierre Thevanez, *What Is Phenomenology? and Other Essays*, trans. James Edie (Chicago: Quadrangle, 1962), 93–112.

5. See *The Phenomenology of Husserl: Selected Critical Readings*, ed. R. O. Elveton (Chicago: Quadrangle, 1970), 259–306.

6. For which see, Rudolf Bernet, Iso Kern, and Eduard Marbach, *An Introduction to Husserlian Phenomenology* (Evanston: Northwestern University Press, 1992), ch. 8 and 9.

7. See Bernard Williams, "Descartes' Use of Skepticism," in *The Skeptical Tradition*, ed. Myles Burnyeat (Berkeley: University of California Press, 1983), 337–40.

8. Jean-Luc Marion, *Sur L'Ontologie Grise de Descartes* (Paris: J. Vrin, 1975), 131–48.

9. L. J. Beck, *The Metaphysics of Descartes*. (Oxford: Oxford University Press, 1965), 28–38; for a detailed study, see Gary Hatfield, "The Senses and the Fleshless Eye," in *Essays on Descartes' Meditations*, ed. A. O. Rorty (Berkeley: University of California Press, 1986), 48–55.

10. Ricoeur, *Husserl*, 31.

11. Erazim Kohak comments on Jan Patocka, the great Czech phenomenologist and close associate of Husserl, that one of the most distinctive aspects of Patocka's belief was "his powerful sense of philosophy as a personal calling, a vocation in the strong sense usually reserved for a religious vocation. . . . The philosopher is presented as radically not of the world though very much in it, in terms more reminiscent of St. Paul than of secular philosophy. In a dramatic turn of phrase, Patocka tells us that not even God can move the philosopher, only reason can." Patocka, *Writings*, 15–16.

12. David Bell, *Husserl* (London: Routledge, 1990), 162; next quote ibid; just the contrary for Gaston Berger. "We have attempted to show that [phenomenology] could not be viewed as a dialectical construction, which could be effected openly, yet abstractly and conceptually. Now we must reject the opposing interpretation, which in order to free phenomenology from verbal trickery, would make it a kind of mystical activity or esoteric discipline." *The Cogito in Husserl's Philosophy*, trans. Kathleen McLaughlin (Evanston: Northwestern University Press, 1972), 50.

13. Soffer, "Neo-Cartsianism," 157.

14. Descartes conducted many inquiries into the behavior of comets; see CSM III, 37.

15. Thevanez, *What Is Phenomenology?*, 104.

16. Martial Gueroult, *Descartes According to the Order of Reasons*. trans. Roger Ariew (Minneapolis: University of Minnesota Press, 1984), II, 260.

17. Williams, "Skepticism," 341; Gaston Berger also emphasizes this outward-return journey, see Berger, *The Cogito*, 73.

18. Ricoeur, *Husserl*, 88.

19. Bernet, Kern and Marbach, *Introduction*, 54; see also Herman Philipse's conclusions on the dilemma posed by transcendental versus psychological constitution of the world, "Transcendental Idealism," in *The Cambridge Companion to Husserl*, ed. Barry Smith and D. W. Smith (Cambridge: Cambridge University Press, 1995), 278–80.

Chapter 2.

1. Williams, "Skepticism," 337–52; E. M. Curley, *Descartes Against the Skeptics* (Oxford: Blackwell, 1978), 1–20; Michael Williams, "Descartes and the Metaphysics of Doubt," in *Essays on Descartes' Meditations,* ed. A. O. Rorty (Berkeley: University of California Press, 1986), 117–39.

2. Francisco Sanchez, *That Nothing Is Known.* Latin text ed. and trans. Douglas Thomson (Cambridge: Cambridge University Press, 1988).

3. Richard H. Popkin, *History of Skepticism from Erasmus to Spinoza* (Berkeley: University of California Press, 1979), 37, 39.

4. C. B. Schmitt, "Rediscovery of Ancient Skepticism in Modern Times," in *The Skeptical Tradition,* ed. Myles Burnyeat (Berkeley: University of California Press, 1983), 237.

5. Gisela Striker, "The Ten Tropes of Aenesidemus," in *The Skeptical Tradition,* 95–115.

6. Sextus Empiricus, *Outlines of Skepticism*, trans. Julia Annas and Jonathan Barnes (Cambridge: Cambridge University Press, 1994), PH I, 8 (standard citation).

7. Ibid., PH I, 21.

8. Ibid., AL I, 182–84.

9. Ibid., PH II, 18.

10. M. F. Burnyeat, "Can the Skeptic Live his Skepticism?" in *The Skeptical Tradition*, 128.

11. Ibid., PH III, 23–25.

12. Ibid., PH III, 41–43; cf. also AP I, 258–60.

13. Ibid., AL I, 80–86.

14. Ibid., AL I, 86.

15. Michel de Montaigne, *The Essays of Montaigne*, ed. and trans. M. A. Screech (New York: Penguin Press, 1991), 491, 500.

16. Ibid., 548.

17. Ibid., 561.

18. E. M. Curley traces a number of borrowings from Montaigne in Descartes' writings: see his *Descartes against the Skeptics*, 13–20.

19. Montaigne, *Essays*, 564.

20. Ibid., 672.

21. Ibid., 637.

22. Ibid., 634.

23. Ibid., 640.

24. Ibid., 649, 652.

25. Ibid., 660, 674.

26. Terence Penelhum, "Skepticism and Fideism," in *The Skeptical Tradition*, 295.

27. Pierre Gassendi, *The Selected Works*. ed. and trans. Craig Brush (New York: Johnson Reprint, 1972), "Letter to de Pribac," 4–5.

28. Ralph Walker, "Gassendi and Skepticism," in *The Skeptical Tradition*, 325.

29. Gassendi, *Selected Works*, 22.

30. Ibid., 42.

31. Ibid., 86.

32. Burnyeat, "Can the Skeptic Live his Skepticism," 143–44, note 8.

33. Gassendi, *Selected Works*, 253.

34. Ibid., 265.

35. Ralph Walker, "Gassendi and Skepticism," 331.

36. Quoted in Walker, "Gassendi and Skepticism," from *Gassendi Opera Omnia* (Lyons, 1658), II: 458.

37. Gassendi, *Selected Works*, 106.

38. Sanchez, *That Nothing Is Known*, 280.

39. Gassendi, *Selected Works*, 108.

40. Ibid., 326.

41. Ibid., 347.

42. Sanchez, *That Nothing Is Known*, 171.

43. On medicine as the ultimate goal, cf. also CSM I, 143; III, 76, 131, 275, 359.

44. Elaine Limbrick, Introduction to Sanchez, *That Nothing Is Known*, 48.

45. Henri Gouhier, *Les Premieres Pensées de Descartes* (Paris: J. Vrin, 1958), 116.

46. Elaine Limbrick, Introduction to Sanchez, *That Nothing Is Known*, 83.

47. Etienne Gilson quoted, Ibid., 83, note 48.

48. Ibid., 199–217.

49. Herbert Spiegelberg, *The Phenomenological Movement*, 3rd ed. (The Hague: Nijhoff, 1982), 1: 160.

50. M. F. Burnyeat, "Idealism and Greek Philosophy," *The Philosophical Review*, 91 (1982), 32.

51. Gueroult, *Descartes*, I, 47.

52. Allen Hance, "Husserl's Phenomenological Theory of Logic and Overcoming of Psychologism," *Philosophy Research Archive*, 13 (1988); and John Metcalfe, "Husserl and Early Victorian Philosophical Logic," *Eidos (Canada)*, 7 (1988); Dallas Willard, "Husserl on a Logic that Failed," *Philosophical Review*, 89 (1980).

53. Herbert Schnadelbach, *Philosophy in Germany 1831–1933*. trans. Eric Matthews (Cambridge: Cambridge University Press, 1984), 72–74; 98–100.

54. Anton Dumitriu, *History of Logic* (Tunbridge Wells, Kent: Abacus Press, 1977), 3: 311–52.

55. Martin Kusch, *Psychologism: A Case Study in the Sociology of Philosophical Knowledge* (London: Routledge, 1995), especially ch. 1 and 2; see also, Jens Cavallin, *Content and Object: Husserl, Twardowski and Psychologism* (Dordrecht: Kluwer Academic, 1997), ch. 2.

56. Sextus, *Outlines*, AL II, 481.

57. J. S. Mill, *Examination of Sir William Hamilton's Philosophy*. 5th ed. (London, 1878), 461.

58. J. S. Mill, *A System of Logic*. 6th ed. (London, 1865), 1: 309–10; for Descartes' position on non-contradiction, see CSM II, 108.

59. F. A. Lange, *Logische Studien* (Leipzig, 1877), 27 ff.

60. Ch. Sigwart, *Logik*. 3rd ed. (Freiburg and Leipzig, 1889–93), Band I, sec. 45. English trans. Helen Dendy. 2nd ed. (London and New York, 1895), 1: 297.

61. Ibid., English trans., 1: 8, 14; for Descartes' remarks on nonrelative truth, see CSM II, 102.

62. English edition: Wilhelm Dilthey, *Descriptive Psychology and Historical Understanding*, trans. R. M. Zaner and K. L. Heiges (The Hague: Nijhoff, 1977); cf. also, John Jalbert, "Husserl's Position between Dilthey and Neo-Kantianism," *Journal of the History of Philosophy*, 26 (1988); and Gail Soffer, *Husserl and the Question of Relativism* (Dordrecht: Kluwer Academic, 1991), ch. 1.

63. English edition: Wilhelm Dilthey, *Introduction to the Human Sciences*, trans. R. J. Betanzos. (London: Harvester, 1990).

64. Hermann Ebbinghaus' rebuttal appeared in *Zeitschrift fur Psychologie und Physiologie der Sinnesorgane*, (October, 1895).

65. Dilthey, *Descriptive Psychology*, 26, 29; emphasis added.

66. Sigwart, *Logic*, 1: 14–15.

67. Popkin, *History of Skepticism*, 8–10.

Chapter 3.

1. Sanchez, *That Nothing Is Known*, 275.

2. Francis Bacon, *The Physical and Metaphysical Works*, ed. Joseph Devey (London: George Bell, 1889), 1, 2; next quote ibid. Descartes approved of the Baconian

program for the recording of astronomical observations, Letter to Mersenne, May 1632, CSM III, 38.

3. A. C. Crombie, *From Augustine to Galileo* (London: Heinemann, 1970), 2: 174–85.

4. Nicholas Jardine, *The Birth of History and Philosophy of Science* (Cambridge: Cambridge University Press, 1988), 9–28.

5. "In the *Dioptrics* and *Treatise on Man*, Descartes took over Kepler's revolutionary theory of vision in a suitably mechanized form [which] Kepler had shown in *Ad Vitellionem Paralipomena* (1604)." John Schuster, "Descartes' Mathesis Universalis," in *Descartes: Philosophy, Mathematics and Physics*, ed. Stephen Gaukroger (London: Harvester Press, 1980), 61.

6. Jardine, *Birth of History*, 137; emphasis added.

7. Demosthenes, *Orations.* trans. C. R. Kennedy (London: J. M. Dent, nd), 129.

8. Dalia Judovitz, *Subjectivity and Representation in Descartes* (Cambridge: Cambridge University Press, 1988), 104.

9. Neal Gilbert, *Renaissance Concepts of Method* (New York: Columbia University Press, 1960); for his synopsis of Galen's medical work, see 17–25.

10. Ibid., 39–45.

11. Diogenes Laertius, *Lives of the Philosophers*, Book IX, sec. 62.

12. Aristotle, *Metaphysics*, 1008b.

13. On the subject of danger at a precipice, see Husserl's comment: "It seems so easy, following Descartes, to lay hold of the pure ego and his cogitations. And yet it is as though we were on the brink of a precipice, where advancing calmly and surely is a matter of philosophical life and death." Husserl CM, 23.

14. On the importance of synthesis and analysis in *Rules for the Direction of the Intellect*, see Stephen Gaukroger, *Descartes: An Intellectual Biography* (Oxford: Oxford University Press, 1995), 124–26.

15. There have been many attempts to interpret Descartes' dream; for a perspicacious and ingenious recent account, see Gaukroger, *Descartes Biography*, 106–11.

16. For which, see Jean-Joseph Goux, "Descartes et la perspective," in *L'Esprit Createur* 25 (1985). Compare also this famous image: "Our language can be seen as an

ancient city: a maze of little streets and squares, of old and new houses, and of houses with additions from various periods; and this surrounded by a multitude of new boroughs with straight regular streets and uniform houses." Wittgenstein, *Philosophical Investigations*, sec. 18.

17. Descartes' solitary imagery in this passage may have derived some of its flavor from an influential Italian theorist of method, Girolamo Borro; see Gilbert, *Renaissance*, 192.

18. On the concept of *bricolage*, see Claude Levi-Strauss, *The Savage Mind* (Chicago: University of Chicago Press, 1966), 16–22.

19. Gueroult, *Descartes*, 1, 203.

20. For which, see Peter Dear, "Mersenne's Suggestion," in *Descartes and His Contemporaries*, ed. Roger Ariew and Marjorie Grene (Chicago: University of Chicago Press, 1995), 44–62.

21. E. M. Curley, "Analysis in the *Meditations*," in *Essays on Descartes' Meditations*, ed. A. O. Rorty (Berkeley: University of California Press, 1986), 153–57.

22. The only other detailed commentary in English on the "Seventh Objections" and "Replies" is Roger Ariew, "Pierre Bourdin and the Seventh Objections," in *Descartes and His Contemporaries*, 208–25.

23. Gassendi, *Selected Works*, 374.

24. John Locke, *An Essay Concerning Human Understanding*, ed. P. H. Nidditch (Oxford: Oxford University Press, 1975), 10, 102.

25. Immanuel Kant, *Critique of Pure Reason*, trans. Norman Kemp-Smith (New York: St. Martins Press, 1965), A236 (B295).

26. G. W. F. Hegel, *Lectures on the History of Philosophy*, trans. E. S. Haldane and F. H. Simpson (New York: Dover, 1955), 3: 217; compare also Nietzsche's *The Gay Science*, various sections in Book Five.

27. Ludwig Landgrebe, "Husserl's Departure from Cartesianism," in *The Phenomenology of Husserl*, ed. R. O. Elveton (Chicago: Quadrangle, 1970), 259–61.

28. Maurice Merleau-Ponty, "Everywhere and Nowhere," in *Signs and Other Essays*, trans. R. C. Cleary (Evanston: Northwestern University Press, 1964), 152.

29. Dorion Cairns, "My Own Life," in *Phenomenology: Continuation and Criticism*, ed. Fred Kersten and Richard Zaner (The Hague: Nijhoff, 1973), 10.

30. Bernet, Kern and Marbach, *Introduction*, 245.

31. Ibid., 2.

31. The claim that Husserl conceives this ordering within the intentional sphere as a hierarchy of levels along Leibnizian lines is quite apparent in sec. 14 of *Phenomenological Psychology*.

Chapter 4.

1. For the place of this lacuna in the text, see CSM I, 77–78.

2. This is not the context for a discussion of an earlier version, the theory of aggregates, for which see David Bell, *Husserl*, 62–71; and Dallas Willard, HSW, 86–91.

3. Herbert Spiegelberg, "From Husserl to Heidegger," *Journal British Society of Phenomenology* (1971) p. 78; this is from Boyce Gibson's Freiburg Journal for those years.

4. Jean-Luc Marion, *Sur L'Ontologie Grise de Descartes* (Paris: J. Vrin, 1975) 131–48.

5. Jean-Luc Marion, "Cartesian Metaphysics and the Role of the Simple Natures," in *Cambridge Companion to Descartes*, ed. John Cottingham (Cambridge: Cambridge University Press, 1992), 115–39.

6. Dennis Sepper, "Ingenium, Memory Art," in *Essays on the Philosophy and Science of René Descartes*, ed. Stephen Voss (Oxford: Oxford University Press, 1993), 142–61.

7. On Lull, see AT X, 157, 165; Agrippa, AT X, 165, 168; Schenkel, AT X, 230. See also, Frances Yates, *The Art of Memory* (Chicago: University of Chicago Press, 1966), 373–75.

8. Sepper, "Ingenium," 151.

9. Dallas Willard, "Wholes, Parts and the Objectivity of Knowledge," in *Parts and Moments*, ed. Barry Smith (Munich: Philosophia, 1982), 382 ff.; see also, Morris Kline, *Mathematical Thought* (Oxford: Oxford University Press, 1972), 1023–39.

10. Jean Piaget and others would later propose a much lower limit of about seven items.

11. Bell, *Husserl*, 54; this overly brief summary of aggregates owes much to Bell's excellent exposition of this topic, 31–59.

12. Husserl, in fact, claimed priority in his discovery of the concept of figural moments or gestalts; see Theodor de Boer, *The Development of Husserl's Thought*, trans. Theodore Pantinga (The Hague: Nijhoff, 1978), 23, note 4, citing LI 442 and 480; see also Husserl's letter to Oskar Kraus, editor of Franz Brentano's *Psychologie von empirischen Standpunkt*, vol. III (1929); English edition, *Sensory and Noetic Consciousness*, trans. Linda McAlister (London: Routledge and Kegan Paul, 1981), 90, note 2.

13. Compare Descartes' analysis of the perception and expectation of proportionality in the unfolding of a sequence of musical tones in the "Compendium Musicae" of 1618, AT X, 94.

14. On the concept of recursion in linguistics, for instance, see Noam Chomsky, *Language and Mind* (New York: Harcourt, Brace, Jovanovich, 1972), 60–65.

15. Willard, "Wholes, Parts," 390.

16. L. J. Beck, *The Method of Descartes* (Oxford: Blackwell, 1952), 72; emphasis added.

17. William Shea, *The Magic of Numbers and Motion* (Washington: Science History, 1991), 148–75.

18. The only comprehensive manner to account for their diverse treatment should be read, of course, to pertain to the continuity of the meaning of simple-complex throughout so many transformations. Such an account is not designed to compete with (in fact, it endorses) the stratigraphic analysis of the composition of the *Rules* which shows that different strata fulfill sometimes divergent purposes for Descartes; see especially Schuster, "Descartes' Mathesis," 41–42, and notes 1–5.

19. Marion, "Cartesian Metaphysics," 131–32.

20. There is a growing body of recent scholarship devoted to demolishing the "legend" or myth of Cartesian dualism regarding mind-body union and resuscitating his original arguments. It's not possible to bring all of them into the current discussion, but these have been the most valuable for our purposes: Gordon Baker and Katherine Morris, *Descartes' Dualism* (London: Routledge, 1996), 163–93; David Yandell, "What Descartes Really Told Elisabeth: Mind-Body Union as a Primitive Notion," in *British Journal of the*

History of Philosophy (5) 1997, 249–73; Marleen Rozemond, *Descartes' Dualism* (Cambridge, Mass.: Harvard University Press, 1998); A. O. Rorty. "Cartesian Passions and the Union of Mind and Body," in *Essays on Descartes' Meditations*, 513–34; "Descartes on Thinking with the Body," in *Cambridge Companion to Descartes*, 371–92.

21. "Descartes seemed prepared to assert as an explicit, positive part of his doctrine that there *could be no* intelligible connection between soul and body. . . . This suggests that the very same argument that is taken by critics of Cartesian Dualism to prove the incoherence of causal interaction could be seen, from his own perspective, as a conclusive reason for denying that there is any such thing as (efficient) causal interaction between body and soul (in either direction)." Baker and Morris, *Descartes' Dualism*, 55.

22. A. O. Rorty, "Cartesian Passions" and "Descartes on Thinking with the Body"; Susan James, *Passion and Action: The Emotions in Seventeenth-Century Philosophy* (Oxford: Oxford University Press, 1997), 94–108; Michel Henry, "The Soul According to Descartes," in *Essays on the Philosophy and Science*, 40–51; and "Videre Videor," in *Genealogy of Psychoanalysis*, trans. Douglas Brick (Stanford: Stanford University Press, 1993), 11–40.

23. A. O. Rorty, "Cartesian Passions," 518.

24. Barry Smith, *Parts and Moments*, 37.

25. Peter Simons speaks of different concepts of whole also, ibid., 121–23.

26. For which see Elmar Holenstein, *Roman Jakobson's Approach to Language* (Bloomington: Indiana University Press, 1976), 164–78.

27. Bell, *Husserl*, 141.

28. See especially Peter Simons, *Parts: A Study in Ontology* (Oxford: Oxford University Press, 1987), 162–71.

29. For a detailed exposition of Husserl's notion of a person as a mindful body, a discussion of the texts in *Ideas Second Book* compatible with our analysis, see David W. Smith, "Mind and Body," in *Cambridge Companion to Husserl*, 323–93.

Chapter 5.

1. Berger, *The Cogito*, 65.

2. See articles by Hintikka, Gewirth, and Kenny in *Descartes: A Collection of Critical Essays,* ed. Willis Doney (New York: Doubleday, 1967).

3. Curley, *Descartes against the Skeptics*, 46–69, 116–24; Marjorie Grene, *Descartes* (London: Harvester Press, 1985), 3–45; Hatfield, "Senses and Fleshless Eye," 45–80.

4. Gueroult, *Descartes*, Introduction.

5. Beck, *The Metaphysics of Descartes*, 22, note 1.

6. Grene, *Descartes*, 5–6, emphasis added; see also Hatfield, "Senses and Fleshless Eye," 53.

7. Lilli Alanen marks the same correlation between the two senses of Cartesian ideas and the noesis-noema distinction in Husserl. See her "Cartesian Ideas and Intentionality," *Acta Philosophica Fennica* 49 (1990), 348–50.

8. "I used the word 'idea' because it was the standard philosophical term used to refer to the forms of perception belonging to the divine mind, even though we recognize that God does not possess any corporeal imagination. And besides, there was not any more appropriate term at my disposal" (CSM II, 127). Regarding which choice, E. M. Curley remarks: "As a Latin term, the word *idea* does not have a home in ordinary language; it is rare in classical Latin, a borrowing from the Greek. . . . Descartes' use of it in connection with human thought was novel and the source of much confusion among his readers." "Analysis in the Meditations," in *Essays on Descartes' Meditations*, 160; see also Michael Ayers, "Ideas and Objective Being," in *Cambridge History of Seventeenth-Century Philosophy*, ed. Daniel Garber and Michael Ayers (Cambridge: Cambridge University Press, 1998), 1062–74.

9. Franz Brentano, *Psychology from an Empirical Standpoint*, ed. Oskar Kraus (London: Routledge and Kegan Paul, 1973), 88–90.

10. Brentano, *Psychology*, 140–41, 180; *Sensory and Noetic Consciousness*, 17–24; *The Origin of Our Knowledge of Right and Wrong*, ed. Oskar Kraus, trans. R. M. Chisholm (London: Routledge and Kegan Paul, 1969), 50–54.

11. Vere Chappell, "The Theory of Ideas," in *Essays on Descartes' Meditations*, 177–98; similar conclusions are reached by Lilli Alanen, "Sensory Ideas, Objective Reality, and Material Falsity," and by A. W. MacKenzie, "The Reconfiguration of Sensory Experience," both in *Reason, Will, and Sensation*, ed. John Cottingham (Oxford: Oxford University Press, 1994), 229–50, 251–72.

12. Richard Aquila, *Intentionality: A Study of Mental Acts* (University Park: Pennsylvania State University Press, 1977), 7–13.

13. Chappell, "Theory of Ideas," 184.

14. MacKenzie argues quite rightly that Descartes held to a componential analysis of idea-contents, though the syntax is never developed, and that 'objective' reality applies to the basic components (or simples). See MacKenzie, "Reconfiguration," 260.

15. Chappell, "Theory of Ideas," 191; on the three-termed relation, see also Husserl, CM, 65–67.

16. Alanen makes a solid case for an understanding of Cartesian ideas as always being presented against a background of other ideas, beliefs, and attitudes in terms of which these ideas are interpreted. Sensations are not just given as such, but are identified only after reflection; she claims that this is "the outcome of a phenomenological reduction of a kind," in "Sensory Ideas," 245.

17. "Abstaining from acceptance of its being. . . . we shift the actual perception into the realm of non-actualities, *the realm of the as-if*, which supplies us with 'pure' possibilities, pure of everything that restricts to this fact or to any fact whatsoever," Husserl, CM, 70; see also Ideas I, 270–74; and Eduard Marbach, *Mental Representation and Consciousness* (Dordrecht: Kluwer Academic, 1993), 61.

18. "Instead of becoming lost in the performance of acts built intricately on one another, and instead of (as it were) naively positing the existence of the 'objects' intended in their sense. . . . we must rather practice reflection, i.e. make these acts themselves, and their immanent meaning-content, our 'object,' " LI, 254.

19. Brentano also clearly highlights the notion of supposition as a form of *as-if* cognition; see his *Psychology*, 284–85.

20. This highly condensed synopsis of the stages of doubt endorses an analysis given by Curley, *Descartes against the Skeptics*, 116–24.

21. Both Descartes and Husserl refer to the unchecked spread of hyperbolic doubt as "contagious" or "infectious" processes; compare the "rotten apples" image in the Sixth Replies, CSM II, 324.

22. "If I abstained. . . . and still abstain from every believing involved in or founded on sensuous experiencing, so that the being of the experienced world would remain unaccepted by me, still this abstaining is what it is; and it exists, together with the whole stream of my experiencing life. Moreover, this life is continually there *for me*," Husserl, CM, 19.

23. For some fine-grained criticisms of this definition, see Ruth Mattern's article in *Essays on Descartes' Meditations*, 479–83.

24. John Burkey, "Descartes, Skepticism, and Husserl," 20.

25. For further comments on the Cartesian notion of volition and its relation to human freedom, see David Rosenthal, "Will and the Theory of Judgement," in *Essays on Descartes' Meditations*, 411–16; Bernard Williams, *Descartes: The Project of Pure Enquiry* (New York: Penguin Press, 1978), 168–83.

26. A great deal of the literature in phenomenology is devoted to the cognitive basis of "attention"; its relation to various topics in Gestalt Psychology is well known; see Brentano, *Sensory and Noetic Consciousness*, 19–23; Husserl, Ideas I, 222–26.

27. "This reflection, like all attentiveness, is no more than the concentration of the whole capacity of intelligence on a single point that then becomes the sharp focus of light, the other points ceasing, or almost ceasing, to receive the light, and finding themselves rejected in the night, meaning in a void of knowledge," Gueroult, *Descartes*, I, 57.

Chapter 6.

1. John Burkey begins his article with the commendable aim of reconstructing a Husserlian reading of Descartes' *Meditations* and to show the "conceptual enticements and limits" which Husserl found so compelling in this text. It is somewhat odd then that almost every quote is from Husserl and only one or two from Descartes; and that a sympathetic, informed commentary on Descartes is almost invisible. "Descartes, Skepticism, and Husserl," 1–27.

2. For which, see Guido Kung, "Phenomenological Reduction as Epoché and Explication," in *Husserl: Expositions and Appraisals*, ed. F. A. Elliston and Peter McCormick (Notre Dame: University of Notre Dame Press, 1977), 338–49.

3. Spiegelberg, *The Phenomenological Movement*, 159–60.

4. Theodor de Boer had access to this diary from which he quotes in his 1966 Dutch work; English trans., 305–6; Ricoeur also locates this dramatic turning point in a "true skeptical crisis," see his *Husserl*, 30–31.

5. Adrien Baillet, *La Vie de Descartes* (Paris, 1691; facsimile reprint, Hildesheim: Georg Olms, 1970), I, 70–83. Despite the fact that Madame Rodis-Lewis discusses new documentary evidence in her excellent new work, there is no further insight on Chandoux beyond Baillet's report; see her *Descartes: His Life and Thought*, trans. Jane Marie Todd (Ithaca: Cornell University Press, 1998), 60–72. Stephen Gaukroger is also content to let this report pass without further corroboration, although he does emphasize this incident's

significance for Descartes' understanding of the skeptical challenge; see his *Descartes Biography*, 183–86. It is certainly strange that in the voluminous correspondence of Berulle, Mersenne, Richelieu, Gabriel Naudé, and others, there is no further reference to this mountebank.

6. Popkin, *History of Skepticism*, 172–77.

7. This assertion is supported by Gueroult's reading: "The fact that the cogito finds in its characteristic of most simple and most general ultimate nature the deep justification of certainty that we are constrained to give to it, proves that the reality it entails is not that of my personal *concrete self*, but that of my *thinking self in general*, as universal condition of all possible knowledge," Gueroult, *Descartes*, I, 30.

8. Landgrebe comments on Husserl's "Lectures on First Philosophy" (HUS VIII): "Husserl's attempts to distinguish these ways. . . . contradict and partly cancel each other so that we cannot come to any confident conclusion as to how many ways Husserl had himself distinguished precisely because he had not reached any final differentiation," in "Husserl's Departure from Cartesianism," 272.

9. For comments on this taxonomy of reductions, see C. W. Harvey, *Husserl's Phenomenology and the Foundations of Natural Science* (Athens: Ohio University Press, 1989), 89; perhaps the most cogent summary of the plus and minus of the three ways is that by Patocka, *Selected Writings*, 301–11; see also Jan Patocka, *An Introduction to Husserl's Phenomenology*, trans. Erazim Kohak, ed. James Dodd (Chicago: Open Court, 1996), ch. 6.

10. "The supposition of non-being [is] part of the substratum of the attempt to doubt. In Descartes, this part is so predominant that one can say that his attempt to doubt universally is properly an attempt to negate universally," Husserl, Ideas I, 59.

11. The standard English translation (CSM I, 206) of this passage obscures this rare use of the term "suspension" by rendering it "supposition," the same term they use to render the French *supposions* in the previous sentence.

12. This interpretation of epoché is supported by Elliston and McCormick, the editors of HSW, 367; and by Spiegelberg, *The Phenomenological Movement*, 134, 715, 724.

13. Harvey, *Husserl's Phenomenology*, 105–6.

14. Thevanez, *What Is Phenomenology?* 97–98; many of Thevanez's brilliant insights are marred by an exaggeration of Descartes' and Husserl's respective positions, so that they always seem to be at two extremes on any given issue.

15. Soffer, "Husserl's Neo-Cartesianism," 147.

16. The symbolic use of parentheses is taken up by Eduard Marbach in his ingenious development of a phenomenological notation; see his *Mental Representation*, 19–40.

17. Though one might claim that Husserl also has a prefigured goal; these analyses are "so many necessary steps for reaching the goal *continually guiding us*, namely the acquisition of the essence of that pure consciousness which will determine the field of phenomenology," Ideas I, 81; cf. also 104.

18. For that matter, it might be a rhizome in the Aristotelian sense: "Philosophy is essentially a science of true beginnings, or origins, of *rizomata panton*. The science concerned with what is radical must from every point of view be radical itself in its procedure," Husserl, HSW, 196.

19. For which see Marion, "Cartesian Metaphysics," 115–39.

20. HSW, 319; Ideas I, 56; Ideas III, 48; CM, 24; Crisis, 77, 153.

21. Descartes' *Meditations* is not the only work which was thought of by its author as a unified interconnection of chains of reasons; "The infinity of tasks disclosed by our extremely general preliminary sketch. . . . are a chain of particular meditations fitting into the universal frame of one unitary meditation, which can always be carried further synthetically," Husserl, CM, 87.

22. This spurious sense of transcendence was first discussed in IP (*passim*); as an absurd notion, "a round square," see Ideas I, 129; CM, 84; it is vitally important to distinguish this excluded sense from Husserl's novel reworking, see Harvey, *Husserl's Phenomenology*, 80–83; de Boer, *Husserl's Thought*, 319–21.

23. Baker and Morris, *Descartes' Dualism*, 154.

24. Berger, *The Cogito*, 110.

25. Gueroult, *Descartes*, I, 30.

26. Husserl manuscript, quoted by Bernet, Kern, and Marbach, *An Introduction*, 62.

27. Walter Soffer also correctly recognizes this ambiguity and states that Husserl's charge that Descartes rescued "a little tag-end of the world" must be withdrawn, "Husserl's Neo-Cartesianism," 156.

28. Gueroult, *Descartes*, I, 34.

29. Compare Husserl's description of the being of the intentional object in consciousness, CM, 42; and Ideas I, 70, note 57; on Descartes' dual notion of idea, Gueroult remarks, "This way of characterizing the necessary nature of idea and correlatively the inclusive nature of its eventual cause, is in some measure phenomenological. . . . The definition of the principle of the correspondence of the idea with what is ideated is none other than a kind of phenomenological description of the idea," *Descartes*, I, 136–37.

30. Burkey, "Descartes, Skepticism, and Husserl," 24.

31. "In general, a real or an ideal being that surpasses the totality of transcendental subjectivity is nonsense and is to be understood absolutely as such," HUS VII, 482. Despite Husserl's repeated denomination of such a concept as absurd, something to be stricken out, Herman Philipse interprets a passage at Ideas I, sec. 58 (quoted above) to mean virtually the opposite: "The contingent regular order in the sensations of transcendental consciousness, which enables it to constitute a world, is a rational ground for assuming the existence of a Divine Being beyond the world. Both for Husserl and for Berkeley, epistemology was the gate to rational theology and metaphysics," in "Transcendental Idealism," 287.

32. This accords well with features of the two principal operations of the intellect, intuition and deduction, in Rule III of the *Rules*.

33. Harry Frankfurt, *Demons, Dreamers, and Madmen* (Indianapolis: Bobbs-Merill, 1970), 170–80; Curley, *Descartes against the Skeptics*, 96–124; Gueroult, *Descartes*, I, 167–74.

34. Gueroult, *Descartes*, I, 170.

35. Bernet, Kern, and Marbach, *An Introduction*, 154–55.

36. In *Erste Philosophie* he claims that he has not argued in a circle, HUS VIII, 69–71; Landgrebe, "Husserl's Departure," 274–76.

37. For detailed exposition of this immense problem in Husserl's later work, see especially an article by Michael Theunissen, "The Original Transcendental Project of Social Ontology: Husserl's Theory of Intersubjectivity" in *The Other*, trans. Christopher Macann (Cambridge, Mass.: MIT Press, 1984); and Alfred Schutz, "The Problem of Transcendental Intersubjectivity in Husserl," in *Collected Papers* (The Hague: Nijhoff, 1966), III, 51–91. In his response to Eugen Fink's comments, Schutz observes that, "Husserl's failure to find a solution to this problem is due to his attempt to interpret the *ontological* status of social reality within the lifeworld as the constituted product of the transcendental subject, rather than explicating its transcendental *sense* in terms of operations of consciousness of the transcendental subject."

38. Ricoeur, *Husserl*, 84–85; see also Thevanez, *What Is Phenomenology?* 108: "The Cartesian ego becomes conscious of its lack of being, of its finitude, of its dependence on the infinite being, which in the *ordo cognoscendi* comes afterwards, but which is nevertheless more primary in the *ordo essendi*. Husserl's transcendental ego more and more acknowledges that it is secondary with respect to the contingent facticity of the *Lebenswelt*, that is to say, of the non-reflexive on the pre-reflexive."

39. Harvey, *Husserl's Phenomenology*, 106–7.

40. Compare Herman Philipse's astute analysis of the five or six steps in Husserl's progressive radicalization of the Cartesian requirement to find an indubitable foundation of knowledge, "Transcendental Idealism," 281–85.

41. Soffer, "Neo-Cartesianism," 157.

Chapter 7.

1. Jaako Hintikka, "The Phenomenological Dimension," in *Cambridge Companion to Husserl*, 93–97; Claire Ortiz Hill, *Word and Object in Husserl, Frege, and Russell* (Athens: Ohio University Press, 1991), 62–67; D. W. Smith, *The Circle of Acquaintance* (Dordrecht: Kluwer Academic, 1989), 20–27.

2. In light of Schlick's general antipathy to phenomenology, it is ironic that he correctly equates intuition with acquaintaince, and conceptual knowledge with understanding, commending Russell's notion, and then *incorrectly* asserts that phenomenology conflates these two functions. Moritz Schlick, *General Theory of Knowledge*, trans. A. E. Blumberg (New York: Springer-Verlag, 1974), 83.

3. C. O. Hill, *Word and Object*, 67–70.

4. D. W. Smith and Ronald McIntyre, *Husserl and Intentionality* (Dordrecht: D. Reidel, 1982), 363–69.

5. D. W. Smith, *Circle of Acquaintance*, 28–30.

6. Gary Hatfield, "The Cognitive Faculties," in *Cambridge History of Seventeenth*, 970.

7. Schuster, "Descartes' Mathesis Universalis," 40–42.

8. For a complete synopsis and discussion of the eight theorems D1–D8 of simple and complex natures in Rule XII, see Chapter 4.

9. This interpretation of perspicacity and discernment as practical techniques which are distinct from, but correlated with, the two cognitive operations is supported by Gueroult, *Descartes*, I, 59–60.

10. Richard Rorty, "Intuition," in *Encyclopedia of Philosophy*, ed. Paul Edwards (New York: Macmillan, 1967), IV, 208.

11. A compatible account of the first five remarks is offered by John Yolton, *Perceptual Acquaintance from Descartes to Reid* (Oxford: Blackwell, 1984), 19–22.

12. Instantaneous: "grasp each truth by means of a single and distinct act" (Rule IX, CSM I, 33); "the whole proposition must be understood all at once, and not bit by bit," (Rule XI, CSM I, 37).

13. Christian Knudsen, "Intentions and Impositions," in *Cambridge History of Later Mediaeval Philosophy*, ed. Norman Kretzmann et al. (Cambridge: Cambridge University Press, 1982), 479–95.

14. Louis Loeb admirably documents the congruence of meaning for "intuition" in Descartes and Locke in *From Descartes to Hume* (Ithaca: Cornell University Press, 1981), 37–43; for an excellent overview of the history of German usage, see F. Kaulbach, "Anschauung," in *Historisches Worterbuch der Philosophie,* ed. Joachim Ritter (Darmstadt, 1971), Band I, 340–46.

15. Hintikka, "The Phenomenological Dimension," 86–87.

16. This passage was deleted from the second edition of Schlick's work, but not due to Husserl's "very sharp comments." Schlick said that "Husserl accused me of having read his book too hastily, but in the very same sentence misquoted my own. Further he complained that I had falsely assumed that 'ideation' was not intended as a real mental act. This was a misunderstanding. . . . The clearing up of this leaves untouched the arguments against phenomenology set forth in the text." Schlick, *Theory of Knowledge*, 139, note 37.

17. "Presentation" is J. N. Findlay's translation for the German *Vorstellung*, otherwise often translated as "idea"; other editors reserve this English term for *Gegenwartigung*, and "presentification" for *Vorgegenwartigung*. See Bernet, Kern, and Marbach's comments on this, *An Introduction*, 144.

18. "Not to say that Husserl's sensitivity and skill in making linguistic distinctions are not among the most extraordinary on record. The *Untersuchungen* abound with examples. The chapter on the thirteen (!) uses of *Vorstellung* (idea) is as richly satisfying as a Bach concerto." Gustav Bergmann, "The Ontology of E. Husserl," in *Logic and Reality* (Madison: University of Wisconsin Press, 1964), 219.

19. On the importance of the notion of the "totalizing act" with regard to intuition of sensible objects in Husserl's early work before 1900, see J. K. Cooper-Wiele, *The Totalizing Act* (Dordrecht: Kluwer Academic, 1989), 74–86.

20. On the difference between intuition of logical categories and intuition of essences, see E. Levinas, *The Theory of Intuition in Husserl's Phenomenology*, trans. André Orianne (Evanston: Northwestern University Press, 1973), 80.

21. John Yolton, *Perceptual Acquaintance*, 26.

22. Martin Jay, *Downcast Eyes: The Denigration of Vision in Twentieth-Century French Thought* (Berkeley: University of California Press, 1994), 69–82.

23. E. M. Curley points out that clarity and distinctness are not used in their technical sense until the piece of wax episode; see *Descartes against the Skeptics*, 72, note.

24. "Husserl generalizes the distinction defended by Stumpf between feelings such as localized pain, which require no cognitive basis, and emotions such as joy and regret, which do have such a cognitive underpinning, so that it applies to perception. Visual sensations—of redness and of form—and tactile sensations—of roughness and smoothness—differ from acts of seeing and touching in the same way in which a localized pain differs from regret. Perceptual sensations and localized pains are non-intentional. Seeing and regret are intentional." Kevin Mulligan, "Perception," in *Cambridge Companion to Husserl*, 182.

25. MacKenzie, "Reconfiguration," 264.

26. Though Descartes is determined not to accept the tradition's framework, it is another issue whether he is successful in resisting its influence; see Stanley Rosen, *The Ancients and the Moderns* (New Haven: Yale University Press, 1989), 22–36. John Cottingham has recently set out to debunk the 'myth' that Descartes was a genuine innovator and that he relies to a great extent on arguments put forward by scholastics and neo-skeptics; his exposition of this claim is almost completely unjustified. See his "A New Start?" in *The Rise of Modern Philosophy*, ed. Tom Sorrell (Oxford: Clarendon Press, 1993), 145–66.

27. M. D. Wilson, *Descartes*, 216.

28. John Yolton, *Perceptual Acquaintance*, 35, 37. This last formulation by John Yolton of "a new doctrine" is supported by Descartes' observation at the very end of the "Second Meditation," regarding the piece of wax, which explicitly equates bodies being perceived *by the intellect alone* with their being understood (CSM II, 22).

29. On the noema and its relation to this earlier notion of intentional content, see Barry Smith and D. W. Smith, "Introduction," in *Cambridge Companion to Husserl*, 22–27; John Drummond, *Husserlian Intentionality and Non-Foundational Realism* (Dordrecht: Kluwer Academic, 1990), ch. 1.

30. Hatfield, "Senses and the Fleshless Eye," 71; Gueroult argues against any interpretation of Descartes' knowledge of self as based on introspection, since this would lead to a psychologistic fallacy, Gueroult, *Descartes*, I, 46–47.

31. Recent publication of Brentano's lectures on *Descriptive Psychology* from the 1890s reveal that Husserl's former teacher relied heavily on a primitive notion of intuition; Husserl may well have attended these lectures, although he had secured his own post.

32. On the dominance of "seeing" and visual terminology in the *Meditations*, see (sic) Michel Henry, "Videre Videor," 11–40.

33. "Pure phenomenology as science. . . . can only be essence investigation, and not at all an investigation of being-there; all 'introspection' and every judgment based on such 'experience' falls outside its framework" *Philosophy as Rigorous Science*, HSW, 183.

34. See Elizabeth Stroker: "Husserl's appeal to intuition, made so often just in his work of 1913, could easily give the impression that our understanding here no longer suffices. Thus one could get the impression that, under the label 'essential insight' (*Wesenschau*), which is talked about so much in the *Ideas*, Husserl propounded an intuitionism whose only source of legitimation seemed to be precisely the evidence, characterized as 'experience of truth,' or even as its 'internalization,' which could presumably be had only by those who are specially gifted, capable of the right insight," in "Husserl's Principle of Evidence," *Contemporary German Philosophy*, ed. D. E. Christensen (University Park: Pennsylvania State University Press, 1982), 115.

35. "Although Descartes did enjoin one to turn inward and to discover the givens of one's own experience, his method cannot patly [patently] be described as introspective. For Descartes was not asking one simply to look within. . . . Rather, he was hoping to help the reader discover, through the process of meditation, a source of impersonal, objective judgements that lies hidden in the intellect," Hatfield, "Senses and the Fleshless Eye," 69.

36. Levinas, *Theory of Intuition*, 91; on the current status of this heated debate, see Hermann Philipse, "Transcendental Idealism," 239–54.

37. For example, by David Bell, *Husserl*, 194–95, who describes the process as "fatuous and utterly naïve," and the theory "an unmitigated failure."

38. Carl Posy argues that this Husserlian notion of intuition is entirely compatible with L. E. Brouwer's mathematical intuitionism; see his "Mathematics as a Transcendental Science," in *Phenomenology and the Formal Sciences*, ed. Thomas Seebohm et al. (Dordrecht: Kluwer Academic, 1991), 107–31.

39. Bernet, Kern, and Marbach, *An Introduction*, 79.

40. Bernet, Kern, and Marbach, *An Introduction*, 188.

Chapter 8.

1. E. R. Callahan, "Conversion," in *New Catholic Encyclopedia* (New York: McGraw-Hill, 1967), IV, 286; and James Strachan, "Conversion," in *Encyclopedia of Religion and Ethics*, ed. James Hastings (Edinburgh: T. and T. Clark, 1911), IV, 105–10.

2. Callahan, "Conversion"; cf. also Rudolf Bultmann, *Theology of the New Testament* (London: SCM Press, 1952), I, 67–73.

3. Robin Lane Fox, *Pagans and Christians* (New York: Penguin, 1986), 271.

4. Plato, *Republic*, VII, 518c–d, trans. Paul Shorey.

5. A. D. Nock, *Conversion* (Oxford: Clarendon Press, 1961), 164–86.

6. As several colleagues have pointed out, it does seem to have made sense to speak of a conversion to Marxism, the one arguable exception, and this probably because it was embraced with an almost religious fervor, if not fanaticism.

7. William James, *The Varieties of Religious Experience* (New York: Scribners, 1902), 189–258.

8. RSV, Luke 9: 24; cf. also Matthew 16; 25, Mark 8: 35.

9. Augustine, *Confessions*, Book VIII, xii, 29; cf. Peter Brown, *Augustine of Hippo* (London: Faber, 1990), 101–14.

10. On Augustine's influence on the design of Descartes' *Meditations*, see especially Stephen Menn, *Descartes and Augustine* (Cambridge: Cambridge University Press, 1998), 209–44.

11. W. W. Meissner, *The Psychology of a Saint: Ignatius of Loyola* (New Haven: Yale University Press, 1992), 69–108; on general aspects of conversion in this period, see

Jean-Robert Armogathe. "La Conversion au XVIIme Siècle," in *Actes du XIIme Colloque de Marseille* (Marseille: CMR, 1982), 29–43.

12. Beck, *The Metaphysics of Descartes*, 28–38, quote 30.

13. Hatfield, "Senses and the Fleshless Eye," 48–55.

14. Dalia Judovitz underscores the discursive weight carried by both rhetoric and argument, *Subjectivity*, 137–57.

15. "There is more than a nominal connection between the *mauvais genie* who appears in the posthumous *Olympica* and the malign demon of the *Meditations*. Both appear in the context of dreams, both raise the problem of providence, both are counterposed to the 'spirit of truth' or to certainty, and in both cases the apparitions seem to represent the religious alternative to philosophy." Hiram Caton, *The Origin of Subjectivity* (New Haven: Yale University Press, 1973), 123, note.

16. On Descartes' dream, see Richard Kennington, "Descartes' Olympica," *Social Research* 28 (1961), 171–204; Bernd Jager, "The Three Dreams of Descartes," *Review of Existential Psychology and Psychiatry* 8 (1968), 195–213; Shea, *Magic of Numbers and Motion*, 115–20.

17. Gaukroger, *Descartes*, 110–12.

18. Hatfield, "Senses and the Fleshless Eye," 47.

19. Walter Conn, *Christian Conversion* (New York: Paulist Press, 1986), 116–17; citing Bernard Lonergan, *Method in Theology* (London: Darton, Longman and Todd, 1972), 238–40.

20. Beck, *The Metaphysics of Descartes*, 74.

21. Husserl was quite explicit in his acknowledgement of this orientation in a revised passage of *Ideas Third Book*, "My way to phenomenology was essentially determined by the mathesis universalis," where he cites Bolzano's *Theory of Science*, mathematics, and theory of propositions as sources; Ideas III, 49.

22. Karl-Otto Apel also calls for the rehabilitation and reconstruction of Descartes' *Prima Philosophia* on the basis of a transcendental pragmatics of language; see "The Cartesian Paradigm of First Philosophy," *International Journal of Philosophical Studies* 6 (1998), 1–16.

23. Bernet, Kern, and Marbach, *An Introduction*, 57.

24. In addition: "In advance 'world' has the meaning 'the universe of the *actually* existing actualities': not the merely supposed, doubtful or questionable actualities, but the actual ones, which as such have actuality for us only in the constant movement of corrections and revisions of validities." Crisis, 146; and "Scientific reason [is] a reason that actualizes genuine cognition by an unremittingly concomitant criticism of cognition." FTL, 128.

25. Bernet, Kern, and Marbach, *An Introduction*, 245.

BIBLIOGRAPHY

Seventeenth Century Texts and Commentary

Alanen, Lilli. "Cartesian Ideas and Intentionality." *Acta Philosophica Fennica*. 49 (1990).

Aliqué, Ferdinand. *La Découverte métaphysique de l'homme chez Descartes*. 2me ed. Paris: Presses Universitaires de France, 1987.

Annas, Julia and Barnes, Jonathan, eds. *The Modes of Scepticism*. Cambridge: Cambridge University Press, 1985.

Apel, Karl-Otto. "The Cartesian Paradigm of First Philosophy." *International Journal of Philosophical Studies*. 6 (1998).

Ariew, Roger and Grene, Marjorie. *Descartes and His Contemporaries*. Chicago: University of Chicago Press, 1995.

Arnauld, Antoine. *Logic, or the Art of Thinking*. [1662] Translated by Jill Buroker. Cambridge: Cambridge University Press, 1996.

———. *On True and False Ideas*. [1683] Translated by Stephen Gaukroger. Manchester: Manchester University Press, 1990.

Baillet, Adrien. *La Vie de M. Descartes*. 2 vols. [1691] facsimile reprint. Hildesheim: Georg Olms, 1972.

Baker, Gordon and Morris, Katherine. *Descartes' Dualism*. London: Routledge, 1996.

Beck, L. J. *The Method of Descartes*. Oxford: Oxford University Press, 1962.

———. *The Metaphysics of Descartes*. Oxford: Oxford University Press, 1965.

Beyssade, Jean-Marie. *La Philosophie première de Descartes*. Paris: Flammarion, 1979.

Brush, Craig. *Montaigne and Bayle*. The Hague: Martinus Nijhoff, 1966.

Burnyeat, Myles, ed. *The Skeptical Tradition*. Berkeley: University of California Press, 1983.

Caton, Hiram. *The Origins of Subjectivity: An Essay on Descartes*. New Haven: Yale University Press, 1973.

271

Clarke, Desmond. *Descartes' Philosophy of Science.* Manchester: Manchester University Press, 1982.

———. *Occult Powers and Hypotheses.* Oxford: Oxford University Press, 1989.

Costabel, Pierre. *Démarches originales de Descartes savant.* Paris: J. Vrin, 1982.

Cottingham, John. *Descartes.* Oxford: Blackwell, 1986.

Cottingham, John, ed. *The Cambridge Companion to Descartes.* Cambridge: Cambridge University Press, 1992.

———. *Reason, Will, and Sensation.* Oxford: Oxford University Press, 1994.

Curley, E. M. *Descartes against the Skeptics.* Oxford: Blackwell, 1978.

Descartes, René. *The Philosophical Writings.* 2 vols. Translated by John Cottingham, Robert Stoothoff, and Dugald Murdoch. Cambridge: Cambridge University Press, 1984–85.

———. *The Correspondence.* Translated by John Cottingham, Robert Stoothoff, Dugald Murdoch, and Anthony Kenny. Cambridge: Cambridge University Press, 1991.

———. *Oeuvres de Descartes.* Edited by Charles Adam and Paul Tannery. New ed. 12 vols. Paris: J. Vrin et CNRS, 1964–76.

Doney, Willis, ed. *Descartes: A Collection of Critical Essays.* New York: Doubleday, 1967.

Ferreira, M. J. *Scepticism and Reasonable Doubt.* Oxford: Oxford University Press, 1986.

Garber, Daniel. *Descartes' Metaphysical Physics.* Chicago: University of Chicago Press, 1992.

Garber, Daniel and Ayers, Michael, eds. *The Cambridge History of Seventeenth-Century Philosophy.* Cambridge: Cambridge University Press, 1998.

Gassendi, Pierre. *The Selected Works.* [1624–58] edited and translated by Craig Brush. New York: Johnson Reprint, 1972.

Gaukroger, Stephen, ed. *Descartes: Philosophy, Mathematics, and Physics.* London: Harvester Press, 1980.

Gaukroger, Stephen. *Cartesian Logic.* Oxford: Oxford University Press, 1989.

———. *Descartes: An Intellectual Biography.* Oxford: Oxford University Press, 1995.

Gouhier, Henri. *Les Premières Pensées de Descartes.* Paris: J. Vrin, 1958.

———. *La Pensée métaphysique de Descartes.* Paris: J. Vrin, 1962.

———. *Cartésianisme et Augustinisme au XVIIme siècle.* Paris: J. Vrin, 1978.

Grayling, A. C. *The Refutation of Scepticism.* London: Duckworth, 1985.

Grene, Marjorie. *Descartes.* London: Harvester Press, 1985.

Grosholz, Emily. *Cartesian Doubt and the Problem of Reduction.* Oxford: Oxford University Press, 1991.

Gueroult, Martial. *Descartes' Philosophy Interpreted according to the Order of Reasons.* 2 vols. Translated by Roger Ariew. Minneapolis: University of Minnesota Press, 1984.

Henry, Michel. *Genealogy of Psychoanalysis.* Translated by Douglas Brick. Stanford: Stanford University Press, 1992.

———. *Phenomenologie Materielle.* Paris: P. U. F., 1990.

Hooker, Michael, ed. *Descartes: Critical and Interpretive Essays.* Baltimore: Johns Hopkins, 1978.

James, Susan. *Passion and Action: The Emotions in Seventeenth-Century Philosophy.* Oxford: Oxford University Press, 1997.

Jardine, Nicholas. *The Birth of History and Philosophy of Science.* Cambridge: Cambridge University Press, 1988.

Judovitz, Dalia. *Subjectivity and Representation in Descartes.* Cambridge: Cambridge University Press, 1988.

Lennon, T. M. et al., eds. *Problems of Cartesianism.* Montreal: McGill University Press, 1982.

Leyden, W. von. *Seventeenth-Century Metaphysics.* London: Duckworth, 1968.

Loeb, Louis. *From Descartes to Hume.* Ithaca: Cornell University Press, 1981.

Marion, Jean-Luc. *Sur l'ontologie grise de Descartes.* Paris: J. Vrin, 1981.

———. *Sur le prisme métaphysique de Descartes.* Paris: P. U. F., 1986.

———. *Sur la théologie blanche de Descartes.* Paris: P. U. F., 1991.

Menn, Stephen. *Descartes and Augustine.* Cambridge: Cambridge University Press, 1998.

Montaigne, Michel de. *The Essays of Montaigne.* Translated by M. A. Screech. New York: Penguin, 1991.

Nadler, Steven. *Arnauld and the Cartesian Philosophy of Ideas.* Manchester: Manchester University Press, 1989.

———. *Malebranche and Ideas.* Oxford: Oxford University Press, 1992.

Nelson, Benjamin. "The Early Modern Revolution in Science and Philosophy." *Boston Studies in the Philosophy of Science* 3 (1967).

Popkin, Richard H. *History of Skepticism from Erasmus to Spinoza.* Berkeley: University of California Press, 1979.

———. *The Third Force in Seventeenth-Century Thought.* Leiden: E. J. Brill, 1992.

Rodis-Lewis, G. *L'oeuvre de Descartes.* Paris: J. Vrin, 1971.

———. *Idées et vérités éternelles chez Descartes.* Paris: J. Vrin, 1985.

———. *L'antropologie cartésienne.* Paris: P. U. F., 1991.

———. *Descartes: His Life and Thought.* Translated by Jane Marie Todd. Ithaca: Cornell University Press, 1998.

Rorty, A. O., ed. *Essays on Descartes' Meditations.* Berkeley: University of California Press, 1986.

Rozemond, Marleen. *Descartes' Dualism.* Cambridge, Mass.: Harvard University Press, 1998.

Sanchez, Francisco. *That Nothing Is Known.* [1581] edited and translated by Elaine Limbrick; Latin text by Douglas Thomson. Cambridge: Cambridge University Press, 1988.

Schmitt, Charles B. *Cicero Scepticus.* The Hague: Martinus Nijhoff, 1972.

Sextus Empiricus. *Outlines of Scepticism.* Translated by Julia Annas and Jonathan Barnes. Cambridge: Cambridge University Press, 1994.

———. *Against the Grammarians (Adversus Mathematicos I).* Translated by D. L. Blank. Oxford: Oxford University Press, 1998.

Shea, William R. *The Magic of Numbers and Motion.* Washington: Science History, 1991.

Sorrell, Tom, ed. *The Rise of Modern Philosophy*. Oxford: Clarendon Press, 1993.

Stroud, Barry. *The Significance of Philosophical Scepticism*. Oxford: Oxford University Press, 1984.

Thorndike, Lynn. *A History of Magic and Experimental Science*, 8 vols. New York: Columbia University Press, 1923–58.

Vuillemin, Jean. *Mathématiques et métaphysique chez Descartes*. Paris: P. U. F., 1987.

Watson, Richard. *The Downfall of Cartesianism*. The Hague: Martinus Nijhoff, 1966.

Webster, Charles. *The Great Instauration*. London: Duckworth, 1975.

Williams, Bernard. *Descartes: The Project of Pure Inquiry*. New York: Penguin, 1978.

Wilson, Margaret D. *Descartes*. London: Routledge, 1978.

Yandell, David. "What Descartes Really Told Elizabeth: Mind-Body Union as a Primitive Notion." *British Journal of the History of Philosophy* 5 (1997).

Yates, Frances A. *The Art of Memory*. Chicago: University of Chicago Press, 1966.

———. *The Rosicrucian Enlightenment*. London: Routledge, Kegan Paul, 1972.

———. *The Occult Philosophy in the Elizabethan Age*. London: Routledge, Kegan Paul, 1979.

Yolton, John. *Perceptual Acquaintance from Descartes to Reid*. Oxford: Blackwell, 1984.

Husserlian Phenomenology

Bachelard, Suzanne. *A Study of Husserl's Formal and Transcendental Logic*. Translated by Lester Embree. Evanston: Northwestern University Press, 1968.

Bell, David. *Husserl*. London: Routledge, 1990.

Berger, Gaston. *The Cogito in Husserl's Philosophy*. Translated by Kathleen McLaughlin. Evanston: Northwestern University Press, 1972.

Bergmann, Gustav. *Logic and Reality*. Madison: University of Wisconsin Press, 1964.

Bernet, Rudolf, Kern, Iso, and Marbach, Eduard. *An Introduction to Husserlian Phenomenology*. Evanston: Northwestern University Press, 1993.

Boer, Theodor de. *The Development of Husserl's Thought*. Translated by Theodor Plantinga. The Hague: Martinus Nijhoff, 1978.

Brentano, Franz. *Truth and Evidence*. Translated by R. M. Chisholm et al. London: Routledge, Kegan Paul, 1966.

———. *The Origin of our Knowledge of Right and Wrong*. Edited by Oskar Kraus. Translated by R. M. Chisholm and E. H. Schneewind. London: Routledge, Kegan Paul, 1969.

———. *Psychology from an Empirical Standpoint*. Edited by Linda McAlister. Translated by A. C. Rancurello et al. London: Routledge, Kegan Paul, 1973.

———. *Theory of Categories*. Edited by Alfred Kastil. Translated by R. M. Chisholm and N. Guterman. The Hague: Martinus Nijhoff, 1981.

Burkey, John. "Descartes, Skepticism, and Husserl." *Husserl Studies* 7 (1990).

Carr, David. "The Fifth Meditation and Husserl's Cartesianism." *Philosophy and Phenomenological Research* 34 (1974).

Cavallin, Jens. *Content and Object: Husserl, Twardowski, and Psychologism.* Dordrecht: Kluwer Academic, 1997.

Dilthey, Wilhelm. *Introduction to the Human Sciences.* Translated by R.J. Betanzos. London: Harvester, 1990.

———. *Descriptive Psychology and Historical Understanding.* Translated by R. M. Zaner and K. L. Heiges. The Hague: Martinus Nijhoff, 1977.

Dreyfus, Hubert, ed. *Husserl, Intentionality, and Cognitive Science.* Cambridge, Mass.: MIT Press, 1982.

Drummond, John. *Husserlian Intentionality and Non-Foundational Realism.* Dordrecht: Kluwer Academic, 1990.

Drummond, John and Embree, Lester, eds. *Phenomenology of the Noema.* Dordrecht: Kluwer Academic, 1992.

Dufrenne, Mikel. *The Notion of the A Priori.* Translated by Edward S. Casey. Evanston: Northwestern University Press, 1966.

Elliston, Frederick and McCormick, Peter, eds. *Husserl: Expositions and Appraisals.* Bloomington: Indiana University Press, 1977.

Elveton, R. O., ed. *Phenomenology of Husserl: Selected Critical Readings.* Chicago: Quadrangle, 1970.

Fulton, John S. "The Cartesianism of Phenomenology." *Philosophical Review* 49 (1940).

Gurwitsch, Aron. *The Field of Consciousness.* Pittsburgh: Duquesne University Press, 1964.

———. *Studies in Phenomenology and Psychology.* Evanston: Northwestern University Press, 1966.

Hance, Allen. "Husserl's Phenomenological Theory of Logic and the Overcoming of Psychologism." *Philosophy Research Archives* 13 (1988).

Harvey, Charles. *Husserl's Phenomenology and the Foundations of Natural Science.* Athens: Ohio University Press, 1989.

Herman, F. W. von. "Husserl et Descartes." *Revue Metaphysique et Morale* 92 (1987).

Hill, Claire Ortiz. *Word and Object in Husserl, Frege, and Russell.* Athens: Ohio University Press, 1991.

Hopkins, Burt C. *Intentionality in Husserl and Heidegger.* Dordrecht: Kluwer Academic, 1993.

Husserl, Edmund. *Cartesian Meditations.* Translated by Dorion Cairns. The Hague: Nijhoff, 1973.

——— *The Crisis of European Sciences and Transcendental Phenomenology.* Translated by David Carr. Northwestern University Press, 1970.

——— *Early Writings in the Philosophy of Logic and Mathematics.* Translated by Dallas Willard. Dordrecht: Kluwer Academic, 1993.

——— *Experience and Judgement.* Revised and edited by Ludwig Landgrebe. Translated by J. S. Churchill and Karl Ameriks. Evanston: Northwestern University Press, 1973.

——— *Formal and Transcendental Logic.* Translated by Dorion Cairns. The Hague: Nijhoff, 1969.

———— *Husserl: Shorter Works*. Edited by Peter McCormick and F. A. Elliston. Notre Dame: University of Notre Dame Press, 1982.

———— *Ideas First Book: General Introduction to a Pure Phenomenology*. Translated by Fred Kersten. The Hague: Nijhoff, 1982.

———— *Ideas Second Book: Studies in the Phenomenology of Constitution*. Translated by R. Rojcewicz and André Schuwer. The Hague: Nijhoff, 1989.

———— *Ideas Third Book: Phenomenology and the Foundations of the Sciences*. Translated by T. E. Klein and W. E. Pohl. The Hague: Nijhoff, 1980.

———— *The Idea of Phenomenology*. Translated by W. P. Alston and G. Nakhnikian. The Hague: Nijhoff, 1964.

———— *Logical Investigations*. 2 vols. Translated by J. N. Findlay. London: Routledge, Kegan Paul, 1970.

———— *Phenomenological Psychology*. Translated by John Scanlon. The Hague: Nijhoff, 1977.

———— *The Paris Lectures*. Translated by Peter Kostenbaum. The Hague: Nijhoff, 1967.

———— *Thing and Space: Lectures 1907*. Translated and edited by R. Rojcewicz. Dordrecht: Kluwer Academic, 1998.

———— *The Phenomenology of the Consciousness of Internal Time*. Translated by J. B. Brough. Dordrecht: Kluwer Academic, 1991.

———— *Husserliana: Gesammelte Werke*. Edited by Walter Biemel et al. The Hague: Nijhoff, 1950–95.

Ingarden, Roman. *Time and Modes of Being*. Translated by Helen R. Michejda. Springfield, Illinois: Charles Thomas, 1964.

Jalbert, John. "Husserl's Position between Dilthey and Neo-Kantianism." *Journal of the History of Philosophy* 26 (1988).

Kersten, Fred. *Phenomenological Method: Theory and Practice*. Dordrecht: Kluwer Academic, 1989.

Kockelmans, Joseph. *Edmund Husserl's Phenomenological Psychology*. Translated by Bernd Jager. Pittsburgh: Duquesne University Press, 1967.

Kottakapally, J. "Husserl's Critique of His Cartesian Way." *International Philosophical Quarterly* 22 (1982).

Kuhn, Rolf. "Zur Methode Descartes et Husserl." *Frei Zeitung Philosophie und Theologie* 38 (1991).

Kusch, Martin. *Psychologism: A Study in the Sociology of Philosophical Knowledge*. London: Routledge, 1996.

Kuspit, D. B. "Epoche and Fable in Descartes." *Philosophy and Phenomenological Research* 25 (1964).

Landgrebe, Ludwig. *The Phenomenology of Edmund Husserl: Six Essays*. Edited by Donn Welton. Ithaca: Cornell University Press, 1981.

Levin, David M. *Reason and Evidence in Husserl's Phenomenology*. Evanston: Northwestern University Press, 1970.

Levinas, Emmanuel. *The Theory of Intuition in Husserl's Phenomenology*. Translated by André Orianne. Evanston: Northwestern University Press, 1973.

Marbach, Eduard. *Mental Representations and Consciousness*. Dordrecht: Kluwer Academic, 1993.

Metcalfe, John. "Husserl and Early Victorian Philosophical Logic." *Eidos*. 7 (1988).

Mohanty, J. N. *Edmund Husserl's Theory of Meaning*. The Hague: Martinus Nijhoff, 1976.

Natanson, Maurice. *Husserl: Philosopher of Infinite Tasks*. Evanston: Northwestern University Press, 1973.

Patocka, Jan. *Philosophy and Selected Writings*. Edited and translated by Erazim Kohak. Chicago: University of Chicago Press, 1986.

————. *An Introduction to Husserl's Phenomenology*. Translated by Erazim Kohak. Edited by James Dodd. Chicago: Open Court, 1996.

Pivcevic, Edo, ed. *Phenomenology and Philosophical Understanding*. Cambridge: Cambridge University Press, 1975.

Ricoeur, Paul. *Husserl: An Analysis of His Phenomenology*. Translated by Edward G. Ballard and Lester E. Embree. Evanston: Northwestern University Press, 1967.

Schnadelbach, Herbert. *Philosophy in Germany 1831–1933*. Translated by Eric Matthews. Cambridge: Cambridge University Press, 1984.

Schuhmann, Karl. *Die Dialektik der Phanomenologie*. The Hague: Martinus Nijhoff, 1973.

Simons, Peter. *Parts: A Study in Ontology*. Oxford: Oxford University Press, 1987.

————. *Philosophy and Logic in Central Europe from Bolzano to Tarski*. Dordrecht: Kluwer Academic, 1992.

Smith, Barry, ed. *Parts and Moments: Studies in Logic and Formal Ontology*. Munich: Philosophia, 1982.

————. *Foundations of Gestalt Theory*. Munich: Philosophia, 1988.

Smith, Barry and Smith, David W., eds. *The Cambridge Companion to Husserl*. Cambridge: Cambridge University Press, 1995.

Smith, David W. and McIntyre, Ronald. *Husserl and Intentionality*. Dordrecht: D. Reidel, 1982.

Smith, David W. *The Circle of Acquaintance*. Dordrecht: Kluwer Academic, 1989.

Soffer, Gail. *Husserl and the Question of Relativism*. Dordrecht: Kluwer Academic, 1991.

Soffer, Walter. "Husserl's Neo-Cartesianism." *Research in Phenomenology* 11 (1981).

Sokolowski, Robert. *The Formation of Husserl's Concept of Constitution*. The Hague: Nijhoff, 1970.

————. *Husserlian Meditations*. Evanston: Northwestern University Press, 1974.

Stroker, Elizabeth. *Husserlian Foundations of Science*, 2d ed. Dordrecht: Kluwer Academic, 1997.

Spiegelberg, Herbert. *The Phenomenological Movement*, 3rd revised ed. The Hague: Nijhoff, 1982.

Tieszen, Richard. *Mathematical Intuition*. Dordrecht: Kluwer Academic, 1989.

INDEX